POMPEY THE GREAT

For Ruthie

POMPEY THE GREAT

A Political Biography

Second Edition

Robin Seager

Blackwell
Publishing

© 1979, 2002 by Robin Seager

350 Main Street, Malden, MA 02148-5018, USA
108 Cowley Road, Oxford OX4 1JF, UK
550 Swanston Street, Carlton South, Melbourne, Victoria 3053, Australia
Kurfürstendamm 57, 10707 Berlin, Germany

First published 1979 by Blackwell Publishing Ltd
Second edition published 2002

3   2007

Tranferred to digital print 2007

Library of Congress Cataloging-in-Publication Data

Seager, Robin.
  Pompey the Great : a political biography / Robin Seager–2nd [updated] ed.
      p. cm.
  Includes bibliographical references and index.
  ISBN: 978-0-631-22720-5 (alk. paper) — ISBN: 978-0-631-22721-2 (pbk. :alk. paper)
  1. Pompey, the Great, 106–48 B.C. 2. Consuls Roman – Biography.
3. Generals–Rome–Biography. 4. Rome–History–First Triumvirate, 60–53 B.C.
5. Rome–History–53–44 B.C. I. Seager, Robin. Pompey. II. Title.

DG258 .S42   2002
937′.05′092—dc21
[B]   2002022773

A catalogue record for this title is available from the British Library.

Set in 11 on 13 pt Bembo
by Kolam Information Services Pvt. Ltd, Pondicherry, India
Printed and bound in Great Britain by
Marston Book Services Limited, Oxford

For further information on
Blackwell Publishing, visit our website:
http://www.blackwellpublishing.com

CONTENTS

PREFACE

I am grateful to the publisher for the opportunity to produce a revised edition of this book, which has now been unavailable for many years, and in particular to Al Bertrand, who first made the suggestion to me and has proved eminently flexible and understanding throughout our subsequent dealings.

The text of the original version has been reproduced essentially unchanged, apart from the correction of misprints and other minor blemishes and the removal of a few obscurities of expression. However, various additions have been made, not least with a view to making the book more accessible not only to scholars and students but to those with a more general interest in Rome and its history.

An Introduction presents a concise narrative of Roman politics from Ti. Gracchus to Sulla. This, it is hoped, will provide a contextual background to Pompeius' career for those relatively unfamiliar with the subject and enable them better to understand the political world in which he set out to make his mark. An Afterword deals with those matters, great and small, on which advances in scholarship have increased our knowledge or caused me to change my opinions since the appearance of the first edition. As further aids to comprehension I have added a Chronological Table and a Glossary of technical terms, while some Latin words and phrases have also been translated where they occur in the text and notes. A further significant improvement, for which I personally can claim very little credit, is the embellishment of the book with a number of maps.

In conclusion I should especially like to thank my editor, Margaret Aherne. Her unerring eye for error and confusion, her imaginative and constructive approach, her patience with my prejudices and her sense of humour have done much to make what might have been a lengthy war of attrition as swift and painless as the Great one's campaign against the pirates.

Robin Seager
Liverpool, December 2001

PREFACE TO THE FIRST EDITION

Books on Caesar and Cicero abound. Even Crassus has now attracted two biographers in quick succession. Yet there has been no life in English of Pompey the Great, though Syme could label the decades of his greatest eminence as 'the domination of Pompeius'. Scholars and students have had at their disposal only foreign works: in German the admirable study by the greatest of all historians of republican Rome, Matthias Gelzer, in French the voluminous compilation of van Ooteghem. Therefore a book in English on Pompeius should need no justification.[1] Nor should the writing of historical biography, at least for anyone who believes with Gelzer that the historian's proper concern is 'was die Menschen der Vergangenheit bewegte, was sie dachten und trieben'. The subtitle of the present work is intended to warn the reader to expect no treatment of the detail of Pompeius' wars and no estimate of him as a commander.

The unremitting burdens of teaching and administration – the former useful at least, sometimes even rewarding, the latter irksome and futile in equal measure – have unduly delayed the writing of this book. It is the more pleasant to give thanks to those whose kindness has helped. A visit to Rome in 1975 was made possible by a grant from the Research Fund of the University of Liverpool. Bruce Marshall presented me with a copy of his book on Crassus before it was generally available, Allen Ward with page proofs of his. Other unpublished material was put at my disposal by Geoffrey Lewis. Pat Sweetingham laboured well beyond the call of duty in producing the final typescript with breathtaking speed. But my greatest debt is to Peter Wiseman and above all to Josette Jackson, who both read the entire book in draft and were responsible for countless improvements in both style and substance.

Robin Seager

ABBREVIATIONS

Abbreviations and short titles not included in this list should be immediately intelligible on reference to the bibliography.

AHR	*American Historical Review*
AJP	*American Journal of Philology*
ANRW	H. Temporini (ed.), *Aufstieg und Niedergang der römischen Welt* I 1, Berlin/New York, 1972
Athen.	*Athenaeum*
CAH	*Cambridge Ancient History*
CM	*Classica et Mediaevalia*
CP	*Classical Philology*
CQ	*Classical Quarterly*
CR	*Classical Review*
CRAI	*Comptes-rendus de l'Académie des Inscriptions et Belles Lettres*
CSCA	*California Studies in Classical Antiquity*
GC	A. H. J. Greenidge and A. M. Clay, *Sources for Roman History 133–70 B.C.*^{2} (ed. E. W. Gray), Oxford, 1960
GR	*Greece and Rome*
ILLRP	*Inscriptiones Latinae Liberae Rei Publicae* (ed. A. Degrassi), Firenze, 1963–5
ILS	*Inscriptiones Latinae Selectae* (ed. H. Dessau), repr. Berlin, 1962
JP	*Journal of Philology*
JRS	*Journal of Roman Studies*
LAAA	*Liverpool Annals of Art and Archaeology*
LCM	*Liverpool Classical Monthly*
MRR	T. R. S. Broughton, *The Magistrates of the Roman Republic*, New York, 1951–60

Philol.	*Philologus*
Phoen.	*Phoenix*
RE	A. von Pauly, G. Wissowa et al. (eds), *Real-Encyclopädie der classischen Altertumswissenschaft*, Stuttgart, 1894–
REA	*Revue des études anciennes*
REL	*Revue des études latines*
RhM	*Rheinisches Museum*
SIG³	*Sylloge Inscriptionum Graecarum³* (ed. W. Dittenberger, F. Hiller von Gärtringen), Leipzig, 1915–24
TAPA	*Transactions of the American Philological Association*

Map 1 _Italy in the Late Republic_

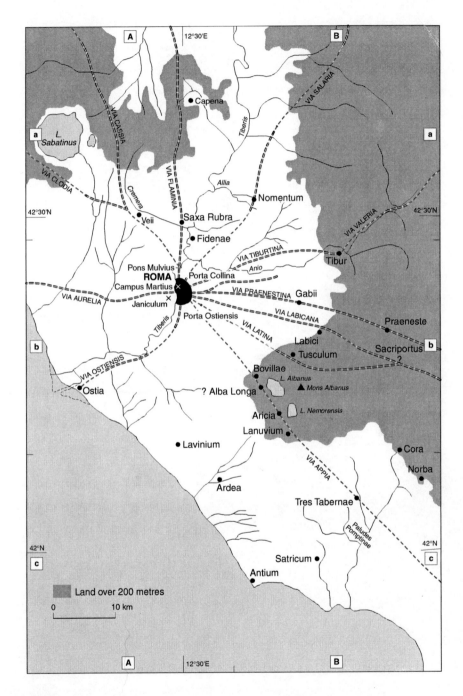

Map 2 *Latium*

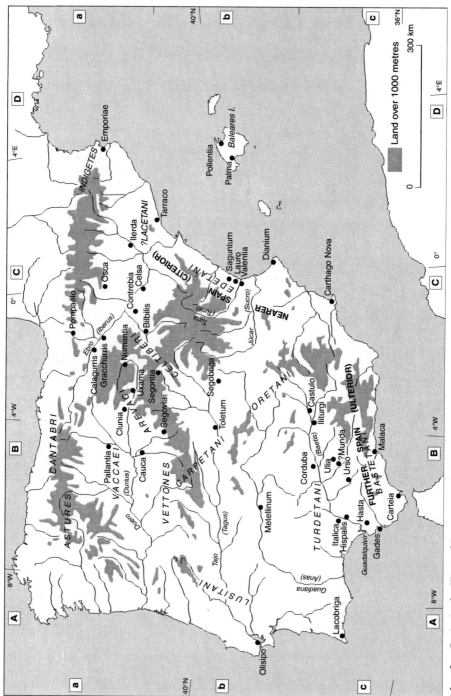

Map 3 *Spain in the Time of Pompeius and Caesar*

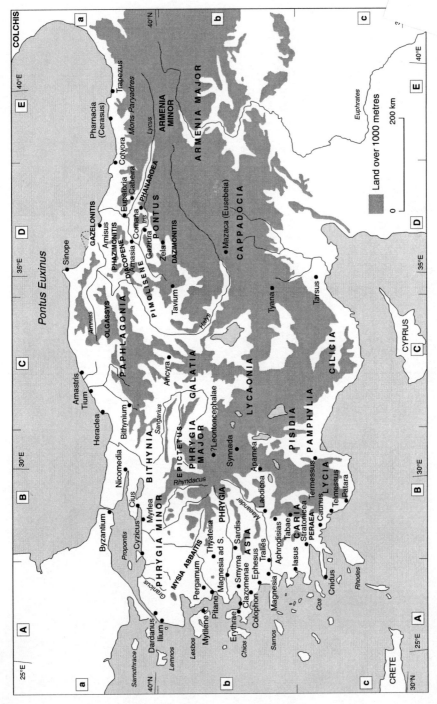

Map 4 Asia Minor

Map 5   *The East*

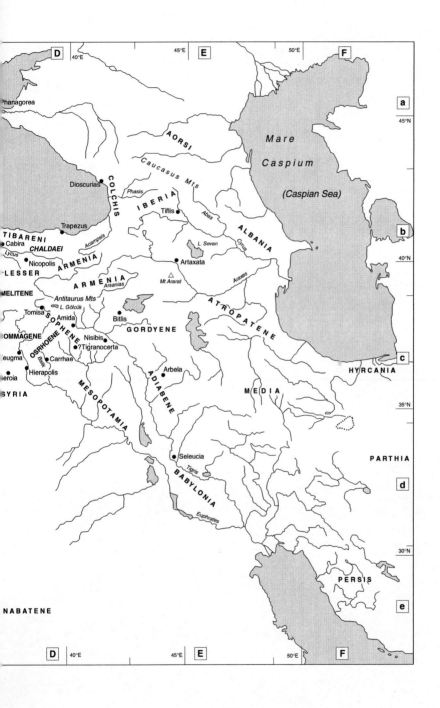

INTRODUCTION
THE HISTORICAL
BACKGROUND – FROM THE
GRACCHI TO SULLA

It was in the civil war that ended in the dictatorship of Sulla that the young Cn. Pompeius took the first steps on the path that led him, by way of two triumphs, to his first consulship in 70. Sulla's victory cast a long shadow over the last decades of the republic. But in his legislation he had been looking backwards, to the upheavals of the past fifty years, during which the supremacy of the senate had been repeatedly challenged, his aim to restore the unquestioned predominance it had, in his perhaps somewhat rose-tinted view, enjoyed before the tribunate of Ti. Gracchus. His measures had a negative and a positive side. He identified those factors that had undermined the senate's power and tried to neutralize them for the future. He also took steps to strengthen it as a body, to make it capable of resisting any challenge that might arise despite his precautions.

Since Sulla's tenure of power and its aftermath are crucial to political developments in the period that embraces the bulk of Pompeius' career, a brief summary of events from Ti. Gracchus to Sulla may help to make that period more accessible, especially to readers with little or no previous acquaintance with Roman history.

TIBERIUS GRACCHUS

Ti. Sempronius Gracchus, tribune in 133, and his younger brother Gaius were men of the highest nobility, linked by birth and marriage with Scipio

Africanus, conqueror of Hannibal, with Scipio Aemilianus, destroyer of Carthage, and with Aemilianus' leading rivals in the senate.

The situation that Tiberius set out to remedy as tribune had arisen gradually. The Roman army was a citizen militia, with a minimum property qualification for service. Since the end of the Hannibalic war a series of protracted wars overseas had kept peasant farmers away from their holdings sometimes for years at a time. Some never came home at all. Others found that in their absence their farms had deteriorated beyond hope of recovery. Such men had no choice but to sell up and drift to Rome or to the nearest town to seek employment. But even Rome had little to offer, though until about 146 a number of major building projects provided some alleviation.

The foreign wars created other problems too. Those fought in the eastern Mediterranean were extremely profitable. But in the distribution of booty, as in most things, Roman society was strikingly hierarchical. So it was the upper class who found themselves with money to spend. Land was the traditional sphere of investment and the rich could benefit from a buyer's market. Moreover, a dispossessed peasant could rarely remain on his former holding as the tenant or employee of the man to whom he had sold it. The wars had also brought in many prisoners, who formed an unprecedentedly large pool of cheap slave labour. Those who had cash to spare to buy up land could also afford slaves to work it.

Thus there came about a widespread change in the ownership of land, from small independent holdings worked by the owner and his family to large estates worked largely by slaves and managed by a bailiff on behalf of an absentee proprietor – the origins of what were later called *latifundia*. This change in ownership did not, however, give rise to a corresponding change in land use, from primarily arable farming to 'ranching', with much increased numbers of livestock being pastured on the land.

There was also a military dimension. Every time a farmer sold all his land, or enough of it to leave him with a smaller holding than the minimum required to make him liable for military service, the army lost a soldier. Not only did the slaves who replaced the free peasants not serve in the army; they might, if they rebelled (as in Sicily in 134), themselves constitute a military threat.

These problems had been noticed before Ti. Gracchus. As consul in 140 C. Laelius, a close friend of Scipio Aemilianus, had planned to take action, but in the face of senatorial opposition had thought better of it. Cynics alleged that this change of heart had earned him his *cognomen* Sapiens, 'the wise'. But Ti. Gracchus was made of sterner stuff.

The details of his agrarian law are controversial, but not crucial here. He sought a solution in the distribution of the *ager publicus*, the public land of the Roman people, acquired largely by right of conquest. Such land might be used in various ways, depending on its location and quality. But the bulk of it was thrown open as common land, with an upper limit of 500 *iugera* on the amount any individual might exploit, on payment of a rent to the treasury of a percentage of produce or a polltax on livestock.

This system had been abused in various ways. By 133 the rents were rarely if ever collected. Nor had the 500 *iugera* limit been observed. The boundaries between private and adjoining public land had also become obscure, whether through conscious deception or genuine confusion, and many occupiers had come to treat the public land they held as if it were their own. A further complication involved Rome's Italian allies. If no Roman took possession of newly acquired public land, inevitably its former Italian owners seized the chance to reoccupy it. Again over time the boundaries between land that was still Italian as of right and land that officially belonged to Rome, though now illegally occupied by Italians, will have become unclear.

Ti. Gracchus introduced a bill to reclaim for the state all public land held by individuals in excess of the legal limit. This was to be distributed in small allotments to those who had lost their land. The allotments were to remain the property of the state and a nominal rent was to be paid. The senators, many of whom were directly affected, were predominantly hostile. So Tiberius took his proposal directly to the *concilium plebis*, without first submitting it to the senate for approval. This was neither illegal nor unprecedented, but highly unusual. The senate persuaded another tribune, M. Octavius, to veto the bill. Tiberius then proposed that Octavius be removed from office for betraying a tribune's fundamental duty to uphold the interests of the people. Octavius was duly deposed and the bill was passed. A commission of three was elected to put it into operation: Tiberius himself, his brother Gaius and his father-in-law Ap. Claudius, the *princeps senatus*.

The senate next tried to sabotage the law by assigning the commission a ludicrously small sum of money. At this point fortune intervened. Attalus III of Pergamum died and left his kingdom to Rome. Thanks to a family connection with Pergamum Ti. Gracchus gained early news of this windfall. He promptly proposed that the royal estate should be used to finance his land commission. This expedient further annoyed his opponents, since it constituted interference by the people in two fields which the senate regarded as its own preserve: foreign affairs and finance.

The activities of the commission were also offensive to many Italians. Italian peasants had suffered just as much as their Roman counterparts from the effects of long fighting overseas, and the Italian towns had been even less able than Rome to cope with the consequent influx of destitute ex-farmers. Yet they were not eligible for allotments under the law. It thus created a new grievance for the Italian lower classes and a new reason for them to hanker after Roman citizenship. The Italian land-owning classes were also upset by the law. The commissioners had received judicial powers to determine in disputed cases what was and was not public land. Italians, even of the upper class, were more vulnerable to pressure and chicanery than Roman citizens. They were therefore bound to suffer disproportionately from the activities of the commission and so to resent even more bitterly their social and political inferiority. Agrarian legisla-tion did not create the Italians' desire for Roman citizenship, but it greatly exacerbated it, and henceforth the two issues more than once arose to-gether.

The dogged ingenuity Tiberius displayed in circumventing opposition probably bears witness to nothing more sinister than determination to get his law passed and make it work. But his enemies claimed that he was aiming to set himself up as a demagogic tyrant. To protect the collective supremacy of the ruling class against the ambitious individual the Roman constitution had two built-in safeguards: any office-holder had at least one colleague who could, if need be, veto his actions, and his tenure of power was of limited duration, normally one year. By deposing Octavius from office Tiberius had nullified the first of these safeguards. For the remainder of his tribunate the senate was powerless to check him. But once he was out of office his opponents could, if they wished, repeal his law and devise appropriate charges to destroy his political future.

Then came the bombshell. Tiberius announced his intention of standing for immediate re-election. He may have had further legislative plans, as his brother later claimed. More probably he merely hoped that a second term would give the furore a chance to die down and free him from the fear of prosecution. But the news inspired in his opponents a nightmare vision of a tribune re-elected year after year as long as he retained the confidence of the plebs, introducing whatever legislation he pleased, unchecked by the veto, while the senate was reduced to the role of impotent spectator.

On the day of the election both sides were on edge and tension soon escalated into violence. A mob led by the *pontifex maximus* Scipio Nasica attacked the tribune and his supporters. Tiberius himself and many of his followers were killed and their bodies thrown into the Tiber. The consul of

132, Popillius Laenas, rounded up many more, who were condemned by a court created by the senate, in defiance of the laws on the right of appeal to the people.

The agrarian law was not repealed. This confirms that it was Tiberius' methods and their possible constitutional implications, more than the content of the law, that had angered and alarmed the senate.

GAIUS GRACCHUS

In 125 the consul M. Fulvius Flaccus, by now a land commissioner, proposed the enfranchisement of those Italians who wanted Roman citizenship, the extension of the right of *prouocatio* to those who did not. This measure was allegedly inspired by Italian complaints about the commission and was intended to neutralize them. But the senate was hostile and packed Flaccus off to protect Massilia from the Gauls.

By this time the younger Gracchus had shown his sympathy for the allies. In 126 a tribune, M. Junius Pennus, had expelled all non-citizens from Rome, probably in response to agitation against the agrarian law. C. Gracchus spoke against Pennus' law before leaving to serve as quaestor in Sardinia. In 125 a single allied city, Fregellae, rose in revolt. The rising was easily crushed by a praetor, L. Opimius, but it is interesting that his enemies accused Gaius of complicity, further evidence of his perceived attitude to Italian aspirations.

Gaius was elected tribune for 123 and embarked, with the active support of some of his colleagues, on a wide-ranging programme designed to relieve urban unemployment and the hardship that arose from the uncertainties of the grain supply, to weaken or at least establish some checks on the collective power of the senate, and to protect himself against assassination and his work against repeal. In so doing he set up a model for later politicians who chose, for whatever reason, to follow the *popularis* path.

To benefit the masses Gaius re-enacted his brother's agrarian law and provided for the building of granaries and roads and the distribution of corn at a cheap fixed price. More striking was his proposal to establish colonies overseas, most controversially on the site of Rome's ancestral enemy Carthage, to be renamed Junonia. This could be seen as an insult to the memory of Scipio Aemilianus, who had placed the devastated city under a curse. Gaius also sought to broaden his support by appealing to the as yet ill-defined equestrian order. The contracts for farming the taxes of the new and extremely wealthy province of Asia (the former kingdom of Pergamum) were to be auctioned at Rome, to the advantage of Roman *publicani*. More importantly, Gaius transferred from the senate to the *equites* the right to serve as jurors in the court that dealt with extortion by provincial governors. Senatorial juries were notorious for acquitting their manifestly guilty friends and relatives. But the law did not ameliorate the lot of the provincials, who now fell victims to a new form of exploitation perhaps worse than what had gone before. Governors eager to line their own pockets knew that if they aided and abetted the excesses of the *publicani* they would have nothing to fear from an equestrian jury if they were prosecuted on their return to Rome. The law also had grave political repercussions. Their status as jurors gave the *equites* an identity and a self-awareness they had not hitherto possessed, and control of the courts became an issue of contention between them and the senate for more than fifty years.

The one element in Gaius' programme still to be brought before the people was the most likely to provoke opposition at all levels. Determined to improve the lot of the Italians, he proposed that the Latins should receive citizenship, the remainder of the allies Latin status. He had been re-elected for 122, apparently without incident. But his position was gravely under-mined while he and Fulvius Flaccus were away from Rome, attempting to establish the colony at Carthage. The senate had learned from the experi-ence of 133. They found a tribune, M. Livius Drusus, not to veto but to outbid Gaius, abolishing the rent on Gracchan allotments and proposing no fewer than twelve new colonies – these were never sent out. Drusus also drove a wedge between the Latins and the other allies by granting the Latins *prouocatio*, even on military service. The consul C. Fannius too spoke against the bill, exploiting the reluctance of the urban plebs to share its few privileges and accusing Gaius of monarchical ambitions. The bill probably never came to the vote, and the collapse of Gaius' fortunes was underlined when he failed to secure re-election for 121.

Early in that year Minucius Rufus proposed the repeal of the law for the colony at Carthage. Had Gaius still been tribune he could have vetoed. But as a private citizen all he could do was demonstrate. The inevitable riot ensued. For the first time the *senatus consultum ultimum* was passed, instruct-ing the consuls to ensure that the republic came to no harm. L. Opimius, the destroyer of Fregellae, enthusiastically complied. Gaius himself and Fulvius Flaccus were killed, along with many of their supporters, and Opimius then led a witch-hunt against the survivors, just as Popillius had done in 132.

MARIUS

The work of the land commission was gradually eroded and finally brought to a halt by a law of 111. But the most noteworthy events of the twenty years between the tribunates of C. Gracchus and Saturninus took place further afield: wars in Gaul against the marauding Cimbri and Teutones and in Africa against the Numidian king Jugurtha, which brought to prominence both the new man C. Marius and his eventual rival L. Cornelius Sulla.

Marius first attracted attention as tribune in 119, with a law to lessen the pressure put by influential men on voters at the elections. But the Jugurthine war brought him fame and his first consulship. Jugurtha's seizure of sole control in Numidia had induced only the most sluggish Roman response. It coincided with the first defeats by the Cimbri and Teutones, which revived old nightmares of the Gallic sack of Rome, while Jugurtha enjoyed the favour of some distinguished Romans and bought the support of many more. Only when he overplayed his hand in 112 with a massacre of Italian businessmen at Cirta did equestrian anger and fear combine with *popularis* rage at the corruption and inertia of the nobles and force the senate to take action. A tribune, C. Mamilius, established a court with equestrian jurors to try those accused of intriguing with Jugurtha, while Q. Caecilius Metellus, *cos.* 109, later to be called Numidicus for his successes, was to prove Rome's first effective commander in the war.

The Metelli liked to take up men of talent who lacked resources, both new men and impoverished aristocrats. Both Sulla and Pompeius were soon to benefit, but at this time the most notable examples were M. Aemilius Scaurus, consul in 115 and *princeps senatus*, and Marius, who held the praetorship in the same year. Marius accompanied Metellus to Africa, where a soothsayer promised him no fewer than seven consulships. He asked Metellus for leave to return to Rome to stand for 107. Metellus, like most nobles, believed that the praetorship should mark the upper limit of a new man's political ambitions and contemptuously refused.

So Marius set about undermining Metellus' position. He convinced the equestrian businessmen at Utica, whose activities had been drastically curtailed by the war, that if he were in command he would quickly finish off Jugurtha. They mobilized their contacts at Rome, in their own class and in the senate, to back Marius for the consulship. *Popularis* agitation on behalf of the new man against the supposedly idle and incompetent noble also told in his favour. Marius was elected and soon afterwards the people appointed him to the command in place of Metellus.

The property qualification for military service had been lowered more than once, but the supply of manpower had constantly decreased. Marius ignored the property qualification altogether and enrolled the *capite censi*. This step was to have dramatic consequences. These men had no land, but some no doubt had once owned land and lost it, and all looked to their commander to secure them allotments at the end of their term of service from a shortsightedly reluctant senate. Their primary loyalty was not to senate and people but to their general, and if one day a general were to ask them to march against Rome, they might well be ready to follow.

In bringing the war to a successful conclusion Marius, as Sallust makes abundantly clear, enjoyed a great deal of good luck. Moreover, the elaborate diplomacy which led to the surrender of Jugurtha by Bocchus of Mauretania, with whom he had taken refuge, was entirely the work of Marius' quaestor Sulla. But for the moment there seems to have been no friction between the two men and Marius returned to Rome as the hero of the hour.

He was soon to find fresh employment. The ending of the Jugurthine war coincided with new disasters in the North. For a time the threat to Italy had receded, as the Cimbri and Teutones turned aside into Spain. But now they had returned, and at Arausio in 105 inflicted Rome's worst defeat since Cannae itself. Two armies, under the consul Cn. Mallius Maximus and the proconsul Q. Servilius Caepio, had been annihilated, in part because the noble Caepio had refused to co-operate with the new man Mallius. Marius, hailed as a potential saviour, was elected to a second consulship for 104, and to ensure that he enjoyed sufficient *auctoritas* to be regarded as supreme commander he was re-elected each year, holding office for five successive years from 104 to 100.

SATURNINUS

During that time Marius formed an uneasy alliance with the third of the great *popularis* tribunes, L. Appuleius Saturninus. Saturninus modelled himself on the Gracchi, particularly on Gaius, and flaunted in his entourage one L. Equitius, who he claimed was an illegitimate son of Ti. Gracchus. But his background was very different (no member of his family had risen beyond the praetorship) and his methods were markedly rougher. When an opponent tried to cut short an assembly by reporting an ominous clap of thunder, Saturninus offered the notorious response: 'If you don't shut up it'll hail as well!'

As quaestor at Ostia in 104 Saturninus was dismissed from his post by the senate. But he secured the tribunate for 103 and introduced a corn law on the Gracchan model and a law to distribute land in north Africa to Marius' veterans of the Jugurthine war, in order, it is said, to secure their good will. This formulation should serve as a warning against the erroneous assumption that Saturninus was no more than an instrument of Marius. Each tried to exploit the other in pursuit of his individual agenda; hence their association was inevitably stormy and shortlived. Saturninus also brought a prosecution against one of the villains of Arausio, Cn. Mallius, while his colleague C. Norbanus arraigned Caepio.

The most important measure of Saturninus' first tribunate was his law to establish a court, with equestrian jurors, to hear cases of treason, *maiestas populi Romani minuta*. (A more literal translation would be 'the diminution of the greaterness of the Roman people'.) The specific offences listed in the law will have pertained to misconduct by governors and commanders in the field. But it was also possible to bring a charge on any grounds that could be presented as a derogation of *maiestas*. This explains why the law was not repealed after Saturninus' death. Instead the senate turned it into a weapon against popular tribunes who resorted to violence in pursuit of their aims. But the vagueness and ambiguity of the law also made it an unreliable tool. Defence counsel could often claim that a client's conduct did not constitute a diminution of *maiestas* but rather upheld or even enhanced it.

Saturninus had annoyed the optimates in 103 enough for the censors of 102 to try to prevent his inclusion on the roll of the senate and expel his friend C. Servilius Glaucia. But Saturninus had sufficient influence with the urban plebs to summon a mob to deter the censors from their purpose.

Glaucia was tribune in 101 and may already have held the office in 104. In one of these years, or perhaps as praetor in 100, he passed a law restoring to the *equites* control of the extortion court, which they had briefly lost in 106, when the consul Caepio either handed it back to the senate or introduced mixed juries. In 101 he presided at the tribunician elections for 100, at which Saturninus secured a second term, though only at the cost of murdering a fellow candidate.

Saturninus brought in further laws for the distribution of land to veterans, in Sicily, Achaea, Macedonia and Cisalpine Gaul. But his fragile alliance with Marius was soon to end. Marius was afraid that his veterans might come to feel greater loyalty to Saturninus than to himself. He also longed to be accepted by the nobility, who looked askance at his association with Glaucia and Saturninus. To protect his agrarian law against repeal

Saturninus had appended to it an oath to maintain it, to be sworn by all senators. It was Marius himself who found a solution. The senators should swear, he said, to observe the law in so far as it was a law. But if the law were rescinded, because it had been passed by violence or against the auspices, the oath would fall with it and they would be absolved. Only Metellus Numidicus spurned this subterfuge and went into exile in preference to taking the oath. His departure highlighted a serious error into which Saturninus had fallen. The law benefited only the veterans, neglecting the urban poor, who became so hostile to Saturninus that many volunteered to fight for Metellus should he choose to resist. The tribunes of the sixties and Caesar in 59 did not repeat this mistake in their agrarian bills.

The last straw for Marius came at the consular elections. Saturninus had already been elected to a third tribunate for 99, with L. Equitius, the bogus Gracchus, as his colleague. Glaucia, already tribune and praetor in successive years, now stood illegally for the consulship of 99. To improve his chances he and Saturninus murdered one of his principal rivals, C. Memmius. In the ensuing riot Saturninus, Glaucia and others took refuge on the Capitol. The *s.c.u.* was passed, and Marius showed no hesitation in acting against his former associates. He forced them to surrender by cutting off their water supply, but promised that they would be given a fair trial. They were imprisoned in the senate house, but when the angry mob climbed on to the building and pelted them to death with tiles torn from the roof Marius did not see fit to intervene.

The reasons for the failure of the Gracchi and Saturninus are clear. The sources of support that a tribune could muster were too disparate in their social background and political concerns and too fickle to be relied on for long. In particular a tribune had no troops at his command, a lack that Saturninus tried in vain to remedy by his appeal to the Marian veterans. Clodius, with his private army enrolled from the *collegia*, was the first to find an answer to the problem, and so survived for another five years after his tribunate. The senate had been frightened and shaken by its confrontations with the tribunes, but had emerged with its collective predominance largely intact. It was an altogether different and graver threat, the rebellious general at the head of an army, that was to bring the republic down.

THE NINETIES

In the nineties Marius faded into the background. Military crises had brought him to unrivalled prominence, but his successes had rendered him obsolete, at least for the time being – a problem that would later confront Pompeius too. In 98 his enemy Metellus Numidicus was recalled, thanks largely to the efforts of his son, whose dedication earned him the *cognomen* Pius. In the same year the consular *lex Caecilia Didia* banned 'tacking', that is, the combination of widely disparate proposals in a single law, so that the people might be forced to pass something it did not want in order to secure some more desirable outcome.

Two interesting *maiestas* trials took place in 95. The first was that of C. Norbanus, who as tribune in 103 had prosecuted Caepio for the defeat at Arausio. The prosecutor was P. Sulpicius, the future tribune of 88. The case achieved fame because of the daring defence by one of the two leading orators of the day, M. Antonius, who exploited the vagueness of the *maiestas* law by claiming that sedition could serve the interests of the state. Norbanus was acquitted. A tit-for-tat case was then brought against Caepio's son, who as quaestor in 103 resorted to violence against Saturninus' corn law. Caepio was defended by Antonius' only rival in the courts, L. Crassus. Again both sides made good use of the law's imprecision, and again the verdict was acquittal.

But the most important event of 95 was the *lex Licinia Mucia*, passed by the consuls L. Crassus and Q. Mucius Scaevola the jurist. This set up a court to investigate cases of allies who had been passing themselves off as Roman citizens. Asconius claims this as the prime cause of the Social War, because of the resentment it aroused among the Italian upper classes. The war did not break out until the end of 91, but the Italians, remembering the fiasco of Fregellae, will have made very thorough preparations for concerted action. They were in fact probably ready for action by 92, but held their hands in the hope that M. Livius Drusus, tribune designate for 91, would be able to do something for them by peaceful means.

The year 92 is notorious for a trial of a different kind, that of P. Rutilius Rufus, *cos.* 105, for extortion in Asia. After his consulship Q. Scaevola had governed the province and had introduced a new edict, designed to protect the provincials against the excesses of the *publicani*. Despite his seniority Rutilius had accompanied him as a legate. On his return Rutilius found himself arraigned for extortion, at the instigation of the outraged and frustrated tax-farmers, before a jury of their equestrian peers.

Rutilius, a Stoic of extreme views, refused to offer serious resistance. Antonius and Crassus both begged to defend him, but in vain; only his nephew C. Cotta was allowed to say a few words. Rutilius was duly condemned and, unable to pay the enormous fine, went into exile, pointedly retiring to Asia, where he was welcomed as a hero by the people he had supposedly oppressed.

This was to the best of our knowledge the first flagrantly unjust verdict brought in by an equestrian jury, though probably only because no other governors had tried to restrain the *publicani*, preferring to aid and abet their depredations. It created a furore and voices were raised to demand the restoration of senatorial juries, most notably that of M. Scaurus, who was prosecuted in this year for taking bribes from Mithradates VI of Pontus. Scaurus, a politician of consummate skill, promptly brought a counter-charge against his accuser, the younger Caepio, and both cases were dropped. But the experience prompted Scaurus to suggest to Livius Drusus that when he became tribune he should return the courts to the senate.

LIVIUS DRUSUS AND THE SOCIAL WAR

Livius Drusus is a complex character. Son of the opponent of C. Gracchus, he seems to have been convinced that he could solve all Rome's political and social problems. His aims in some ways prefigured those of Sulla, for he too wished to reinforce the supremacy of the senate. In the interests of concord he set out to alleviate the various grievances of *equites*, plebs and Italians. His chosen instrument was the tribunate, to the confusion not only of modern scholars but also of his own contemporaries, many of whom could not fathom the paradox of a tribune passing laws clearly modelled on those of the Gracchi in order to restore and uphold the *auctoritas* of the senate. That the very men he was trying to benefit failed completely to understand what he was doing is highlighted especially by Velleius Paterculus, whose percep-tively sympathetic remarks on Drusus may owe their inspiration in part to the tribune's kinship with Velleius' hero Tiberius' mother Livia.

To win the support of the common people Drusus passed corn and agrarian laws. Then he set out to end the struggle between *equites* and senate for control of the courts. Whether he proposed to share the courts between the orders or to double the numbers of the senate by adding to it 300 *equites* and then to restore the courts to this inflated senate is unclear: the confusion of the sources permits no confident conclusion. What is certain is that, far from achieving a reconciliation between *equites* and senate, Drusus aroused the bitter resentment of both and lost a great deal of his support. The *equites* were further offended by a law, perhaps retro-spective, that made equestrian jurors liable to bribery charges. Even the allies were alarmed by another of his measures, to establish colonies (probably those originally provided for by his father) in Italy and Sicily. They were afraid that the law would reopen the question of *ager publicus* still illegally occupied by Italians.

So by the time Drusus finally approached the question of Italian enfranchisement the omens were far from propitious. If all had gone according to plan, senate, *equites* and plebs, duly sweetened by the measures passed in their interests, would have been ready to accept, even if without enthusiasm, the extension of the citizenship. Instead, Drusus had alienated virtually all strata of Roman society and even the Italians themselves were now deeply suspicious. His situation worsened with the death of his principal supporter in the senate, L. Crassus. If the enfranchisement bill was ever brought before the people, it was rejected.

Such of Drusus' laws as had been passed were now declared invalid by the senate at the instigation of his most vociferous opponent, the consul L. Marcius Philippus, both on religious grounds – Philippus was an augur – and because they allegedly offended against the *lex Caecilia Didia*. Drusus offered no resistance. But this passivity did not save him from the fate of his distinguished predecessors. He too was murdered, though not in a riot, but stabbed one day on his way home from the forum.

The Italians must have felt that there was now no hope of achieving their aspirations by peaceful means, and war broke out before the end of the year. The vast majority, whatever their social standing, wanted Roman citizenship. Only a minority of diehards came to feel over the course of the war that they were fighting for their independence. But different aspects of citizenship mattered to different categories of Italians. The upper classes wanted to be placed on a footing of at least nominal social and legal equality with their Roman counterparts. Many will have wanted to vote, some at least to embark on a career in Roman politics. Those who had been abroad will have had an unofficial taste of what citizenship meant, since Greeks and others in the East tended to play safe by treating anyone from Italy as a Roman. The poor will have wanted to share in land distributions and the other material benefits reserved for the Roman plebs. All, whatever their rank, will have wanted protection against the arbitrary outrages to which Roman officialdom was prone when dealing with lesser breeds without the law.

The year 90 began in recriminations. A tribune of supposedly dubious ancestry, Q. Varius, set up a *quaestio* manned by equestrian jurors to hear charges against those who had stirred up the allies to rebel. Many, though not all, of those condemned were former friends of Livius Drusus, on whom the *equites* were happy to take vengeance for his attempt to deprive them of the courts. The episode is also noteworthy for an incident that neatly encapsulates the meaning of *auctoritas*. In a public meeting Varius dared to suggest that the aged M. Scaurus was guilty of fomenting sedition. Scaurus confronted his accuser and spoke briefly: 'Q. Varius, a Spaniard, claims that M. Scaurus, *princeps senatus*, stirred up the allies to revolt. M. Scaurus, *princeps senatus*, denies it. There are no witnesses. Which, citizens, is it fitting you should believe?' It may be assumed that at this point Varius started running.

A *lex Iulia* late in 90 and a *lex Plautia Papiria* in 89 enfranchised virtually all those who had not taken up arms or were prepared to lay them down. These laws did not represent a Roman change of heart; they were merely a response to a conspicuous lack of military success in the first year of the war. But in 89 the tide turned. Two commanders in particular distinguished themselves: Sulla and Pompeius' father, Pompeius Strabo. Strabo also seized the chance to extend his patronage by granting Latin rights to the people of the Transpadane region.

For many Italians, as indicated above, the vote was not the principal motive for seeking citizenship. But it was this aspect of enfranchisement that most concerned the Roman ruling class. A huge influx of new potential voters would place great strain on traditional networks of patronage and *clientela* and, on a cynical level, make bribery much more expensive. Legislative and electoral assemblies would thus become much more difficult to control. Once concessions had been made on the citizenship issue, the senate therefore made every effort to delay their implementation and minimize the disruption caused by the influx by confining the new citizens to a small minority of tribes.

SULLA'S FIRST CONSULSHIP

The eyes of would-be commanders were soon to be fixed on another war, potentially rich in glory and profit. The expansion of Mithradates VI of Pontus, and in particular his invasion of Bithynia, could not be overlooked. The command would naturally go to a consul of 88. So the elections of 89 were hotly contested. Not all those who wished to stand were legally entitled. Pompeius Strabo was eager for an immediate second consulship, while C. Caesar Strabo had not yet held the praetorship. Both were suppressed, Caesar Strabo thanks to the efforts of a tribune of 88, P. Sulpicius, a friend of Livius Drusus who was determined to distribute the new citizens fairly throughout all the tribes.

The successful candidates were Sulla, who thus earned a fitting reward for his successes in the Social War, and Q. Pompeius Rufus, another associate of Drusus and Sulpicius. Sulpicius might therefore have hoped for the support, or at least the neutrality, of both consuls. Instead he found that both opposed him. So he turned to another man who was dreaming of a Mithradatic war, Marius. Despite his advanced age Marius saw in the prospect of a new major conflict the chance to revive his waning prestige and win fresh laurels. The arrangement was simple. Marius would use his influence to force through the distribution law. In return Sulpicius would pass a bill transferring to Marius the command against Mithradates, which by now had been allotted to Sulla.

These measures were carried out, in an atmosphere of increasing violence. Eventually Sulla decided it was unsafe to remain in Rome. But the triumph of Sulpicius and Marius was shortlived. Sulla, determined not to yield, took a step from the consequences of which the republic was never to recover. He already had an army encamped outside Nola, one of a few places still in arms after the Social War, which he had meant to use as the nucleus of the force he would lead to Asia. Now he told the troops what had happened. Marius, he said, would not trust them. So they would be deprived of the lavish booty they would have won in an easy campaign against effete and unwarlike enemies. (This estimate of the opposition was to prove conspicuously false, but Sulla, like many others at Rome, may well have believed it at the time.)

The army responded as Sulla intended and clamoured for him to lead them to Rome, there to reclaim his and their rights. The enormity of this action cannot be overstated. Sulla's officers would have none of it, with the sole exception of his quaestor, L. Licinius Lucullus. Nor did the senate welcome him as a saviour from tyranny. Even those who disliked Marius and Sulpicius did not see the march on Rome as an appropriate solution. The common people put up a desperate but hopeless resistance, but Sulla took the city with relative ease.

Sulpicius' legislation was rescinded and he, Marius and some of their supporters were declared public enemies. Sulpicius was hunted down and killed, while Marius eventually escaped to Africa. It may be that Sulla now passed a series of laws that prefigured the reforms of his dictatorship. If so, the details are obscure. But fortunately any measures he enacted in 88 were in force for so short a time that our ignorance of them is of little practical importance.

Sulla could not stay long in Rome. His pose as the champion of law and order did not allow him to keep an army in the city, and without it he did not feel safe. The Marians were gathering in Africa, there were rumours of plots in Rome itself, and Pompeius Strabo had an army close enough at hand to take advantage of Sulla's example. The reliable Pompeius Rufus set out to take over Strabo's troops, only to be murdered by them, with Strabo's connivance and probably at his instigation. So Sulla quickly departed to fight Mithradates.

Before he left he had been obliged to allow free elections. The consuls elected for 87, L. Cornelius Cinna and Cn. Octavius, were not to his liking. But all he could do was to make them swear an oath that they would not interfere with his arrangements while he was away. He can hardly have expected this oath to be honoured; it will have been no more than a ploy to seize the moral high ground.

CINNA AND CARBO

On taking office Cinna revived the plan to distribute the new citizens throughout all the tribes. He clashed with Octavius and there were further outbreaks of violence. Cinna was driven from the city, but he knew what to do next. He too had a small force at Nola, with which he took refuge, and set about raising men and money from Italy on the strength of his claim to be the champion of the new citizens. He was soon joined by Marius. The brief and ill-documented civil war that followed, in the course of which Pompeius Strabo fell victim to the plague, ended with the capture of Rome by Marius and Cinna and the death of Octavius.

The purge of their enemies that followed was more drastic than anything that Rome had yet witnessed, though it pales into insignificance beside the slaughter that Sulla perpetrated on his return from the East. Among the victims were M. Antonius and L. Crassus. Cinna had himself elected to an immediate second consulship for 86, with Marius as his colleague. So Marius achieved the seventh consulship promised by the omens, though he died when the year was only a fortnight old.

The years of Cinna's predominance, during which he and his associate Cn. Carbo virtually monopolized the consulship, are difficult to write about because of the profound hostility of the sources. This bias is easily explained: Sulla won, and Sulla wrote an autobiography, which came inevitably to dominate the tradition. Though Sulla had been declared a public enemy, it seems that Cinna was prepared to co-operate at least until the problem of Mithradates had been dealt with. In 86 L. Valerius Flaccus and C. Flavius

Fimbria were sent out to the war with instructions to liaise with Sulla if he were willing or, if he refused, at least to fight Mithradates first.

But Sulla remained intransigent. Indeed his faithful subordinate Lucullus deliberately allowed Mithradates to escape from Pitane rather than co-operate with Fimbria. In his letters to Rome Sulla made his position clear. On his return he would take vengeance on his enemies for their actions against him, but he had no quarrel with anyone else, including the new citizens. In 85 he made a peace with Mithradates at Dardanus that even his own loyal army saw as bordering on treason, and set about reorganizing the wartorn provinces and preparing for the civil war to come.

Cinna and Carbo at last put into practice the distribution of the new citizens and began to raise troops in the hope of meeting Sulla in the Balkans. But Cinna was murdered in a mutiny shortly after the young Pompeius had left his camp and withdrawn to Picenum to await develop-ments. When Sulla finally landed in Italy in 83 he was joined by various noteworthy figures who brought with them forces of their own, most notably Metellus Pius, M. Crassus and of course Pompeius. He made agreements with the Italian peoples, promising not to take away their hardwon citizenship, though the Samnites seem to have been excluded, probably because Sulla refused to acknowledge the validity of their surren-der to Marius in 87.

The civil war was brief. Of Sulla's opponents Carbo was driven out of Italy first to Africa and then to Sicily, where he was later hunted down by Pompeius, while his colleague in the consulship of 82, the younger C. Marius, was besieged in Praeneste. Their most able lieutenant, Q. Sertorius, fled to Spain, where he remained a thorn in the side of Rome for another ten years. When Sulla took Rome he and his supporters indulged in an orgy of killing. Then he set off for Praeneste. In a desperate attempt to raise the siege a Samnite army marched on Rome. Sulla was forced to turn back, but succeeded in crushing the opposition at the battle of the Colline Gate, though much of the credit for the victory belonged to Crassus. Soon afterwards Praeneste fell and Marius was killed.

SULLA'S DICTATORSHIP

Even before Sulla became dictator, the senate had passed decrees validating all his acts, in the past and for the future. Among the first was the most notorious, the establishment of the proscriptions, ironically undertaken to impose some semblance of order on the previously indiscriminate killing of opponents. Several lists were posted. The lives (if they had not already been killed in the fighting) and property of those whose names appeared were forfeit and their descendants suffered various political disabilities. Only men of senatorial and equestrian rank were named. Sulla was not concerned with the rank and file, who had merely followed the lead of their betters. The criterion was simple: to have been on the wrong side in the civil war. But it is clear that the lists were tampered with in pursuit of private feuds and financial gain, not only in Rome but all over Italy.

Sulla then recommended the appointment of a dictator to set the state in order, and made it discreetly clear that he would not refuse the task. He was duly elected, with an *interrex* presiding, since the consuls were absent and perhaps both already dead. No time limit was set on his appointment, but neither he nor anyone else believed that he was being given power for life. Nobody knew how long he would need to carry out his mission, but all will have taken it for granted that once he had done so he would abdicate, as indeed he did.

His principal objective was to restore the collective supremacy of the senate. He therefore set out to remove all the threats to that supremacy that his knowledge of recent history could identify. Popular tribunes had undermined the senate and irritated Sulla himself, so he abolished the legislative powers of the tribunate and banned ex-tribunes from holding any higher office. The multiple consulships of Marius, Cinna and Carbo had given individuals too much power, so he revived old laws on the ages at which magistracies could be held and the interval that must elapse before iteration. To ensure that the senate was kept up to strength for the future he raised the number of quaestors elected each year from twelve to twenty and allowed them to enter the senate at the end of the year instead of waiting for enrolment at the next census.

But the senate needed more immediate reinforcement. Civil war, the proscriptions and natural wastage had reduced it to not much more than half its paper strength of three hundred. Sulla first brought its numbers back up to the three hundred mark, then doubled its size by promoting a further three hundred *equites*. The courts were then restored to this much enlarged senate and the whole system of criminal justice was revised and expanded. This measure was only a partial success. The gulf between senate and *equites* seems to have been bridged to a large extent, but the new senate was too large and socially diffuse to function as a coherent whole. The old nobility must have felt nothing in common with the vast mass of new members, and increasingly the upper echelon dominated the proceedings of the senate and dictated its policy in so far as it had one.

The common people suffered from the abolition of the corn dole. But the measure that had the most far-reaching consequences for the poor was the seizure of land all over Italy from cities and peoples that had supported the Marians to provide land for the settlement of Sulla's veterans. This created economic and social problems and resentments that occasioned intermittent upheavals for another twenty years.

There was, moreover, one threat to the predominance of the senate that Sulla could not legislate effectively against, though he tried, re-enacting and expanding the existing law on *maiestas*. That was the menace of a contumacious proconsul, at the head of an army more loyal to himself than to Rome. Sooner or later a new Sulla would appear, one who was not paradoxically devoted to shoring up a tottering senate. The threat of prosecution for treason would serve as no deterrent to such a man, whose actions would be determined not by considerations of legality but by purely pragmatic calculation of his chances of success in civil war. If he won he would not be prosecuted. If he lost he would be unlikely to live long enough to face a court.

Sulla cannot have been unaware of the danger. But he could fairly claim that he had given the senate a chance. It was now up to the senate and those who came forward to lead it to seize that chance and resist in the name of *senatus auctoritas* the machinations of over-ambitious individuals. So, by the end of 81 at the latest, Sulla laid down his dictatorship. In 80 he held a second consulship, with Metellus Pius as his colleague. It seemed that constitutional normality, law and order, and the fabric of society had been successfully restored. A budding orator from Marius' home town, Arpinum, in his defence of Sex. Roscius of Ameria, saw fit to enlighten the nobility with a scathing sermon on the duties of their exalted station. Sulla, like others, might have marvelled at the young man's impudence, but he could have had, as Cicero surely knew, no quarrel with the sentiments expressed.

FURTHER READING

Cambridge Ancient History IX^2, ed. J. A. Crook, A. W. Lintott, E. Rawson, Cambridge, 1994.

R. J. Evans, *Gaius Marius, a political biography*, Pretoria, 1994.

M. Gelzer (trans. Seager), *The Roman nobility*, Oxford, 1969.

A. Keaveney, *Sulla, the last republican*, London, 1982.

—— *Rome and the unification of Italy*, London, 1987.

D. Stockton, *The Gracchi*, Oxford, 1979.

L. R. Taylor, *Party politics in the age of Caesar*, Berkeley, 1949.

T. P. Wiseman (ed.), *Roman political life 90 B.C.–A.D. 69*, Exeter, 1985.

1

CN. POMPEIUS STRABO

The Pompeii were late arrivals on the political scene at Rome. The first consul of the name, Q. Pompeius, achieved the office in 141 and survived defeat before Numantia to play a prominent part in the opposition to Ti. Gracchus and hold the censorship in 131.[1] The degree of his kinship with Pompeius Magnus is obscure, though it was certainly not close; indeed most of the family relationships of the Pompeii are a matter for conjecture.[2] But only one member of the *gens* was to be significant in shaping the destinies of the young Cn. Pompeius: his father Cn. Pompeius Strabo, consul in 89.[3] Strabo's estates and the centre of his influence were in Picenum, but the origins of the family must have lain elsewhere, for the tribe of the Pompeii, the Clustumina, is not found in that region. Nevertheless it may be regarded as certain that Strabo was established there before the Social War, and that his appointment to operate in Picenum reflects the senate's awareness of his power in the area.[4]

In the first year of the war Strabo, as a legate of the consul Rutilius Lupus, had at first been defeated on his home ground and shut up in Firmum, but he broke out and drove the enemy back to Asculum. This victory, Rome's first major success of the war, inspired the senate to put off mourning and return to its normal attire.[5] But it was in his consulship that Strabo really came to the fore first as the general who did more than any other to bring the war to a successful conclusion,[6] then as a sinister and disruptive force in politics. Sole consul for most of his term of office after the death of his colleague L. Porcius Cato, who had fallen fighting the Marsi,[7] Strabo's military achievements included the subjection of the Vestini, Paeligni, Marrucini and Marsi,[8] and culminated in the bitterly contested siege of Asculum, the stronghold of the Italian leader Vidacilius.[9]

But his efforts against them in war must not be allowed to obscure Strabo's manifest awareness of the importance of ties with Italian notables to the influence and standing of a Roman politician. The young Cicero served in Strabo's army against the Marsi, and was present at a parley between Strabo and his brother Sextus and the Marsic leader P. Vettius Scato, who had enjoyed ties of *hospitium* with his Roman opponent before the outbreak of war. Cicero remarks on the absence of ill-feeling that characterized the talks.[10] It is surely no accident that Picenum, the scene of Strabo's greatest success, was also the chief source of his own power and of the *clientela* that was his most useful legacy to his son.[11]

Two actions in particular during his consulship reveal Strabo's constant eagerness to broaden that *clientela*. A famous inscription records his grant of citizenship as a reward for distinguished service to a squadron of Spanish cavalry, in accordance with the terms of the *lex Iulia* of 90.[12] This rudimentary link with Spain was to serve as a pointer to the young Pompeius, who is attested as a member of his father's *consilium* on the occasion of the grant.[13] Apart from other individual grants of citizenship – one to P. Caesius of Ravenna is recorded[14] – Strabo passed a law which was designed to extend his own influence from Picenum into the lands beyond the Po. Latin status was accorded to the towns of the Transpadane region, and their leading citizens were henceforth able, like those of other Latin colonies, to achieve Roman citizenship by holding municipal office.[15] Once again Pompeius was to profit by his father's forethought: the Transpadana, along with Picenum, was always to figure as one of his principal sources of manpower.[16]

On 25 December 89 Strabo celebrated his triumph over Asculum.[17] Later writers revel in the paradox, which may be apocryphal, that P. Ventidius, who was himself to triumph over the Parthians in 38,[18] was carried as a baby in arms among the prisoners in Strabo's triumphal procession.[19] Strabo then returned to his army as proconsul.[20] His presence in the neighbourhood of Rome posed a problem for the new consuls of 88, L. Cornelius Sulla, whose achievements in the South in 89 had in some degree matched those of Strabo himself in the North, and Strabo's distant relative Q. Pompeius Rufus, whose son was married to Sulla's daughter.[21] Strabo had already made his ambition clear, for before his return to Rome to celebrate his triumph he had made an abortive attempt to secure an immediate second consulship, on the model of Marius' string of consulships from 104 to 100.[22] Although he remained quiescent throughout the traumatic time of Sulla's clash with the reforming tribune P. Sulpicius,[23] his struggle with Marius for the command against Mithradates (which Strabo too may have coveted), and his march on Rome,[24] Sulla, restored to the consulship, still saw Strabo and his army as a threat: all the more so since he was only too well aware that he had just set a lethal example of what a general with loyal troops at his back might accomplish. He went so far as to introduce a law to recall Strabo to Rome, but Strabo blocked the attempt by putting up a friendly tribune, C. Herennius, to veto the measure.[25]

So a successor was found for Strabo: the consul Pompeius Rufus was appointed, probably by the senate, to take over command of his army.[26] But again Strabo was equal to the occasion. Since legal means of obstruction had proved ineffective, violence would serve, and Strabo's troops were ready to prove their loyalty. Strabo welcomed Rufus to his camp, but the next day, when Rufus was about to conduct a sacrifice, Strabo withdrew from the scene, ostensibly to demonstrate his lack of official standing, whereupon the men crowded round the consul and killed him.[27] Strabo continued in his command, but made no move. He had no wish to fight Sulla if he did not have to, and no doubt he hoped that Sulla, rather than challenge him again, would take the easy way out and go off to fight Mithradates, as in fact he did.[28] For the moment, it was better to bide his time and wait upon the likelihood of trouble after Sulla's departure, in the impending consulship in 87 of his own erstwhile legate L. Cornelius Cinna.[29]

Cinna's expulsion from Rome by his colleague Octavius gave Strabo his opportunity. When Cinna and Marius advanced on the city, Strabo at first sat on the fence. Hostile sources were to put the blame on him for the failure to nip the attack in the bud: by cultivating both sides, it was said, Strabo allowed Cinna and Marius to gain strength, and did not lend his aid to Octavius and the optimates until it was already too late.[30] It was only when the plight of the city induced the senate to ask him to come to the help of the state that Strabo pitched camp outside the Colline Gate.[31] It may be at this point, if there is any truth in the story at all, that Cinna bribed L. Terentius, a companion of the young Pompeius, to kill him, while other accomplices were to set fire to Strabo's tent, a plan thwarted by Pompeius.[32] Even now Strabo did not move until Marius had seized Ostia.[33] He then fought against Cinna's ally Sertorius. However, he was still not prepared to commit himself fully. When Marius occupied the Janiculum, Strabo detached six cohorts from his army to assist Octavius and himself took part in the battle, hoping to secure his second consulship from the senate as the price of his co-operation. But this same hope then led him to prevent Octavius from following up their initial success, for fear that the war might be brought to an end before the consular elections,[34] since too swift a decision would rob his help of its market value.[35] The lack of sympathy for his aspirations shown by the defenders of the city, and perhaps the fear that the likely election of Metellus Pius to the consulship of 86 would lead to his own supersession and prosecution,[36] encouraged Strabo to turn his attention more seriously than before to the prospect of a deal with Cinna. It was he who now persuaded the senate to give a hearing to Cinna's envoys, while he began secret negotiations with Cinna behind Octavius' back.[37]

But Strabo's intrigues were cut short by his death. Plague ravaged both armies, and Strabo fell ill.[38] C. Cassius was sent to take command of the army until such time as Strabo was fit to resume duty, and for a moment this unwelcome news revived the general, but Cassius saw that his end was near. For three days Strabo lingered on, then he died.[39] His funeral was disturbed by rioting, as the mob pulled his body from its bier and dragged it through the mud on a hook, till the tribunes and some other senators restored order and covered the body with their cloaks. Two motives are cited for this popular hatred of Strabo: his avarice and his persistent refusal to come to the aid of the state in its hour of need.[40]

Of the activities of the young Pompeius during his father's lifetime almost nothing is known. Born on 29 September 106,[41] he received his early military training at Strabo's hands[42] and served in his army during the Social War, when his presence at the siege of Asculum is guaranteed by the record of Strabo's *consilium*, in which his son duly figured.[43] He was also present during the *bellum Octavianum*.[44] But his father's career and untimely death left Pompeius in a curiously anomalous position. He was a *nobilis*,[45] but he could not look forward to the easy and automatic career to which a scion of the aristocracy might normally feel himself entitled.[46] The relative novelty of the Pompeii, Strabo's unpopularity,[47] his untimely death and the disturbed nature of the times all combined to deprive Pompeius of that nexus of friendships and connections both inside and outside the senate, often reaching back many generations, on which the power of a *nobilis* was habitually founded. Noble though he was, Pompeius was left with his own way to make in politics. But Strabo had bequeathed him one immeasurable advantage: lands in Picenum and immense influence in the towns of that region, which would form the nucleus of Pompeius' support not only in peace but in war.[48] His career also offered several useful pointers to his son, and time was to prove that Pompeius had noted them all. The value of loyal troops as a lever against the senate or as a safeguard of one's own position, the possible benefits to be gained from playing off one side against the other in times of tension and civil strife, the need to be timely and steadfast in betrayal, the need to build up by all the means at his command the web of friendships at Rome that Strabo had lacked, the importance of money but also the need for discretion in its acquisition,[49] the value of influence in the provinces, especially those that were sources of manpower, and perhaps above all the importance of public opinion:[50] all these were lessons that the young Pompeius learned and never forgot.

2

POMPEIUS, CINNA AND SULLA

The *Cinnanum tempus* was to prove eventful for the young Pompeius. The hatred aroused by Strabo during his lifetime was not extinguished by his death or the disturbances at his funeral. When Cinna captured Rome, his bodyguard broke into Pompeius' house and ransacked it, though that need not prove any special personal rancour either on their part or on Cinna's. In 86 an action was brought against Pompeius, apparently for *peculatus*, to recover booty and cash allegedly due to the treasury from the siege of Asculum, which had somehow found its way into Strabo's own possession and so might now be recovered from his heir.[1] But the exercise served chiefly to show that Pompeius already enjoyed powerful support. His advocates included the censor L. Marcius Philippus, the great orator Q. Hortensius, and Cn. Papirius Carbo, soon to be chosen by Cinna as his colleague in the consulship of the following year.[2] This was not the last time that Philippus was to intervene effectively to further Pompeius' career. The presence of Carbo is perhaps more striking, for his appearances in the courts during these years were few, and it suggests that Pompeius enjoyed the good will of the regime.[3] As a further insurance Pompeius had become engaged to the daughter of the president of the court, P. Antistius. One of Strabo's freedmen was made the scapegoat, and after his inevitable acquittal Pompeius was escorted home by a crowd which ironically sang the wedding march. The marriage took place a few days later.[4]

Given these indications of favour, it is perhaps not surprising that Pompeius next appears in 84 in Cinna's camp, when it had finally become clear that the efforts of the senate and magistrates at home to come to some arrangement with Sulla were doomed to failure.[5] What happened when he arrived there is shrouded with mystery. It seems that he heard something which made him fear or pretend to fear for his life, and in consequence quietly withdrew to a place of safety. His unexplained absence was noted and gave birth to a rumour that Cinna had had him murdered. It was, according to Plutarch, this suspicion that gave rise to the mutiny which ended in Cinna's death.[6] The tale as it stands leaves many questions unanswered. First and foremost, why should Cinna's troops care whether Pompeius had been murdered or not? This seemingly anachronistic estimate of his importance may cast doubt on the authenticity of the whole story. But even if there is a kernel of truth, did Pompeius really fear for his life, and, if so, did he have cause? Did he, or anyone else, deliberately spread the rumour that he had been murdered, to stir up the simmering hostility to Cinna? It is hard to see what Pompeius himself stood to gain from Cinna's death: the only immediate beneficiary was Carbo, who was left for the rest of the year as sole consul. But it would be wild speculation indeed to suppose that Carbo, and even more so that Pompeius or both in conjunction deliberately set out to encompass Cinna's downfall.

For the moment Pompeius was content to sit on his estates in Picenum and await developments.[7] But once Sulla had landed in Italy no sane man could have any doubts as to the eventual result of the civil war, and Pompeius, like many others, saw this as the opportune moment for spectacular commitment to Sulla's cause. Like M. Licinius Crassus and Metellus Pius, he assembled a private army from his clients and hastened to put himself at Sulla's disposal.[8] Whatever doubts Sulla may have had about Pompeius' allegiance because of his own earlier brushes with Strabo,[9] he accepted the offer of a legion as sufficient proof of good will, and at their meeting he paid Pompeius a striking compliment. As was only proper, Pompeius addressed him as *imperator*, and Sulla, with prophetic tact, returned the salutation.[10]

Pompeius' services to Sulla during the brief civil war were noteworthy, and brought him into contact with both Crassus and Metellus Pius.[11] He recruited more men, and by the time of Sulla's victory his private army amounted to three legions.[12] This gave Sulla the problem of what to do about him.[13] He could not be liquidated, like the wretched Lucretius Afella,[14] but he could hardly be left politically on the loose: Sulla will have remembered his father only too well. A solution was provided by that ever opportune device, the political marriage. In 82 Pompeius was offered the hand of Sulla's stepdaughter Aemilia, child of his wife Metella and her previous husband M. Aemilius Scaurus, the consul of 115, the most versatile and unscrupulous politician of his day.[15] She was already married to and indeed pregnant by M'. Acilius Glabrio, the son of the colleague of C. Gracchus. But the need to accommodate Pompeius was paramount, and Glabrio was persuaded to divorce his wife, while Pompeius divorced

Antistia. The match will have suited not only Sulla, but also Aemilia's Metellan relatives. It had long been the habit of the Metelli to bind to themselves by marriage men whose talent outran their financial and political resources. Scaurus and Sulla, as well as Marius, had themselves fallen into this category.

On a practical level it seemed best to Sulla to find Pompeius further immediate employment. So Pompeius' position was for the first time placed on a legal footing. He was invested with praetorian *imperium* by a decree of the senate and sent in pursuit of Carbo, who had fled, when the resistance to Sulla collapsed, first to Africa, then to Sicily.[16] The chase was soon over. Carbo was captured, and despite his pleas for mercy he was put to death and his head sent to Sulla.[17] His defence of Pompeius in 86 might have given him cause to hope,[18] but Pompeius was never to show any hesitation in betraying old friends when the occasion demanded. For him his link with Carbo must merely have underlined the need to prove his loyalty to Sulla by a suitably harsh and dramatic gesture. Carbo's exact position at the time is unclear. He is described as consul at the time of his death, which at least serves to date that event before the end of 82, but, unlike others among Pompeius' early victims, he is also labelled, by sources concerned to justify Pompeius' behaviour, as one of the proscribed.[19] If this is correct, as seems highly likely, it would be a curious oversight if the senate had neglected to deprive him of his consulship, as it had done Cinna in 87.[20]

With Carbo dead, Pompeius and his legate and brother-in-law C. Memmius devoted themselves to the organization of Sicily.[21] From the outset of his career Pompeius showed himself acutely aware of the need to seize every chance to extend his *clientela*.[22] He imposed rigid standards of conduct on his troops in Sicily, sealing their swords in their scabbards and demanding an account of every broken seal.[23] Of the many connections he formed on the island at this time, the most noteworthy was that with Sthenius of Himera.[24]

Before the question of his return to Rome could arise, Pompeius received a letter from Sulla and news of a further decree of the senate, empowering him to proceed to Africa to wipe out the 'Marian' resistance there led by Cn. Domitius Ahenobarbus.[25] So he left Memmius in charge of Sicily and proceeded with all possible speed to Africa.[26] Domitius had secured the support of the king of Numidia, Hiarbas, but according to Plutarch it took Pompeius only forty days to overcome all opposition, capture Domitius' camp, put Hiarbas to death and replace him with the more suitable Hiempsal.[27] Domitius too, like Carbo, was put to death.

Once again his status as one of the proscribed is cited to justify Pompeius, but the act was to have political repercussions later.[28]

The victory over Domitius was a turning-point in Pompeius' career. As far as Sulla was concerned he had served his purpose and must now be translated back into private life. So Pompeius received another letter from the dictator, instructing him to disband all his forces except one legion and with this token force to await the arrival of a successor.[29] But Pompeius was determined not to be so easily removed. He knew that he could not hope to face Sulla in open war, but he also knew that Sulla would be reluctant to destroy the impression of peace and restored constitutional normality by using force to crush a man who had rendered such outstanding service to his cause.[30] At the end of the African campaign his troops had hailed him not only as *imperator* but also for the first time as Magnus,[31] and calculation as well as conceit will have told him that a confrontation was well worth the risk. Once he had decided on this course, he pursued it with both subtlety and vigour. His troops demonstrated angrily at Sulla's attempt to remove him.[32] No doubt they had been discreetly encouraged to do so by Pompeius: another lesson learned from his father.

Sulla gave way, and Pompeius returned to Italy at the head of his army. Instead of giving rein to his resentment, Sulla made a point of flattering the young hero and addressing him as Magnus, and instructed those around him to do likewise.[33] But Pompeius was not satisfied, and demanded a triumph.[34] Technically the claim had some justification, since the operations against Hiarbas provided the formal requirement of a *bellum externum*.[35] At first Sulla refused, no doubt resenting Pompeius' presumption and finding a technical excuse: Pompeius was not a senator. Pompeius persisted, arrogantly warning Sulla that more men worshipped the rising than the setting sun.[36] The situation had been made more difficult for Sulla by the death in childbirth of Pompeius' wife Aemilia.[37] The gamble paid off: Sulla swallowed his pride, though not his resentment, and with an exasperated cry of 'Let him triumph!' withdrew his opposition.[38]

So Pompeius achieved the first extraordinary landmark of his extraordinary career: a triumph in his twenties, the first ever to be celebrated by an *eques*.[39] During the preparations for the ceremony he showed that he could control his men when he wanted to. The troops had threatened to seize and divide amongst themselves the spoils that were destined to grace the procession, but Pompeius quickly suppressed the outbreak, thus earning the admiration of P. Servilius Vatia, the consul of 79, who had previously been among the most outspoken opponents of his claim.[40] Only one element of farce marred the proceedings. Pompeius had planned an innovation: his chariot was to be drawn not by horses but by four elephants. Unfortunately the city gate was too narrow for the elephants to pass through, and so, after two attempts, this piece of ostentation had to be abandoned.[41]

The date of this first triumph is known: 12 March.[42] But the year is disputed, and although the date of Pompeius' birth, 29 September 106, is certain,[43] this is of little help, since his age at the time of the triumph is variously given as twenty-three, twenty-four, twenty-five and twenty-six.[44] These ages give a choice between 82 (which can of course be ruled out), 81, 80 and 79 for the year of the triumph. The case for 79 has been convincingly refuted,[45] but choice between 81 and 80 remains possible. The speed of Pompeius' operations in Sicily and Africa makes it just possible to fit not only the campaign but also the delays and negotiations over the triumph into the first two months of 81, and despite examples of triumphs delayed for far longer periods the earlier date is perhaps to be preferred.[46]

Sulla also provided Pompeius with a new wife, drawn once more from the immediate circle of the Metelli: Mucia, half-sister of two Metelli who were in due course to reach the consulship, Celer, consul in 60, and Nepos, consul in 57.[47] So by 80 Pompeius had already established himself in the kind of position that he was always eager to attain: not that of one who wished to overthrow the state, but one for whom the state had to be ready and at least in appearance willing to make allowances and bend the rules almost to breaking-point. His equestrian triumph marked him out as such a man. On the political level he had challenged Sulla and won, and this gave him the confidence to do so again if the need arose. But at the same time it cannot be too firmly stressed that it was in serving Sulla and destroying his enemies that Pompeius had acquired the strength to face up to him.[48] In 80 and for a further decade Pompeius was a Sullan: an ambitious, arrogant and unmanageable one, it is true, but nevertheless, for what the label is worth, a Sullan.[49]

3

THE RISE TO THE CONSULSHIP

Fresh opportunities were soon to arise for Pompeius to further his military ambitions. At the consular elections of 79 Sulla had not tried to exercise improper influence, and the outcome had not been to his liking. One place had fallen to Q. Lutatius Catulus, son of Marius' rival, who was to prove himself the backbone of the optimates for nearly two decades. But the other consul designate was M. Aemilius Lepidus, whose candidature had displeased Sulla and had brought about a new clash between him and Pompeius, which led Sulla to rebuke him bitterly and cut him out of his will.[1] Pompeius had backed Lepidus for the consulship,[2] perhaps in the belief that Lepidus would probably cause some sort of trouble, and that an unsettled situation of any kind was likely, in some way, to further his own rise. That is not to say that he ever intended to give his support to political or social revolution: it was as the champion of Sulla's senate, albeit in defiance of Sulla's regulations, that he made his early career.

Lepidus lived up to expectations. He threatened to repeal Sulla's acts and recall the survivors of the proscriptions, took up the cause of the dispossessed, whose land had been seized and bestowed on Sulla's veterans, and perhaps passed a law restoring distributions of cheap corn; though at first he appears to have opposed the restoration of tribunician power, it is possible that later he changed his mind.[3] Not surprisingly he quarrelled with Catulus, in particular over the question of a state funeral for Sulla, when the former dictator died in the course of the year.[4] On that issue Catulus carried the day, and Pompeius played a part in ensuring that the ceremony went off in an orderly fashion.[5] But greater danger was to come. A rising broke out in Etruria, where Marius had enjoyed considerable support and repression had been correspondingly harsh.[6] Men who had lost their land, their citizenship or both attacked the Sullan veterans at Faesulae, and the senate viewed the outbreak with sufficient alarm to send both consuls to suppress it.[7] But in Etruria the consuls clashed with one another.[8] Lepidus turned back towards Rome, and Catulus prepared to use force to resist his advance.[9] But the senate, horrified at the prospect of renewed civil war, put pressure on both consuls to swear an oath that they would not take up arms against each other.[10] Perhaps to placate him and get him out of the way, Lepidus was also assigned an important province: Gallia Transalpina, while Cisalpina too appears in the following year under the control of his legate M. Junius Brutus.[11] Then, since Lepidus had not yet held the consular elections, the senate summoned him to do so.[12] Instead, Lepidus marched on Rome at the head of the insurgents he had been sent to suppress, demanding an immediate second consulship.[13] Despite his lack of serious troops he presented a threat that could not be disregarded.[14] He had inherited *clientela* in the Cisalpine region, and if he succeeded in maintaining control there he could establish a link with the rebel Sertorius in Spain.[15] Some senators were in favour of coming to terms,[16] but an old friend of Pompeius, L. Philippus, carried the day in favour of a harder line: the *senatus consultum ultimum* was passed and Catulus was commissioned to put down his former colleague.[17]

To assist him the senate appointed Pompeius.[18] The precise nature of his position is uncertain. His *imperium* was surely praetorian, as it had been in Sicily and Africa under Sulla: what is in doubt is whether he was a legate of Catulus or once again enjoyed an independent command.[19] The only evidence which has been thought to shed light on the problem is unfortunately ambiguous. When the rising had been put down, Catulus instructed Pompeius to dismiss his troops, but Pompeius refused.[20] It has been claimed that Pompeius must have been Catulus' legate for Catulus to have the right to order him to disband, on the other hand that he must have been independent to dare to refuse. Neither argument is compelling. Catulus might well feel that *maior potestas* was sufficient to justify his giving Pompeius orders, whatever the source of Pompeius' own authority, while Pompeius' attitude is likely to have been determined by a calculation of what he could get away with rather than the technical niceties of the situation. The problem must therefore remain unsolved.

The campaign itself presented no great difficulties.[21] Catulus occupied the Mulvian bridge and the Janiculum, a battle was fought, and Lepidus was driven back.[22] Only now, when blood had been shed, was the rebellious proconsul declared a *hostis*.[23] After retreating to Etruria, he sought refuge in Sardinia, where ill health and, allegedly, a broken heart soon ended his life.[24] Those of his supporters who escaped made their way to Spain to join Sertorius.[25] Meanwhile his legate Brutus attempted to hold Mutina against

Pompeius, but without success, and his fate added another scalp to the belt of the *adulescentulus carnifex* ('the youthful butcher'): he surrendered, but was put to death, in some accounts while attempting to escape.[26] Technical justification may have existed: it is highly likely, though no such decree is recorded in our sources, that he, like Lepidus, had been declared a *hostis*.[27]

Hitherto Pompeius and Catulus had co-operated well enough, but now Pompeius showed himself contumacious. The revolt was over, and there was no further call for him to remain in arms, but when Catulus ordered him to disband his troops he refused.[28] It would be out of place to speak here of a threat of civil war, just as it would have been in 81. Pompeius did not have the strength to challenge the senate, even if his troops had been prepared to follow him against the state, and his age and lack of experience, despite his military achievements, made him a most implausible potential dictator.[29] Nor did he wish to overthrow the Sullan system: his entire career down to 70 was made in defending the Sullan oligarchy from those who rebelled against it.[30] His objective was clearly limited, and its nature is plain enough. One major theatre of war remained: Spain, where Metellus Pius had been engaged for two years in the struggle against Cinna's hench-man Sertorius.[31] It is not unlikely that Pius had already asked for help.[32] The only question in 77 was who should be sent to reinforce him. The natural answer would have been the consuls, who had at last been elected, but they refused to go.[33] Excessive significance should not be attached to this action.[34] Their names may invite speculation: Mam. Aemilius Lepidus Livianus and D. Junius Brutus, homonymous with Lepidus and his legate. But nothing suggests that similar designs or sympathy with Sertorius should be imputed to them: disinclination to undertake a difficult, dangerous and unrewarding war is surely enough to explain their reluctance.[35] Their attitude gave Pompeius his opportunity, and it is reasonable to suppose that he must have known of it when he took his stand against Catulus. He must also have known that a substantial body of opinion in the senate would be prepared not only to tolerate his contumacy but reward it with further employment as hatchetman extraordinary. The principal spokesman of that view was again the influential L. Philippus, who used the consuls' refusal to go to Spain as his cue for a famous witticism, when he proposed that Pompeius should be sent out to assist Pius *non pro consule sed pro consulibus*.[36]

The task was not an easy one, but despite the military problems Pom-peius found time to strengthen his influence in ways that he had already employed in Sicily and Africa and was to use on a far grander scale in the East. He built up *clientelae* all over Spain, which remained loyal even in the civil war against Caesar, despite Caesar's efforts to establish his own influence during his governorship in 61.[37] Known names among Pompeius' officers reveal the nature and limitations of his friendships at this time. Most famous is the scholar M. Terentius Varro, who served for several years and remained a faithful supporter.[38] D. Laelius was killed in 76 at the battle of Lauro, but his son preserved the family's connection with Pompeius.[39] A graver loss in the next year was Pompeius' brother-in-law C. Memmius, quaestor in 76, but now a casualty at the battle of the Turia.[40] The year 75 also marks the first appearance in Pompeius' service of L. Afranius, the archetype of the 'Pompeian', if that much abused label has any value at all: the military man from Picenum who owed his entire political career to the patronage of Pompeius and so remained obstinately loyal.[41] Towards the end of the war Pompeius had as his quaestor C. Cornelius, the future tribune of 67.[42] Men of distinguished family are, however, conspicuous by their absence: neither Pompeius nor this war can have seemed likely to provide prospects of even temporary profit or advancement such as might have tempted a *nobilis*.

Meanwhile at Rome several issues began to emerge. Agitation for the restoration of the tribunician power began in 76, but its mouthpiece, the tribune Sicinius, was somehow silenced by the consul C. Scribonius Curio, who had been prominent under Sulla in the Mithradatic War.[43] Nevertheless in 75 a major concession was made: the consul C. Aurelius Cotta, despite noble opposition, removed the ban on the tenure of higher office, with which Sulla had turned the tribunate into a political dead end.[44] It was inevitable that pressure would henceforth increase and that the full restoration of legislative powers would follow in the not too distant future.[45] Attempts to portray Cotta as a moderate rest on a misunderstanding: the craving for *gratia* of a man with the careers of two brothers to advance as well as his own is sufficient explanation of his actions.[46] But more pressing problems than the rights of tribunes existed to occupy the consul's mind. Corn was in short supply, and high prices provoked rioting.[47] The war in Spain was going badly, and in a speech put into Cotta's mouth by Sallust it is said that both Pius and Pompeius were clamouring for money, reinforcements and supplies, while Rome might also find herself needing armies in Asia and Cilicia because of the ominous growth of the power of Mithradates.[48] Sulla's heirs were indeed soon to be faced with the legacy of the Peace of Dardanus.

Matters were brought to a head in 74, in the consulship of Sulla's most trusted henchman, L. Licinius Lucullus, and C. Cotta's brother Marcus. A letter came to the senate from Pompeius; Sallust's version is preserved.[49] In it a vigorous appeal for help, which claims to be only the most recent of many, is followed by a somewhat oracular warning: if the required assistance is not forthcoming, then against Pompeius' will his army and with it the whole Spanish war will move to Italy.[50] It would surely be quite mistaken to see in these words a veiled threat by Pompeius to ally himself with Sertorius and join him in an invasion of Italy. The mention of his army suggests that he may have meant that his troops might mutiny and make it impossible to carry on the war. The further implication that this would leave Sertorius free to follow him home is a gross exaggeration: Sertorius had won battles, but was in no position, even if Metellus and Pompeius withdrew, to move on to the offensive and invade Italy. Nevertheless, Pompeius' missive produced results. Strenuous efforts were made to supply the men and materials needed for Spain, not least by the consul Lucullus.[51] He had just, by dint of sedulous and sordid intrigue, secured for himself the command against Mithradates, to be shared with his colleague M. Cotta,[52] and had no desire to see his prospects of glory in the East dashed by untoward developments in Spain.[53] There is, however, nothing to support the conjecture that Pompeius had hitherto been deliberately starved of supplies and men.[54] Whatever the resentment and alarm provoked by his appointment or the lack of experienced and able men that had made it necessary, he was after all fighting for Sulla's friends against Sulla's enemies, and it would have been folly on their part to act in a way that would have diminished his chances of success. The difficulties that faced the Roman forces in Spain – and it is worth remembering that both commanders had complained, and not Pompeius alone – were not of the senate's making.

　　Nor is there anything to commend the view that the commands of Lucullus and Cotta against Mithradates and of the praetor M. Antonius against the pirates[55] were intended to create a balance of power between these unquestionably loyal men in the East and the unreliable Pompeius in the West.[56] Not only was Pompeius' loyalty to the Sullan senate beyond reasonable question; the idea of meeting an assumed potential threat from Spain by sending loyal generals to perform arduous tasks at the opposite end of the empire simply makes no sense. If there were fears at Rome that the Spanish war might, as Pompeius had warned, shift to Italy, the proper place for such a reliable man was Cisalpine Gaul. In this connection it is worth noting that Lucullus' original province was indeed Cisalpina.[57] But that need not indicate doubts about Pompeius' loyalty, merely a fear that, as he himself affected to believe, he and Metellus would prove unable to contain Sertorius in Spain. Above all, this view of the appointments of 74 makes the tacit assumption that the senate had chosen to create the commands when it did. This is only partially true in the case of Antonius and quite untrue in that of Lucullus and Cotta. The initiative belonged not to Rome but to Mithradates, who had picked his moment to renew the war precisely because he hoped that Rome, already heavily committed in Spain, would find her resources insufficient to oppose him effectively.[58]

While Pompeius and Metellus gradually gained the upper hand in Spain, the question of the tribunate continued to dominate politics at Rome. In 74 L. Quinctius led the campaign, but his efforts were crushed by Lucullus.[59] Quinctius patiently nursed his resentment till the chance for revenge came during his praetorship in 68.[60] The cudgels were taken up in 73 by the historian C. Licinius Macer, and it is now that the sources for the first time link the name of Pompeius with the question of the tribunician power. In the speech that Sallust puts into his mouth, Macer claims that the optimates were using Pompeius' name as an excuse for putting off any action.[61] If this is true, it could hardly have carried conviction. It would be quite absurd for the senate to pretend that it was powerless to act in defiance or even in ignorance of Pompeius' wishes. If so crude a delaying tactic was in fact employed, it can only have produced understandable exasperation. More interestingly, Macer goes on to assert that Pompeius would undoubtedly use his influence to secure the restitution of the tribunes' legislative powers.[62] It is hard to know how much credence to attach to this.[63] There is no other discernible link between Macer and Pompeius either at this time or later, and although it is possible that Pompeius had already decided what line he would take on his return and had communicated this to the tribune, it is more likely that Macer was taking Pompeius' name in vain, in the hope that he would in consequence feel bound to lend his support to the cause, so as not to disappoint the popular expectations that had been aroused in his absence and without his consent.

In Spain Pompeius' successes in 73 were crowned in 72 by the final defeat of Perperna after the murder of Sertorius. As a result Sertorius' papers fell into his hands, but in the interests of concord and his own future influence he was tactful enough to destroy them, allegedly unread.[64] The consuls of the year, L. Gellius Publicola and Cn. Cornelius Lentulus Clodianus, passed a law to ratify grants of citizenship made in Spain by both Pompeius and Pius.[65] Pompeius made lavish use of the opportunity this gave him for patronage.[66] The most distinguished recipient of the citizenship was L. Cornelius Balbus of Gades.[67] To celebrate his victory Pompeius set up a trophy in the Pyrenees, claiming the capture of 876 towns from the Alps to the boundaries of Hispania Ulterior.[68]

But before he could think of claiming the triumph he had earned, he was summoned to Italy by the senate to perform a further task, the execution of which was to have far-reaching consequences.[69] Since 73 Italy had been troubled by the slave rebellion of Spartacus.[70] First several praetors and then the consuls of 72 had failed to make any headway against the rebels. After the failure of Gellius and Clodianus the war was entrusted to Crassus, who had held the praetorship in the previous year.[71] By early 71 the revolt was virtually crushed, and little remained for Pompeius to do.[72] However, the senate's summons was of value to him, since it justified him in keeping his army together instead of disbanding it as soon as he entered Italy.[73] He arrived in time to mop up a band of fugitives in the North, and with an equal absence of tact and scruple used this trifling achievement to diminish the credit undoubtedly due to Crassus and claim for himself the glory of ending the rebellion.[74] In fact the honours that Crassus received were all that he had a right to expect and more: an ovation, with the special distinction of a laurel wreath.[75] But he was jealous, however unjustly, of Pompeius' Spanish triumph,[76] and his resentment was deep and enduring: despite periods of uneasy co-operation there was from this point on no love lost between the two men.

For both Pompeius and the senate and people of Rome the inevitable and urgent question was: what now? Once the answer had been found, it no doubt seemed both obvious and ineluctable. Pompeius and Crassus were elected consuls for 70.[77] It is worth stressing the difference in their respective situations. Crassus had fulfilled all the technical requirements: he had been praetor in 73, and his achievement against Spartacus as well as his family background made him an obvious candidate for office.[78] Pompeius, on the other hand, was too young for the consulship and had held none of the requisite preliminary offices.[79] But the senate passed a decree exempting him from the provisions of the *lex annalis* and allowing him to stand in absence.[80] It has been suggested that Pompeius and Crassus extorted their consulships from a reluctant senate and people by the threat of force.[81] In the case of Crassus that is patently absurd. Nor will it hold water for Pompeius. It is true that he kept his army together until the celebration of his triumph on the last day of 71, claiming that he was waiting for Pius.[82] It had therefore been in existence at the time of the senatorial decree which authorized his candidature and of the election itself. But to try to gain the consulship by the threat of force would have been a hazardous enterprise out of all proportion to the reward, for Crassus and eventually Metellus would surely have resisted, and it can hardly have seemed necessary. To the people Pompeius was a hero, while to many in

the senate the consulship, abnormal though it was, must have seemed no
more than a just reward for his services to the state. Even those who feared
the possible results of so blatant a breach of Sulla's ordinances must have
realized that no lesser acknowledgement was possible. It was hardly plausible
to ask a man who had commanded a proconsular army for the past seven years
to submit himself as a candidate for the praetorship.[83] It is surely reasonable
to assume that majority opinion, both inside and outside the senate, saw
Pompeius' consulship as necessary and proper, even if not desirable.[84]

That Pompeius would not be inactive as consul was indicated by a speech
he made while designate.[85] Three matters, he promised, would receive
his attention: the tribunician power, the courts, and provincial government. The question of control of the courts, dormant since Sulla's revival
of senatorial juries, had been raised again in 74 by the scandalous trial of
Oppianicus.[86] The issue had been fortuitously linked with that of the
tribunate, largely by the accident that Quinctius had played a major role in
agitation on both matters. Provincial government and its problems had been
brought to the notice of the public, and of Pompeius, chiefly by the conduct
in Sicily of C. Verres. It was perhaps inevitable that among the victims of the
governor's judicial and administrative eccentricities clients of Pompeius
should be numbered, and in 72 Verres interfered with one of the most
influential of them, Sthenius of Himera.[87] The consuls Gellius and Lentulus,
who were well disposed towards Pompeius, introduced a decree of the
senate in Sthenius' favour, but Verres' father succeeded in protecting his
son's interests.[88] In the following year the matter was taken up by Pompeius'
adherent the tribune M. Lollius Palicanus, who was also active in the cause of
tribunician power.[89] It was therefore only proper that Pompeius should
demonstrate his readiness to protect his clients from oppression.

As consuls Pompeius and Crassus co-operated only once,[90] to pass a law
restoring the legislative powers of the tribunes.[91] The senate offered no
objection, for the necessity of the reform was generally accepted.[92] No
doubt both men expected to profit in the future from tribunician legislation,
and neither would have been prepared to see the other secure for himself all
the popular good will that such a measure would bring.[93] The question of the
courts, however, was not settled until the autumn.[94] It seems that, despite his
promise of 71, Pompeius had much less interest in this subject.[95]

Cicero insists on the link between the fate of senatorial juries and the
verdict in the trial of Verres, claiming that an honest decision by a senatorial
court might stave off the otherwise inevitable loss of control.[96] It is unlikely
that there is any truth in this. What is more puzzling is whether the
eventual solution, embodied in a law by the praetor L. Cotta, brother of

the consuls of 75 and 74, had been preceded by a harsher proposal. Cicero several times speaks in the *Verrines* as though the threat which the senate was facing was not merely the sharing of the courts but total transfer to the *equites*.[97] That talk along these lines was in the air in the spring and summer of 70 is more than likely, but it may never have got as far as even a tentative formal proposal, while it is possible that Cicero in a polemical context was prepared to represent the effects of the *lex Aurelia* as tantamount to a total transfer of the courts, as do certain later and unreliable sources.[98] Cotta's bill divided the juries into three: senators, *equites* and *tribuni aerarii*.[99] It is possible that the measure had Pompeius' blessing in something more than a purely passive sense, if there is any truth in the suggestion that this tripartite division was not of Cotta's own devising but was the work of Palicanus.[100]

Pompeius' reasons for taking an interest in the trial of Verres have already been enumerated. But that interest was tacit: he played no active part in the proceedings. Cicero certainly had motives enough of his own for taking the case: the ties he had established in Sicily, the prospect of scoring off Hortensius, and the chance of acquiring praetorian standing in the senate.[101] Neither at the time nor later did he claim to have been acting in Pompeius' interests. The trial then cannot be seen as a head-on confrontation between Pompeius and the Metelli.[102] But the Metelli and their friends were vigorous in support of Verres. Their motive is obvious: with three brothers all in search of office in quick succession, the family fortunes needed supplementing, and the purity of the source could not be scrutinized too closely.[103] So Hortensius undertook Verres' defence. L. Metellus, who succeeded Verres in Sicily, hindered Cicero's investigation at every turn. He attempted to prevent the destruction of Verres' statues, cajoled and threatened potential witnesses, quashed a decree which revealed that honours paid to Verres had been extorted by force, and wrote to Pompeius and Crassus on his behalf.[104] Every effort was made to secure the postponement of the trial until 69, when Hortensius was to share the consulship with Q. Metellus, who also threatened Cicero's witnesses, and the lot had conveniently assigned the *repetundae* court to the third brother, M. Metellus.[105] There was also an attempt to rob Cicero of the right to prosecute; the name of the would-be *praeuaricator*, Q. Caecilius Niger, is suggestive.[106] Cicero, as is well known, defeated all these manoeuvres and secured Verres' condemnation. Pompeius might be well satisfied, both with the result and with the fact that he had had to make no effort and incur no overt enmity in order to bring it about. Nor need we suppose that the Metelli were greatly upset by their defeat: they had already done well enough out of

Verres, and once the effort to save him had been made and failed, they might well reflect that they were better off without him.

The result of the trial of Verres was not the only matter that Pompeius could look back on with satisfaction as his consulship drew to a close. The censors of the year had been his friends, the consuls of 72, and their conduct of the census may well have fostered his *clientelae*, especially in the Transpadane region.[107] They had also pandered to his vanity by staging a *transuectio* of the *equites*, at which Pompeius was able proudly to declare that he had not only performed the military service required of him by the law, but had done so under his own command.[108] The censors then escorted Pompeius home, accompanied by a cheering crowd. Again, in the field of display, his triumph had been followed in the summer by the games he had vowed to hold if he defeated Sertorius.[109] But on a more practical level he had not succeeded in obtaining grants of land for his veterans. A tribune, Plotius or Plautius, proposed a measure to provide land for the troops who had served under Pompeius and Metellus Pius, but on the ground that the treasury could not bear the expense the bill was dropped or, if passed, not put into operation.[110] So Pompeius will have known better than to exaggerate his influence in Roman politics. The meteoric and military nature of his rise had deprived him of all experience of senatorial practice, and he lacked the web of connections, painstakingly spun, that would enable him to influence senatorial debates and manipulate popular assemblies. When he entered the senate for the first time as consul his knowledge of senatorial procedure had indeed been so small that his friend Varro had had to compose a handbook to enable him to take his place without embarrassment.[111] As a consular he could look forward to dignity, but less power than most of his nominal peers. Yet the foundation had been laid for his future achievements: the tribunician power had been restored, and Pompeius was prepared to wait in patience till the time came to use it. At the end of 70 he could afford the empty gesture of a public reconciliation with his colleague Crassus, especially since it was Crassus who made the first move.[112]

4

THE COMMANDS AGAINST THE PIRATES AND MITHRADATES

After his consulship Pompeius refused to take a province and withdrew from the political scene. His position acknowledged his extraordinary career and brilliant military achievements. He was now a consular, one of the *principes ciuitatis*, and unique amongst them by reason of his youth and his omission of the cursus demanded by Sulla's legislation.[1] But he had neither the experience nor the influence at Rome to play an effective part in senatorial politics or, more important, to exercise control over elections, and as yet there was no opportunity for him to exploit the restored legislative powers of the tribunes. So he preferred to bide his time and wait for another command to come his way. The obvious theatre for such a command was Asia Minor, where Lucullus was still engaged in the war with Mithradates. But in 69 the time was not yet ripe to press for Lucullus' supersession, so Pompeius was content to remain in the background.

For their part the optimates were not prepared to make any fresh concessions to Pompeius' ambition. They had acquiesced in his consulship, but that office marked the summit of a conventional career in public life, and in their eyes he had no right to expect anything more. He was a consular, and with that he must, like any other consular, rest content. But it was not only an attempt to secure a new command that the optimates were determined to resist; they were also bound to hinder Pompeius' efforts to assert himself at elections and in the courts. They were bent on preserving their predominance in the workings of the state, but the events of 70 had made it much more difficult for them to retain control. The completion of the enfranchisement of Italy by the censors of that year had created a mass of new voters unfettered by established bonds of *clientela*, and their sweeping expulsion of senators meant that competition would become more bitter than ever as the victims struggled to recover their lost dignity. Every move by Pompeius to advance adherents of his own constituted an additional complication that would further weaken the already shaky optimate hold. So it was inevitable that they should try to keep him in his place, not necessarily through personal hostility but simply to safeguard their own political position.[2]

In 69 M. Fonteius, governor of Transalpine Gaul in the middle seventies, was prosecuted for extortion in his province. During his time in Gaul Fonteius had been active in supplying corn and troop reinforcements for the war in Spain.[3] It has been argued that the prosecution should be seen as an attempt by the Metelli to take revenge on a supporter of Pompeius for Pompeius' hostility to Verres in the previous year.[4] So extreme a statement rests on two unlikely assumptions: first that Pompeius had been deliberately starved of supplies in the Spanish war, second that the prosecution of Verres had been a direct and open trial of strength between the Metelli and Pompeius.[5] There is nothing to connect the prosecutors of Fonteius, M. Laetorius (or Plaetorius) and M. Fabius, with the Metelli or any other supposed enemy of Pompeius.[6] Nor did the Metelli involve themselves in the case.[7]

Pompeius too took no active part. Cicero defended Fonteius, but that will not serve to prove Pompeius' involvement. Cicero, as a spokesman of equestrian interests, had reasons enough of his own to take the case, for Fonteius had favoured Roman businessmen, the Roman colony of Narbo and the friendly city of Massilia, to the detriment of the Gauls: Narbo, Massilia and the traders all backed him at the trial.[8] Nor is the defence of Fonteius ever listed as a service to Pompeius, as it would have been if Pompeius had openly supported him. But Cicero did make play with Pompeius' name, praising his achievements in Spain, to which Fonteius had contributed, and claiming the good will of his officers and men.[9] It is fair to suppose that he did so with the approval of Pompeius, who would hope to see Fonteius acquitted, but had no reason to give him his overt support, since he was in little danger of condemnation.[10]

The elections of these years reveal the weakness of Pompeius' position in urban politics and the struggle of the optimates to retain control. The year 69 saw Q. Hortensius and Q. Metellus as consuls, with M. Metellus as praetor. For the consulship Pompeius had been able to produce no challenger, though his adherent M. Palicanus, the tribune of 71, succeeded in securing the praetorship.[11] A third Metellus, Lucius, the praetor of 71, followed his brother Quintus in 68, but death came to weaken the power of the Metelli.[12] Lucius died early in his year of office and Marcus, the praetor of the previous year, never reached the consulship. The other consul of 68, Q. Marcius Rex, was reliable, and so was one at least of the consuls of 67, C. Calpurnius Piso. About the other, M'. Glabrio, there might have been doubts: he had presided without bias at the trial of Verres in 70.

Throughout these years bribery was rife. C. Piso himself had achieved office only as the result of massive payments, first to the voters, then to potential accusers.[13] This and other matters that recalled the events of 70 were to engage the attention of a tribune of 67, C. Cornelius, who set out, in the face of optimate opposition, to put a stop to bribery and various other forms of corruption.[14] Cornelius had served as quaestor under Pompeius, probably in the Spanish war,[15] and Pompeius may well have had an interest in his measures. Piso's opposition to the bribery law – though popular pressure forced him to introduce a watered-down version himself – confirms that it was above all the optimates who were resorting to bribery to keep out any candidates associated with Pompeius.[16] Against his candidate for the consulship of 66, Palicanus, Piso adopted more direct measures: he refused to accept Palicanus' nomination and announced that if he were nevertheless elected he would not declare the result.[17]

Of more immediate concern to Pompeius was the attack on Lucullus by another friendly tribune of 67, A. Gabinius.[18] The campaign to undermine Lucullus' position in Asia Minor had begun in 69.[19] Criticism came from equestrian sources and from the general's own troops.[20] The *equites* brought the same charges against him as they had against Q. Metellus in the Jugurthine War: Lucullus was deliberately prolonging the war to retain his command and enhance his glory.[21] A more cogent, if less publicized, motive for equestrian discontent was Lucullus' attempt to check the excesses of the publicans in Asia,[22] and to bring the province some measure of financial relief from the ravages of war.[23] For Lucullus' troops too the war had been long and arduous, and in their estimation their commander had failed to enrich them sufficiently with plunder.[24] Lucullus was not disposed to court the favour of his men and was unable to win their affections.[25] In particular they resented his refusal to quarter them during the winter among the pleasures of the Greek cities.[26] Already in 69 the province of Asia was withdrawn from Lucullus' command,[27] and the mutinies of late 69 and early 68 in Pontus and Gordyene encouraged Lucullus' enemies at Rome.[28] Prominent among them was L. Quinctius, praetor in 68, who had clashed with Lucullus in 74, when as tribune he had agitated for the restoration of the tribunician power and had been suppressed by the consul.[29] Now he saw the chance of revenge, and worked energetically to bring about Lucullus' supersession.[30] While Quinctius and others intrigued at Rome, the troops in Asia Minor were encouraged to mutiny by Lucullus' brother-in-law

P. Clodius. He worked in particular on the men who had served with Fimbria – they had been in Asia Minor for eighteen years – and contrasted the plight of Lucullus' army with the happy position of Pompeius' Spanish veterans, who were enjoying civilian life with grants of land.[31] The campaign of 68 had not been a great success: the capture of Nisibis was outweighed by failure in Armenia and loss of territory in the north.[32] So a further blow was struck against Lucullus. Cilicia was removed from his command and assigned to the consul Marcius Rex.[33] On his way to Cilicia, Marcius refused a request for help from Lucullus, who was finding the mutiny at Nisibis hard to suppress.[34]

At the outset of his tribunate Gabinius introduced a law which assigned Bithynia and Pontus to the consul of 67 M'. Glabrio.[35] The news increased the reluctance of Lucullus' troops to obey him, and they simply refused to follow any further.[36] Glabrio's own performance was singularly undistinguished.[37] Though his inertia need not have stemmed from the belief that he had been appointed merely as a caretaker until such time as Pompeius was ready to take over, his lack of achievement worked to Pompeius' advantage.[38] It has been denied that Pompeius intrigued against Lucullus and inspired Quinctius' and Gabinius' attacks, on the ground that he cannot have predicted the disasters that befell Lucullus during 67.[39] The argument is not cogent. Metellus Numidicus suffered no disasters in Africa, but Marius nevertheless plotted his removal on precisely the pretexts that had been urged against Lucullus since 69. Quinctius at least had reasons of his own to hate Lucullus, but Gabinius was surely acting on Pompeius' behalf and with his approval. It was still too early for Pompeius to move in, but he knew how to be patient, and now that Lucullus had been stripped of his provinces he could afford to be, especially as Gabinius' next move was designed to secure him another special command to deal with a more pressing problem.

Piracy had been a constant plague in the Mediterranean for over a generation. M. Antonius in 102 and his son in 74 had been totally ineffective in their efforts at suppression; indeed Rome's subjects found the younger Antonius a worse menace than the pirates.[40] P. Servilius in the seventies had been more successful, but his campaigns had brought no lasting solution.[41] Since the outbreak of the Mithradatic war the problem had grown worse, for the pirates had flourished in concert with the king. Their organization grew elaborate and efficient, and Rome's failure to check them fostered an ostentatious arrogance. From the pillaging of famous shrines in Greece and Asia Minor they had progressed to raids on Italy itself, capturing two praetors, Sextilius and Bellienus, and, ironically, a daughter of the elder Antonius. Other distinguished captives were Caesar and Clodius. They loved to mock the power of Rome: when they captured a Roman they would grovel before him and beg for Rome's mercy before making him walk the plank.[42] By 67 the matter was urgent for another, even more important reason. The activities of the pirates had disrupted trade in the Mediterranean to such an extent that the corn supply of Rome was threatened.[43]

To deal with piracy Gabinius proposed a law.[44] One man, chosen from among the consulars, was to be given the task of clearing the sea, with the right to appoint fifteen legates with praetorian *imperium*, to fit out a fleet of two hundred ships, to levy troops as required, and to draw upon the treasury at Rome and the resources of the publicans in the provinces.[45] The command was to last three years.[46] The commander's *imperium* was to cover all the sea east of the Pillars of Hercules, all islands, and the coasts of the mainland, including Italy, up to a distance of fifty miles inland.[47] The law did not mention Pompeius by name, but it was obvious that, if it was passed, he would be appointed to the post by popular demand.[48]

Opposition in the senate was almost universal. It is said that the only senator to speak for the law was Caesar, who was eager to win popular support.[49] The consul C. Piso was violently hostile. He warned Pompeius that if he tried to set himself up in defiance of the senate as a new Romulus, the fate of Romulus might be in store for him.[50] Hortensius too spoke at length against the bill in the senate and repeated his arguments when it came before the people. He put the opposition case in a nutshell: if such power was to be granted to a single man, then Pompeius more than any other was worthy of it, but in the interests of security no such grant should be made.[51] The senate furiously turned on Gabinius and the tribune was almost lynched. In reply the mob attacked the senate and seized C. Piso, and had Gabinius not intervened to pacify the crowd, the consul would have been killed. The opposition therefore turned to the other tribunes of the year, hoping to persuade one or more of them to veto the measure. Two came forward, L. Trebellius and L. Roscius Otho.[52]

Pompeius was very eager for the command.[53] The task suited his great talent for the organization and co-ordination of large-scale operations over a wide area, and it had popular appeal, for the pirates' interference with the corn supply made it possible to present acceptance as dictated by concern for the public welfare. But it was always his way to hang back and feign reluctance, so that honours might appear to be forced on him against his will, and the violent opposition of the mass of the senate made him all the more keen to do so on this occasion.[54] In a speech before the people he rehearsed his achievements in Sicily, Africa and Spain, but claimed that he had now done enough, maintaining with tongue in cheek that it would not be hard to find some other commander.[55] Gabinius then performed his part in the charade, extolling Pompeius' ability and begging him not to be deterred from his duty by the carping of envious opponents.[56] When Trebellius tried to speak against the bill, he was shouted down by the angry crowd, and so he interposed his veto. Gabinius countered in dramatic fashion, resorting to a device that had been used only once before, by Ti. Gracchus in 133.[57] He proposed that Trebellius should at once be deprived of his office, and the tribes began to vote on the measure. At first Trebellius stood firm, but when the first seventeen tribes had voted against him and only one more vote was required for his deposition, he withdrew his veto. Roscius then tried to register his disapproval, but he too was threatened by the crowd and could do no more than to raise two fingers in the air, signifying once again by this gesture that in the view of the bill's opponents such power was too great to be entrusted to any one man.[58]

Gabinius then turned to Catulus and invited him to speak, in the hope that the danger to the tribunes would compel him now to support the bill, however reluctantly, and that the rest of the senate would follow his lead.[59] Catulus spoke, but not in a vein to please Gabinius. His authority was sufficient to gain him a hearing, and he reiterated the objections to the proposal. No one man had ever held so many commands in succession, and this concentration of power was a bad thing, for it led to a shortage of experienced commanders, from which Rome had already suffered during the Sertorian war.[60] Extraordinary commands bestowed on private citizens were a dangerous expedient, to be avoided whenever possible. Nor could a single man control so great a war. It might be argued, Catulus admitted, that the provision of fifteen legates answered that objection, but he would prefer to see a number of independent commanders. As a last resort he posed a question. What if Pompeius was killed? Who could replace him? The reply from the crowd was unanimous: Catulus himself.[61]

Opposition proved vain, and the law was passed.[62] It was followed by at least one further law, which appointed Pompeius, and perhaps a second, increasing the forces to be placed at his disposal to 500 ships, 120,000 infantry, 5,000 cavalry, 24 legates and two quaestors – forces far in excess of anything that might be required.[63] Popular confidence in Pompeius was so great that on the very day of his election the price of bread dropped.[64]

A major and probably insoluble problem remains: the status of Pompeius' *imperium* in relation to that of other governors in the provinces he might be called upon to visit. Our sources contradict one another. Velleius says that Pompeius, like Antonius in 74, was granted *imperium* equal to that of other proconsuls.[65] Tacitus states on the other hand that when the *imperium* of Cn. Corbulo was declared *maius* under Nero it was thereby raised to the same level as the power bestowed by the people on Pompeius for the pirate war.[66] It has been claimed that Tacitus is correct, that Pompeius' *imperium* was in fact *maius*, that is greater than that of the governors with whom he might come into contact, and that Velleius meant no more than that Pompeius' *imperium*, like Antonius', was proconsular.[67] The arguments are not cogent. Nothing in Catulus' speech in Dio makes it a more suitable reply to a proposal of *imperium maius* than to one of *imperium aequum*.[68] Nor need the reference to Asia in the preamble to Pompeius' triumph[69] indicate that he intervened in that province by virtue of superior *imperium*. Pompeius listed all the regions he had fought in and benefited by his campaigns.[70] His intervention in Asia could quite well have been by arrangement with a friendly governor whose *imperium* was equal to his own. Velleius may therefore be allowed to mean what he says.

No clue to the riddle can be found in Pompeius' dealings with Metellus in Crete.[71] Certainly he claimed that his own authority extended to Crete and interfered with the activities of Metellus, sending a legate, L. Octavius, to receive the surrender of the Cretan communities.[72] He is also said to have written to Metellus instructing him to refrain from further military action and to the Cretans encouraging them to ignore Metellus.[73] But Metellus refused to give in and drove Octavius out of Crete.[74] Pompeius' interference in Crete does not prove that his *imperium* was greater than that of Metellus, though it may fairly be said that if it was not the tone he adopted was extremely tactless. But neither does Metellus' refusal to obey him prove that Pompeius' *imperium* was only equal to his own. Metellus was stubborn, and he knew that he could be sure of powerful support at Rome. The great majority of senators disapproved of Gabinius' law, and even Pompeius' friends were displeased by his behaviour.[75] So even if Pompeius did have a technical right to give him orders Metellus might have calculated that disobedience in the cause of dignity was a risk well worth taking. In the absence of convincing support from other sources for either view, decision between Velleius and Tacitus can only be arbitrary. It is perhaps slightly more plausible that, since Antonius had encountered no problems of precedence, Gabinius judged that Pompeius too would find *imperium aequum* adequate to his needs.

The freedom to choose his legates gave Pompeius his first real opportunity for patronage, which could be used to repay old debts and attempt to create new obligations.[76] Both the censors of 70, Lentulus Clodianus and Gellius Publicola, accepted posts, as did one of the younger Metelli, Nepos, the future consul of 57. Two Manlii Torquati served; one of them, Lucius, reached the consulship in 65. Other men who were to attain the highest office were Cn. Lentulus Marcellinus, consul 56, and M. Pupius Piso, consul 61. Two scholars of distinction also appear on the list: Pompeius' old associate M. Varro and the historian Cornelius Sisenna.[77] It is striking that the roll includes none of the hard core of Pompeius' supporters, the military men from Picenum like Afranius and Petreius. Pompeius was more concerned to seize the chance of establishing distinguished connections, and he had probably decided that his plan to deal with the pirates would not require men of great military experience.

He set about his task with consummate skill. The coasts of the Mediterranean were divided into thirteen regions and each region was assigned to a legate.[78] Early in spring Pompeius began to sweep the pirates eastwards.[79] His most urgent duty was to reopen the links between Rome and the sources of her corn supply, and so he concentrated first on the corn-growing provinces of Sardinia, Sicily and Africa.[80] The opening stage of the campaign was a brilliant success: in the space of forty days the pirates were driven back to Cilicia.[81] But this did nothing to blunt the hostility of the consul C. Piso. Undaunted by his failure to prevent the passage of the law, Piso set about hindering Pompeius as much as he could, interfering with his recruiting and discharging men whom Pompeius had already enlisted both in Italy and in Piso's own province of Cisalpine Gaul.[82] This obstruction caused Pompeius himself to return to Rome, where Gabinius was ready to adopt strong measures and bring a law before the people to deprive Piso of his consulship. But Pompeius was reluctant to go to such extremes and succeeded in arranging matters to his own satisfaction. From Rome he proceeded to Brundisium and sailed for Cilicia.[83] He had sent letters requiring assistance to all the kings, potentates and cities of Asia Minor;[84] even Lucullus co-operated, providing Pompeius with funds, as he made a point of recording later at his triumph.[85] Within three months the war was over. The pirate fleets had been crushingly defeated in a single great battle and their last stronghold, Coracesium, had fallen.[86] Pompeius was duly saluted by his men as *imperator*.[87]

Yet more striking than Pompeius' military success was his treatment of his prisoners. His wisdom and humanity are thrown into relief by certain remarks made a few years earlier by Cicero in the *Verrines*. By common consent a more humane man than most Romans of his age, Cicero nevertheless makes it clear that captured pirates could expect the harshest of treatment and that he himself entirely approved.[88] Pompeius did not share the prevailing attitude. The captured pirates were settled at various points in Asia Minor; Pompeius removed temptation from their path by shifting them away from the sea to inland sites more suited for agriculture.[89] This policy not only rehabilitated the pirates but also attempted to repair the desolation caused by the Mithradatic war in certain areas of southern Asia Minor.[90] Among the towns which received settlers in this way were Mallus, Adana, and Epiphaneia; Pompeius also refounded the abandoned city of Soli in Cilicia, renaming it Pompeiopolis.[91] The largest single settlement, however, was not in Asia Minor but in Greece, at the depopulated town of Dyme in Achaea.[92] The settlements in eastern Cilicia, which was nominally still in the hands of the rapidly disintegrating Syrian royal house, the Seleucids, suggest that Pompeius had already decided that this region must be brought under direct Roman control and by his arrangements proposed to force the senate's hand on annexation.[93]

The sweetness of Pompeius' success was soured by his clash with Metellus in Crete. The island had become a centre of piracy second only to Cilicia, and it had been declared a consular province for 68. At first it had fallen to the lot of Hortensius, but the orator had no wish to leave Rome and ceded it willingly to his colleague Metellus.[94] Metellus set about subduing Crete with such ferocity that when Pompeius received his command under Gabinius' law the Cretans, envying the lenient treatment that their colleagues in other areas were getting from Pompeius, appealed to him to intervene.[95] Tact might have indicated a refusal, but whatever the degree of his *imperium* Pompeius undoubtedly had the right to operate in Crete and was reluctant to pass over this chance to extend his *clientela*. So he accepted the surrender of various communities and sent his legate L. Octavius to Crete to receive their submission. Metellus, resenting this interference in his province, seems to have made a point of attacking those towns that had come to terms with Pompeius, despite the efforts of another Pompeian legate, the historian Sisenna, to persuade him to moderation. When he failed in this, Sisenna took no further action, but Octavius established himself at Lappa and showed ready to fight Metellus. The proconsul accepted the challenge and Octavius was driven out. By this time Sisenna had died, and Octavius, taking over his army, gave help to Metellus' victims and occupied Hierapytna with the pirate leader Aristion until Metellus' approach forced them to escape by sea.[96] Worse trouble might have ensued: Pompeius was on the point of sailing to Crete when news reached him of his appointment to command against Mithradates.[97] Metellus, left to his own devices, went on to conquer the whole island and take the name Creticus,[98] but he was long pursued by Pompeius' rancour. His triumph was delayed until 62, and two of the most prominent Cretan pirates, Panares and Lasthenes, did not appear in it, for Pompeius persuaded a tribune to remove them from Metellus' custody on the ground that they had surrendered to him, not to Metellus.[99]

Pompeius' achievement against the pirates was bound to be exaggerated. Eulogists proclaim that no pirate was ever seen in the Mediterranean again.[100] Cicero himself maintains that after Pompeius there were no pirates in Asia, dismissing the claim that there were as a malicious attempt to diminish his glory.[101] But he admits that there was still need for L. Flaccus to be diligent against pirates when he governed Asia in 62.[102] Later it is recorded that Syria was ravaged by pirates at the time of Gabinius' restoration of Ptolemy Auletes.[103] Their activities provoked complaints against the governor not only from the provincials but also from the publicans, who found it impossible to collect the taxes.[104] But such a resurgence of piracy was inevitable, especially perhaps in Syria, where Pompeius' arrangements were to be much more hasty than elsewhere.[105]

At the beginning of 66 Pompeius was in a position to lay claim to the command against Mithradates and Tigranes. His own success against the pirates contrasted sharply with the setbacks that Lucullus had suffered during 67, and Pompeius at last judged that the time was ripe to strike.[106] In December 67 one of the new tribunes, C. Manilius, had introduced a bill to distribute freedmen equally throughout all the thirty-five tribes.[107] There were violent disturbances, and on 1 January 66 the senate passed a decree annulling the bill.[108] Despite the anger of the people and an attempt by Manilius to claim that the idea stemmed from Crassus, the bill was dropped and Manilius turned to more important matters.

He proposed that the provinces of Cilicia, Bithynia and Pontus should be assigned to Pompeius, together with charge of the Mithradatic war.[109] The bill aroused considerable opposition. Those who feared and resented Pompeius' ambition felt that Lucullus was being cheated of the glory of finishing a war he had already won, and there were even voices raised in defence of the claims of Rex and Glabrio, despite their incompetence.[110] The leaders of the resistance were again, as in the previous year, Catulus and Hortensius.[111] Unmoved by Pompeius' achievement against the pirates, they argued now, as they had then, that so much power should not be granted to a single man. But this time there was more support for the bill inside the senate. Caesar backed Manilius,[112] as he had Gabinius, but now he was not alone. Four consulars gave the measure their endorsement: C. Curio, *cos.* 76, C. Cassius, *cos.* 73, Lentulus Clodianus, *cos.* 72 and, most significant of all, Servilius Isauricus, *cos*. 79.[113] Only Clodianus had any previous link with Pompeius, legislating in his favour in 72 and holding the censorship when Pompeius was consul in 70. It is reasonable to suppose that the others, despite their politics – Curio had served under Sulla and supported Verres, and Cassius had been consul with Lucullus' brother Marcus – respected Pompeius' achievement and felt that he had earned his new command.[114] Servilius more than any other man, thanks to his own experience in Cilicia, was in a position to judge the true value of Pompeius' work.

Perhaps even more important, Cicero, now praetor, spoke in support of the bill before the people.[115] He had exercised caution in the previous year, though now he lavished retrospective praise on Gabinius.[116] His acquisition to Pompeius' cause was of great publicity value, for Cicero was a champion of law and order, a paragon of respectability. His stand was thus likely to weigh heavily with moderate opinion, which might have been alienated by the readiness of Gabinius and Manilius to ignore legal technicalities and resort to violence.[117] He based his case firmly on considerations that would appeal to his own most loyal supporters, the equestrian businessmen and tax-farmers.[118] Asia was by far Rome's richest province, and the war had brought the loss of vital revenues from it.[119] Financial reverses in Asia had even affected credit in Rome itself.[120] Rome's reputation too was at stake, as was the safety of her friends and allies and of Roman property abroad,[121] while Pompeius, the only commander feared by the enemy, was being demanded as general not only by the *equites* but by all men, citizens and allies alike.[122] Whatever the qualities required in a commander or a governor – wisdom, expertise, courage, authority, good luck, moderation, humanity – Pompeius possessed them all, as he had proved repeatedly throughout his career.[123] He was in fact the greatest general of all time.[124]

With those who might object Cicero took various tones. The Metelli were given short shrift: Pius got no mention in Cicero's eulogy of Pompeius' achievements against Sertorius, while Pompeius' clash with Metellus in Crete was presented to redound to his credit.[125] Lucullus on the other hand was treated with some respect, though Cicero found the task an awkward one. He praised Lucullus' campaigns against Mithradates and insisted that no opponent of Manilius' bill could value him more highly.[126] But his mild assertion that under Lucullus Roman troops had shown rather too much interest in the question of booty, while their morale had become open to question, carries no more conviction than his claim that the present ousting of Lucullus was due to nothing more than a traditional Roman reluctance to leave the same man in command for too long a time.[127] As for

Catulus, his argument that no break with tradition should be envisaged could be countered by appeal to precedents that had worked out well: the sending of Scipio Aemilianus against Carthage and Numantia and the commands of Marius in the Jugurthine and Cimbric wars.[128] Nor, Cicero claimed, was Catulus being consistent. Pompeius had already held extraordinary commands, he had triumphed before he had become a senator, and had reached the consulship without holding any other office. All these unprecedented honours had been granted with Catulus' approval and authority.[129] It was therefore illogical for him now to oppose the people's will, while the people was right to stand by the judgement it had made on Pompeius in voting for the *lex Gabinia*, a judgement which Pompeius' performance had fully justified.[130]

The law was passed by all the tribes, and Pompeius learned of it in time to be distracted from a confrontation with Metellus in Crete. As before, he pretended displeasure at the new burden that was being thrust upon him, but his eagerness for the Mithradatic command had been so obvious for so long that he succeeded only in exasperating his friends.[131]

Once again Pompeius' *imperium* poses a problem. The sources are even less informative than before. Only Appian makes a specific statement: Pompeius' power under Manilius' law was the same as it had been against the pirates.[132] Unfortunately he does not say whether that was in his view *aequum* or *maius*. It is therefore methodologically unsound to combine Appian with Velleius and say that under the *lex Gabinia* Pompeius' *imperium* was *aequum* and must, since it remained unchanged, have been *aequum* under the *lex Manilia* too,[133] as Appian may, for all we know, have believed, like Tacitus, that it was *maius* under the *lex Gabinia*. If, as seems more likely, it was *aequum* against the pirates, the arguments that Manilius left it unaltered are weak. It is claimed that the amount of detail employed when *imperium maius* was tentatively proposed for Pompeius in 57 suggests that that was the first time the concept had been framed, and that no clash like that between Pompeius and Metellus in Crete was to be expected in Asia Minor, so that Manilius would not feel the need of a safeguard.[134] But by its very nature *imperium maius* always had to be defined with detailed precision: thus the use of detail in 57 does not show that there had been no earlier formulation. Even if no clash was likely in Asia, the stalemate in Crete had demonstrated the need for *imperium maius*, and Manilius might have been expected to take precautions against any possible recurrence.[135] Thus, though certainty is impossible, it seems on balance more plausible that Pompeius' *imperium* was now declared *maius*.

Pompeius was granted a further power, that of making peace and war on his own initiative without reference to the senate and people at Rome.[136] The significance of this clause, which was to provide a precedent for Augustus, should not be exaggerated. In practical terms it represented sound common sense. Pompeius would be operating over a wide area. He would come into contact with all manner of potentates with whom the military needs of the moment might make it expedient to wage war or conclude an agreement. Communications would always be slow, sometimes perhaps difficult. If on each occasion he had to seek authority from home, the situation might well have changed completely by the time a reply was received, and valuable diplomatic and military opportunities prove irrevocably lost. It was therefore vital that Pompeius should be free to make his own decisions on the spot. The senate was not thereby deprived of its right to discuss any arrangements to which he might wish to give a more permanent character. When the war was over and Pompeius came home he would have to submit his acts for ratification, and there would then be time for the senate to debate them at leisure.

The legates who had served under Pompeius against the pirates probably retained their commands,[137] while others were added. Gabinius, who had been debarred from service as a legate under his own law, probably took the opportunity to join his patron and so avoid the risk of prosecution for the upheavals of his tribunate.[138] Pompeius' trusted lieutenant L. Afranius also now joined him, and Metellus Nepos was followed by his brother Celer, soon to be consul in 60. These men exemplify the varying degrees of commitment to Pompeius that existed among his legates. Afranius and others like him owed their entire careers to their service in Pompeius' wars and had little hope of public office without his continuing and energetic support. Men such as Celer and Nepos on the other hand had no need of Pompeius to secure them the consulships for which they had been destined in their cradles; as long as it suited their convenience they might ride for a while on his shoulders, but from them he could expect no loyalty when he had served their turn.[139]

5

POMPEIUS IN THE EAST

On receiving the command against Mithradates, Pompeius must have been well aware that only the death or capture of the king would produce an end to the war that would satisfy the Roman people and bring further lustre to his own reputation.[1] Mithradates had been let off the hook too many times for any settlement that left him in power, or even at large, to be generally acceptable, and if Pompeius was to prove that he was greater than Sulla and Lucullus, then he had to achieve the final solution to the problem. Moreover, the criticisms already brought against him in Rome made him realize that, if possible, the task before him must be shown to be of some magnitude.[2]

If therefore it ever took place, his alleged first step, the sending of Metrophanes to Mithradates with a friendly message,[3] could only have been intended to lure the king into a false sense of security while Pompeius made his preparations. But even this is still difficult to accept. Metrophanes' mission is mentioned only by Dio, whose account at this point does not inspire confidence, and its fate is left unrecorded. More important, if the mission had succeeded, it would have brought an immediate but inglorious end to the war, and that Pompeius certainly did not want. If Mithradates had responded favourably and made peace before Pompeius had struck a blow, this would have proved his enemies' claim that the king had already been defeated before Pompeius took over. Pompeius would hardly have taken that risk at the outset: a little later, when Mithradates tried to sound out the possibility of settling for a draw, he deliberately set terms that would compel the king to fight on. It therefore seems likely that Metrophanes' mission should be relegated to the realm of fiction.[4]

Pompeius' immediate concern was rather the attitude of Phraates III of Parthia. Lucullus had entered into negotiations with the Parthian king, who had sent an embassy with an offer of friendship and alliance. But the embassy which Lucullus had dispatched in return had found out that Phraates was also in touch with Tigranes of Armenia, demanding the cession of Mesopotamia in return for his help against the Romans. The eventual agreement had secured Phraates' neutrality, and may also have established the Euphrates as the frontier between the Roman and Parthian spheres of influence.[5] It is uncertain whether Pompeius or Phraates took the initiative in renewing this agreement, but for the moment it was in the interests of both that it should be maintained, and Pompeius extracted from Phraates a guarantee that he would not only not attack the Romans but would move against Armenia.[6] This arrangement could clearly be of only short-term benefit to either side: Phraates might be happy to have the blessing of the Roman in his quarrel with Tigranes, while Pompeius could hope for profit by exploiting the feud between Parthia and Armenia to contain and weaken Tigranes while he himself dealt with Mithradates, but lasting agreement over the fate of Armenia, should Phraates prove too successful, was hardly likely.

Mithradates had at first hoped for Parthian support,[7] but the success of Pompeius' negotiations with Phraates at once inspired him to try to cut his losses: he sent an embassy enquiring on what terms Pompeius would be prepared to make peace.[8] This put Pompeius in a quandary. If the war was brought to an end without a blow, the gibes that had been uttered against him would seem well founded. It was therefore vital to him that Mithradates should fight on, and so he had no choice but to offer terms that the king would be bound to reject.[9] So he demanded that Mithradates should surrender unconditionally and hand over all deserters.[10] The news of this ultimatum provoked a mutiny in Mithradates' camp, and so, if the king had been in any doubt, his hand was forced: he was compelled to pretend that his envoys to Pompeius had in reality been sent merely to spy out the land.[11]

With the danger of an embarrassingly easy victory thus averted, Pompeius set out from Cilicia for Galatia, to approach the awkward matter of asserting his new authority. Glabrio, who had never even taken command of his troops, and Marcius presented no problem. But the premature assumption that the war was over had led to the sending out of a senatorial commission to organize Lucullus' conquests,[12] and the commission was still trying to go about its business. Pompeius' attitude was ruthlessly uncompromising. He was determined from the first that the organization of Roman rule in the East was to be his work alone, and he was equally bent on denying Lucullus all opportunity for patronage. So he systematically reversed the commission's decisions and the edicts of Lucullus, issuing counter-edicts of his own.[13] Such behaviour made it unlikely that a reconciliation between the two men could be achieved; nevertheless, well-meaning or malicious friends arranged a meeting.[14] Omen-spotters noted that the laurels of Pompeius' lictors were fresh and green, whereas those that preceded Lucullus were dry and withered.[15] At first the two were studiously polite to one another, but the tone soon changed. Pompeius accused Lucullus of avarice and mocked him as a Xerxes in a toga; Lucullus retorted that Pompeius lusted only after power and likened him to a vulture that killed no prey of its own but feasted only on other creatures' kills.[16] When he departed, Pompeius naturally took with him all the troops who had been under Lucullus' command, except for sixteen hundred men whom he left him as a guard of honour.[17]

Pompeius now set out in pursuit of Mithradates. An initial Roman victory drove the king to seek sanctuary with Tigranes, only to find that the Armenian had betrayed him and set a price upon his head.[18] Tigranes' motives were probably complex. He was faced with the rebellion of his own son, and suspected Mithradates of complicity in the rising,[19] but it was probably calculation of his own best interest that finally determined his decision. If he believed that Mithradates ultimately stood no chance against Pompeius, then in the face of his son's intrigues with Phraates (see below) his own best chance of survival must already have seemed to lie in offering as little resistance as his self-respect would allow in the hope of inspiring Pompeius to leniency. So Mithradates fled northwards to Colchis and the Bosporus,[20] where Pompeius, after a vain attempt to catch him,[21] was content to leave him for the moment while he turned his attention to Tigranes.[22] The family struggle between the king and his son played into Pompeius' hands. Young Tigranes had persuaded his father-in-law Phraates to invade Armenia, despite some hesitation on the Parthian's part because of his agreement with Pompeius,[23] and together they advanced on the capital, Artaxata. But Tigranes got the better of his son in battle, and the versatile prince therefore went over to Pompeius, with the blessing of Phraates, who was beginning to be alarmed about the possible effects of Pompeius' displeasure.[24]

Pompeius exploited this happy situation with ruthless duplicity. He must already have realized that he was no longer bound to treat Phraates and the young Tigranes with the same degree of circumspection, now that Mithradates had been driven out of Asia Minor, but he hid his change of attitude until Armenia was safely in his hands. For the moment the prince was made welcome and used as a guide as Pompeius in his turn advanced on Artaxata.[25] King Tigranes, who had no doubt been even more convinced of the wisdom of his calculations by the Parthian invasion of Armenia, surrendered without a fight and in an elaborately staged meeting outside Artaxata abased himself before Pompeius, laying his diadem at his conqueror's feet. Pompeius magnanimously restored the crown to his head and confirmed him in his kingdom.[26] But it remained to consider just what the limits of that kingdom were to be. Pompeius' decisions ran as follows. Tigranes was to retain his ancestral realm of Armenia, but was to lose the additional territories he had acquired during the war. These comprised principally Syria from the Euphrates to the sea, parts of Cappadocia and Cilicia, and Sophene.[27] He was also to pay an indemnity of six thousand talents.[28] Tigranes could hardly have hoped for better terms, but his son was bitterly disappointed and resentful. He had already incurred Pompeius' displeasure by a show of resentment when Pompeius had confirmed Tigranes in his kingdom instead of setting him up in his father's place.[29] Now he again showed his dissatisfaction on hearing that of all the territories taken from his father he was to have only Sophene.[30]

This decision is rather puzzling. It was the only one of the regions removed from Tigranes on which Pompeius made an immediate public pronouncement. That in itself is understandable, since Sophene protected Armenia to the Southwest, and Pompeius' policy required the maintenance of Armenia as a strong buffer. But the grant to young Tigranes is odd, given the prince's unreliability and his ties with Phraates. It is perhaps legitimate to conjecture that Pompeius never saw this as more than a very temporary measure and was from the first confident and indeed determined that he would find some pretext for altering the arrangement. If so, the pretext was not long in presenting itself. Sophene held several of Tigranes' royal treasuries, from which Pompeius urgently needed the money. Determined that these funds should remain in his own hands, the prince made efforts to escape, which resulted in his arrest and imprisonment.[31] After some delay, the money found its way into the hands of the king, who passed on to Pompeius more than had been required of him, a prudent gesture which stimulated Pompeius to enrol him as a friend and ally of the Roman people and remove the threat of his son by dispatching the latter under guard to Rome, eventually to grace his triumph.[32] Sophene was restored to Tigranes; no doubt Pompeius calculated that his feud with Phraates would make him keen to keep it out of Parthian hands.[33]

Pompeius' attitude to the young Tigranes not unnaturally alarmed Phraates, who tried in vain to intercede for his son-in-law.[34] When the Parthian anxiously enquired about the present position with regard to the Euphrates frontier, Pompeius made the ominously oracular response that he would abide by whatever frontier seemed just to him.[35] It does not of course follow that he was contemplating a fullscale invasion of Parthia. But just as the removal of Mithradates as a serious threat had left him with no motive to be lenient with young Tigranes, especially when his father had proved so co-operative, he knew that he would not require Parthian help and saw no further need to make concessions even on paper.

So, by the end of 66, Pompeius could view his achievement with considerable satisfaction. Of the two opponents he had been commissioned to deal with, Mithradates had been driven out of Asia Minor and could never again be expected to present any real threat to Roman interests, while Tigranes had been reduced to complete dependence on Rome. Nevertheless he could not rest on his laurels. To enhance his own reputation and meet the demands of Roman public opinion, Mithradates had to be finally eliminated. Therefore the Iberian and Albanian campaigns of 65 appear to represent a diversion.[36] To a certain extent Pompeius' hand was forced: the fear of a Roman invasion in pursuit of Mithradates inspired the Albanians to attack first.[37] He may also have felt the temptation to rival and outdo Alexander, to conquer regions where even Alexander had never set foot.[38] But the reduction of Albania and Iberia should not be written off as mere ostentation.[39] These kingdoms prolonged the protective screen on the eastern and northeastern flanks of Pontus, for Pompeius had planned, at least in outline, what he was going to do with Mithradates' kingdom, even before its subjection had been completed.[40] He may also have been keen to explore the possibility of trade between Pontus and India.[41] But however great his desire for glory, it did not turn his head. For the sake of his men, who had endured considerable hardships, he was prepared to turn back without reaching the Caspian.[42]

On his return he was confronted with a choice of courses as far as Mithradates was concerned: he could either mount an invasion of Bosporus or blockade his enemy and turn his attention elsewhere. He seems first to have thought of invasion, and got as far as Colchis, the submission of which meant that the eastern frontier of Pontus was now secure from the Euxine to the Caspian. Then the difficulties of the prospective campaign and a new development caused him to change his mind and opt for a blockade. So he returned to Pontus and in autumn 65 completed its reduction. The new development was the continuing quarrel between Tigranes and Phraates. This now centred on Gordyene, which Phraates invaded.[43] But the successes of Pompeius and his legates during 65 had made the Parthian even more anxious to maintain peaceful relations with Rome, and he sent envoys to renew his treaty.[44] Pompeius was even less ready than before to take account of Parthian sensibilities, and in the dispute over Gordyene he could have no doubt where Rome's interests lay. He demanded its cession to Rome, and when the envoys were inevitably unable to return any answer, he sent Afranius to take possession of the land by force.[45] Afranius accomplished his mission without encountering resistance, and Gordyene was duly handed over to Tigranes.[46]

Pompeius then established himself in the spring of 64 at Amisus, where no fewer than twelve native kings came to pay court to him as he began to make his dispositions for the future of what had been Mithradates' king-dom.[47] It may have been at this time that Mithradates made a final attempt to salvage something from the wreck of his fortunes by sending an embassy to Pompeius, requesting that he too should be allowed to keep his ancestral kingdom as a tributary of Rome. Pompeius countered by demanding that Mithradates should present himself in person and plead his case, but the king was too wily to fall into such an obvious trap.[48]

From Amisus Pompeius moved southwards towards Syria,[49] to which his quaestor M. Aemilius Scaurus had already been sent ahead in 66.[50] He could still do nothing about Mithradates except to keep him penned up in Bosporus, and meanwhile it was highly desirable that the disturbed state of affairs in Syria should be reduced to some sort of order.[51] On his way he reduced to submission Antiochus of Commagene,[52] while the establish-ment of friendly relations with Osroene also probably belongs to this time.[53] That Pompeius never considered any other solution to the prob-lems of Syria but annexation is clear from the fact that he dated his possession of the country from the moment that Tigranes surrendered to him in 66.[54] In his eyes the Seleucid claim had been extinguished by Tigranes' conquest, and Tigranes' rights had now passed to Rome in similar fashion.[55] When he reached Antioch, he granted an audience to Antiochus XIII, who had been recognized as king by Lucullus, but treated his pretensions with the utmost contempt, accusing him of spending his reign hiding in Cilicia and insisting that annexation was essential if Syria was not to remain a prey to the incursions of Jews and Arabs.[56]

Meanwhile Pompeius' relations with Phraates had continued to deterior-ate. At Amisus he had refused to address Phraates by his customary title King of Kings, which had provoked an embassy of complaint from the Parthian to forbid him to cross the Euphrates. An arrogant reply had angered Phraates, and at the same time as Pompeius advanced into Syria he made another attack on Gordyene.[57] Tigranes' appeal for help put Pom-peius in a difficult position. He may or may not have lacked the personal confidence to undertake a fullscale Parthian war,[58] but he was certainly aware that he could expect criticism from home if he embarked on another seemingly irrelevant adventure in the pursuit of renown while the neglected Mithradates was still at large.[59] So he produced excuses: he had no authority to fight Phraates, and he had already achieved enough to satisfy his own desire for glory.[60] The most he was prepared to do for his client was to send a commission of three to arbitrate.[61] The arbitration was accepted by the kings, who duly settled their differences: Tigranes was angry at Pompeius' failure to provide material support, but realized that he could accomplish nothing without the backing that he was clearly not going to get, while Phraates had no wish to provoke Rome by a serious attempt to destroy her most important buffer-state.[62]

In the South two areas still presented problems in 63: Judaea, which was torn by the Hasmonaean civil war,[63] and Nabataea, whose king Aretas was in the habit of making incursions into what was now Roman territory and had intervened in Judaea. When Scaurus had been sent to Damascus in 66, both contenders for the Jewish throne, Aristobulus and Hyrcanus, had canvassed his support, and Aristobulus had succeeded in winning it.[64] But when Pompeius himself came to Damascus, both men appealed to him afresh, and though he seemed to favour Hyrcanus,[65] he refused to give an immediate decision in the matter, claiming that he must deal with Aretas first.[66] Aristobulus retired first to Alexandrium; then, when Pompeius ordered him to give up his garrisons, he withdrew to Jerusalem, and Pompeius set off in pursuit.[67] At Jericho he heard the news of the death of Mithradates, which must have brought him considerable relief, since in the past three years he had made no progress whatever with the task of securing the king's person.[68] Meanwhile Aristobulus had fortified Jerusalem. Pompeius besieged the city, and Aristobulus was rash enough to leave it to engage in negotiations, which ended in his arrest.[69] Resistance was weakened by considerable internal dissension between the partisans of the two brothers and those who would have preferred theocracy.[70] Nonetheless the siege lasted three months before the city was taken with considerable slaughter.[71] Pompeius desecrated the sanctuary of the temple, probably out of intellectual curiosity, but refrained from plundering its treasures.[72] Hyrcanus was duly established in power, but only as high priest, not as king.[73]

The news of Mithradates' death deterred Pompeius from any further action against the Nabataeans, a task which was left to Scaurus.[74] Pompeius himself returned in haste to Amisus to complete his administrative arrangements.[75] He found that the body of Mithradates had been sent to Sinope by his son Pharnaces, and granted it honourable burial. Pharnaces hoped for a

reward for his part in Mithradates' downfall: he put his request in the form
of alternatives, the first wildly optimistic, that he should be restored to his
father's kingdom, the second more plausible, that he should be allowed to
retain Bosporus. Pompeius confirmed him in the latter and acknowledged
him as a friend and ally of the Roman people, but deprived him of the city
of Phanagoria, which was left in the hands of a friendly dynast, Castor.[76]

In spring of 62 Pompeius distributed lavish rewards to his troops,[77] and
then set out in leisurely fashion to return to Rome. Among the places he
visited were Mytilene, the home of his personal historian Theophanes,
which was granted its freedom as a compliment to its distinguished citizen,[78]
Rhodes, where he received a tutorial from the ailing Posidonius, who also
agreed to write a history of his achievements,[79] and Athens, which was
given a donation of fifty talents.[80]

The most elaborate aspect of Pompeius' settlement of the East was his
organization of Pontus.[81] Here he displayed all his administrative skill. To
turn Pontus into a viable Roman province, it was necessary to create
authorities with whom a Roman governor could deal for administrative,
judicial and fiscal purposes.[82] To this end Pompeius divided the province
into eleven communities, each with an urban centre.[83] The degree of
detailed organization required no doubt varied from place to place. At
Zela, for instance, Pompeius made considerable additions to the city's
territory and settled more people within the walls to create a more cogent
administrative centre.[84] Magnopolis was the name he gave to a city which
had been begun by Mithradates under the name Eupatoria and which he
merely completed, while Cabira was enlarged and renamed Diospolis.[85]
Characteristic of his methods and indicative of what underlies much talk of
foundations is his treatment of Phazemon: the village of Phazemon
was declared a city, Neapolis, and its territory was renamed accordingly.[86]
Levantine hyperbole and Pompeius' own desire to rival Alexander inspire
suspicion of his claims to be a great founder of cities.[87] Only one perhaps
was a genuine creation: Nicopolis in Armenia Minor, established after the
expulsion of Mithradates from Pontus.[88] But the comprehensive nature and
intrinsic merit of Pompeius' charter for Bithynia and Pontus are perhaps
best demonstrated by its durability. Various citations from it are to be found
in the administrative questions with which the younger Pliny persistently
plagued his master Trajan,[89] and Dio a century later notes that Pompeius'
arrangements were still in force in his own day.[90]

Within what was to become the province of Pontus one local dynast was
favoured by Pompeius: Archelaus of Comana, who was appointed to the
priesthood there and strengthened by the grant of additional lands.[91]

Certain other areas were too underdeveloped to lend themselves to direct Roman rule, and these were used by Pompeius to reward local potentates who had served him well.[92] The more backward parts of Paphlagonia were granted to Attalus.[93] The tetrarchs of Galatia were confirmed in their kingdoms, and one in particular, Deiotarus, was richly rewarded, receiving various tracts of land in Pontus and the kingdom of Armenia Minor.[94] To the East Aristarchus was established in Colchis.[95] To the South Cappadocia, where Ariobarzanes had been restored after the surrender of Tigranes, was reinforced by the gift of certain Cilician strongholds,[96] while another buffer serving both Cilicia and Syria, Commagene under its king Antiochus, was given the important city of Seleucia on the Euphrates.[97] Within the province of Syria some local dynasts, such as Sampsiceramus at Emesa, were left in power, though Seleucia in Pieria was declared free, while various cities in Coele Syria were detached from Judaea and assigned to the Roman province.[98] But in general Pompeius' arrangements here bear the marks of incompleteness, in sharp contrast with the meticulous nature of his work in the North.[99] The difference is particularly acute in Judaea, where Pompeius rebuilt Gadara as a favour to his influential freedman Demetrius and planned other similar works of rehabilitation, but had no time to put his schemes into operation, though some of them were eventually brought to fruition by Gabinius during his governorship of Syria.[100]

The net result of Pompeius' settlement was to ring the southern shore of the Euxine and the coast of Asia Minor with provinces: Pontus, Bithynia, Asia, Cilicia and Syria. He could thus truly say that he found Asia a border province and left it in the centre of the empire.[101] Next, protecting the territory held directly by Rome from the threat of possible invasion by northern tribesmen or further south by the Parthians, comes an inner ring of client kingdoms: Bosporus, Colchis, Armenia Minor, Paphlagonia, Galatia, Cappadocia, Commagene, the Syrian and Cilician princedoms, and Judaea, with Armenia and its dependent Sophene thrusting deep into Parthian territory as an additional protection. Nor was the importance of the client kings only strategic. Pompeius devised the useful expedient of making the kings pay tribute, and a large proportion of the enormous new revenues that accrued to the treasury from his conquests must have been drawn, not from lands that had passed under direct Roman control, but from the tribute of client kingdoms.[102]

If the system betrays a strategic weakness, it is in the South, where Pompeius' arrangements were less well planned and more hastily carried out, and the inner ring of defences seems more fragmented and so potentially less stable. To the Northwest Syria was well protected by Cappadocia, Commagene and Osroene, and to the South by Judaea, but to the East and Southeast it was not adequately guarded. So it was Syria, in the years after Pompeius' departure, that was most prone to disturbance by brigands and internal strife and to the threat of Parthian invasion. That Pompeius' ordinances were to some extent eroded was, however, due in part to circumstances for which he cannot fairly be blamed. His triumph celebrated his conquests, not his settlement, and the attitude of mind which found expression in that fact led to neglect of the diplomatic relationships on which the smooth working of the settlement depended.[103] But that did not stem from Pompeius' conscious choice. The values of his age and his class dictated the form in which he sought to achieve and perpetuate his fame, as a great *imperator*, not as an administrator, and unlike Augustus he never held the lasting power that would have allowed him to oversee and maintain the workings of the system he had created.

Nevertheless it was not only the Roman state that was to profit from Pompeius' conquests. Honours were heaped upon him in unprecedented measure.[104] The wealth that accrued to the conqueror himself was sufficient to make him the richest man in Rome: a king like Ariobarzanes could be in his debt and find himself hard pressed to raise the interest.[105] But more than wealth Pompeius had acquired *clientelae* on a scale hitherto unwitnessed. Not merely individuals and cities but provinces and kingdoms acknowledged him as their patron. When the civil war with Caesar finally came, it could be taken for granted by all concerned that all the resources of the East, in money, manpower and ships, would be at Pompeius' beck and call.[106]

6

ROME IN THE ABSENCE OF POMPEIUS

The consular elections for 66 had again brought no success for Pompeius. Indeed, the chief virtue of one of the candidates elected, L. Volcacius Tullus, may have been precisely that he had no Pompeian ties.[1] But the next elections brought a dramatic development. The candidates initially elected, P. Autronius Paetus and P. Cornelius Sulla, a relative of the dictator, were also free of the taint of a Pompeian connection,[2] but they were prosecuted for *ambitus*, condemned and unseated. At the by-election, after the presiding consul Volcacius had refused to accept Catilina's candidature, their original rivals L. Manlius Torquatus and L. Aurelius Cotta were elected in their stead.[3] So for the first time since 70 men associated with Pompeius had reached the consulship, though even now only by resorting to desperate measures. Torquatus had served with Pompeius in the East, and his wife came from Picenum, while Cotta, who may have had difficulty in attaining the consulship at all, had been responsible as praetor in 70 for the reform of the juries.[4]

In the courts enemies of Pompeius and defenders of the Sullan order had been eager for revenge on the popular tribunes of 67 and 66. Cornelius was the first to be attacked, but the initial assault ended in farcical failure. Two brothers, P. and C. (or L.) Cominius, prosecuted him for *maiestas*, but on the day fixed for the hearing they found that the president of the court, P. (or L.) Cassius, had failed to appear, while their own safety was threatened by rioters.[5] Only the intervention of the consuls, who were present as witnesses for Cornelius, saved them from violent handling. On the next day Cassius put in an appearance, but this time the Cominii failed to turn up: probably they feared another riot, though there was a suspicion that they had succumbed to bribery. The charge against Cornelius was therefore dropped.[6]

Next it was Manilius' turn: the charge brought against him, when his tribunate expired, was *repetundae*.[7] The choice of court is surprising and requires explanation, since Manilius' law on the distribution of freedmen had given rise to considerable rioting and so a charge of *maiestas* or *uis* would have been in order.[8] One reason may have been that such a charge might provoke a counter-prosecution against L. Domitius Ahenobarbus, who had played a prominent part in the violence of December 67.[9] Moreover, Cicero was president of the *repetundae* court, and so, if the case was tried before him, he would be unable to act as counsel for the defence. He might of course exert his influence on Manilius' behalf, but perhaps the prosecutors thought that he would do less damage to their cause as president than as advocate. However, on 27 December Cicero showed no good will towards Manilius.[10] Manilius had been demanding the customary delay of ten days, perhaps in the hope that Cicero would defend him if the trial were postponed until 65. But Cicero refused, and fixed the trial for 29 December, apparently with the intention of rushing it through.[11] At once he found himself the butt of an angry crowd, for Manilius had considerable popular support, since it was felt that he was suffering for his services to Pompeius. Cicero was summoned to a public meeting called by the new tribunes, at which he was forced not only to excuse his actions but also to express his disapproval of the prosecution and to commit himself, for the first time, to active support of Manilius by promising to defend him in 65.[12] In January 65 Manilius was prosecuted, this time for *maiestas*.[13] The praetor C. Attius Celsus urged Cicero to undertake the defence.[14] His standing is obscure. He may have been president of the *maiestas* court, but this is unlikely, since the president when Cornelius was tried again later in the year was Q. Gallius.[15] Perhaps his province was *repetundae*. This would not only provide a further reason for Manilius' eagerness to postpone the original *repetundae* trial, if he knew he could expect a friendly praetor in 65, but would also explain what is otherwise puzzling: why Manilius' enemies changed their tactics and switched from *repetundae* to *maiestas*. At the trial Manilius led an attack on the prosecutor, Cn. Minucius, which was beaten off by his old adversary Domitius, and the proceedings broke up in disorder.[16] But a further attempt, perhaps on 5 February, succeeded: both consuls were present in accordance with a decree of the senate, and this time there was no violence. Manilius failed to appear and was condemned in absence.[17]

Pompeius seems to have been ready enough to sacrifice Manilius, whose turbulent nature made him a dubious asset.[18] Nor indeed is there any indication that he exerted himself on behalf of Cornelius. However, belated success against Manilius gave the opposition heart to make another attack on his predecessor, and about this trial information is relatively full. Cornelius was defended by Cicero, and though the speeches are lost a number of fragments and much of Asconius' commentary survive.[19] The charge was still *maiestas*, and both sides proceeded with equal sophistry and cynicism. The prosecution witnesses were pillars of the Sullan oligarchy: Hortensius, Catulus, Metellus Pius, M. Lucullus and Mam. Lepidus.[20] There can be no doubt that they would have preferred, as Cicero claimed,[21] the faceless tribunes of the seventies, yet they solemnly rose to defend tribunician *maiestas*, which Cornelius had infringed by ignoring the veto of his colleague Servilius Globulus. Cicero's reply was no less disingenuous. It could hardly be treason, he averred, for a tribune to read aloud from a piece of paper![22] But it was not this feeble piece of verbal trickery that impressed the jury. Cornelius' cause had popular support, for his law on *ambitus* had been much desired by the people, quite apart from his ties with the popular hero Pompeius.[23] Cicero spoke in a strongly popular vein, and much of his speech was devoted to praise of the achievements of the absent Pompeius.[24] It was Cornelius' old link with Pompeius that won him the support not only of the *equites* and *tribuni aerarii* on the jury but also of a number of the senators: those who were not, as Asconius puts it, associated with the *principes*.[25] It is significant that Globulus himself had no taste for the way in which his brush with Cornelius was being exploited to mount an attack on the power of the tribunate: he appeared as a witness, but for the defence.[26]

The success of Cicero's defence of Cornelius won him popular favour and made him virtually certain of Pompeius' backing in his campaign for the consulship, but the optimates had been displeased, as Vatinius was to remind Cicero in 56, and it was now more than ever necessary for him to convince them that his excursions into popular oratory did not represent his true political position but had been undertaken solely to secure Pompeius' good will, which he could not do without.[27]

Another tribune of 66, C. Memmius, had pursued a feud against the Luculli, prosecuting Marcus, though without result, for his activities under Sulla, and successfully delaying the decree of a triumph to Lucius for his achievements against Mithradates and Tigranes.[28] Plutarch claims that he aimed at winning Pompeius' favour, but any tie between them was not strong enough to deter Memmius from tampering with Pompeius' wife.[29]

Meanwhile Pompeius' old rival Crassus set about strengthening his own position against the day of Pompeius' return from the East. Early in 65 he sponsored a motion in the senate to send Cn. Calpurnius Piso as *quaestor pro praetore* to Hispania Citerior, where Pompeius had acquired great influence during the Sertorian war.[30] Piso was believed to be hostile to Pompeius, but he did not survive long in Spain before he was killed by some native cavalrymen. Rumour had it that they were faithful clients of Pompeius and did the deed with his blessing: they may well have hoped to please him, and probably succeeded, though it is highly unlikely that they were acting under instructions.

As censor Crassus directed his efforts towards two further ends, but with a similar lack of success. His first move was intended to reinforce his own *clientela* and undermine that of Pompeius in an area that was of vital military importance to Rome both as a reserve of manpower and because of its strategic position, the Transpadane region. It had long been a source of strength for Pompeius. Now Crassus attempted to enfranchise the Transpadani,[31] but a further influx of new citizens, so soon after the enfranchisement of Italy belatedly completed by the censors of 70, was unwelcome to the Sullan oligarchy, which was already finding the enlarged assemblies difficult to control by the traditional means of patronage and bribery. Fortunately for them the other censor was Catulus, and his stubborn opposition forced Crassus to abandon the proposal. Next he turned his attention to Egypt, urging the annexation of that kingdom. The wealth of the country and its abundant corn made it an attractive prize, and the proposal brought together Crassus and Caesar, who was aedile in 65. It was suggested that Caesar should be commissioned to supervise the annexation, which suffices to show that the intention was not to create a military command to rival that of Pompeius, for such a command would not have been entrusted to a man of merely aedilician standing.[32] But once again Catulus stood firm against his colleague, and the Egyptian scheme too came to nothing.[33] Cicero too committed himself on this issue, opposing Crassus in his speech *de rege Alexandrino*, but there is nothing to suggest that he construed this stand as a service to Pompeius.

Nevertheless, he could hope for Pompeian support at the consular elections of 64, and consequently for that of much of the urban plebs, because of his defence of Cornelius and his contribution to the passing of the *lex Manilia*.[34] But at the same time, if he was to be elected, he needed the backing or at least the neutrality of the nobles, both young and old, many of whom might look with disfavour on his Pompeian past.[35] He was well aware of the difficulty of reconciling these potential sources of support. In discussing his chances with Atticus he singled out as vital the attitude of L. Domitius, the future consul of 54.[36] Domitius was powerful, rich and arrogant, and had very good reasons to dislike Pompeius. Yet the triumphant outcome of Cicero's election campaign proves that he must have secured the backing both of Pompeius and of Pompeius' most distinguished opponents, Domitius and men of like stamp. The explanation is probably to be found in two related factors: the candidature of L. Sergius Catilina and fear of the possible intentions of the absent Pompeius.[37] Catilina had once, like the young Pompeius, been a member of Strabo's *consilium* at Asculum.[38] There is no evidence of any more recent link with Pompeius,[39] but Catilina could not be regarded as reliable, despite a longstanding connection with Catulus.[40] His conduct as governor of Africa had aroused the wrath of that province's most distinguished patron, Metellus Pius, and he had previously made himself notorious under Sulla.[41] Now, proud, ambitious and deeply in debt, he might well welcome with open arms a new Sulla who could secure his position and gratify his desires. Such a man could not be allowed to hold the consulship at a time when Pompeius might return from the East. Men were suspicious of Pompeius' intentions. True, he had shown no sign of wanting to seize power when he came back from Spain in 71, but then his strength had been such that the outcome would have been in doubt. Now, if Pompeius decided to imitate Sulla, he would have the military strength to crush any resistance. It would therefore be folly to permit the election of a consul whose conduct would at best be likely to provide an excuse for Pompeius to use force on the pretext of restoring order and who might well be inclined to encourage and abet him in any attempt he might make to win absolute power. Cicero on the other hand, despite his links with Pompeius, would never support a Sullan *coup d'état*. His devotion to law and order and the sanctity of private property was unswerving. Should Pompeius return while Cicero was in office, it might even be hoped that the orator would act as a moderating influence on him should one prove needful. So both adherents of Pompeius and those who feared him combined to sweep the new man to the head of the poll. The election, like others in the sixties, was attended by heavy bribery, but this seems to have been undertaken chiefly in the interest of Catilina and his running-mate C. Antonius, for when the senate attempted to put a stop to it obstruction came from the tribune Q. Mucius Orestinus, who was in all probability the brother of Catilina's wife Aurelia Orestilla.[42]

The manner of his election left Cicero with a problem that was to plague him throughout his consulship. If he devoted himself to energetic defence of the interests of Pompeius, he would offend those optimates who had assisted his election but were reluctant to see Pompeius' position strengthened still further. If on the other hand he opposed the designs of Pompeius' friends, then Pompeius would have just cause on his return to accuse him of ingratitude. So Cicero had to walk a tightrope, and the first crisis of his year of office called for all his skill in this regard.

Several of the tribunes of 63, led by P. Servilius Rullus, introduced an agrarian bill.[43] It proposed the establishment of a commission of ten, with praetorian *imperium*, whose power was to extend throughout the empire. This commission was to be elected not by the whole people but by seventeen of the thirty-five tribes chosen by lot and voting under the presidency of Rullus himself. Their task was to raise money from various sources, including the sale of certain categories of public land in Italy and abroad, and with the funds so acquired to buy up land for distribution to the poor. The measure was clearly meant to provide land for Pompeius' veterans when the war in the East was over, though the urban proletariat was also to share in the benefits of the law. Its promoters had no doubt realized the danger of courting the veterans to the exclusion of the city plebs, for a split between these two groups of supporters had contributed to the fall of Saturninus in 100.[44]

Cicero attacked the bill first in the senate and then before the people. He based his case on two propositions: first, the measure was for various reasons inimical to the interests of Pompeius;[45] second, it would not benefit the people. Only the first point is relevant here.[46] Cicero insisted on his own and the people's devotion to Pompeius and remarked that he had won his consulship with Pompeius' backing.[47] To show that the proposal damaged Pompeius he brought various arguments. The diverse means by which Rullus' commission was to raise money to purchase land for allotment interfered with Pompeius' rights in his provinces. Thus provision was made for the sale of territories that had belonged to Mithradates in Paphlagonia, Pontus and Cappadocia, while the war was still in progress and before Pompeius had made his report or arrangements had been made for the future administration of these regions. At this time Pompeius ought still to be exercising full control.[48] The clause that new revenues accruing to the state after 63 should be used to buy land was also presented by Cicero as an interference with the conquests of Pompeius.[49] More important, Pompeius, whom the people would have entrusted with any mission, was excluded from membership of the agrarian commission by the clause in the bill which laid down that candidates must stand for election in person.[50] There was thus a danger that his veterans would be lured away from their allegiance to him and would come to look elsewhere for their land if they saw so much power in the hands of the Rullan commission while Pompeius was barred from serving.[51] Even a clause that seemed to promise Pompeius a privileged position was interpreted by Cicero as an attempt to discredit him. He was exempted from the provision that booty in the possession of commanders should be made available to the commission for the purchase of land. But, said Cicero, Pompeius did not want special treatment, which was calculated only to stir up ill feeling against him.[52]

The case that the bill was directed against Pompeius will not bear examination. Indeed, it seems far more likely that Rullus and his colleagues were acting on Pompeius' behalf.[53] Pompeius need have no objection to the use of the revenues from his conquests if his own veterans would ultimately benefit, while if reliable men controlled the commission's operations there would be no call for him to occupy a seat on it himself. The possibility remains, however, that what began as a measure designed to further Pompeius' interests was seen by his rivals as an opportunity to curb him. Cicero hinted laboriously that behind Rullus stood Crassus and Caesar: those who had failed in 65 to lay hands on Egypt openly were now trying to do so by more devious means and were aiming through the agency of the commission to secure tyrannical power for themselves.[54] This allegation may be completely false, or it may be that Crassus at least saw the chance of diverting the bill from its true purpose and by securing control of the commission acquiring a corner in land for distribution. Possession of such a bargaining counter would put him in a very strong position when Pompeius returned and the veterans' demands had to be met. Such a development might go some way towards explaining the speed and ease with which the bill was dropped once Cicero had turned the mass of the people against Rullus.

Next politics moved into the realm of farce. An elderly senator, C. Rabirius, was prosecuted for his part in the death of the popular tribune L. Appuleius Saturninus, who had been lynched along with a number of his followers after a riot on 10 December 100.[55] The initiator of the prosecution was the tribune T. Labienus, who charged Rabirius with the obsolete offence of *perduellio*. Procedure and penalties were equally archaic: the appointment by the urban praetor of *duumuiri* to pronounce a verdict, and death by crucifixion if Rabirius was condemned. Duumvirs were duly appointed by L. Valerius Flaccus: L. Julius Caesar, consul in the previous year, and his young and distant relative C. Caesar. It is unlikely that the charade would have been carried to its gruesome conclusion, but Cicero intervened in the senate and put a stop to the attempt to impose the death penalty. Rabirius had already appealed to the people against the verdict of guilty pronounced by the duumvirs, so Cicero once more spoke on his behalf, contriving at once to defend the authority of the senate as vested in the *senatus consultum ultimum* and to present himself as a true *popularis* by contrast with the bloodthirsty tribune.[56] The proceedings ended as they had begun, in farce: a praetor, Metellus Celer, lowered the red flag flown on the Janiculum – a signal that Rome was being attacked and that the citizens must all rush to defend the walls.[57]

This ludicrous episode may bear some relation to the bill of Rullus. If Rullus and his colleagues had in fact, despite Cicero's claims, been acting in Pompeius' interests, then the Rabirius affair may have been staged as an entertainment designed to rehearse *popularis* themes in a manner that would require no positive action but might serve to take the minds of the disappointed masses off Rullus' failure. Certainly three of the men involved may be linked with Pompeius at about this time. Labienus came from Picenum and passed legislation in Pompeius' favour during his tribunate. Later, despite his service in Gaul with Caesar, he joined Pompeius at the outbreak of the civil war.[58] It is true that he also had a personal interest in the trial: his uncle Q. Labienus had been among those who had died with Saturninus.[59] Caesar had backed the *lex Gabinia* and *lex Manilia*, and supported Labienus' laws in 63. He also testified against C. Piso, the consul of 67, whose hostility had given Gabinius and Pompeius so much trouble.[60] Finally, Metellus Celer had served with Pompeius in the East, and retained Pompeius' good will when he came to stand for the consulship of 60.[61] But if the Rabirius trial was mounted by friends of Pompeius, it is only fair to say that Cicero is unlikely to have given offence by his stand on behalf of the defendant. Since the trial was never meant to be carried through to the bitter end, it mattered little that Cicero had twice exercised a vital influence on the course of proceedings.

In the latter part of the year Cicero had more serious matters to contend with. Catilina was standing once more for the consulship, with a programme designed to exploit and exacerbate social discontent in Rome and the Italian countryside. In Etruria support for his candidature was mobilized by L. Manlius, a former centurion in Sulla's army. Others who might hope to benefit from a violent upheaval found their leader in L. Cornelius Lentulus Sura, consul as long ago as 71 but expelled from the senate in 70 and now praetor. To what extent these various groups of malcontents were welded into a single force by Catilina in the service of a coherent master-plan for revolution need not be considered here.[62] Cicero claims that it was so, but even if the 'Catilinarian conspiracy' was largely a figment of Cicero's imagination, his reasons for conjuring it into existence were cogent, while if the conspiracy really existed essentially as he portrayed it, the motives that dictated his policy, so far from losing their force, would become all the more pressing. He was faced with a confused and threatening situation. Discontents festered beneath an outwardly calm surface, ready to break out into the open. Cicero's overmastering fear was that a catalyst would be supplied by the return of Pompeius, who might at worst unite all the malcontents under his own leadership, at best exploit the need to crush unrest as a pretext for keeping his army together and staging a *coup d'état*. This is the key to Cicero's policy in the autumn and winter of 63. His urgent desire was that all the potential troublemakers in the state should without delay come out into the open and unite – that the wicked, as he says, should put a wall between themselves and the good.[63] If that happened, and happened quickly, it would be possible for the forces of law and order to crush any rising before Pompeius' arrival. When the great general landed in Italy he would be confronted with peace and concord on every side and would find no emergency to exploit for his own ends.

As leader of the rising he was eager to provoke Cicero cast Catilina. He emphasized that those he labelled Catilina's supporters were men who needed a new Sulla to set them on their feet: bankrupts, spendthrifts and gamblers, men lusting after honours or the profits of proscriptions, and Sulla's own veterans, who had failed to make a success of farming on the holdings bestowed on them by their commander. Such men might well favour Sulla's former henchman Pompeius should he show signs of imitating his master's example.[64] But Cicero was determined that they should never have the chance. Hence his relentless campaign to drive Catilina into open revolt and his exultation at its success.[65] Once Catilina had committed himself to the field, his small and ill-equipped force was doomed to annihilation before much time had elapsed.[66] Meanwhile in the city Lentulus and his confederates, while trying to stir up revolt among the Allobroges in Gaul and to establish a link with Catilina, played into Cicero's hands and were unmasked. When the senate debated their fate on 5 December Cato carried the day for their execution despite the opposition of the praetor designate Caesar.

On another matter, however, Cato's notorious rectitude came close to upsetting Cicero's calculations.[67] If Pompeius were to return in 62, it was desirable that the consuls in office to receive him should be reliable men. Those elected seemed eminently suitable. D. Junius Silanus, despite his pusillanimous conduct in the debate of 5 December, was closely linked with Cato and husband of Servilia, former wife of that M. Brutus whom Pompeius had put to death in 77. L. Licinius Murena, first of his family to attain the highest office, was a military man, a former legate of Pompeius' enemy Lucullus, the votes of whose veterans had contributed to his election.[68] Cicero could be well pleased with this result. But then the son of an unsuccessful candidate, the jurist Ser. Sulpicius Rufus, prosecuted Murena for *ambitus*, and Cato lent his weight to the accusation, apparently for no better reason than that it was true. Cicero sprang to Murena's defence and secured his acquittal without undue difficulty, assisted by two other advocates of note who had no affection for Pompeius, Hortensius and Crassus.[69] The same preoccupations inform the *pro Murena* as are found in the *Catilinarians*: the need for concord, calm and a reliable consul, ostensibly as a safeguard against Catilina, in reality as a safeguard against Pompeius.[70]

So Murena was saved, but trouble might still come in 62 from two other sources: the praetor Caesar and the tribune Metellus Nepos. The year 63 had been a great one for Caesar. He not only secured the praetorship for 62 but was also elected *pontifex maximus*, defeating two men whose distinction and service to the state might have been thought to give them claims far more convincing than his own, Catulus and Servilius Isauricus.[71] His involvement in the events of the year shows Caesar chiefly concerned to reinforce the links with Pompeius that he had forged in 67 and 66.[72] His part in the Rabirius trial has already been noted, and when two tribunes, Labienus the prosecutor of Rabirius and T. Ampius Balbus, passed a law giving Pompeius the right on his return to wear triumphal dress at the games and the *toga praetexta* and a gold crown in the theatre, Caesar gave them his support.[73] He also appeared as a witness against C. Piso, the consul of 67, though his action here will have been dictated less by a desire to please Pompeius, who seems to have taken no interest in the trial, than by an eagerness to win favour for himself in Cisalpine Gaul, the scene of Piso's excesses. Cicero defended Piso and secured his acquittal, but Pompeius can hardly have resented this stand. Piso had done Cicero valuable service at the time of his election campaign, and Pompeius will have understood that the debt had to be paid.[74] Besides, Piso's acquittal was in no sense a blow to his own prestige or a threat to his future prospects.

Metellus Nepos was on the surface a more serious threat to Cicero. Like his brother Celer he had been serving as a legate of Pompeius in the East, and was given leave to return to Rome and stand for the tribunate of 62.[75] Taking office on 10 December 63 he and a colleague, L. Calpurnius Bestia, at once attacked Cicero for his execution of the conspirators in the city, and when Cicero laid down his office at the end of the year Nepos by his veto prevented him from delivering the lengthy speech that he had prepared for the occasion.[76] In January he took more positive steps, bringing forward two proposals: first, that Pompeius should be recalled to Italy to put down Catilina, who was still in the field; second, that he should be allowed to stand in absence for the consulship.[77] It is hard to know to what extent Nepos was acting on direct instructions from Pompeius.[78] He must have left his commander in the East some months before the Catilinarian danger had developed, though no doubt he had been in subsequent communication with Pompeius by letter. But given the delays involved it would be only reasonable for Pompeius to allow him a fairly free hand to exploit the situation as seemed best in the light of developing circumstances.[79] If the tactic adopted by Nepos was the floating of alternative proposals, one less extreme than the other, to test public opinion and give Pompeius the chance of eventually appearing to exercise moderation by opting for that which had aroused less disquiet, this would accord with Pompeius' methods on other occasions. On the other hand, if the proposals were presented not as alternatives but as cumulative, Nepos might have been trying to recreate for Pompeius the situation of 71.[80] Then Pompeius had kept his army together, with the slave revolt of Spartacus as his justification, and then too he had stood for the consulship in absence. If the tribune had been successful in pushing through his measures, the scene would have been set for a repeat performance, with Catilina now filling the role that had been played in 71 by Spartacus, and this may indeed have been Pompeius' objective at this time.

Nepos enjoyed the support of Caesar, who also clashed again with Catulus.[81] Catulus, smarting at his defeat in the pontifical election, had tried to persuade Cicero to frame Caesar on a charge of complicity in the revolutionary designs of Catilina,[82] so Caesar had good reasons of his own to counter-attack. Catulus had been entrusted by the senate with the task of restoring the temple of Jupiter on the Capitol. The work was by now almost complete, but Caesar intervened to deprive Catulus of the credit and transfer completion of the operation to Pompeius. It is significant that, although Caesar's motive for attacking Catulus was personal, he chose a method of expressing his hostility that was once again calculated to win Pompeius' favour.[83]

However, there was strong opposition. One of Nepos' colleagues in the tribunate was Cato, who had stood for office with the expressed intention of thwarting whatever undesirable proposals Nepos might bring forward.[84] He proved a highly effective opponent, but Nepos, who throughout his career seems to evidence a taste for trouble, did not give way easily, and the struggle between the two reached such proportions that the *senatus consultum ultimum* was passed and both Caesar and Nepos were suspended from office by the senate.[85] Pompeius cannot have been pleased by this development. The result of Nepos' violent behaviour must have been to discredit any proposal associated with his name, so that his potential usefulness will have been reduced to nothing.[86] It may be that the manner of Nepos' failure and a desire to live down the memory of it played some part in dictating the posture of extreme moderation and conciliation that Pompeius in fact adopted when he returned.

Caesar and Nepos reacted very differently. Caesar retired into private life and gave assurances of his future good behaviour, and as a result was duly reinstated in office.[87] Nepos fled to Pompeius.[88] In 49 two tribunes took refuge with Caesar, in circumstances not dissimilar, and Caesar used the defence of tribunician rights as a pretext for embarking on civil war. If in 62 Pompeius had felt any inclination to invade Italy and seize power, as he was now for the first time militarily strong enough to do, the senate's treatment of Nepos would have given him an excuse. But Pompeius did nothing of the sort, and there is not the slightest hint that the thought of fighting in Nepos' cause ever crossed his mind.

Early in 62 he may have received a more distinguished visitor. At this time Crassus left Rome, allegedly because he was afraid of Pompeius or at least wished to give that invidious impression.[89] But neither explanation will stand up, since Crassus went to Asia.[90] One of his motives will no doubt have been to investigate the economic situation,[91] but it is not unlikely that he met Pompeius. What they may have talked about is not clear, but there are certainly no grounds for positing any agreement between them for positive co-operation on Pompeius' return.[92]

As to the manner of that return, Pompeius' behaviour over Nepos gave indisputable proof that his intentions were entirely peaceful. He expected a certain position of honour in the state, and he had practical demands to make – the ratification of his acts and the provision of land for his troops – that he took it for granted would be met, but he had no thought of fighting to achieve these ends. Yet even before he himself reached Italy he received a clear indication that all would not be easy. To further his purposes in 61 he naturally wanted to ensure that at least one consul would be friendly. His candidate was his legate M. Pupius Piso. Piso was duly sent ahead to ensure that he arrived at Rome in time to hand in his nomination, but Pompeius also submitted a request to the senate that the elections should be postponed till after his own arrival, to give him the chance to canvass for Piso in person. The senate rejected the request, and the leading spirit behind its decision was Cato.[93] It was thus made plain to Pompeius well in advance that, when the time came to press for his requirements in the senate, he might expect opposition, and might expect Cato to lead it.

7

THE RETURN OF POMPEIUS

When Pompeius reached Brundisium towards the end of 62 his behaviour was more conventional, more overtly conciliatory than it had been on his return from the Sertorian war in 71. Then, even after the defeat of Spartacus, he had kept his army together until his triumph. Now he disbanded his troops immediately on landing.[1] Several reasons may have contributed to this change. Pompeius did not intend to seize power, but his capacity to do so in 62 was far greater than it had been in 71, and it is easy to imagine that the fearful expectations aroused by his advent were in their turn correspondingly more acute. It was not only Pompeius' increased strength that might inspire disquiet; he was coming from the East, from a war against Mithradates, and that ominous coincidence was bound to stir memories of Sulla, under whose banner Pompeius had once served, even in men whose reason might tell them that open resort to violence was not Pompeius' way. Knowing that the alarm he caused was greater than it had been before, Pompeius had good reason to try to demonstrate that such fears were devoid of justification. As early as the spring of 62 he had written publicly, giving a guarantee to those who were prepared to believe him that he had no intention of making trouble, but was dedicated to the preservation of *otium*.[2] No doubt the conduct of the over-enthusiastic Metellus Nepos had made some such gesture a matter of urgency. This letter had given much pleasure to Cicero, who knew Pompeius well enough to expect no less of him, but others had been less happy. Cicero's fears in 63 had not been groundless: many who were discontented with their lot, those whom Cicero describes as Pompeius' *ueteres hostes, noui amici* ('old enemies, new friends'), had hoped and believed that he would come home like Sulla and make their fortunes for them in the process.[3] To them his declaration of his peaceful intentions had come as a bitter blow.

Pompeius was also perhaps more confident than he had been in 71. He was now a consular of eight years standing, and his successes in the East and the adulation they had earned him cannot have been without their effect on his already redoubtable conceit. But if confidence may have led him to disband his army, his response to the political situation at Rome reveals a curious mixture of overconfidence and insight. His first action was to divorce his wife Mucia, on whose conduct during his absence rumour cast the gravest suspicions. To replace her he selected a niece of Cato, daughter of the consul D. Silanus and Servilia, and requested the hand of her sister for his eldest son.[4] Pompeius' vanity is striking. It was rash in the extreme to dispense with Mucia before making sure of the match with the Juniae. Perhaps past experience enhanced his inherent belief that an alliance with Rome's greatest general must prove irresistible, for in the eighties Sulla and the Metelli had been only too ready to ply him with brides to secure his loyalty. More important is the motive that dictated Pompeius' choice. It has often been seen as the reflection of a shift in the balance of power within the upper strata of the senate, a decline in the numbers and authority of the Metelli and a corresponding increase in the influence of Cato and his friends. Such schematism is to be resisted: the gulf between 'Metellans' and 'Catonians' implied by this view simply did not exist.[5] Pompeius' reason was less general, more ruthlessly practical. Cato's attitude to the candidature of M. Piso had shown, as had his vigorous and effective opposition to Metellus Nepos, that he was likely to prove a thorn in Pompeius' flesh. From Pompeius' point of view a marriage alliance was the obvious means of neutralizing Cato, if not of actually gaining his support. That at least was certainly how Cato himself saw the matter, and he refused to allow his freedom of political action to be circumscribed in this way.[6] Both girls were eager for the match, and so, more surprisingly, was their mother, despite Pompeius' previous lethal intervention in her domestic affairs (above, p. 71), but Cato firmly refused to allow it, and Pompeius found himself rebuffed.

The incident was little short of a political disaster. By divorcing Mucia Pompeius had run the risk of offending her half-brothers Celer and Nepos at a time when Celer's attitude was vital, since he was a candidate for the consulship of 60 and his stance might have a decisive effect on the success or failure of Pompeius' dealings with the senate. At the same time Cato's behaviour had shown that Pompeius' worst fears of opposition from that quarter would be realized, since if Cato had not already been determined to resist Pompeius' demands when he put them to the senate, he would have had no reason to react as he had done to his proposal. The great man had made a fool of himself, and the immediate future looked stormy.

By late January 61 Cicero was in private already critical of Pompeius, but his attitude may have been to a large extent dictated by Pompeius' failure to lavish adequate praise on the achievements of his consulship. Pompeius and Cicero were the two vainest men in Rome, and Cicero's remarks in the *Fourth Catilinarian*, where he praised Pompeius for his victories abroad but trumpeted his own successes at home as equally great, if not greater,[7] cannot have failed to touch Pompeius on a sore spot. He made friendly overtures to Cicero now, for he was well aware of the power of Cicero's tongue and he knew that he would need every friendly voice he could muster if his objectives were to be achieved. Nervousness and embarrass-ment may well have made his advances sound as insincere as in fact they were. At all events Cicero claimed that Pompeius praised him only because he was afraid to criticize and claimed to see through the profess-ions of friendship to the envy and resentment that lurked beneath. His crushing verdict on Pompeius at this time, *nihil come, nihil simplex, nihil ἐν τοῖς πολιτικοῖς inlustre, nihil honestum, nihil forte, nihil liberum*, though stimulated by pique and shaped by malice, is valid testimony to the awkward situation in which Pompeius found himself.[8]

Though his head was full of his own concerns, he found when he reached the neighbourhood of the city that other men had no time to give him the attention he thought he deserved, for Rome was in the grip of a highly entertaining political and religious scandal.[9] At the end of 62 the rites of the Bona Dea, from which all males were rigorously excluded, had been celebrated in the house of the *pontifex maximus* Caesar. Pandemonium had broken out when it was found that the ceremony had been polluted by the presence of the notorious P. Clodius, disguised as a woman. Opinions varied as to whether his quarry had been Caesar's wife Pompeia or simply one of the maids. Caesar seized the chance to utter a famous quotation and divorced Pompeia, but did not pursue the matter further. Others, however, saw an opportunity to remove a dangerous figure from the political scene or simply to create an awful example to check impiety and sexual licence in the young. The matter was raised in the senate by Q. Cornificius, but the consuls were divided. M. Valerius Messalla, backed by Cato, was hostile to Clodius, but Piso, though forced to join Messalla in bringing a motion, worked to frustrate his own proposal out of friendship for Clodius.[10] This explanation of his behaviour is quite sufficient: it should not be seen as a clue to Pompeius' attitude, for it is clear from his subsequent reaction that Pompeius knew little of the affair and cared less.

However, it was forced on his notice on his first public appearance, which pleased nobody, if Cicero is to be believed. It held out no hope of revolution or reform to the poor or the discontented, but good men found it lacking in weight.[11] It is unlikely that Pompeius had wanted to speak at all. The tribune Fufius Calenus, encouraged by Clodius' friend M. Piso, brought him before a public meeting and asked him if he thought it was just for the praetor presiding in a court of law to handpick his jury, as the senate had decreed should take place in the trial of Clodius for sacrilege. Pompeius, who was probably ill-informed about the details of the case and not very interested, extolled the authority of the senate in general terms.[12] But he was not to be allowed to get off so lightly. In the senate it was not Clodius' supporters who tried to make him commit himself, but the consul Messalla who asked him what he thought of the whole affair and in particular his views on the composition of the court. Pompeius again refused to be drawn, speaking in praise of all decrees of the senate, and remarking in an aside to Cicero as he sat down that surely he had said enough about the matter.[13] The watchful Crassus saw a chance to play on Cicero's easily wounded vanity and drive a wedge between him and Pompeius. His apparent approval of Cicero's consulship had won Pompeius some applause, but he had not been fulsome. Crassus now launched into an elaborate speech in praise of Cicero's achievements and drew the reaction he had hoped for from Pompeius. Cicero noted Pompeius' annoyance, but was unsure whether the cause was anger at seeing Crassus get the credit which he could have had for himself had he spoken more generously, or envy at the senate's high regard for Cicero's deeds.[14] Both factors may well have played a part.

Meanwhile the protagonists in the Bona Dea affair kept up a lively campaign. Inside the senate Clodius had little support except for Piso, Fufius and C. Curio, the consul of 76. Outside he organized public meetings and attacked Messalla, Lucullus and Hortensius, while a band of young aristocrats led by Curio's son demonstrated in his favour. Despite the efforts of Piso and Curio, the senate voted for the specially constituted court, and Fufius conceded defeat.[15] Then Hortensius abruptly changed his position and devised a compromise bill for Fufius which substituted a normal jury. It seems he was afraid that Fufius would veto the motion of the consuls and eager that Clodius should at least come to trial. Perhaps too he believed that it would make no difference, since Clodius' guilt was manifest. Cicero was not so sanguine, and events were to prove him right. Clodius was defended by Curio, large sums were expended on his behalf, and the jury acquitted him by 31 votes to 25.[16] In the course of the trial Cicero took a stand that was to have catastrophic results for his own future. His testimony destroyed Clodius' alibi, and from that day Clodius was determined to have his revenge.[17] But despite the outcome of the trial Cicero was euphoric. He continued to attack the villains of the piece in the senate, somehow depriving the consul Piso of the province of Syria and in his own estimation at least shattering Clodius.[18] He also enjoyed the benevolence of the masses, who believed that he was on uniquely good terms with Pompeius. Indeed their outward amity was so great that young Curio and his friends tried to provoke Pompeius by addressing him as Cn. Cicero.[19] But Pompeius had cause to bridle his vanity and cultivate Cicero, for he had so far made no progress at all towards the achievement of his ends. Piso had proved an egregious failure, and despite the escape of Clodius Cicero had given repeated proofs of the power of his oratory. For the moment he was clearly to be humoured.[20]

With the year half over and nothing accomplished, Pompeius decided to cut his losses and hope for better service from the magistrates of 60. His former legate Metellus Celer was standing, and Pompeius continued to lend him his support.[21] But Celer was hardly to be relied upon. He might co-operate with Pompeius for as long as it suited him, but he did not need him in order to secure the consulship that he thought of as his birthright, and there was no guarantee that he would use it to further Pompeius' ends, especially since the divorce of Mucia might well have offended him gravely. More trustworthy from Pompeius' point of view was L. Afranius. But like other men who owed their success in life to Pompeius' patronage Afranius had no personal influence or ancestral connections.[22] Only massive bribery could ensure his election. His opponents did their best to resist: two decrees of the senate were proposed by Cato and his brother-in-law Domitius Ahenobarbus, and the tribune Lurco received a special dispensation to bring an *ambitus* bill before the people after the announcement of the elections.[23] A clause in the senatorial decrees, that enquiries should be made into the conduct of magistrates at whose houses the distributors of bribes carried on their operations, reflected the rumour that the consul Piso was attempting to make up for his own lack of success in securing Pompeius' objectives by organizing the campaign for a suitable successor. But Cato's efforts proved vain, and Afranius was elected with Celer.

The celebration of his third triumph, timed to coincide with his forty-fifth birthday, gave Pompeius a brief respite from the problems of politics. The festivities occupied two days, 28 and 29 September.[24] In the inscription recording the dedication of his spoils to the goddess Minerva he claimed to have received the surrender of more than twelve million people and over fifteen hundred towns and fortresses, to have sunk or captured almost eight hundred and fifty ships, and to have conquered all the lands from Lake

Maeotis to the Red Sea.[25] The announcement of the triumph mentioned his suppression of piracy, his restoration to Rome of command of the sea, and the defeat of Mithradates and Tigranes, and listed the regions and peoples he had subdued: Asia, Pontus, Armenia, Paphlagonia, Cappadocia, Cilicia, Syria, the Scythians, Jews and Albani, Iberia, Crete (he still nursed his grudge against Metellus) and the Bastarnae.[26] Another inscription, perhaps from the temple of Venus Victrix dedicated in 55,[27] gave more details of the kingdoms and provinces over which he had extended his protection and the kings and tribes he had conquered. He boasted that he had extended the boundaries of the empire to the ends of the earth and did not overlook the tangible benefit this had brought to the revenues of the Roman people.[28] Similarly the placards carried in the procession commemorated not only the nations over which he had triumphed but revealed that he had almost doubled Rome's provincial income and was in addition bringing to the treasury booty to the value of twenty thousand talents.[29] All the treasures of Mithradates, later to be dedicated on the Capitol, graced the celebration,[30] the major events of the war were represented by tableaux,[31] and even trees found a place.[32] But most striking of all was a giant float which described itself as a trophy of the inhabited world, a piece of ostentation which belies the apparent moderation of Pompeius' refusal of all surnames drawn from his conquests.[33] Many distinguished prisoners and hostages preceded the victor's chariot, including the young Tigranes and Aristobulus.[34] Pompeius himself appeared in a cloak that he claimed had once belonged to Alexander.[35] The end of the proceedings once again revealed his humanity: all the prisoners were sent home at the state's expense except the kings, and even of these only Aristobulus was put to death.[36]

Towards the end of 61 came the first of the developments that were to play so dramatic a part in shaping the history of the last decade of the republic. The equestrian tax-farmers who at the most recent auction had purchased the right to collect the taxes of the usually highly profitable province of Asia found that because of the ravages of the Mithradatic War the province was exhausted.[37] So far from making the customary enormous profit, they would be unable to cover their costs. Instead of accepting the results of their own miscalculation with as much equanimity as they could muster, the *publicani* had the impudence to go to the senate and ask for a rebate. They had the support of Crassus, who was eager to extend his influence and no doubt had a financial interest in the matter.[38] Cicero too defended their claim in the senate. He regarded it as outrageous, but felt that the need to preserve concord between the orders, which had been artificially forged in 63 by the threat to private property and law and order, but which he saw fit to make a lasting political goal, outweighed the moral consideration. However, the consul designate Metellus Celer spoke against the *equites* at the beginning of December, as would have Cato had time allowed.[39] Pompeius, who probably saw the affair as yet another irrelevancy likely to delay still further the accomplishment of his own ends, seems to have offered no opinion, though he remained on outwardly friendly terms with Cicero.[40] But the bond between senate and *equites* was already severely strained by the threat of an enquiry into the bribery at the trial of Clodius, which the equestrian jurors saw as a reflection on the dignity of the whole order, and in January 60 Cicero lamented that the *concordia ordinum* had been shattered.[41]

Pompeius now at last made an attempt to secure land for his veterans and the ratification of his acts. The prospects were not good. Afranius was proving an even more disastrous failure as consul than his predecessor Piso had been, while his colleague Celer, who had broken completely with Pompeius, was effectively hostile. The agrarian law was introduced by a tribune, L. Flavius: its content was modelled on the bill of Plotius in 70, which had been intended to provide land for the veterans of the Sertorian war, but as in the bill of Rullus the urban plebs was also to benefit.[42] Opposition to the bill, and to the ratification of Pompeius' arrangements in the East, came not only from Cato and Celer, but also from Crassus and Lucullus, who dragged himself away from his fishponds to attend the senate and thwart systematically the man who in his opinion had robbed him of the glory of ending the Mithradatic War.[43] The matter was made worse by Pompeius' own highhanded attitude: he asked the senate to ratify his acts *en bloc*, without considering the detail of his arrangements. Lucullus on the other hand insisted that each item be scrutinized and discussed at length. Such discussion could have dragged on indefinitely, and Pompeius in frustration was eventually compelled to let the matter drop. Even Cicero tried to sit on the fence, proposing numerous modifications in Flavius' bill, which he hoped would earn him the favour of landowners without alienating Pompeius or the people.[44] Despite Pompeius' eagerness that the measure should go through, the majority of the senate was hostile, suspecting his intentions.[45] So, when Flavius lost patience with Celer and carried him off to prison, the senate was ready to meet there at the consul's summons. The tribune, however, placed his bench across the prison entrance and his sacrosanct person on the bench, whereupon Celer solemnly ordered the prison wall to be breached. Embarrassed by this constitutional farce, Pompeius was compelled to tell Flavius to set his opponent free.[46] Cato also kept up his stand on the Asian taxes, preventing any decision in the matter: Cicero castigated his conduct as more honest than wise.[47] It is hardly surprising in the circumstances that Pompeius was prepared to swallow his pride in an attempt to keep Cicero's support. Cicero had resented Pompeius' long silence on the subject of his own achievements, but in March he remarked with satisfaction to Atticus that Pompeius had now more than once made speeches in the senate giving him credit for saving the empire.[48] But Cato won the day. By June both the question of the Asian taxes and Flavius' agrarian bill had been dropped.[49] Pompeius had been humbled. He kept up his links with Cicero, though Atticus was afraid that the closeness of their association would discredit Cicero with the optimates.[50] Cicero, however, was sanguine: he felt that he himself was the only man to deserve the name of optimate since the death of Catulus, and insisted that it was not he who had made concessions to Pompeius, but Pompeius who had made a move away from *popularis* levity towards moderation and respectability.[51]

Thus when Caesar returned from his praetorian province of Hispania Ulterior the political situation that confronted him was full of possibilities for a man of imagination and daring. Pompeius had been alienated from the senate by the consistent and successful opposition to his efforts to acquire land for his veterans and secure the ratification of his acts. Crassus and the *equites* had been offended by the attempt to rake up the Bona Dea trial and the senate's refusal to make any concession in the matter of the Asian taxes. If one man was responsible for this dangerous state of affairs, it was Cato, who had baulked Pompeius, Crassus and the *publicani* at every turn. Small wonder that Cicero accused him of doing harm, because he behaved as if he were living in Plato's republic.[52]

Caesar's return aroused considerable interest. Confident as ever of his own influence for good, Cicero hoped to win him for the optimate cause, just as he thought he had already won Pompeius.[53] That Caesar had his eye on the consulship had been common knowledge for some time. Cicero had remarked in December 61 that Pompeius' close friend L. Lucceius was eager to stand and was meditating an electoral compact either with Caesar, to be arranged by Q. Arrius, or with Caesar's principal rival, Cato's son-in-law M. Calpurnius Bibulus.[54] But a slight hitch developed in Caesar's plans. His treatment of the unfortunate Spaniards had moved them to rebel; indeed it is not unlikely that he had deliberately provoked them beyond endurance in order to win the glory of a successful war.[55] His suppression of the rebellion he had caused had duly won him a triumph, but he reached the vicinity of Rome somewhat later than he had planned and found that there would not be time for him both to prepare for and celebrate his triumph and to hand in his nomination for the consular elections by the appointed day. So he wrote to the senate with the not unreasonable request that he be allowed to stand in absence and so be able to enjoy his triumph in the normal manner.[56] But the request was opposed, almost inevitably, by Cato, and once again Cato got his way.[57] It is hard to see the point of this petty and shortsighted policy. No doubt Cato and everyone else assumed that no man, especially one so dedicated to personal glory as Caesar, would forgo the honour of a triumph. But even if Caesar had reacted as expected and given up his chance of standing for 59, there would have been no long-term gain: the problems that might arise in the consulship of one who had already proved himself disquietingly energetic and ambitious would only have been postponed for a year.

However, Caesar shattered expectations by abandoning, not the consul-ship, but his triumph.[58] Instead he entered the city without pomp and presented his candidature by the appropriate date. The campaign was a furious one. Cato and his friends threw all their weight behind Bibulus. Cato communed with his conscience and decided that in such a situation bribery was in the interests of the state, and so no expense was spared.[59] Caesar found a source of funds by concluding the projected arrangement with the wealthy Lucceius, whereby they pooled their resources: Caesar's energy and influence in return for Lucceius' money.[60] But Caesar's sights were set higher. He had exerted himself in Pompeius' interest in the past; now was the time for Pompeius to repay the debt. With Crassus too he had co-operated before, and Crassus had paid off his numerous and pressing creditors and so enabled him to leave for Spain in 61.[61] Crassus, like Pompeius, had good cause to help Caesar now. Both men, as Caesar was quick to realize, would want a return for their investment, and both at this moment had specific ends, of which the senate had frustrated them, but which they could hope to achieve through the agency of a friendly consul, a consul, unlike Piso and Afranius, of talent and determination. When Caesar approached Pompeius and Crassus he no doubt promised that if elected he would see to it that Pompeius' acts were ratified, that land was provided for his troops,[62] and that the improvident *publicani* of Asia were reimbursed at least in part. Both men were impressed, and both gave him their backing. Pompeius may have felt misgivings. A man like Caesar was a dangerous tool. A tribune who passed a helpful law was no problem: such a man could be helped to the praetorship or simply forgotten. A consul was a different matter. There might still be little or no cause for alarm if he were a nobody like the wretched Afranius. But a consul of lofty lineage and loftier ambition might require an imposing reward for his services in the shape of a noteworthy provincial command, which might prove the first step on the road to rivalry. But even if Pompeius gave a thought to the distant future, as things stood he had no choice. He had tried to gain his ends by employing tribunes and consuls of no consequence, but thanks to the relentless opposition of Cato, Celer, Lucullus and the rest the methods that had worked in 67 and 66 had led to abject failure in 61 and 60. He had no alternative but to raise the level of the struggle and trust himself to a consul of a different stamp, regardless of the possible consequences, if he was not to recede into insignificance, his credit with the veterans and the common people destroyed, his godlike stature in the provinces and kingdoms of the East undermined, and his self-respect in shreds. For the coalition that Roman hindsight was to see as the cause of the civil war of 49 Cato must bear much of the blame, for it was Cato who ineluctably drove Pompeius into Caesar's arms.[63]

The result of the election was perhaps predictable. The Roman people had little interest in policies, and though it was happy to take Lucceius' money it did not know his name. Of the candidates who presented themselves, Caesar and Bibulus were the most distinguished and both paid well, so Caesar and Bibulus were elected. Many men must have voted for them both, however absurd this may appear to modern eyes.[64] Before the election the senate had decreed that the consuls of 59 should have as their province *siluae callesque*, the forests and cattle tracks of Italy.[65] This has often been seen as a proleptic effort to deprive Caesar of a worthwhile provincial command, but this is unlikely. At the time when the allocation was made, in accordance with the law of C. Gracchus, Caesar had not yet been elected, and even if the optimates had already felt certain that he was bound to take one place, they would not have wanted to rob their own candidate Bibulus of a proper command. Besides, they must have realized that the expedient would prove futile, since the possibility had to be reckoned with that Caesar would obtain a province, as in fact he did, by a law of the people, regardless of the senate's arrangements. The true explanation lies in a desire to comply with the *lex Sempronia* of C. Gracchus (which ordained that consular provinces should be assigned before the consuls concerned were actually elected) in a manner which could subsequently be revoked without the need for any general redistribution of provinces. The consuls were in effect being held in reserve because of the unsettled situation in Gaul during the spring of 60. In March there had been great fears of a Gallic war, inspired by the beginnings of the Helvetian migration and the defeat of the Aedui.[66] The senate had reacted in near panic, proposing that the consuls should draw lots for the Gallic provinces, that a levy should be held and all leave cancelled, and envoys sent to ensure the loyalty of the Gauls. Yet by May the news from Gaul was of peace.[67] However, the situation remained unsettled, and in the circumstances the senate's decision was a wise one. If further trouble ensued, the consuls of 59 could be sent to Gaul and *siluae callesque* could revert to quaestors without upsetting whatever arrangements for praetorian provinces might have been made in the meantime.

Caesar then had come to the consulship with the individual backing of Pompeius and Crassus. But he nurtured a more ambitious design: to increase their political effectiveness and his own by reconciling them and persuading them to work together.[68] Pompeius and Crassus were not of course open enemies, but their co-operation in 70 had been uneasy and brief, and Crassus had been unfriendly since Pompeius' return. Their aims in 60 were by no means incompatible, but there was always a danger that Crassus in particular might work to keep Caesar from satisfying Pompeius out of jealousy, malice or sheer love of intrigue. So Caesar set about his task. His appeal was, as it had to be, strictly practical. He pointed out that if the three of them agreed to work together, no force in Rome could stand against them and they could control the city.[69] As events were to show, this forecast held good only while Caesar was in office, and even then only at the cost of much effort and great unpopularity, but the objectives of all three partners were short-term, and it is perhaps unlikely that any of them gave much thought to the ultimate future of their coalition.[70]

So was born the compact which modern scholarship has misleadingly dubbed the 'First Triumvirate'. The date of its formation remains problematical.[71] Certainly negotiations were not completed until well after Caesar's election to the consulship, perhaps even not until after he had entered office.[72] In December 60 Cicero received a visit from the Spaniard L. Balbus, friend and confidential agent of both Pompeius and Caesar.[73] He promised that as consul Caesar would take the advice of Cicero and Pompeius in all matters of state, and would try to reconcile Pompeius and Crassus. Caesar's eagerness to add Cicero to the coalition was no doubt shared by Pompeius, if not by Crassus, and is not hard to explain. Both men had had ample cause in recent years to acknowledge the power of his oratory. If he could be persuaded to use it to further the purposes of the coalition, this would be an invaluable gain. Moreover, Cicero was a paragon of respectability, and his adhesion might therefore serve to win support among moderate men in Rome and all over Italy, support of which, if Cato and Bibulus were resolute in keeping up their opposition, the three might well find themselves sorely in need.

8

THE CONSULSHIP OF CAESAR

Caesar wasted no time in setting about his programme of legislation. The first of his two agrarian laws was already a topic of discussion in December 60, and if the tribune P. Vatinius, rather than Caesar himself, was the formal proposer of the bill, it may already have been promulgated at the time of Cicero's visit from Balbus.[1] Caesar was determined to prevent his opponents from claiming that he had ridden roughshod over the prerogatives of the senate. He brought the law before the house in January, encouraging debate and promising to excise or amend any clause to which cogent rational objections were made.[2] To their chagrin the optimates found that there was nothing in the terms of the law, which had been drafted with great care and had no doubt taken account of the objections raised in 63 and 60 to the proposals of Rullus and Flavius, against which complaint could reasonably be brought. Even Cato was forced to take refuge in the unsatisfactorily vague generalization that agrarian laws were not in the interests of the state.[3] However, the lack of concrete objections did not silence the opposition; indeed, pique and frustration made them all the more determined to resist, and throughout the month of January they successfully employed in the senate the delaying tactics that had served them so well in the previous year.[4] Indeed, when Cato embarked upon another filibuster, Caesar was provoked into having him arrested and ordering his removal to prison, but when the senate showed its willingness to follow him there, he was forced to rescind the order.[5] So, abandoning the senate, Caesar turned to the people, and appealed in public to Bibulus to withdraw his opposition.[6] But Bibulus remained obdurate, and Caesar at last called upon Pompeius and Crassus.

Until now they had remained in the background. It is significant that at the time of Cato's arrest in the senate he was outspokenly supported by M. Petreius, a faithful adherent of Pompeius.[7] Petreius' attitude makes it clear that not only the reconciliation of Pompeius and Crassus but even the extent to which Pompeius as an individual was committed to Caesar, whatever his methods, was still unknown, not only to the general public, but even to men on whose loyalty Pompeius could hope to rely. Now both he and Crassus expressed their approval of the bill, and Pompeius, though embarrassed by the violent turn events had taken, made it plain, with some pomposity, that if force was used to obstruct the passage of the law he would not hesitate to use force in his turn to secure its adoption.[8] Bibulus still maintained his opposition, but on the day appointed for the voting on the law he retired from the fray when a bucket of manure was emptied over his head.[9] This display of violence dispelled all resistance, even that of Cato, and the law was duly passed.[10] Next day Bibulus appeared in the senate and tried to secure its annulment, but he could find nobody willing to introduce a motion.[11] So he withdrew to his house and spent the rest of the year watching the sky for unfavourable omens, which had the effect of rendering all the rest of Caesar's legislation technically invalid.[12]

The terms of the law require little comment.[13] As in other recent proposals, the beneficiaries were to include the urban plebs as well as Pompeius' veterans, and money to purchase land for distribution was to be drawn from the revenues of Pompeius' Eastern conquests. The commission appointed to administer the law was unusually large: it consisted of twenty members. But there appears to have been an inner commission of five, which controlled operations.[14] Pompeius himself was one of the five, and it is reasonable to conjecture that Crassus was another. The relationship between the two commissions is not entirely clear, but it is certain that they were not created by the first law and the *lex Campana* respectively. Both the twenty and the five were active in Campania: Suetonius reports that Atius Balbus, who was one of the twenty, operated in that region, and so too did Pompeius himself. Moreover, the five are mentioned as already in existence in April, before the passing of the *lex Campana*, while Cicero describes the post offered to him as both a quinquevirate and a vigintivirate. The most economical conclusion therefore seems to be that the five were part of the twenty and that both were established under the first law.[15] The clue as to the special status of the five is perhaps given by the *elogium* of one of their number, Messalla Niger the consul of 61.[16] He is described as *Vuir a.d.a.i.*; it may then be the case that only the five were equipped with judicial powers. In an effort to protect the law against repeal or annulment on technical grounds, Caesar included in its terms an oath to abide by its provisions, to be taken by all senators. For some time Celer, Cato and Favonius held out, but they eventually gave in and swore.[17]

Next Caesar and Pompeius arranged the recognition by Rome of Ptolemy XIII Auletes as king of Egypt.[18] Their principal motive for this step was the huge fee offered by the unwanted ruler, though not all the money was forthcoming at once, and some of it was never paid.[19] This matter may have been attended to in February, the month in which the senate normally dealt with foreign embassies and foreign business in general. If, however, it was postponed until March, it may have been conjoined with the ratification of Pompeius' acts in the East. This was carried by Caesar after opposition had been cowed, probably towards the end of March. The granting to the *publicani* of a rebate of one third of the purchase price on the contract for the Asian taxes was probably passed at about the same time; indeed, since it too concerned an Eastern province, it may even have been inserted as a clause in the law that confirmed Pompeius' acts, thus giving rise to the charge that Caesar (or Vatinius) had violated the *lex Caecilia Didia*, which prohibited 'tacking'.[20] It would certainly have been sound tactics for Caesar not to keep Crassus waiting, when Pompeius had been satisfied, for the measure which had chiefly moved him to join the coalition.

The last of Caesar's laws to be enacted in part to serve the interests of his fellow dynasts was passed in late April or early May: a second agrarian law providing for the division of the rich *ager Campanus* into twenty thousand allotments. Preference was to be given to men with families of three or over, a clause that prefigures the social legislation of the principate.[21] Most of Pompeius' veterans had been dealt with under the earlier agrarian law, and the intended beneficiaries of the *lex Campana* were to be drawn principally from the urban poor of Rome, though a few Pompeian troops were included.[22] The law was again protected by an oath.[23] The Campanian land was a delicate subject. The rent from it had long constituted a vital contribution to the always inadequately replenished treasury, and attempts to use it for public distribution had always aroused the most violent opposition. Ti. Gracchus had made a start in 133, but the force of public opinion had driven the Gracchan commission to look elsewhere, and C. Gracchus may even have formally exempted Campania from the activities of his commission.[24] Sulla too had left it alone, and Rullus' attempt in 63 to make it available for distribution had provided Cicero with one of his most powerful weapons against the tribune.[25] Cicero was once again predictably disturbed, though he tried to draw comfort from the belief that the Campanian land would accommodate only five thousand settlers, so that many would be disappointed and in consequence turn against the coalition.[26] The threat to the treasury now was deemed even greater than it had been before, since another source of revenue, the *portoria* of Italy, had been abolished by Metellus Nepos in 62.[27]

Now that the material claims of Pompeius and Crassus had been satisfied, it was time for Caesar to look to his own future. Some time in May the tribune Vatinius introduced a law that granted Caesar the governorship of Gallia Cisalpina and Illyricum for five years, with an army of three legions.[28] The significance of these provinces has been debated. Cisalpina was vital for several reasons. It was a great reservoir of manpower, and its position made it possible for the governor to keep an eye on events in Italy and Rome and, if the need should arise, to offer a threat. In 59 it was a strong source of influence for Pompeius, who had built on *clientelae* inherited from his father, but in 65 and 63 Caesar had already begun to take an interest in the region on his own account.[29] As things stood, Pompeius might feel that his own connections in the province would serve if necessary as a check on Caesar, but the longer Caesar stayed there and the more active he showed himself, the more likely he was to undermine Pompeius' position and emerge as a serious rival. Militarily Cisalpina would be a suitable base for operations against the Gauls, which seemed likely to be called for on more than one front. The movements of the Helvetii were still causing alarm, and there can be little doubt that Caesar intended from the first to campaign against them. His sponsorship of the German prince Ariovistus as a friend and ally of the Roman people,[30] a cynical move meant only to secure the German's neutrality until the Helvetii had been dealt with, points clearly in that direction. But an attack on Noreia by the Boii suggested the likelihood of trouble in another quarter, and the presence of Caesar's legions at Aquileia at the beginning of 58 indicates that the Helvetii had at least for the moment been thrust out of the limelight.[31] Also to be connected with the disturbed situation in the North is the foundation by Vatinius of a colony at Novum Comum.[32] The grant of Illyricum is somewhat puzzling. Some have thought that it, rather than Gaul, was intended to furnish Caesar's chance of military glory in the shape of a campaign against the Dacians, but the uncertain chronology of the Dacian monarchy brings this into doubt, and Caesar's failure ever to reach Illyricum puts his own views beyond recovery. But in the late republic, perhaps from the time of Sulla, Illyricum could be attached to another province, Macedonia or Gallia Cisalpina, for no special purpose other than administrative convenience, and it may be that this was the true cause in 59 and that the search for a specific explanation is misdirected.[33]

Subsequently the senate added to Caesar's command, giving him Gallia Transalpina and an additional legion on the motion of Pompeius.[34]

Pompeius' own motives are unlikely to have differed greatly from those of the mass of the senators who found the proposal acceptable, though he may have felt that it would do no harm to his interests if Caesar spent as little time as need be in Cisalpina. But the major reason for the appointment was military. It was obvious, not least to Pompeius, that there would be a Gallic war of some sort: even if men did not foresee anything of the magnitude that actually transpired, Caesar's desire for glory and his success in provoking war in Spain in 61 were a sufficient guarantee of action. Any war in Gaul was likely to require the active co-operation of the governors of Transalpine and Cisalpine Gaul. It is clear that the migration of the Helvetii, although it was in fact a very different and a relatively minor affair, had awakened memories at Rome of the dark years when the Northern frontier had been repeatedly threatened by the wandering hordes of the Cimbri and Teutones, a bogey that Caesar was to exploit for his own purposes when he came to write the *Bellum Gallicum*.[35] The worst disaster of the Cimbric War, at Arausio in 105, had been caused by the inability of two Roman commanders to work together. If Transalpina was to have a separate governor in 58, it would in theory at least be natural to declare it consular, but the prospect of fruitful co-operation in the field between Caesar and Bibulus after what had passed between them at Rome during their year of office could hardly have been more remote. Indeed, there were probably few eligible men who could be trusted to work with Caesar, or with whom Caesar could be trusted to work. One distinguished member of Bibulus' circle, Servilia, grand-daughter of Q. Caepio, consul in 106 and chief architect of the defeat, was a walking reminder of Arausio to anyone who might otherwise forget it. To Pompeius therefore and to many men of sense, whatever their personal opinion of Caesar, a divided command may not unreasonably have seemed a sure recipe for a new disaster, and it will have been in the need for a unified command to face the overestimated threat from the Helvetii that Pompeius found a convincing justification for his proposal when he defended it in the senate.

So by May Pompeius found himself in possession of all the material objectives, the desire for which had moved him first of all to back Caesar for the consulship and then to accede to Caesar's suggestion of a coalition with Crassus. Yet he had little cause for satisfaction on all but the narrowest of fronts. He had no doubt expected on his return from the East to secure his ends quickly, with a minimum of opposition, and then to be held in awe as Rome's leading citizen. Such a position of abstract supremacy would have contented him: he had no further practical ambitions, at least for the moment. Instead he had met with insults and obstruction so effective that he had had to resort to extreme measures, the eventual repercussions of which were still to be experienced. In consequence his popularity, which should have reached new heights, was at its lowest ebb.

For the first three months of the year there is no detailed information about Pompeius' reactions to the turn events were taking. But it is not hard to imagine the pain and humiliation he must have felt in increasing measure as the struggle to secure the passage of the agrarian law attained ever more violent proportions, until he was finally forced to commit himself openly, with a pomposity that attests his embarrassment, and so expose himself to the full brunt of public hostility. Once the sequence of Cicero's correspondence is resumed in April, allusions to the unpopularity of the dynasts and Pompeius' unhappy frame of mind occur in almost every letter.

The matter uppermost in Cicero's mind, and one which was to exercise Pompeius and Caesar too, was of course Clodius' continuing campaign to carry out his *transitio ad plebem* as a first step to winning election as tribune and revenging himself on Cicero.[36] The affair was brought to a head in March by the trial of Cicero's consular colleague C. Antonius. It might have been expected that both Pompeius and Caesar would lend some support to the prosecution.[37] Pompeius had been thought to be hostile to Antonius even before his own return from the East,[38] though there is nothing to suggest that he had given him any thought in the meantime, while Caesar had prosecuted him in 76.[39] It had been the censors of 70, who had links with Pompeius, who had included Antonius in their purge of the senate.[40] Nevertheless Cicero felt obliged to defend him on the strength of his grudging and mercenary assistance at the time of the Catilinarian crisis, but he approached the task with undisguised distaste.[41] That in itself need not have occasioned the dynasts' displeasure. They were quite capable of understanding Cicero's obligation to Antonius, they may well have known too the reluctance he felt at being called upon to fulfil it, and Antonius' condemnation, while it might have given them pleasure, was hardly vital to their interests. If Cicero had confined himself to the business in hand, it is safe to assume that his appearance for the defence would have provoked no noteworthy reaction.

But with characteristic rashness Cicero allowed his own eloquence to carry him away, and gave vent to his anger at the violent methods adopted by the coalition, the undermining of the senate's authority and the threat to the freedom of the state.[42] The outburst was ill-timed. Caesar's patience had been exhausted by the mindless opposition to the agrarian bill, Pompeius had been attacked and humiliated too often. It appears that Cicero had played no part in the campaign against the dynasts in January, but if now, when the opposition seemed at last to be cowed, he proposed to add his powerful voice to its ranks, Pompeius and Caesar could expect further trouble that they were not prepared to endure. So they reacted dramatically; indeed, they over-reacted in a fashion that shows how the events of the past three months had frayed their nerves and blunted their judgement. Cicero's unguarded remarks were uttered in the morning. In the afternoon of the same day Clodius' adoption was carried out, with Caesar presiding as *pontifex maximus* and Pompeius officiating as augur.[43] As a short-term move, to terrorize Cicero into silence, the adoption was entirely successful, but it is impossible to believe that Pompeius and Caesar had considered fully the broader implications of their action, and much of their behaviour in the months that followed suggests that they regretted their impetuous response.[44] Now that Clodius was eligible for the tribunate, it could be taken for granted that, if he stood, he would succeed in gaining election. He had substantial connections and sources of support of his own, and if the dynasts turned against him he could rely on the enthusiastic backing of their numerous enemies. Nevertheless, when Pompeius and Caesar came to try to undo what they had done, there were various lines of approach open to them. First, it might be possible to prevent Clodius from standing for the tribunate. Secondly, some means of removing Cicero from Rome might be found, in the hope that Clodius' desire for revenge would cool. Lastly, if all else failed, attempts might be made to persuade Clodius to forgo the pleasures of vengeance.

From Pompeius' point of view there can be no doubt that the first solution of the problem was the most attractive. He stood to gain nothing whatever from Clodius' tribunate, and while he can hardly have predicted the campaign which Clodius was in fact to mount against him, his violent and volatile nature might well have led Pompeius to expect some trouble from him. Cicero's presence in Rome on the other hand might well prove valuable to him when the time seemed ripe, with Caesar out of the way, to make a serious attempt to recover his respectability. So Pompeius took steps. In April Cicero reports a proposal that Clodius was to be sent on an embassy to Tigranes.[45] Clodius was highly annoyed: the coalition was offering him none of the posts he might have chosen, such as a place on the agrarian commission, and a mission to Armenia did not suit his plans at all. So he succeeded in evading it, to the displeasure of Pompeius and Caesar.[46] The scheme was probably devised by Pompeius. If the tribunician elections took place at the usual time, in July, it was highly likely that Clodius would be unable to get back in time to stand: Pompeius' loyal client Tigranes would surely manage to arrange honorific delays – or worse

– to ensure that his patron's desires were fulfilled. But a second avenue was already being explored: a *libera legatio* for Cicero, or perhaps an embassy to Alexandria, to the dynasts' new client Ptolemy Auletes.[47] But Cicero was reluctant to accept. He wanted to see the sights of Alexandria, but not as a favour from Pompeius and Caesar, for fear that the optimates, and especially Cato, would interpret the mission as a bribe to secure his support or at least his neutrality – Cicero's mercurial temperament was not at that moment capable of conceiving that his safety might be at stake. That Pompeius had a hand in this scheme too is shown by Cicero's remark that if Theophanes talked to Atticus about it (presumably to ask him to persuade Cicero to accept), he should not go so far as to reject it out of hand.[48]

Already by April the coalition was faced with many other problems. External opposition might have been crushed at the price of great unpopularity, but there were signs that relations between the partners were not easy. Cicero at Antium remarked to Atticus that the one hope of salvation for the state lay in dissension among the dynasts,[49] and he had some reason to hope. The forthcoming consular elections might lead to disputes among their supporters: there was a rumour that Pompeius and Crassus themselves intended to stand for a second joint consulship, but Cicero had also heard that the jurist Ser. Sulpicius was to stand again in conjunction with Pompeius' faithful supporter Gabinius.[50] This would mean that Crassus' friend Q. Arrius would have to be disappointed.[51] A vacant augurate too might lead to unhealthy competition – the one prize, Cicero admits, with which he himself might have been tempted.[52] There is no reason to doubt that the signs of a rift which Cicero claimed to detect were real enough, even though the motives of his informant, Clodius' friend the younger Curio, may not have been entirely disinterested.[53] Some trouble among the quinquevirs was also being hinted at.[54] Curio soon declared his hatred of the coalition still more forcefully, and the band of young men that had plagued Cicero in 61 now turned its attention to Pompeius.[55] Cicero was in confident mood. The prudent Atticus had been engaging in negotiations with Clodius, but Cicero was tempted to hope that they would fail,[56] feeling in his present buoyant frame of mind that Clodius would be too weak to hurt him, since he was bound to face the opposition of the optimates if he stayed on good terms with the dynasts, or of the dynasts if he broke with them.[57] Underlying all these speculations is the constant insistence that the coalition's excesses had lost it the support of the masses, who saw that power had not been transferred from the senate to the people but had instead been restricted to only three men, and so resented the domination of the three even more than they had the previous supremacy of the senate.[58]

The inevitable explosion was soon to come. Clodius moved on to the attack, declaring that he would stand for the tribunate with the sworn intention of rescinding Caesar's legislation.[59] Caesar's response was little short of hysterical as he stormed that he had never passed a law about Clodius' adoption. Cicero gleefully remarked that he was ready to swear that Pompeius had visited him at Antium and told him how he had officiated as augur.[60] Clodius' new hatred of Caesar was allegedly shared by Curio, who gave Cicero his information, C. Memmius and Metellus Nepos.[61] But if Clodius, two of his closest friends and a man linked with them chose to attack Caesar in this way, their motive is not hard to discern. The dynasts had made it clear to Clodius that they would have liked to prevent his becoming tribune, and that since they had failed in this they wanted to stop him from taking revenge on Cicero. Clodius' threat to repeal Caesar's laws should be seen as a warning: if the coalition did not back down and allow him his head, it could expect serious trouble from him during his tribunate.[62]

The unpopularity of the dynasts was by no means confined to Rome. In the last week of April Cicero was at Formiae, where he found, as he had at Antium, great unrest.[63] Pompeius was deeply hated, and his surname Magnus a dead letter. The singling out of Pompeius in this talk of unpopularity is striking. There are probably several contributory causes. It indicates that the public saw Pompeius as the senior partner and chief beneficiary of the coalition, and so assigned the greatest responsibility to him. But it also reflects the opposition's knowledge that of the three Pompeius was by temperament by far the most concerned about public opinion, by far the most likely to be hurt and perhaps even moved to change his stance as a result of public obloquy and humiliation.[64] A further factor for which allowance must be made is that Cicero was more interested in Pompeius than in Caesar or Crassus, but that interest itself was dictated not only by his personal ties with Pompeius but at least in part by his awareness that Pompeius was the most vulnerable of the three to pressure of this kind. The fear that Pompeius would in some way resort to violence first appears in Cicero's correspondence at the end of April and is directly linked with the persistence of verbal attacks as well as with the danger that Caesar's laws might be repealed.[65] What exactly Cicero was afraid of is difficult to determine, and it is correspondingly hard to see what Pompeius could have done at this point to improve his position. A resort to violence, presumably in practical terms the use of his veterans to seize a dictatorship, would, if it had succeeded, have brought him absolute power, but lack of power was not Pompeius' problem. He had already attained his material ends; what he wanted now was acceptance and respect from the optimates and the restoration of his old standing with the masses, and a dictatorship would not bring him these: indeed, its effect would be quite the opposite. The only possible gain for him would be the opportunity to follow Sulla's example and exact a bloody vengeance from his critics, but that would have been alien to his nature and to his conception of his own position in the state. Yet the only way in which he could have silenced criticism, the abandonment of the coalition, would have meant at this time intolerable humiliation and the risk of losing his practical gains if the optimates, as was not unlikely, did not prove conciliatory but tried to follow up such a moral victory to the limit. No matter how unhappy he was, for the moment Pompeius had no choice but to remain in his present allegiance.

Nevertheless his attitude gave Caesar cause for alarm. At the beginning of May Cicero displays Pompeius taking refuge in sophistries.[66] Beneath the pose of bombastic superiority to mundane questions, the underlying desire to dissociate himself from the violence and illegalities of the preceding months is plain. He admitted that he approved of Caesar's legislation, but insisted that Caesar alone must be ultimately responsible for his actions. Such matters as tribunician vetoes, unfavourable omens, or whether it would have been safe for Bibulus to show his face in public were no concern of his. At this time Cicero had just heard the news of Pompeius' betrothal to Caesar's daughter Julia.[67] The match and its timing must surely be seen in the light of Caesar's alarm at Pompeius' increasing discontent. The manner of its making indicates that it cannot have been conceived long before its execution: Julia was already betrothed at the time to Q. Servilius Caepio,[68] and that agreement had to be broken to make way for more important considerations. Caesar plainly felt it vital to create some new bond between himself and Pompeius and so was ready to run the risk of offending a less prominent adherent. As for Pompeius, his acceptance of the alliance shows that, however much he fulminated, he knew, when he took the trouble to think calmly, that for the moment he was stuck with Caesar. Personal factors may of course have contributed to his decision: there is every evidence that the marriage was a happy one and so calculated from Caesar's point of view to serve its political purpose admirably. At about the same time Caesar strengthened his own position in another direction through a marriage alliance with a distinguished noble family.[69] His bride was Calpurnia, daughter of L. Calpurnius Piso Caesoninus, a candidate for the consulship of 58.

Other signs of the reinforced link between Caesar and Pompeius soon appeared. From now on Caesar did Pompeius the honour of asking him to give his opinion first in the senate, whereas hitherto Crassus had enjoyed this privilege.[70] It may also have been at this time that he made Pompeius his heir.[71] Crassus and his associates also suffered more tangible rebuffs: Caesar's new connection with L. Piso meant that Arrius' chances of the consulship completely disappeared, while Crassus' former legate C. Pomptinus found himself not only deprived of Gallia Transalpina to make way for Caesar, but also insulted, along with Arrius, by Vatinius and others.[72] It is hardly surprising that Crassus is later said to have been delighted by Pompeius' difficulties.[73]

But Caesar was not the only one who had cause to worry about the possible behaviour of Pompeius. Clodius too was still concerned to revenge himself on Cicero, but despite his threats Pompeius and Caesar were still recalcitrant. Any notion of preventing Clodius from standing for the tribunate had by now been dropped, but when Cicero's correspondence resumes at the beginning of July the old expedient of a *libera legatio* was still being canvassed, together with a new possibility created by the *lex Vatinia*: a legateship with Caesar in Gaul.[74] This latter solution would undoubtedly have suited Caesar better; for Pompeius it would have had much less appeal. In Gaul Cicero would have been under Caesar's eye, unable to tempt Pompeius towards respectability, whereas if he were to be useful to Pompeius, he could be so only in Rome. Clodius now confined himself to uttering threats against Cicero.[75] Open opposition to the coalition was voiced only by his friend Curio, who was consequently treated as a hero by the optimates, while the praetor Fufius, who in 61 as tribune had saved Clodius from a handpicked jury and tried in 59 to retrieve equestrian honour by enacting that the votes of the three decuries of jurors should be separately recorded,[76] was publicly jeered and hooted.[77] Such demonstrations were, as Cicero bitterly remarks, of no practical use, any more than the stand of Juventius Laterensis, who withdrew his candidature for the tribunate rather than take the oath to observe the *lex Campana*.[78] Nevertheless, though he no longer hoped for the break-up of the coalition, the dynasts' unpopularity was so universal that Cicero was afraid that they might have to resort to desperate measures in order to retain control.[79] Pompeius remained the chief target for attack: at the *ludi Apollinares* the actor Diphilus drew thunderous applause for the line *nostra miseria tu es magnus* ('through our suffering you are great', with a play on Pompeius' *cognomen* Magnus) and others that could be taken as gibes against Pompeius.[80] The audience had already made its views clear before the performance, when Curio had received a standing ovation on his arrival, the sort of reception, as Cicero says, that Pompeius himself used to get in happier times, while Caesar had been greeted with stony silence.[81] Pompeius had not been present: he was at Capua on the business of the land commission. But Caesar had not been amused by the demonstration, and it was understood that he had written to Pompeius at once.[82] He already had another source of discomfort: the edicts of Caesar's colleague Bibulus, who since his withdrawal to watch the sky had passed his time by composing diatribes against the coalition.[83] Cicero again judged the exercise futile, but Bibulus too was a popular hero, though the obscenity of his elucubrations may do much to explain the enthusiam of his public.[84]

But despite his other preoccupations Pompeius still proclaimed his loyalty to Cicero, insisting that Clodius would not dare to proceed against him.[85] Cicero believed that he meant what he said, but that Clodius had deceived him. Meanwhile Caesar kept open his offer of a legateship in Gaul, but Cicero felt that he preferred to fight.[86] Atticus was inclined to doubt whether Pompeius was as well disposed towards Cicero as he claimed, but at this stage, before Clodius had brought any further pressure to bear, he may well have been sincere, though he was already protesting too much, undertaking to defend Cicero to the death if Clodius attacked him.[87] Cicero still saw no hope of a change: nothing was now so popular as hatred of the *populares*, but active resistance could only lead to a massacre.[88] He paints a vivid picture of Pompeius' position.[89] Pompeius had always been used to the trappings of glory and was not accustomed to unpopularity. Now he was broken in mind and body and did not know where to turn. The way forward was a perilous and steep descent, while to go back would argue inconsistency and lack of courage. The *boni* hated him, and even the wicked were not his friends. He had ventured to speak at a public meeting on 25 July, but he had been totally demoralized, a pitiful sight that could give pleasure to no-one but Crassus.[90] Cicero was deeply moved, though his friends felt that he should have been pleased because of the part Pompeius had played in Clodius' adoption,[91] and more and more afraid that Pompeius might do something desperate. Meanwhile the crowds continued to flock to read Bibulus' latest edicts.[92] Their only practical content had been a postponement of the consular elections till 18 October, and when Caesar had tried to persuade a public meeting to join him in a protest to Bibulus he had met with a hostile response.[93]

In August Clodius hesitated to commit himself, threatening first the dynasts, because of their unpopularity, then Cicero and the *boni*.[94] Pompeius negotiated with him and reported his satisfaction to Cicero.[95] He had pointed out that he himself would be open to accusations of treachery if he allowed Clodius to injure Cicero when he had made the attack possible by facilitating his adoption. Both Clodius and his brother Appius had given him guarantees, and Pompeius declared that if Clodius broke faith he would prove that his friendship with Cicero took precedence. But Cicero knew better than to trust Clodius' promises and was eager for Atticus to come to Rome and try to discover from Clodia what her brother's real intentions were.[96] He was now sure that Pompeius was not only unhappy but deeply regretted the course he had taken.[97] He longed to be restored to the position he had held before, openly confessing his grief to Cicero and asking him in vain if he could think of a way out.[98] The more he came to regret the turn events had taken and to long for a return to the days of his glory, the more he was drawn to Cicero, who was not only prepared to lend a sympathetic ear to his troubles but might prove invaluable in arranging a reconciliation with the optimates. As Clodius continued to brag to all and sundry that he would have his cherished revenge, telling a different tale only to Pompeius,[99] he must have realized that it was high time for him to take drastic action to rid Pompeius of these yearnings for respectability and to cure him of his affection for Cicero.[100]

A few weeks before the consular elections he struck, and to good effect.[101] He himself remained in the background, leaving the execution of his scheme in the capable hands of Curio. A certain L. Vettius told young Curio of a plot to murder Pompeius. Curio informed his father, who in turn told Pompeius, and the matter was brought before the senate. Vettius eventually revealed that a band of young men led by Curio, together with Bibulus, had planned to murder Pompeius. Next day Caesar and Vatinius produced Vettius in public, and more names, including that of Cicero, were added to the list.[102] Though Clodius' name does not appear in Cicero's allusions to the affair, to regard it as his brainchild makes excellent sense.[103] The Curiones were his friends; the lists of alleged conspirators included several enemies of his as well as enemies of Pompeius. Most important, the effect of the story, if Pompeius believed it, would be to make him afraid of the optimates and Cicero. He would therefore become disenchanted with the plan of seeking a reconciliation with the optimates and so would cease to look on Cicero as a potentially useful go-between. His motive for protecting Cicero from Clodius would thus disappear. Since the Vettius affair was so aptly designed to further Clodius' objectives, it is unreasonable to deny his responsibility, especially when it is noted that the pattern of events in 59 is exactly repeated in 58, when Clodius' part is fully attested throughout: first a threat by Clodius to rescind Caesar's legislation, then, when that again proved ineffective, an assassination scare to neutralize Pompeius.

Clodius had calculated well. Pompeius was always liable to be impressed by suggestions that his life was in danger.[104] He continued to praise Cicero and assure him of his support, but in the last months of 59 there are signs that his suspicions had been awakened and that his feelings towards Cicero had changed. The warning signals came at the trial in October of L. Valerius Flaccus, a loyal associate of Cicero's as praetor in 63, but now brought to book for extortion in Asia.[105] His guilt was manifest, but Cicero felt obliged to undertake the defence in company with Hortensius, who lavished praise on his fellow advocate's achievements as consul.[106] Yet there was a strong belief that Pompeius was behind the prosecution. The principal accuser was D. Laelius, son of a man who had fought and died in Pompeius' service during the Sertorian war.[107] In Asia itself it was openly said that Pompeius had asked Laelius to mount the prosecution and had put all his influence and resources at his disposal.[108] One of the *subscriptores* was called L. Balbus: if he was L. Cornelius Balbus, friend of Pompeius and Caesar, then this would serve as further evidence of Pompeius' interest, but the identification is uncertain and perhaps unlikely.[109] But another very close associate of Pompeius was an important prosecution witness: L. Lucceius, Caesar's unsuccessful running-mate in the consular elections of 60.[110] Cicero was manifestly justified in feeling that his consulship was on trial and his whole position under attack, though he tried to put on a bold front and tell young Laelius that Pompeius could not possibly approve.[111] In the circumstances Flaccus' acquittal will have been small comfort.

Meanwhile Clodius and his friends kept up the pressure on Pompeius, insinuating to his suggestible mind that Cicero represented a serious threat to his safety.[112] It is hard to know what, if anything, Pompeius actually believed of the barrage of rumours, anonymous messages and furtive conversations that warned him against Cicero. It is true that he was always ready to believe that his life was threatened, yet it is difficult to credit that even he can have suspected Cicero of plotting against him: it is not easy to imagine what plausible motive might be cited. Cicero once halfheartedly exculpates Pompeius by suggesting that he was convinced by the rumours, not that he was really plotting against him, but that Clodius and company were out to kill him and put the blame on Cicero.[113] But even that is hard to accept, and it may be that Pompeius by the end of 59 had already moved a long way towards the position that he certainly adopted in the first months of 58, that is, that his own best interest lay in betraying Cicero, at least for the time being. The Vettius scare also had another consequence

which must have encouraged Pompeius. The long-delayed consular elections had resulted in the elevation of the dynasts' candidates, Caesar's
father-in-law L. Piso and Pompeius' henchman Gabinius.[114] But Gabinius'
election was not allowed to pass unchallenged. The young C. Cato tried to
prosecute him for *ambitus*, but found that the praetors were unwilling to
grant him a hearing. Outraged by this treatment and seeing the hand of
Pompeius in this shielding of his former legate, Cato vented his spleen at a
public meeting, in the course of which he attacked Pompeius as a *priuatus
dictator*. In July or August such an outburst would have won applause, but
the suspected threat to his life in September appears to have restored some
at least of Pompeius' popularity, and Cato was lucky to escape being
lynched.[115]

So, as he and Caesar continued to give Cicero assurances of their good
will,[116] Pompeius could await the new year, the impending tribunate of
Clodius, and Caesar's departure for Gaul with more confidence and higher
hopes than might have seemed possible in the summer. He had secured the
material objectives for which he had laboured in vain since his return from
the East, and he had weathered the immediate political storm. The long-
term consequences of his pact with Caesar were still hidden in the future.
The only immediate threat of trouble must have seemed to reside in the
turbulent Clodius, and to Pompeius, as he made his calculations, it will
have appeared that by abandoning Cicero to his fate he could insure himself
against attack from that quarter.

9

THE EXILE OF CICERO

Clodius began his tribunate with a spate of legislative activity.[1] Much of it was of no immediate concern to the dynasts, though the introduction of free distributions of corn and the restoration of the political potential of the *collegia* increased Clodius' hold over the urban masses and made it possible for him to build the private army which was to make him a force to be reckoned with in politics even when he was out of office.[2] The measures to prevent the kind of religious obstruction to which Bibulus had resorted in the previous year might indeed have won the approbation of both Caesar and Pompeius,[3] though it is true that the banning of such tactics for the future underlined that they had hitherto been valid and so served as a reminder that the laws of Caesar and Vatinius in 59 were all open to annulment on technical grounds, a point the potential value of which Clodius had no doubt already perceived.

For the moment all that affected Pompeius was the campaign against Cicero. Clodius based himself on solid traditional ground, highly proper to a holder of his office, reaffirming the right of appeal to the people which had been defended by the great tribunes of the past and which Cicero had violated by his execution of Lentulus and his confederates.[4] The attitude of the consuls was of course vital, and Clodius took careful precautions. On the same day as the bill on *prouocatio* he promulgated a measure granting special commands to both the consuls for five years: Piso was to have Macedonia and Gabinius Syria, which he preferred to Cilicia.[5] It appears from Cicero's unending diatribes that Piso confined himself to gloomy and oracular discouragement, but Gabinius was violently hostile, lending open support to Clodius and exerting his consular authority against all who demonstrated their sympathy for Cicero.[6] No doubt Gabinius had his own reasons for helping Clodius, apart from the prospect of his province: his whole career reveals his concern for the victims of Rome's equestrian tax-gatherers, and the chance to hurt Cicero, so often the mouthpiece of the *publicani*, must have pleased him.[7] Nevertheless, his behaviour may serve as a useful guide to Pompeius' real attitude at this time and help to penetrate the twin veils of Cicero's self-deception and Pompeius' deviousness. For later in the year, when Clodius attacked Pompeius, Gabinius remained loyal to his patron and, unlike Piso, broke violently with the tribune.[8] It is therefore likely that his vigorous support of Clodius indicates that Pompeius had finally decided to sacrifice Cicero. The calculation, though cynical, was sound. If he allowed Clodius to have his way, he could hope that in return the tribune would cause him no trouble, while in the fullness of time, when Clodius was out of office, he could work to secure Cicero's return and so lay claim to his gratitude for the future.[9] So it seemed to Pompeius that it would pay him to be keener in restoring Cicero than in retaining him.[10] He could not know that Clodius would not keep his part of the bargain.

Thus, when the crisis came, Cicero was faced with Pompeius' 'sudden defection'.[11] It was of course not only Pompeius who let him down. Many of his aristocratic friends, irked by Cicero's talent, his vanity and the sharpness of his tongue, were not sorry to see him in trouble.[12] Their attitude may indeed have helped to fix that of Pompeius. It might suit his book to move away from Caesar and back into the fold of respectability, and if the *boni* were content to take a more or less covert delight in Cicero's discomfiture, then it was not for him to spoil their enjoyment. Not all the stories retailed by the sources are likely to be true: it is hard to believe that Pompeius was so embarrassed that when Cicero tried to call on him he fled out of the back door as the visitor was admitted at the front.[13] But his hypocrisy is beyond doubt. When a deputation of senators, including two consulars, M. Lucullus and L. Torquatus, and a praetor in office, Lentulus Marcellinus, came to his Alban estate to plead for Cicero, he referred them to the consuls, saying that he himself could do nothing against Clodius' violence unless he had official authorization from the senate, but that if the consuls came to the defence of the republic in accordance with a senatorial decree, then he too would take up arms.[14] This high-sounding legalism was the thinnest of cloaks for his obvious determination to let matters take their course: he can have been in no doubt as to the nature of the consuls' response.

So Cicero yielded to the storm and withdrew into exile.[15] Caesar, who had been in the neighbourhood of the city with a small detachment of troops, now left for Gaul at the beginning of March after heated exchanges with the praetors C. Memmius and L. Ahenobarbus.[16] Pompeius may have felt that he might now have some breathing space, but he was soon to be disappointed. The first signs of the coming upheaval occurred not long after Caesar's departure, when Clodius took steps to neutralize Cato. Cato had always been an outspoken opponent of extraordinary commands. More important, it was highly likely that, once Clodius was out of office, Cato would take the lead in any campaign to rescind his legislation. Clodius' device to counteract these dangers was a supremely elegant improvisation. He had already passed a law providing for the annexation of the kingdom of Cyprus. The original plan had been that this task should be performed by Gabinius as governor of Cilicia, but when Gabinius changed his province he lost interest. So Clodius seized the chance to press upon Cato a special command of his own, as *pro quaestore pro praetore*, to take over Cyprus and restore some exiles to Byzantium.[17] If Cato accepted the commission, as his sense of public duty was bound to compel him to do, he would in future be muzzled on the topic of extraordinary commands, while in order to uphold the validity of his own acts he would be forced on his return to defend Clodius' legislation against attack.[18]

This brilliant scheme had one flaw: the annexation of Cyprus was an interference with Pompeius' settlement of the East. It was bound to wound Pompeius' vanity and make him suspicious of Clodius' intentions, and more was soon to follow. Pompeius had confirmed that loyal friend of Rome's generals in the East, King Deiotarus of Galatia, as high priest of the Magna Mater at Pessinus. Clodius, in return for a consideration, deprived Deiotarus of the honour and gave it instead to a rival, Brogitarus, who also received the title of king.[19] But the worst insult of all was still to come. Pompeius had restored Tigranes to the Armenian throne, but he had brought the king's son to Rome as a hostage. The prince was being lodged at the house of Pompeius' adherent L. Flavius, now praetor. Clodius organized his abduction and despite Pompeius' demands refused to return him. The subsequent attempt to spirit young Tigranes away involved a skirmish on the Appian Way, when Flavius tried to recover the prince by force, in which several of the participants were killed, among them M. Papirius, a friend of Pompeius.[20] It is probably true that Clodius was well paid for his services, but the enterprise must have been to his taste. He had an eye for a *quid pro quo*, and he had not forgotten the scheme of *Clodius ad Tigranem*. This incident not only angered Pompeius greatly, but provoked the breach between Gabinius and Clodius.[21] Clodius, undismayed, riposted with vigour: his gangs attacked the consul and broke his *fasces*, and he consecrated Gabinius' property.[22]

The motive for these virulent attacks on Pompeius invites conjecture. If Pompeius had already begun by late spring to show signs of moving to

secure Cicero's recall, then of course Clodius' actions would need no
further explanation: he would have been trying to deter Pompeius from
such a course. But it is hard to believe that without provocation Pompeius
would have taken the initiative, since it must have been obvious to him that
if he did take up the cudgels on Cicero's behalf he would unleash on
himself the full force of Clodius' wrath. It is therefore likely that Clodius
took the lead in attacking Pompeius, and that Pompeius' first moves to
bring about Cicero's recall were, as Dio says, a response to the Tigranes
affair.[23] Indeed it is probable that Clodius' behaviour made Pompeius move
much earlier than he would otherwise have done. Why then did Clodius
provoke Pompeius? It may be that he saw in him a rival for popular favour
and sought to undermine his position by making him appear ridiculous.[24]
The public humiliation of Pompeius would certainly appeal to his enemies
among the optimates, whose shortsighted delight in Clodius' baiting of
him, which was later to draw such bitter reproof from Cicero,[25] made them
an important source of potential support for the tribune. That such an
attack would have the result of inspiring Pompeius to work for Cicero's
recall must have been plain to Clodius from the first, but he reckoned that
he would come out on top in any trial of strength, a calculation which in
the short term at least proved correct.

In the light of these considerations it is possible to interpret a proposal on
which information is regrettably slight. The break between Pompeius and
Clodius weakened Clodius' position, but he still enjoyed the tacit support
of the absent Caesar. If, however, a wedge could now be driven between
Clodius and Caesar, the tribune's strength would be still more drastically
curtailed. Such was the aim of a move which may have been initiated at this
time. The suggestion was floated that Caesar should re-enact his laws in a
different manner: that is, without the violence and breaches of legal and
religious rules that had vitiated their original passing.[26] The point of this
suggestion will surely have been that all Caesar's measures except one
would have been re-enacted: the adoption of Clodius would have been
omitted. The legislation of 59 would then have been declared invalid,
Clodius' adoption and with it his election as tribune and all his legislation
would be rendered null and void, and his principal hold over the
dynasts would be broken. The most obvious beneficiary of this proposal
would have been Cicero, and it may have been the work of his friends in
the senate as the movement for his recall began to gather momentum in the
early summer. But Pompeius too might have lent his backing, since its
success would have freed him from the nuisance of Clodius while leaving
his material interests securely protected. Clodius replied as he had done in

the previous year, when Caesar had thought better of his adoption. He had argued irrefutably that all Caesar's legislation must stand or fall together; his adoption could not be singled out and treated as a special case.[27] Now he brought Bibulus and the augurs before a public meeting to swear that Caesar's laws had been passed in defiance of the omens and declared once again that, since all the laws were therefore invalid, they should all be rescinded by the senate, adding ironically that if that happened he would carry Cicero home on his own shoulders.[28] No more was heard of the proposal; perhaps Caesar himself made it clear that he had no wish to be turned into a *bonus* at such a price.

But Pompeius saw fit to ignore Clodius' warning. At the end of May Cicero had not been hopeful.[29] Atticus had been negotiating with Pompeius, whose friends Varro and Hypsaeus had been active on Cicero's behalf, but Cicero, though he had written to Pompeius, regarded the lack of any serious enquiry into the Tigranes affair as proof that Pompeius was weak and that Clodius could get away with whatever he pleased. Nevertheless Pompeius lent his support to the proposal of the tribune L. Ninnius for Cicero's recall, which was brought before the senate on 1 June, but vetoed by Aelius Ligus.[30] At this time Atticus regarded the attitude of Hortensius and the optimates as of primary importance,[31] an observation which dispirited Cicero still further, as he blamed Hortensius and the rest for his exile. Sunk in pessimism, he thought that Pompeius' protestations were insincere. Ninnius' effort had come to nothing, and things were hanging fire in the senate. Nor could matters be expected to improve in the latter half of the year, after the elections, for Clodius would still be tribune, and one of the consuls designate would be his friend Metellus Nepos.[32] Atticus was more concerned with the present: the quarrel between Pompeius and Clodius was likely to afford the optimates so much amusement that any inclination they might have had to oppose Clodius would be blunted. But he could also hold out one piece of hope: Pompeius had apparently given him to understand that he thought the matter should be raised again in the senate after the elections.[33]

Cicero's despair makes it hard to unravel the progress of Pompeius' calculations. Clodius' behaviour is perhaps a safer guide. Whatever Cicero's suspicions and doubts, Clodius at least had none. The results of the elections in the main favoured Cicero: the other consul designate, with Nepos, was P. Cornelius Lentulus Spinther, and several of the tribunes would take his part, including P. Sestius and T. Annius Milo.[34] Yet Cicero continued to fear the worst, claiming that Clodius would still be a force as a *priuatus* and that some tribune would be found to veto any favourable measure. But Clodius felt that the time had come to dampen Pompeius' enthusiasm. His tactics were exactly the same as in the previous autumn. Now, as then, he had begun by issuing a threat to attack Caesar's legislation if his plans were hampered. When that threat was ignored, he turned once again to threats of violence, to make Pompeius fear for his life. The 'plot' was even more ludicrous than the Vettius scare had been, yet it proved even more effective. On 11 August Pompeius attended a meeting of the senate. In or near the building a slave of Clodius was apprehended carrying a dagger, to which he had conveniently called attention by dropping it. The dagger was brought to the consul Gabinius, and interrogation of the slave revealed, predictably enough, that he had been sent by Clodius to assassinate Pompeius.[35] Pompeius reacted remarkably, even for a man with his exaggerated fear of plots against his life. He went straight home and barricaded himself within doors, where he remained for the rest of the year.[36]

No doubt his anger at this humiliation sharpened his determination to bring Cicero home, and there is no reason to doubt the sincerity of the assurances passed to Atticus by Varro.[37] But he was not prepared to break with Caesar, and refused to divorce Julia when this was suggested to him by the tribune Q. Terentius Culleo.[38] Indeed his insistence that he had to have Caesar's agreement was not just a pretext to cover his inaction.[39] It was perhaps in November that the tribune designate Sestius was sent on a mission to secure Caesar's consent, which was grudgingly given.[40] But Cicero still did not trust the dynasts, though the favourable attitude of Spinther, who according to Atticus was completely in Pompeius' power, was cheering, while Q. Cicero held out hopes that Nepos might be persuaded to change his mind.[41] Meanwhile, the tribunes designate were preparing their proposals, and Cicero, mercurial as ever, began to find fault with their timidity and lack of concern for his property, just as he had with the bill to recall him brought forward at the end of October by eight tribunes of 58.[42] But in December came a good omen: Nepos, won over by Pompeius and Spinther, declared that as consul he would not oppose Cicero's restoration.[43]

Once Clodius was out of office, the movement for Cicero's recall swiftly gained strength.[44] On 1 January L. Cotta gave it as his opinion that a decree of the senate would suffice, since Clodius' law had no validity, but Pompeius wisely argued that a law should be passed, partly as proof of the solidarity of the movement, partly to ensure that no attack could later be made invoking the slogan of popular sovereignty.[45] The first tribune to bring forward a bill was an adherent of Pompeius, C. Messius, followed on

25 January by Fabricius.[46] The only weapon left to Clodius now was violence, and he wielded it to the best of his considerable ability. A bloody riot stopped the passage of the bill. But Pompeius now made up for the inertia he had displayed over the previous six months and transformed the campaign for Cicero's return from an issue that interested only the senate to one in which the whole of Italy became involved. Strong men were summoned from his estates and the regions where his influence was great to swell the gangs that Sestius and Milo were recruiting to meet the *operae Clodianae* on their own ground.[47] Pompeius himself toured the cities and countryside of Italy, mobilizing his vast *clientelae* to come to Rome and lend their voices and votes to the cause.[48] So at last in June the senate voted, on the motion of both consuls with Pompeius' support, that Cicero should be recalled.[49] One senator voted against: whatever else he was, Clodius was no coward. The decree was then ratified by the people, and Cicero returned, making a leisurely progress from Brundisium and carefully timing his arrival in Rome to coincide with the celebration of the *ludi Romani*.[50]

The circumstances of Cicero's return provided the occasion for a new command for Pompeius. Corn was in short supply, and the price was high.[51] On 7 September, two days after Cicero had delivered his speech of thanks and self-congratulation in the senate, there were riots outside the theatre and then outside the senate. Their instigator was Clodius, who claimed that Cicero was responsible, since the shortage had been caused by the influx of people drummed up from all over Italy to vote for his recall. In the short term he was no doubt partly right, but a series of bad harvests, the difficulties of transport and the exigencies of middle men had produced a far more serious situation than could be attributed to such an ephemeral cause.[52] People and senators alike saw the answer in a special commission for Pompeius, whose desire for such a post was in no doubt. The people called on Cicero to speak in favour, and he did so eloquently: if Pompeius had reckoned that his efforts would bear rich fruit, he did not have long to wait for his reward.[53] Clodius, who resented the interference with his own corn law, brought various objections. He claimed that the shortage had been engineered to justify the creation of a special command, accused Cicero of betraying the *auctoritas senatus* and trotted out the old maxim that so much power should not be placed in the hands of any one man.[54] Nor were all the consulars as enthusiastic as Cicero. Only two were present in the senate when a decree was passed on his motion, authorizing an approach to Pompeius and the passing of a law to grant the command.[55] They said that they were afraid to attend the senate because of the popular disturbances, but displeasure too may have played a part in keeping them away. However, they all turned up on the next day to hear what powers Pompeius would see fit to request.[56]

His personal demands were reasonable enough. He asked for fifteen legates, naming Cicero as the first of these and proclaiming that he would regard him as his second self. So Spinther and Nepos drafted a bill giving Pompeius control of the corn supply throughout the Roman world for a period of five years. It was at this point in the proceedings that Pompeius resorted to his old technique of flying a kite to test the wind of public opinion before committing himself. The tribune Messius brought forward an alternative proposal which would have given Pompeius far greater powers, powers disproportionate in both scope and kind to the nature of his task: control of the treasury, a fleet, an army, and *imperium maius* in all the provinces – that is, in all probability, almost a duplicate of his command against Mithradates.[57] As usual there were doubts as to what Pompeius really wanted. He himself declared that he was satisfied with the consuls' proposal, but his friends suggested that he would prefer Messius' bill if public opinion would tolerate it. However, it soon became clear that opposition to Messius was too widespread, and so Pompeius accepted the consuls' version, claiming that this was what he had wanted all along. It is indeed possible, though perhaps not likely, that Messius' bill was intended from the first merely to facilitate this eventual posture of moderation and devotion to the public good.[58]

From both the practical and the political point of view the *cura annonae* was admirably suited to Pompeius' needs. Like the campaign against the pirates in 67, the organization of the corn supply presented chiefly problems of logistics and co-ordination over a wide area, precisely the kind of task for which he had already proved himself supremely gifted. He took the duties of his post seriously, and was frequently to be found away from Rome on business connected with it.[59] It is perhaps for that reason that despite his obvious reluctance to cut himself off from politics at Rome, no permanent dispensation for him to enter the city without laying down his *imperium* was included in the terms of the law; instead, he received an *ad hoc* dispensation whenever circumstances made his presence in the city essential.[60] He approached the problem of the corn supply in exactly the same way as he had that of piracy, dividing up the corn-producing regions of the Mediterranean between his legates, while he co-ordinated their efforts and operated on a roving basis wherever his presence was needed.[61] Unfortunately the names of only two of his fifteen legates are known, Cicero and his brother Quintus.[62] Cicero's own place was largely honorific, but Quintus performed more conventional duties, serving in Sardinia. But

Pompeius had not only secured a mission that he knew he could perform well, so that success gave him the promise of yet more glory;[63] there were further advantages to be won on the propaganda front. Even more than the command against the pirates, the *cura annonae* was a *popularis* matter, for to the common people of Rome the price of corn was perhaps the most important single item in politics. By accepting such a post and by preferring or pretending to prefer this relatively modest and unmilitary role to the armies and fleets dangled before him by Messius, he was proving once more that he was dedicated above all else to the welfare of the masses and valued the opportunity to serve the people more highly than the splendours of command.

So as the year drew to a close Pompeius could feel largely satisfied with recent events. After the setbacks and humiliations of 58 he had recovered a large part of his prestige and power. His major undertaking of the spring and summer, the recall of Cicero, had been brought to a triumphant and glittering conclusion, and already he had benefited greatly from the orator's gratitude. Yet there were still disquieting factors in the background: the growing strength of Caesar in Gaul, the jealousy of Crassus, and the impotent but bitter fury of Clodius. The coalition had played very little part in the events of 57. Crassus seems to have preserved an almost total inertia throughout the struggle that had led up to Cicero's return;[64] Caesar had given a belated and reluctant consent. Neither will have been unduly pleased to see Pompeius once more placed on a pinnacle of power and popularity, the ascent of which he had achieved without their assistance. At this point Pompeius perhaps began to wonder whether the coalition had served its turn. It was the refusal of the optimates to concede his requirements and grant him political acceptance on his own valuation that had driven him to accept Caesar's overtures in 60, but now it seemed worthwhile to test their reactions once more and see if their attitude had changed. It would be necessary to move with the most delicate caution. Caesar in Gaul might be a threat on the horizon to Pompeius' own supremacy, but he was also his trump card in his dealings with the *boni*. To sacrifice Caesar to the simmering wrath of Cato and his friends by renouncing his friendship and abetting his recall would be an act of folly as great in its way as the other extreme course of severing all links with the optimates and making himself in effect dependent on Caesar. Some bait must be found with which to tempt the *boni* and see if the way lay open to realize Cicero's dream, the return of Pompeius from his primrose path of *popularis* levity to safety and respectability in the optimate fold.

10

THE CONFERENCE OF LUCA

Pompeius fixed on the question of the Campanian land.[1] The choice was an excellent one, for several reasons. Attempts to remove the *ager Campanus* from the censors' control and use it for distribution had always aroused the most violent opposition. Quite apart from its economic value, the Campanian land seems to have acquired an almost symbolic significance.[2] After so many threats had been warded off in the past, Caesar's interference had inspired perhaps more resentment than any other aspect of his legislation. To offer it back to the treasury would therefore be a potent demonstration of Pompeius' good will. Nor was its financial importance irrelevant. To carry out his task as curator of the corn supply effectively, Pompeius needed money, for which he was dependent on the senate. The funds that had been voted to him in September were now running out, and it is likely that the senate was showing itself in no hurry to grant him any more. From this point of view the return of the Campanian land to the censors could be seen as a *quid pro quo*, the restoration to the treasury of an important source of revenue, in return for which Pompeius could fairly press his claim for additional money to buy corn. Finally, if part of the legislation of 59 was to be sacrificed, it was the *lex Campana* that would do least damage to Pompeius' own material interests. It is likely that a few of his veterans had received allotments in Campania,[3] but the vast majority had been catered for by the earlier agrarian law; most of the beneficiaries of the *lex Campana* had been members of the urban proletariat. Pompeius' *clientela* would therefore suffer very little harm if the law were repealed.[4]

He moved with customary caution to test senatorial reactions. At a moment when he himself was absent from Rome on business connected with the corn commission, one of the new tribunes for 56, P. Rutilius Lupus, whose links with Pompeius were only later to become fully apparent,[5] raised the question of the Campanian land in the senate.[6] He clearly spoke with great care and considerable skill, taking pains to disguise his role as Pompeius' agent: he praised Cicero, made occasional gibes at Caesar, and appealed to the absent Pompeius as if he had no notion what his reaction to the proposal would be. At the end of his speech he declared that he would not ask the senators to give their opinions, so that nobody need run the risk of incurring ill feeling; both their violent remarks in the past and their present silence made it clear to him what their sentiments were. The consul designate Lentulus Marcellinus, who had already shown himself a forceful figure in the senate, gave the tribune both a warning and discreet encouragement. Lupus, he said, should not make deductions from the senate's present silence. Others no doubt felt, as he did himself, that the question of the Campanian land could not properly be discussed in Pompeius' absence.

Thus to a certain extent Pompeius' caution had defeated its own ends. The senate's interest was obvious, but it seemed likely that he would have to give some sign of his own opinion before the proposal would be taken seriously. What might have ensued is beyond conjecture, for at this point the problem of the *ager Campanus* was thrust into the background by a more explosive matter, the fate of Ptolemy Auletes of Egypt, whose costly restoration in 59 had proved unacceptable to his people and in consequence shortlived.[7] The question had ostensibly been settled in 57 by the senate, which on the motion of the consul Lentulus Spinther had decreed that the king should be returned to his throne by the next governor of Cilicia, Spinther himself.[8] But Auletes wanted to be restored by Pompeius: he may well have felt that Pompeius, who had had his money, owed it to him to make effective delivery. He came to Rome in person and set about bribing all and sundry who might prove useful to work against Spinther and in favour of Pompeius.[9] When the people of Alexandria sent envoys to counteract his intrigues, the king succeeded in arranging the murder of a number and bribed or terrified the rest into quiescence.[10] Pompeius' sympathies were clear, though not openly expressed: he gave the king his hospitality, and it was at his Alban villa that an agreement was made between Ptolemy and the financier C. Rabirius Postumus.[11] The bulk of the senate, however, partly, as Cicero claims, from malice, partly from resentment of Auletes' outrageous behaviour, took refuge behind a convenient oracle, discovered by the tribune C. Cato, which declared that the king should not be restored 'with a multitude'.[12] This was interpreted to mean an army, with the result that, if this view prevailed, there would be no way in which the restoration of Auletes could be used as a pretext for the creation of a military command. The principal aim of this ploy was to render the task unattractive to any man of excessive ambition and above all to Pompeius. But it also displeased Spinther, who no doubt had hopes of extracting some military glory from the exercise.[13]

Cicero's position was well defined. Spinther's vital contribution to his own recall from exile obliged him to support his claim, and he viewed Pompeius' interest in the affair with great distaste. The events of December must have filled him with hope that Pompeius could, by way of the repeal of the Campanian land law, be shepherded back into the fold. But if Pompeius now abandoned this policy in favour of bludgeoning his way to a military command in defiance of senatorial sensibilities, that dream would vanish into thin air. So Cicero spoke very freely in urging Pompeius to shun the infamy that support of Auletes must bring with it.[14] But for the moment, as he admitted, Pompeius gave him no ground for complaint: both in private conversation and in the senate he showed no sign of seeking the command for himself, devoting all his eloquence to backing Spinther's claims. Early in January Hortensius, Cicero and Lucullus combined to table a motion that Spinther should perform the restoration, using whatever force was necessary. This was ruled out on the religious objection, which was firmly sustained by the consul Marcellinus, whom a private grudge rendered hostile to Spinther in this matter. The three consulars therefore amended their motion to retain Spinther as the agent, but without the use of an army.[15] The issue was, however, complicated by various other proposals.[16] Crassus suggested that the task should be entrusted to three legates chosen from among men already vested with *imperium*, while Bibulus preferred three *priuati*. As Cicero pointed out, Crassus' motion, unlike that of Bibulus, did not exclude Pompeius. But no doubt he had an ulterior motive. Any proposal dividing the task between three people was bound to make it seem less attractive: little profit and less dignity would accrue to the beneficiaries of Crassus' motion, if it were passed. It is perhaps worth asking who would have been the most likely or rational choices as legates. Pompeius was not excluded; Spinther was on the spot and had a claim, while on paper at least the obvious choice for a third would be the governor of Syria, Gabinius. But to send three consulars on such a dubious mission would have been grotesque, and it may be that Crassus merely hoped to embarrass Pompeius, who would have been bound to refuse, yet might have found it difficult to explain why without laying himself open to charges of arrogance and ambition. Bibulus' alternative was plainly an attempt to defuse the situation still further by rendering the mission unappealing while excluding Pompeius on technical grounds just to be on the safe side. It is not surprising that the remaining consulars gave it their support, with the exception of the hardheaded Servilius Isauricus, who went further, proposing that Ptolemy should not be restored at all.

It was perhaps the danger embodied in Servilius' proposal that stimulated Pompeius' supporters to come out into the open. His name was mentioned by the tribune Rutilius, and a motion that he should restore the king was brought by Volcacius Tullus, with the backing of Pompeius' former legate Afranius.[17] This naturally aroused suspicions about Pompeius' real desires, which were confirmed by the open efforts of Libo, Hypsaeus and others close to him. All this might have benefited Spinther, but as Cicero observed Pompeius' enemies were also suspicious of Spinther because of his authorship of the bill giving Pompeius control of the corn supply, and in consequence were afraid that by supporting him – or Cicero – they might find themselves somehow serving Pompeius' interests. When the senate met on 13 January the day was largely taken up with a clash between Marcellinus and another tribune, L. Caninius Gallus.[18] Next day three motions came before the house, those of Bibulus, Hortensius and Volcacius. Crassus seems to have allowed his motion to drop. It was then demanded that Bibulus' motion should be divided into its component elements. The first part, that because of the oracle no army should be sent, was passed; the second, that three legates should restore the king, was overwhelmingly defeated. Hortensius' proposal, that Spinther should perform the task but without an army, should have come up next for discussion, but at this point Rutilius intervened, claiming that he had a prior right to take a division on the proposal that favoured Pompeius. This provoked an outcry. The consuls, though they would not give way, did not protest too much, since they had wanted Bibulus' motion to pass and were happy that the day should be wasted in technical squabbles. Otherwise, according to Cicero, there would have been a powerful majority for Hortensius' proposal, despite some overt support for Volcacius.[19]

That evening Cicero dined with Pompeius and seized the chance to plead Spinther's cause yet again. Despite the conduct of his friends, Pompeius still wore the mask: as Cicero wrote to Spinther, when he listened to Pompeius himself, he could acquit him of the slightest suspicion of desire for the command, but when he looked at his associates, he realized that Spinther's chances had been long since undermined. All that he could find to console himself with was the thought that, unless there was a resort to violence, no *popularis* activity would come to anything, despite the efforts of Caninius and C. Cato.[20] Though Cicero more than once mentions them together, it is unlikely that the two tribunes were acting in concert. Caninius wanted to introduce a bill to give Pompeius the task of restoring

Ptolemy, albeit with no army and only two lictors.[21] C. Cato, on the other hand, was eager to strip Spinther of his *imperium*,[22] but had been responsible for the unearthing of the oracle and was shortly to show himself violently hostile to Pompeius. But in the senate on 15 January both responded to the optimate obstruction of their own measures by announcing that they would not allow any law to pass before the elections.[23] The attitude of the tribunes ensured that no progress was made, though Bibulus, whose motion had been shattered, as Cicero boasted, on the previous day, showed himself moderate in defeat. Writing to his brother, who was in Sardinia, on 17 January, Cicero was pessimistic about Spinther's chances.[24] Summing up the struggle, he saw only two possible candidates, Spinther and Pompeius. He claimed still to be unable to discern what Pompeius really wanted, though he had no doubts about his friends. The king's other creditors too were openly working to undermine Spinther's position. So the mission seemed almost in Pompeius' grasp, though Cicero still found hope in the possibility of a compromise solution.[25]

At the beginning of February events took a dramatic turn. On 2 February Pompeius appeared in court on behalf of Milo, who had been charged with *uis* by Clodius.[26] The court convened again on 6 February.[27] Pompeius tried to speak in Milo's defence, but as soon as he rose Clodius' gangs shouted him down. Pompeius struggled to make himself heard and courageously went on with his speech above the din. When he sat down, Clodius got up, to a comparable reception from Cicero and his supporters. Clodius lost his temper and a two-hour slanging match ensued. He then turned to his chorus and asked: 'Who is starving the people to death?' 'Pompeius!' 'Whom do you want to go to Alexandria?' 'Crassus!' Crassus was indeed present, but whether he really wanted to restore Auletes himself is doubtful.[28] However, he was certainly eager to spoil Pompeius' chances, and it was probably with his blessing that Clodius used his name. A riot followed, and then a meeting of the senate was summoned, though Pompeius did not attend, but retired to his house in high dudgeon.[29] Cicero too avoided the meeting, so as not to be forced to choose between keeping silence on issues of such moment and a defence of Pompeius that would offend the optimates, for as usual when Clodius turned his fire on Pompeius, Bibulus, Curio and Favonius, joined now by the son of Servilius Isauricus, were egging him on in their habitual shortsighted manner.[30] On 7 and 8 February the senate met, in the temple of Apollo outside the *pomoerium* so that Pompeius could attend without securing a dispensation.[31] Both sessions were concerned with the disturbances of 6 February. At the first Pompeius delivered a weighty speech, but no decree was passed.

At the second, however, the senate voted that events of 6 February had been *contra rem publicam*. C. Cato delivered a violent attack on Pompeius and with some subtlety followed it with copious praise of a reluctant Cicero, thus exploiting a device that Crassus had employed to good effect in 61.[32] His hypocritical diatribe against Pompeius for betraying Cicero in 58 was received with attentive delight by his audience. But Pompeius replied with striking effect, putting the blame for Cato's behaviour squarely on Crassus, whom he described but did not name, and announcing that he would take greater care of his life than had Scipio Aemilianus. This thinly veiled accusation that Crassus was plotting to murder him was amplified by Pompeius in a private conversation with Cicero. He now believed that Crassus was scheming against his life and, backed by Curio, Bibulus and the rest, was directing and financing the attacks of Clodius and C. Cato, and that his whole political position was threatened, for the masses had been turned against him by Clodius, the nobles were hostile and the senate would not give him a fair hearing.[33] Moreover, the distasteful turn events had taken convinced him that the matter of Egypt was best dropped.[34] This led Cicero to hope that Spinther might yet be entrusted with the mission, and he tried to persuade Ptolemy to give this solution his backing, now that he could no longer cherish any hope of being restored by Pompeius.

It is not surprising that Pompeius had lost interest in Egypt. He was now forced to concentrate all his efforts on re-establishing himself at home. The question of Ptolemy had proved a damaging interlude for him: it had given his enemies the chance to humiliate him in public, it had strained his relations with Cicero and others who wanted to be his friends, and it had enabled Clodius to destroy a large part of his popular support. But despite his immediate difficulties Pompeius still held a trump card, his friendship with Caesar. The time, however, was not yet ripe to play it. For the moment all attention was fixed on the forthcoming trials of the two gang-leaders who had done so much to thwart Clodius in 57 and secure Cicero's recall, Milo and Sestius. Violence was inevitable, and Pompeius took steps to ensure that he would come out on top: while Clodius strengthened his own bands, he summoned men not only from his country estates and his home territory of Picenum, but from as far away as Cisalpine Gaul.[35]

The trial of Sestius was a triumph for Cicero, who was able to deliver a political credo and to lacerate his old enemy Vatinius, who testified for the prosecution.[36] Defended not only by Cicero but also by Hortensius, Pompeius and Crassus, and assisted by a probably collusive prosecutor, Sestius was overwhelmingly acquitted on 11 March.[37] Meanwhile Marcellinus was effectively using religious devices to keep C. Cato in check, while nothing more was heard of Caninius' proposal to send Pompeius to Egypt.[38] It was at this point that Cicero decided to solve Pompeius' problems for him and to revive once more his plan for bringing Pompeius and the optimates together. He must have known that it would not be easy. Pompeius had good cause for resentment against the *boni* and indeed against the senate as a whole: Cicero's one complaint against the otherwise excellent Marcellinus was that he was too rough with Pompeius in the house.[39] Nor were the immediate omens good. The acquittals of Sestius and Milo had inspired the latter to organize the prosecution of a henchman of Clodius, Sex. Cloelius.[40] Cicero had disapproved, and events had proved him right. Cloelius, despite his manifest guilt, was narrowly acquitted, and the count showed that he owed his escape to the senatorial jurors.[41] Cicero had no doubt that this verdict had been dictated by their hostility to Pompeius and consequent readiness to acquit a friend of Clodius. But there were still grounds for hope. Pompeius' relations with Crassus had never been worse, and his loss of popular support was due at least in part to his stand on behalf of Milo and Sestius.[42] So Cicero tried to turn back the clock to the end of 57, when the rift between Pompeius and the *boni* had seemed on the point of being mended. The proposed means then had been the repeal of the Campanian land law, and it was again to this that Cicero looked to restore the situation.

It is unlikely that Pompeius himself played any part in the revival of the question of the *lex Campana* which Cicero proposed in the senate on 5 April.[43] Nevertheless he may have been well pleased at Cicero's initiative, for two reasons. In the first place, as the debate of 5 April made clear, the subject of the Campanian land was still intimately connected with finance, and in particular with the availability of money to buy corn.[44] A decree was passed, allotting Pompeius HS 400,000; it would be interesting to know who proposed it, for it represents a major overture, since Pompeius had as yet given no sign that he was still prepared to consider the repeal of the *lex Campana*. It would be a rash man who was prepared to gamble that his attitude would be the same now as it had been in December 57, after all that had transpired in the meantime, and even then he had not openly committed himself. To give him the money before he had shown his hand was a calculated risk, and it is hardly surprising that the ensuing discussion on the Campanian land was, in Cicero's phrase, more like a public meeting than a senatorial debate. The second attraction that the proposal will have had for Pompeius was that it gave him a great opportunity to put pressure on Caesar. A short while ago he had been isolated, and he might then have seemed to be entirely dependent on maintaining his tie with Caesar. But

Cicero's *démarche* had to some extent opened his options once again and put him back in his favourite position of being able to play off Caesar against the *boni*. He could now point out to Caesar and Crassus that the way was again open for him to renounce the coalition. They could reply that the optimates might still refuse, but the consequences, if Pompeius' overtures were accepted, would be too grave for them to take such a risk. For Crassus the end of the coalition would mean the loss of any hopes he might have of raising himself to a position of parity with his erstwhile partners, while for Caesar it could spell total disaster, so both men might be expected to take notice. Whatever Cicero had intended, he had created a golden opportunity for Pompeius to recover the initiative when he seemed to have lost it completely. Even the timing played into Pompeius' hands; he was due to leave Rome on 11 April for Sardinia.[45]

In his long defence of his political activities written to Spinther in December 54 Cicero, concerned to argue that his motives had throughout demonstrated an unselfish independence of spirit,[46] claimed his revival of the question of the *ager Campanus* as an all-out attack on the unity of the coalition.[47] Since his objective was to win Pompeius away from Crassus and Caesar, the claim, though tendentious, is not entirely unjustified. His action was certainly seen as a major threat by the other member on the spot. As soon as he heard of the proposal, Crassus set off to inform Caesar, who was still in winter quarters at Ravenna.[48] Caesar too realized the seriousness of the threat and was furious at Cicero's interference. He hurried across the breadth of Italy to catch Pompeius before he could set sail.

Such is the prelude to what is often called the conference of Luca. Whether what happened at Luca deserves that imposing name is another matter. In the later sources the meeting takes on the appearance of a planned summit conference, at which the big three settled their differences and ordained the course of affairs for the foreseeable future while magistrates and senators kicked their heels outside, waiting to hear what had been decided.[49] This picture must be largely fantasy. In the first place there was plainly no planning: the meeting at Luca was the result of an almost panic response by Crassus and Caesar to a sudden and drastic threat to their interests. Nor is it certain that Crassus was at Luca at all. The late sources all say that he was, and few modern scholars have questioned this verdict.[50] That he should have been present is at first sight plausible. His own interests were very much at stake, and they were certainly taken account of at Luca: he emerged with the prospect of a second consulship and a major command in which to win military glory. But Cicero's letter to Spinther in 54, the only almost contemporary account, strongly suggests that Crassus did not accompany Caesar to Luca.[51] His possible failure to do so can be explained in the light of his present relations with Pompeius. These had never been more strained: indeed the quarrel between Crassus and Pompeius must have greatly encouraged Cicero's hopes of breaking up the coalition. Both Crassus and Caesar may have felt that in the circumstances a meeting between Crassus and Pompeius could only make matters worse and that it would prove a task too great even for Caesar's diplomatic talents to reconcile them if they met face to face. If on the other hand Caesar alone met Pompeius, he might be able to save the situation. Crassus could trust Caesar to protect his interests simply because his objectives had to be secured if the public purpose of the meeting, a demonstration that the dynasts were still friends, was to be achieved. The obvious practical proof of this reconciliation would be a joint consulship for Pompeius and Crassus, to be followed by commands that further asserted their mutual parity and good will. Caesar was not eligible for a consulship, nor did he want one at this time: his own aim was a renewal of his command in Gaul. Besides, there was no public quarrel between Caesar and his partners: it was Pompeius and Crassus who had, if all went well, to give proof of their renewed alliance. So the only scheme that Caesar could rationally propose to Pompeius was bound to give Crassus what he wanted. Therefore, whatever his personal feelings, he could leave the matter in Caesar's hands without qualms. If something of this kind passed between Crassus and Caesar at Ravenna, it may well be the case that the later sources were misled, that the impression given by Cicero's letter to Spinther is correct, and that the 'conference' of Luca consisted of a meeting between only two of the dynasts, Caesar and Pompeius.

What was agreed between them is fortunately less obscure.[52] First of all, it was essential that the coalition should be shown to be still in existence. Therefore the reconciliation of Pompeius and Crassus was to be manifested in a joint consulship for 55. Whether the provincial commands that were to follow were also decided on at Luca is less certain. There is no reason why they should have been, for the matter was of no urgency, and neither Pompeius nor Caesar had time to waste. As consuls Pompeius and Crassus would see to it that Caesar's command was renewed for a further five years. The political situation at Rome was also to be tidied up. Pompeius will have promised to impress on Cicero that no further attacks on Caesar's laws or on his position in general would be tolerated.[53] In return he will have insisted that Crassus should withdraw his support of Clodius and that pressure should be brought to bear to make him stop his attacks. Then Pompeius sailed for Sardinia. There he had a serious talk with Cicero's

brother Quintus and made it clear to him how matters stood.[54] Both
Quintus and a friend, L. Vibullius, were dispatched with messages to Cicero,
telling him not to raise the question of the Campanian land in Pompeius'
absence. It was a bitter blow. When the senate duly met on 15 May, the
eagerly awaited debate never took place.[55] Though what had happened at
Luca was not yet common knowledge, the coalition was obviously still in
existence. Cicero's dream and with it his political independence were utterly
destroyed.

It remains to consider why Pompeius yielded to Caesar's arguments. He
could still have chosen to repudiate the coalition and to hope that concessions in the matter of the Campanian land would restore his position in the
senate, while the voting of funds for the buying of corn would enable him
to recover his popularity with the masses and so counteract the activities of
Clodius. But such a policy had little to recommend it. He had no guarantee
that the repeal of the Campanian law would win over the *boni*, whose
behaviour in recent months must have made this seem more than doubtful.
Clodius would certainly continue to harrass him, and the optimates might
well continue to applaud. Caesar too would be deeply alienated, and there
was also his perhaps genuine fear of Crassus. Thus if things turned out
badly, acquiescence in Cicero's proposal might leave Pompeius even worse
off than before: weak and humiliated in the senate, subject to constant
attacks from Clodius, at odds with Caesar, and in fear of his life from
Crassus. But to patch up the coalition would bring positive gains: his
friendship with Caesar would be preserved, the threat from Crassus, real
or imaginary, would be removed, and Clodius might be brought to heel.
The optimates would still be hostile, but that was a relatively small price to
pay. On balance there could be no doubt in Pompeius' mind. Both for the
present and for the future his best policy lay in preserving his association
with Caesar and Crassus. All three dynasts emerged from the meeting at
Luca strengthened: Crassus gained most, but Pompeius was the strongest.
He had demonstrated to Caesar and Crassus that the existence of the
coalition depended on him and to the *boni* that it still kept him independent
of them. At some subsequent date he might yet have to choose between
Caesar and the senate, but for the time being he could maintain himself
against either, and when the moment came his choice would be free.

11

THE SECOND CONSULSHIP AND THE GROWTH OF ANARCHY

Both Clodius and Cicero accepted the new situation. All that Clodius could do to sugar the pill was to parade his new-found friendship for Pompeius in such a fulsome and exaggerated manner that its insincerity was blatant.[1] But for Cicero things were much worse. Pompeius' behaviour over the Campanian land had made him look an utter fool, and the optimates, who had always resented his talent and his vanity, took great pleasure in his discomfiture, which compensated them for the loss of their other chief source of entertainment, Clodius' attacks on Pompeius.[2] Feeling that he had been betrayed by them again, just as he had been in 58 and 57, Cicero decided to make the best of a bad job. But he soon found that mere neutrality would not be enough: the dynasts wanted positive benefits from his oratory.

The first to profit was not Pompeius but Caesar. Cicero repeatedly spoke on his behalf in the senate in the early summer, supporting the grant of a *supplicatio*, the sending of ten additional legates to Gaul and the release of funds to pay Caesar's legions, and then successfully opposing an attempt to nip the arrangements made at Luca in the bud by depriving him of one or other of the Gallic provinces.[3] Despite his annoyance at the treatment he had received from the *boni*, his lack of political independence left him bitterly discontented.[4] In July his new dedication to Pompeius was displayed in a less public sphere than the senate house. Now that Pompeius had lost interest in the Egyptian question, he again assured Cicero of his devotion to Spinther's interests. This encouraged Cicero to suggest that Spinther should go ahead, ignoring the notorious oracle, and restore Auletes himself.[5] The advice was probably disinterested and sound enough, but his insistence that Pompeius had at heart been on Spinther's side even in the difficult days of Caninius' agitation does not ring true and contradicts the doubts he expressed at the time. It looks as if Pompeius was hoping that

Cicero would use his influence with Spinther to restore harmony between them and Cicero was doing his best to oblige. In the autumn he had to defend the coalition against another form of attack. Since Pompeius and Caesar had proved too strong to be vulnerable to a direct assault, an alternative strategy was adopted by their enemies: the prosecution of their friends and adherents. The chosen victim was their trusted negotiator L. Balbus, who had assisted in the organization of the coalition and owed his citizenship to Pompeius' good offices.[6] That citizenship was now called into question, but Cicero, Pompeius, who challenged his critics to attack him directly, and Crassus all spoke for the defence, and Balbus was acquitted without undue difficulty.[7]

Although the dynasts could resist attacks, it did not prove easy for them to achieve the ends they had set themselves at Luca. At no time during the period of their uneasy co-operation did they find it possible to exercise anything approaching effective control over elections at any level, and this was never made clearer than at the vital time in 56 when it was essential to their plans that Pompeius and Crassus be elected to the consulship of 55. Other candidates were in the field, notably Pompeius' enemy Domitius Ahenobarbus, who had already attacked Caesar as praetor in 58 and was now sworn to recall him from his command and take over himself.[8] Pompeius and Crassus plainly felt unsure of success if they stood in the normal manner. Despite widespread speculation they refused to commit themselves when Lentulus Marcellinus asked them if they were going to stand, though the people pressed them to reply: Pompeius would not give a direct answer, while Crassus enigmatically declared that he would do whatever seemed best for the good of the state.[9] So the official date for the handing-in of nominations passed without their showing their hand. Then, when it was too late, they attempted to stand, but Marcellinus as presiding consul refused to accept their candidature.[10] This, given his attitude to Pompeius earlier in the year, is not surprising and must surely have been expected by Pompeius and Crassus. It seems certain that they never intended to risk a conventional election and deliberately delayed the submission of their names for that reason. It now became necessary for them to prevent Marcellinus from holding the elections before the end of his consulship. This they duly proceeded to do, using all manner of obstruction, including violence.[11] The point of the manoeuvre is lost to our sources, though a faint echo survives in Dio. If the consuls failed to secure the election of their successors, the task passed to a series of *interreges*. An *interrex* held office for only five days, and only patricians were eligible for the office. It would therefore be fairly easy to prevent the holding of the elections by a hostile *interrex*, and once an *interrex* friendly to Pompeius and Crassus took office their election was assured, barring successful obstruction by their opponents, for interregal elections followed an archaic pattern: the *interrex* proposed only two candidates to the people, so Pompeius and Crassus would face no rivals. Even so, when the elections finally took place early in 55, it was necessary to resort to considerable violence to drive off the opposition and ensure that hostile voters stayed away: Domitius himself was wounded and his linkboy killed.[12]

Elections for the praetorship underlined the weakness of the dynasts' hold over the machinery of government. Only violence and blatant corruption on the part of Pompeius prevented the election of Cato and secured that of Vatinius.[13] Bribery had no doubt been rife on all sides: it was Pompeius' old legate Afranius who on 11 February proposed a decree against bribery in the senate,[14] but it may have been the adherents of the coalition who had most to fear. The failure to hold the elections in 56 had of course created a problem. Normally there was a sufficient interval between the election of magistrates and their entry into office for proceedings for bribery to be brought against them. But since 55 had begun without magistrates it was obviously desirable that once elected they should take office without further delay, which would mean that they escaped the risk of prosecution. So the senate tried to add a rider to Afranius' decree, enacting that the newly elected praetors should not take office for sixty days, to allow the possibility of proceedings. But Pompeius and Crassus refused to countenance this, which confirms that it was their own supporters who would have run the greatest risk of condemnation. The elections for the aedileship were also attended by violence: Pompeius himself came home with blood on his toga, which so alarmed the pregnant Julia that she suffered a miscarriage.[15]

Once they were secure in office, Pompeius and Crassus took steps to combat disorder. Such lip-service to law and order was seemly and natural: neither wanted to overthrow the constitution. It should not of course be assumed that they would have hesitated for a moment to engineer breaches of their own legislation if they had thought that these could be successfully arranged to further their own interests or those of their supporters, or that either their friends or their enemies would have found this surprising.[16] Pompeius passed a law on bribery at elections and also a law on the composition of juries which had a similar objective, the reduction of bribery in the courts.[17] The three classes of jurors established by L. Cotta in 70 were retained, but in future only the wealthiest members of each group were to serve, presumably on the rather unrealistic assumption that rich men would be less prone than poorer ones to succumb to bribes. Crassus produced a law of similar bent, designed to curb the use of the *collegia* in canvassing.[18] This too would further the general tendency of restoring order to political and forensic life, and might also serve the particular purpose of reducing Clodius' independence.

There remained the question of provinces for Pompeius and Crassus. It is unlikely that any specific arrangements had been made at Luca; when Cicero visited Pompeius at Naples late in April it seems that nothing had yet been settled.[19] The two men had a long talk about public affairs, with which Pompeius claimed to be very dissatisfied. Cicero, however, was reluctant to believe that he was telling the truth on any of the matters they discussed, which included the possibility of a provincial command. Pompeius expressed his lack of interest in both Syria and Spain,[20] and his worries about the elections: the prospect that M. Valerius Messalla would stand for the consulship of 54 appeared to displease him greatly.[21] But despite this pretence Syria and the two Spanish provinces were the subject of a law introduced by the tribune C. Trebonius to assign to the consuls extraordinary commands on the pattern of those granted to Caesar in 59 and to Gabinius and Piso in 58.[22] The choice of provinces is interesting.[23] Crassus wanted the chance to win military glory, and his selection of Syria made it clear that he intended to find it in an invasion of Parthia, though the terms of Trebonius' law mentioned no such project.[24] That he received the opportunity marks a concession on the part of Pompeius, since it meant the replacement of Gabinius as governor of Syria, even though he had spent only three years in the province. Pompeius' own choice of the two Spains is more significant. They offered no scope for brilliant conquests, but he hardly stood in need of further laurels in that quarter. He had already built up a large following there during the Sertorian war, and Caesar's unpopular tenure of Ulterior can have done little to undermine it. So Pompeius will not have chosen Spain to restore an influence that had never been seriously threatened. His motive must have been strategic: he wanted the Spains simply in order to control them, should control of the Western provinces become important. If this is so, it may be the first sign that Pompeius had considered the possibility that it might one day come to war between Caesar and himself – or at least between Caesar and the state, since for the moment he was merely strengthening his hand, not committing himself to one side or the other in any eventual conflict. The commands were to run for five years in the first instance, and Pompeius and Crassus were to enjoy the same right to make peace and war without immediate reference to the senate and people as had been vouchsafed

once before to Pompeius by the *lex Manilia*.[25] The motive will have been
the same now as it had been then: to allow the commander on the spot
diplomatic freedom of movement so that valuable opportunities might not
be missed through delays caused by protocol or slow communications.

The law did not pass without considerable opposition. Two tribunes,
C. Ateius Capito and P. Aquillius Gallus, had to be deterred by force, while
Cato and Favonius also spoke against the bill. Events followed a familiar
course: Cato attempted his usual filibuster, which as usual led to his arrest.
Ninnius, the tribune of 58 who had co-operated with Pompeius in his
efforts to recall Cicero, was also prominent now among the coalition's
opponents.[26] Once the law had been forced through, Pompeius and
Crassus turned their minds to Caesar and passed a law granting him an
extension of his command in both Gallic provinces and Illyricum for a
further five years.[27] Both Cato and Cicero are said to have warned Pompeius that he was setting a rod in pickle for his own back.[28]

He tried to restore his popularity by a lavish building programme, on a
scale which Cicero, though he hesitated to say so, plainly thought excessive.[29] As well as a portico and a temple of Venus Victrix he gave the city its
first permanent stone-built theatre, for which he incurred the wrath of
traditionalists.[30] Cicero declared that the games which accompanied the
dedication of the temple and the theatre were the most elaborate he had
ever seen, but Pompeius was not entirely successful in winning popular
favour: his *uenatio* featured elephants as a special attraction, but the crowd
sided with the beasts against the hunters.[31]

Although they could enforce their will on major issues, the dynasts found
that their supporters were still vulnerable in the courts. In October Cicero
complained to a friend that he had been forced to defend the tribune of the
previous year, Caninius Gallus.[32] More dramatically, an accusation was
brought before the censors by Helvius Mancia against Pompeius' close
friend L. Libo.[33] Pompeius came to Libo's aid and attacked Helvius, who
replied with a superb piece of invective that recalled all the victims of the
adulescentulus carnifex. It may also have been in this year that Pompeius and
Cicero both spoke in defence of Ampius Balbus.[34] Nor did the consular
elections, which did not take place till November, bring any comfort. One
consul, Ap. Claudius Pulcher, eldest brother of Clodius, was an opportun-
ist,[35] but the other was the sworn enemy of Pompeius and Caesar,
L. Domitius Ahenobarbus, while Cato himself this time secured the praetorship.

Meanwhile relations between Crassus and Gabinius had become strained
to breaking-point. Gabinius had probably not pleased his successor by

carrying out on his own initiative the long-delayed restoration of Ptolemy Auletes.[36] To make matters worse, he had been contemplating an invasion of Parthia.[37] So Crassus launched an attack on him, in company with Cicero. Then suddenly Crassus' attitude changed completely; he joined Pompeius in defending Gabinius and poured virulent scorn on Cicero the 'exile'.[38] No doubt Pompeius had persuaded him to stifle his resentment towards Gabinius, and with the assistance of a strong letter from Caesar he also forced the unfortunate Cicero into a reconciliation with Crassus.[39] But Gabinius was not mollified; when Crassus sent a legate ahead to take over the province, he refused to receive him.[40] There was also considerable opposition to the levies conducted by both Pompeius and Crassus, and when Crassus eventually set off for the East in the middle of November, Ateius Capito first tried to prevent his departure by putting him under arrest and then, when this move failed, pronounced solemn curses on him and his expedition.[41]

Pompeius, however, did not go to Spain. Instead he set a precedent by choosing to govern both provinces through legates, while he himself remained in the vicinity of Rome, where he could keep his eye on political developments.[42] This expedient was for him no more than a useful way of reconciling his own interests with his duties to the state as governor and curator of the corn supply, but it was later to be systematized and elevated into a mode of government by Augustus, when a grateful and frightened senate bestowed on him a provincial command as great as the combined holdings of Pompeius, Caesar and Crassus in 54, which no man could hope to control singlehanded. So Pompeius was at an advantage against both Crassus and Caesar, but the times were not easy. As consul Domitius immediately unleashed attacks on both Caesar and Crassus.[43] When Crassus was target he found support from his colleague and various consulars, and Cicero was called on to perform wonders of hypocrisy in defence of Crassus' dignity in the senate.[44] In February Domitius also attacked Gabinius, whose firm treatment of the *publicani*, as well as his restoration of Auletes, made him a tempting victim. At the same meeting the senate heard an embassy from Tyre, apparently favourable to Gabinius, since a counter-embassy appeared from the *publicani* of Syria.[45]

In June 54 came the first faint rumours of dictatorship. This theme, which was to recur so often, arose from the growing anarchy that was hampering the day-to-day government of the republic.[46] But for the moment the rumour remained a rumour, while attacks on the supporters of the coalition continued. C. Cato and Nonius Sufenas were brought to trial, but both were acquitted on 4 July.[47] The closeness of the verdict – a

majority of only four votes – reveals yet again the uncertainty of the
dynasts' control over the courts, but the result was enough to make Cicero
despair. Nevertheless, the new concord between Pompeius and Crassus
sufficed to effect an official reconciliation between C. Cato on the one
hand and Cicero and Milo on the other.[48] Another associate of Pompeius
to find himself threatened was C. Messius,[49] who as tribune in 57 had been
responsible for the rejected proposal that would have reinforced the cu-
ratorship of the corn supply with an army and a fleet. Ap. Claudius had sent
him on a mission to Caesar, but the strength of the opposition had been
such that he had been recalled by an edict of the praetor P. Servilius
Isauricus, who had already shown himself hostile to Pompeius in the
senate.[50] Cicero was again called on to speak for the defence, though this
time he may have done so with more enthusiasm than usual since Messius
had also tried to introduce a bill for his recall. Far less attractive was the task
forced on him in August by Pompeius and Caesar of defending his old
enemy Vatinius,[51] though Vatinius was quite prepared to bury the hatchet
and remained sincerely grateful to Cicero for securing his acquittal.[52]

Meanwhile the consular elections for 53 had seemed likely to produce a
close contest.[53] The issue was complicated by impending proceedings in
the courts: one of the candidates, M. Aemilius Scaurus, who had for a short
time been Pompeius' brother-in-law, had served under him as quaestor in
the East and had married Mucia when Pompeius divorced her, was being
prosecuted for extortion in his praetorian province of Sardinia.[54] The
others were M. Messalla, at whose candidature Pompeius had already
expressed disquiet a year before,[55] Cn. Domitius Calvinus, who as tribune
in 59 had opposed the coalition,[56] and C. Memmius, hostile to the dynasts
as praetor in 58, but now enjoying the backing of Caesar's troops and
exploiting the influence of Pompeius in Gaul.[57] Bribery reached unprecedented levels as the candidates made alliances that cut across their previous
and present associations. On 15 July the rate of interest doubled, as the
result of a pact between Memmius and Calvinus designed to secure them
the support of the consuls.[58] This seems to suggest that Memmius put more
faith in his old ties with enemies of the coalition – Calvinus and Ahenobarbus – than in the coalition itself. The chances of Scaurus and Messalla
correspondingly diminished.[59] Pompeius was said by Cicero to be furious.[60] The reason is not immediately obvious, but can perhaps be divined.
The elections were problematical for the dynasts: of the candidates only
Scaurus could perhaps be trusted, and he had not covered himself with
glory in Sardinia. Memmius was a recent acquisition, and his new association with Calvinus must have made him seem unreliable. That Pompeius

should be angry at this apparent double-dealing on Memmius' part is quite understandable, and his two public attitudes at this moment, support for Scaurus, but of such a nature that men doubted whether it was sincerely meant, and open hostility to Messalla, fit perfectly with this assumption. There is certainly nothing to suggest a divergence of interest between him and Caesar.[61]

The outrageous bribery provoked debates in the senate, and the elections were postponed until September.[62] This meant that the trial of Scaurus would come up before the elections, which Cicero regarded as dangerous for his client.[63] But in September scandal broke. The whole scheme was revealed by Memmius to a stunned senate. If he and Calvinus became consuls, they would either provide three augurs to attest the existence of a *lex curiata* empowering Ahenobarbus and Appius to go to their provinces, when no such law had been passed, and two consulars to claim they had put their names to a decree of the senate on the requisitions for the consular provinces, when the senate had not even discussed the subject, or they would pay a huge sum to both.[64] It is at this point that a possible difference of opinion between Pompeius and Caesar arises. Memmius made his confession *auctore Pompeio*, and Caesar was gravely displeased by it.[65] He had naturally put himself completely out of the running for the consulship, which meant that, if the dynasts were to have a candidate at all, it could only be Scaurus, whose ties were all with Pompeius, not with Caesar. That Caesar should have been annoyed at this is intelligible enough; it remains to ask why Pompeius acted as he did. It does not follow from the fact that Caesar was angry that Pompeius was necessarily trying to put him at a disadvantage. Another result of the revelation of the deal was the disgrace of Ahenobarbus and Appius, and that should have pleased both Caesar and Pompeius.[66] Perhaps Pompeius had calculated that the candidates were too unreliable and the scandal attending the election was too flagrant for any result to benefit the coalition, and had therefore decided that both his interests and Caesar's would best be served by using the incident to discredit Domitius and Claudius. So the elections were postponed yet again, while preparations were made to prosecute the candidates.

Meanwhile Scaurus had been acquitted of extortion on 2 September.[67] But the trial had not gone according to the defendant's expectations. He had hoped for the support of Pompeius and feared the hostility of Cato, who was presiding praetor, for both the prosecutor L. Valerius Triarius and his mother Flaminia were on intimate terms with Cato's sister Servilia.[68] But Pompeius offered Scaurus no help, while Cato remained strictly neutral.[69] Despite Asconius' conjecture, Pompeius' motive is unlikely to have been resentment at Scaurus' implied judgement on his divorce of Mucia; he probably simply felt that Scaurus was better dropped. Nevertheless, the list of those who appeared for the defence at the trial provides a useful indication of the complexity of political obligations at Rome and the folly of any simplistic interpretation in terms of 'factions'.[70] The six defence advocates included Clodius as well as Cicero and Hortensius, while Milo appeared as a defence witness along with C. Cato, who owed Scaurus a service, and the nine consulars who testified to Scaurus' character, mostly by letter, numbered among them not only Pompeius, who was prepared to go this far, but also Servilius Isauricus, L. Piso, Volcacius Tullus, Metellus Nepos, L. Philippus and the aged M. Perperna.[71] It is not surprising that Scaurus was acquitted by a large margin, with only eight votes out of seventy for condemnation.

The month also saw the eagerly awaited return of Gabinius, who approached the city on 19 September.[72] Three groups of accusers competed for the pleasure of prosecuting him: L. Lentulus, who had already charged him with *maiestas* and wanted to deal with the *repetundae* charge too, Ti. Claudius Nero, and C. Memmius, a tribune, with the support of L. Ateius Capito.[73] Lentulus was of course pursuing the feud he had begun in 59, when his father failed to win the consulship in competition with Gabinius and he himself had tried to prosecute Gabinius for *ambitus*.[74] Though he had had to allow Gabinius' recall from Syria to give scope to the military ambitions of Crassus, Pompeius was eager to save his loyal adherent if he could, and so he urged Cicero to forget his own grievances against Gabinius, in the hope that he might even go so far as to undertake the defence. But Cicero proved understandably reluctant.[75]

Gabinius slipped into the city by night on 27 September.[76] When summoned by the praetor C. Alfius to appear on the charge of *maiestas* he was almost attacked by a hostile mob. On 10 October he was furiously reviled in a public meeting by the tribune Memmius.[77] On the next day Cato as praetor presided over a *diuinatio* between Memmius on the one side and Nero and his supporters, two young Antonii, Gaius and Lucius, on the other, to decide who should have the right to bring the *repetundae* charge.[78] Presumably Lentulus had dropped out, perhaps under pressure to allow others a chance. At this point Cicero thought that Gabinius was doomed, unless Pompeius managed to carry the day in defiance of the will of gods and men. Meanwhile Gabinius had at last steeled himself to enter the senate.[79] The house was almost empty, but when he tried to slip out the consuls kept him back and brought in the representatives of the *publicani*. Cicero too attacked with a will, stinging Gabinius into calling him an exile.

At this outrage Gabinius was almost lynched by a host of angry senators and *publicani*. Ap. Claudius too inveighed against him on the theme of *maiestas*.[80] Nevertheless Cicero had decided to deny himself the pleasure of appearing for the prosecution, for he did not trust the jurors and was unwilling to provoke an open clash with Pompeius, since there was already friction between them over the behaviour of Milo.

Shortly before he was due to stand trial for *maiestas* Gabinius was charged again, this time with *ambitus*, by P. Sulla, with the support of his stepson Memmius, his cousin L. Caecilius Rufus, and his son.[81] On 21 October, two days before the *maiestas* hearing, Cicero felt that the outcome was still in doubt.[82] All classes in the state hated Gabinius, the prosecution witnesses were highly damaging, the president, Alfius, was reliable, but the prosecutors were lacking in fire, the jury mixed, and Pompeius was working hard to win their favour. These doubts were to prove well founded: on 23 October Gabinius was acquitted.[83] Cicero suggested various reasons – he had had to put up with some criticism for failing to prosecute.[84] Lentulus and his fellow prosecutors had put up a pitiful performance, the jury had proved totally corrupt, Pompeius had done his work well, and, perhaps most significantly, men feared that if he did not have his way over Gabinius he might be moved to work towards a dictatorship.[85] Cicero singles out for comment the behaviour of two of the jurors, Calvinus and Cato.[86] Calvinus voted for acquittal very ostentatiously; Cato was the first to report the result to Pompeius as soon as the votes were counted. Calvinus' attitude is interesting; no doubt he hoped to secure Pompeius' support for his consular campaign now that Pompeius had lost interest in Scaurus. That Cato wished to bring good news is hardly likely; the tone in which he made his announcement was more probably one of anger and disgust. Cicero's defence of his own conduct (he had served as a prosecution witness, but had borne himself with great moderation) underlines the importance that Pompeius attached to Gabinius' acquittal.[87] He felt that, if he had appeared for the prosecution, Pompeius would have come into the city to defend Gabinius, broken off their friendship, and become reconciled with Clodius. As he bitterly remarked, Pompeius had not tolerated dissent on his part in 59 and 58, when he was stronger and under no obligation, so how could he hope to resist now that he was weak and Pompeius supremely strong?

Nevertheless Cicero was confident that Gabinius would be condemned on the other charges, especially that of *repetundae*. At first, despite Pompeius' urging, he still rejected the idea of defending Gabinius as the road to eternal disgrace.[88] But although Cicero, eager to justify himself, might claim that he was all-powerful,[89] Pompeius knew otherwise, and he viewed the impending *repetundae* trial with grave alarm. He now brought such pressure to bear on Cicero that the orator was compelled to yield and defend his old enemy.[90] Envoys from Alexandria appeared at the trial, but they spoke in Gabinius' favour; the prosecutor claimed that they too had succumbed to Pompeius' influence.[91] But whether or not Cicero exerted himself and in spite of Pompeius' testimony, this time the *publicani* were not to be denied. Gabinius was condemned and went into exile.[92]

By this time there had come a vital blow to the renewed alliance between Pompeius and Caesar and to the stability of the coalition as a whole.[93] Pompeius' wife Julia died in childbirth.[94] There can be no doubt that Pompeius had been devoted to her and that she had constituted a powerful bond between her father and her husband.[95] Her death did not of course immediately dissolve the ties between Pompeius and Caesar: no change, however slight, can be discerned in Pompeius' attitude towards Caesar as a direct consequence of his bereavement.[96] Nevertheless, it opened up an opportunity for him to alter the balance of power, should he wish, by a new marriage that might lead him away from Caesar and towards the optimates. But for the moment he showed no inclination to investigate this possibility, while Caesar will have hoped that the bond between them might, when a decent interval had elapsed, be renewed in another form.

All the candidates for the consulship were now awaiting prosecution: Calvinus by his fellow-candidate Memmius, Memmius himself by Q. Acutius, Messalla by Q. Pompeius Rufus, and Scaurus once again by Triarius.[97] The matter aroused much interest, for, as Cicero wrote to his brother, either distinguished men must fall or the rule of law must perish.[98] Attempts were being made to delay the trials, and there now seemed little hope of the elections taking place before the end of the year. The consuls were eager to hold them, but the candidates worked for delay, especially Memmius, who still put his hopes (vainly in Cicero's judgement) in the arrival of Caesar in his winter quarters. The likeliest pair to succeed now seemed to be Calvinus and Messalla, a result unlikely to give Pompeius much pleasure. By late November there had been little change.[99] Cicero still felt that Messalla and Calvinus were certain to be elected and that Memmius, still vainly hoping for Caesar's return, and Scaurus, abandoned by Pompeius, had no chance.[100] Rumours of impending dictatorship grew stronger, strong enough for Pompeius to deny publicly that his ambitions ran in that direction, but as Cicero remarked, earlier he had not said that he would refuse.[101] As ever Cicero found it difficult to say what Pompeius wanted, but, as he observed, as long as the case for dictatorship was loudly argued by his absurdly self-opinionated cousin C. Lucilius Hirrus, it would be impossible for Pompeius to convince anyone that he did not want to be dictator.[102] The prospect alarmed not only the *boni* but above all Milo, to whom Pompeius' hostility was constantly increasing.[103] Pompeius characteristically withdrew from the scene to await developments, but it was clear that the time was not yet ripe: though Hirrus was ready to bring in a bill, there were various opponents prepared to veto it, the *principes* were hostile, and the people showed no interest.[104]

So the year 53 began without consuls, and eventually Pompeius, as proconsul, was called upon by the senate to assist with the holding of elections.[105] He complied, though there was still no hint that he might find the dictatorship offered to him to put a stop to the growing anarchy. Messalla and Calvinus at last secured their consulships with the year already half over.[106] Then from the East came devastating news: the death of Crassus in the disastrous defeat by the Parthians at Carrhae.[107] The blow to Rome's military pride was shattering. On the practical level the threat to the Eastern provinces was far less than was feared in the initial panic, as the Parthians showed no inclination to follow up their success with any vigour. But for the political situation at Rome Crassus' death was heavy with consequences. It is easy in the light of hindsight to say that from this moment on the eventual confrontation between Pompeius and Caesar was inevitable. That is perhaps too facile: if Caesar's enemies among the optimates had been less relentless, if Caesar had been less obsessed with his own *dignitas*, if Pompeius had been prepared to share his position of distinction in the state, the ultimate evil of civil war at least might have been avoided.[108] But the danger of a split between Caesar and Pompeius was certainly increased by the elimination of Crassus, and such a split was more likely to be disastrous in its results than it would have been before.

Caesar certainly had everything to gain by remaining on good terms with his erstwhile son-in-law, and he now proposed that Pompeius should marry his great-niece Octavia, who was at present the wife of C. Claudius Marcellus, soon to be consul in 50, while he himself would divorce Calpurnia and marry Pompeius' daughter, who was married to Faustus Sulla.[109] Pompeius, however, refused, though for the moment he took no alternative action: it was only after he had been elected to the consulship in 52 that he married Cornelia, daughter of the noblest man in Rome, Q. Caecilius Metellus Pius Scipio Nasica, born a Scipio and adopted by Metellus Pius.[110] His response has normally been seen as a move away from Caesar and a step towards reconciliation with the optimates. This interpretation has recently been challenged in favour of the suggestion that Pompeius wished to maintain his bond with Caesar, but disagreed with Caesar as to how this might best be achieved.[111] Whereas Caesar had wished simply to bind Pompeius to him, Pompeius on this view will have seen Caesar's proposals as a waste of their dynastic resources and recommended instead a marriage for himself on the same pattern as Caesar's own union with Calpurnia in 59. The thesis is not without its attractions: it is possible that Caesar's greater sense of insecurity would have led him to calculate their mutual interest in a manner very different from Pompeius. But the readiness of the optimates early in 52, even before the marriage with Cornelia, to make greater concessions than ever before to Pompeius suggests that they at least saw his refusal of Caesar's offer as a step in their direction, and it is likely that Caesar felt the same. That Metellus Scipio was on doubtful terms with Cato is true, but of little importance: even opposition to Caesar was not enough to turn the optimates into a monolithic bloc, and in any event Pompeius still had a long road to travel before he would need to make a choice between Caesar and the optimates. His position had shifted somewhat, but he was still firmly placed between Caesar on the one hand and the *boni* on the other.

12

THE THIRD CONSULSHIP AND THE APPROACH OF CIVIL WAR

The events of December 53 and January 52 played into Pompeius' hands.[1] The elections for the consulship of 52 had been delayed, and the campaign was again marked by bribery and violence on a large scale.[2] All the candidates were of interest to Pompeius in one way or another: his former legate P. Plautius Hypsaeus and Metellus Scipio were standing, in opposition to Milo.[3] To make matters more complex, Clodius was standing for the praetorship, and his hatred of Milo made him lend his support to Hypsaeus and Metellus. The turn of the year came with no consuls or praetors yet elected. This state of affairs displeased Milo, but was agreeable to Metellus and Hypsaeus, and at this point Pompeius demonstrated his favour to them by joining the tribune T. Munatius Plancus in blocking moves to hasten the appointment of an *interrex*.[4]

Then on 18 January Clodius and Milo clashed on the Appian Way near Bovillae;[5] Clodius was wounded and carried to a nearby tavern, where he was attacked and killed on Milo's orders.[6] When the body was brought to Rome, Clodius' widow Fulvia played her part in stirring up the mob and was joined next day by the tribunes Plancus and Q. Pompeius Rufus. Pompeius himself addressed the meeting, attacking Milo, but if Asconius is to be believed, his only interest in the affair was still to exploit it in support of Hypsaeus and Scipio.[7] The people carried Clodius' body into the senate house and cremated it on an impromptu funeral pyre; the blaze destroyed the *curia* and raids were also made on the houses of Milo and M. Aemilius Lepidus the *interrex*. *Fasces* were carried to the homes of Hypsaeus and Scipio, then to the gardens of Pompeius, while the crowd demanded that he should be appointed either consul or dictator.[8] Later on the same afternoon the senate met, and the *senatus consultum ultimum* was passed, in a form which by its abnormal wording underlined the seriousness of the situation: that the *interrex*, the tribunes and Cn. Pompeius, who was in the vicinity of the city with proconsular *imperium*, should see to it that the state came to no harm.[9] The subsequent decree that Pompeius should levy troops throughout Italy highlights the fact that of those authorities appealed to in the *senatus consultum ultimum* he was the only one with the necessary power to take steps to restore order.[10]

Outrage at the destruction of the senate house caused a swing in public opinion in Milo's favour, and he abandoned the idea of going into voluntary exile. He did not lack for champions: both Caelius and Cicero sprang to his defence and claimed, with no plausibility, that Clodius had laid an ambush for him.[11] Meanwhile *interrex* followed *interrex*, and still no elections were held. While Pompeius gathered forces, the legal battles began.[12] Clodius' nephews, the sons of his brother Gaius, were joined by L. Herennius Balbus in attacking Milo, who had the support of Cicero, Hortensius and Cato, while Caelius led a counter-attack against Hypsaeus and Pompeius Rufus. Pompeius' attitude, however, gave Milo great cause for alarm. Three hostile tribunes, Plancus, Rufus, and the future historian C. Sallustius Crispus, had asked him at a public meeting if it was true that he had heard that Milo was plotting to kill him, and Pompeius had replied that he had.[13] Whether he believed the rumour is unclear, but on 22 January he refused to grant Milo an interview.[14] So Milo sent a message, volunteering to withdraw his candidature if Pompeius so desired.[15]

But by now Pompeius had realized that the situation could be exploited for his own benefit as well as that of Scipio and Hypsaeus, and concern, real or feigned, for his own security encouraged him to think of destroying Milo. First he mounted his constitutional high horse, proclaiming that it was not for him to deprive the Roman people of its freedom of choice by decreeing who should stand and who should not. A second message, carried by his cousin Hirrus, urged Milo not to threaten his reputation by trying to drag him into the affair.[16] A month after Clodius' death Metellus Scipio made a speech in the senate which was taken as giving a further indication of Pompeius' own views on the matter. In an altercation with M. Brutus, Scipio complained about the death of Clodius and exploded Milo's claim to have acted in self-defence.[17]

More and more voices were now raised to the effect that the only solution for the troubles of the state was to make Pompeius dictator.[18] The optimates, however, devised a compromise plan. When the subject was raised in the senate; Bibulus, supported by Cato, proposed a strange contradiction in terms: Pompeius should be appointed consul without a colleague.[19] He was duly proclaimed by the *interrex* Ser. Sulpicius Rufus on 24 Interc. and took office at once.[20] It must have been pleasant for him to see Cato and Bibulus humble themselves in this way. Nevertheless, the significance of the appointment must not be exaggerated.[21] It acknowledged that only Pompeius could deal with the present emergency, but it was conceived of by all concerned as only an emergency measure, just as much as a dictatorship would have been if that alternative had been chosen, and it will certainly have been taken for granted that as soon as the crisis abated Pompeius would arrange for the election of a colleague. The choice of the paradoxical sole consulship rather than the dictatorship was not without point. It avoided the evil memory of Sulla and served to remind Pompeius, if that were necessary, that he was not Sulla and was not meant to be, while in practical terms his powers even without a colleague were less than they would have been as dictator in two important respects: he would be liable to tribunician veto and he could be called to account for his actions.[22] Moreover, the consulship gave Pompeius more time to solve the immediate problems and also facilitated the eventual transition back to administrative normality. Unless he had been granted a dictatorship with no time limit, as Sulla had been, he would as dictator have had to resign at the end of six months, presumably after arranging for two consuls to hold office for the remainder of the year. One of these of course might have been himself, but it was preferable on every count for the dictatorship to be avoided and for Pompeius to take the consulship from the first.

Once in power, he acted swiftly.[23] Three days after entering office he brought two proposals before the senate, which were then duly promulgated as laws. The first was *de ui* and dealt specifically with recent events: the brawl on the Appian Way, the burning of the senate house, and the attack on Lepidus' house. The second dealt with *ambitus* and was retrospective to 70, which alarmed the friends of Caesar. In both cases harsher penalties and a quicker procedure were provided for than under the existing legislation. Hortensius tried to move that the proceedings *de ui* should take place *extra ordinem*, but in the normal standing court, but Fufius Calenus demanded that the motion be divided, and Plancus and Sallustius then vetoed the second clause.[24] The threat to Milo was plain, and Caelius, the most outspoken of his supporters, reacted vigorously, claiming that he was being persecuted and trying to obstruct the passage of the laws. Pompeius was forced to show his hand, declaring that if he were compelled to do so he would defend the state by force of arms.[25] The reasons for his hostility to Milo were probably complex. He gave every impression of being afraid that Milo was plotting against his life: he did not live at home, but remained in his gardens, surrounded by a strong bodyguard of troops, and on one occasion he suddenly dismissed the senate because Milo's arrival was expected.[26] The evidence for his fear of assassination is too strong to allow the dismissal of this conduct as sheer hypocrisy, but he had surely decided that the time had come to get rid of Milo. While Clodius had been alive and hostile, Milo had been useful as a counter, but by killing Clodius he had, as far as Pompeius was concerned, destroyed the only justification for his own existence. He was now nothing but a rival to those candidates for office whom Pompeius preferred to support, a liability and a potential threat to Pompeius himself. Now that the affair of Bovillae had given Pompeius the chance to remove him, he used it ruthlessly. Meanwhile, the war of words continued, with Plancus, Rufus and Sallustius on the one side, Caelius, Cato and Cicero on the other.[27] Most energetic of all was Plancus, who threatened to prosecute Cicero and kept up the refrain that Milo was plotting against Pompeius. Pompeius was impressed, or claimed to be so, and increased his bodyguard.[28]

The presidency of the court to be set up under the *lex de ui* was the object of a further law: the president was to be elected by the people from among the consulars.[29] Pompeius' old enemy Domitius Ahenobarbus was elected, but according to Cicero Pompeius approved. The jurors, hand-picked by Pompeius, were said to be men of surpassing distinction and honesty. Three charges were then brought against Milo, *de ui, de ambitu,* and *de sodaliciis*; it was expected that the charge of *uis* would come up first and be successful, so that Milo could then be condemned in absence on the other two counts.[30] When the preliminaries were over, the trial began.[31] On the first day supporters of Clodius created sufficient disturbance to alarm Pompeius, who was by the treasury, and he promised Domitius that next day he would appear in person with a detachment of troops to ensure order. This secured quiet for the next two days of testimony, though at the end of the third day Plancus did his best to stir up the crowd, which had been moved by the testimony of Fulvia. It was clear that there might be trouble on the next and final day, 7 April, but Pompeius took careful precautions.[32] *Tabernae* were closed throughout the city, and troops were placed in the forum and at all the approaches to it. He himself took up his position in front of the treasury, as on the previous day, with a heavy guard. But not even fear of the surrounding troops could keep the friends of Clodius quiet when Cicero rose to speak for the defence.[33] Their threats, and more important perhaps the knowledge that, despite his protestations to the contrary, the troops were there primarily to make sure that Milo was condemned,[34] robbed Cicero of his customary eloquence and he gave a poor performance: the *Miloniana* as we have it is the speech that he would have delivered in normal circumstances.[35]

Milo was duly condemned and retired into exile at Massilia.[36] The significance of Pompeius' attitude is shown by the outcome of the trials that followed. Milo's henchman M. Saufeius, who had led the attack on the inn at Bovillae, was prosecuted twice, first under the *lex Pompeia*, then under the *lex Plautia*; he was defended by Cicero and Caelius and was acquitted on both occasions. On the other hand, Sex. Cloelius, the notorious associate of Clodius, was condemned by an overwhelming majority, and many other adherents of Clodius suffered a similar fate.[37] It is clear that, where Pompeius did not intervene to influence the result, opinion was favourable to Milo and his supporters, hostile to Clodius and his. Indeed, Pompeius soon found his own friends under vigorous attack in the courts. He had by now married Cornelia, the daughter of Metellus Scipio, but both Scipio and Hypsaeus were arraigned for *ambitus*. Pompeius chose to be cynically inconsistent. Metellus could be of great value to him, so he rescued him by choosing him as his colleague in the consulship for the remaining five months of the year.[38] Whether he previously went so far as to summon the jury to his house and harangue it on Metellus' behalf, so that the prosecutor bowed to the inevitable and dropped the charge, is uncertain.[39] But Hypsaeus was relatively unimportant, and so could be sacrificed, while Pompeius' decision to share his consulship with Scipio would mean that Hypsaeus might feel that he had a grievance and so would become a liability. So Pompeius greeted his appeal for help with icy contempt, and he was condemned.[40]

The disturbances of recent months were not the only subject on which Pompeius was to legislate. Provincial government and the appointment of provincial governors also attracted his attention, and this was a matter of vital importance for his present and future relations with Caesar. By now Caesar was beginning to think of a second consulship when the Gallic war was over. From his point of view the essential problem can be succinctly stated. If he returned from Gaul and stood for the consulship in the normal way, even if his command were prolonged until the summer in which he could legitimately stand for the consulship of the following year, namely the summer of 49, he would be liable to prosecution by his enemies in the interval between his surrender of his *imperium* and his entry into office. It was therefore necessary for him to devise some means whereby no such interval ensued and he could instead proceed directly from proconsulship to consulship. To achieve this he needed to retain his *imperium* – though not necessarily his provinces or his army – until such time as he could enter Rome and assume the consulship as he crossed the *pomoerium*. The first requisite for this was a dispensation to stand for the consulship in absence.

That Caesar's thoughts were running in this direction was made clear early in 52. All ten tribunes of the year combined to produce a proposal that Caesar should return to Rome as Pompeius' colleague for the remainder of the year. But he had not yet finished his work in Gaul and preferred to have greater manoeuvrability. So he persuaded them instead to bring in a bill permitting him to stand for the consulship in absence when the period of his command was approaching its end.[41]

They did so, and despite the violent opposition of Cato the bill became law. It had the support of Pompeius, who was certainly not prepared at this stage to abandon Caesar.[42] But his own measures on the provinces were less favourable to Caesar in their implications. Two laws are relevant. The first was designed to reinforce a decree of the senate passed in the previous year.[43] By its terms, instead of the system hitherto in force, whereby a magistrate proceeded, if he chose, to the governorship of a province immediately after his year of office in Rome, an interval of five years was to elapse between the tenure of an urban magistracy and any subsequent provincial command. It would be absurd to suggest that this measure was conceived as a devious means of undermining Caesar's position. The motive publicly proclaimed was the desire to cut down bribery and make urban office less tempting as a passport to extortion abroad, and there is no reason to doubt the truth of this. Nevertheless, the law did work to Caesar's disadvantage. To carry things over during the transitional period and remedy the already desperate shortage of provincial governors, all men of consular and praetorian rank who had never governed a province were constrained in order of seniority to do so now. Under the old system devised by C. Gracchus one of Caesar's provinces would have had to be declared consular before the elections took place in the summer of a given year. The consul who received it would then hold office for a year before going out to Gaul. Thus if the elections took place at the proper time, even if his successor left Rome before the end of his year in office, as was not unlikely in the circumstances, Caesar would have had something approaching eighteen months warning of his impending supersession, during which time he could wind up affairs in the province – or prepare for civil war if he felt so inclined. But under Pompeius' new system of appointing governors no such warning need be given. A successor nominated under the new law could set off for Gaul as soon as his bags were packed. This implication may not have been intended. But Caesar's supporters found it difficult to acquit Pompeius of double dealing when he brought in another law, requiring that all candidates for magistracies should hand in their nominations in person.[44] The inconsistency with the law of the ten tribunes was glaring, and Caesar's friends were not slow to point it out. Pompeius' response was striking. He insisted that he had not meant to deprive Caesar of his personal privilege, and after the law had been passed and engraved he caused a codicil to be added to it, declaring Caesar exempt from its provisions.[45] Technically of course this rider had no legal force, for it had been authorized by neither senate nor people, and Caesar's enemies were soon to show that in their estimation it was no more than a meaningless graffito.[46] Pompeius cannot have been unaware of this, and it is necessary to enquire whether any rational stance can be discerned beneath the apparent inconsistencies of his behaviour at this time.

It seems most likely that by these manoeuvres he wanted to demonstrate his superior power and his freedom to act as he pleased to both Caesar and the optimates. His support of the law of the ten tribunes and his addition of the rider to the law on personal candidature were to Caesar a conditional promise of continued backing, but at the same time a clear warning that his present position and indeed his political existence depended on Pompeius' good will. To the optimates they were an indication that for the moment they could not expect him to abandon Caesar, but must acknowledge his *auctoritas* as the supreme force in the state. Thus Pompeius reckoned to assert his dominance over both parties. Both would be compelled to look to him, Caesar for protection both now and on his return, the optimates for the preservation of order and perhaps the eventual removal of Caesar, should Pompeius ever commit himself wholly to their side. As long as he could maintain this position, Pompeius could rest content. The *res publica* now relied on him for its survival, in peace as it had done in war, and provided that the fact was admitted he was quite prepared to act effectively to preserve it. He had no wish to see the constitution overthrown; it must rather be stretched by common consent almost, but not quite, to breaking-point to accommodate his own unique pre-eminence. In 52 he came close to this ideal, but his supremacy was of its very nature unstable. It depended on his holding the balance between Caesar and the optimates, but neither of the victims of his machinations could be happy with the situation as it was, and events were not likely to stand still.

As in his previous consulships, Pompeius took steps to commemorate his own achievements: a temple was dedicated to Victoria.[47] He also provided for his own future less ambiguously than he had done for Caesar's: his tenure of the Spanish provinces was renewed for a further five years.[48] When the tribunes of 52 who had harried Milo were attacked in the courts as soon as they were out of office, his attitude was again inconsistent. He made no move to protect Pompeius Rufus, but was eager to save Plancus if he could. Despite the clause in his own law abolishing the use of character witnesses, he sent a letter extolling Plancus to be read in court. Cato, who was one of the jurors, sat with his hands ostentatiously over his ears and was removed for his pains, but the vote was still for condemnation.[49]

Nothing that Pompeius had done in 52 was calculated to deter Caesar's enemies from their efforts to remove him from Gaul. M. Claudius Marcellus, consul in 51, began his attempt early in the year, calling down upon himself the wrath of Caesar's secretary Hirtius.[50] Hirtius describes Marcellus' initiative as illegal and premature. This is of course a Caesarian view, but it is also the simple truth. On no possible interpretation of the *lex Licinia Pompeia* could Caesar's second term in Gaul be regarded as expired even at the end of 51, still less at the time when Marcellus began his campaign. Marcellus himself must have realized this, as his grounds for bringing forward his proposal show. He claimed that the Gallic war was over and that Caesar's army should therefore be disbanded.[51] The argument has the air of a conscious counter to the objection, implied or expressed by Caesarian supporters, that the motion was premature. Marcellus might well have suggested in reply that there was no need for Caesar to use up his full time in Gaul, since there was nothing left for him to do there. Another point made by Marcellus also has the appearance of an answer to a Caesarian objection: he asserted that in his view the *absentis ratio* was to be rejected because the law of Pompeius had annulled the law of the ten tribunes.[52] Again it seems likely that Caesar's friends had pointed out that the proposal would deprive Caesar of the privilege guaranteed him by the tribunician law and that Marcellus was attempting to answer them. If he mentioned Pompeius' codicil exempting Caesar from the law, he no doubt did so only to deny that it had any legal force.

Marcellus was opposed not only by a number of tribunes but also by his colleague, the jurist Ser. Sulpicius Rufus.[53] Nor could Pompeius let such a proposal go unanswered: he can have had no hesitation in objecting to it. It disregarded the law he and Crassus had passed in 55 and the law of the ten tribunes, to which he had given his backing, and it flouted his *auctoritas* by ignoring his codicil. His own *dignitas*, more than loyalty to Caesar, dictated the only possible response. On 1 March in the senate he declared his opposition to Marcellus,[54] obviously with sufficient force to cool the consul's ardour, for the letters of Caelius to Cicero in Cilicia reveal that the matter was first put off till 1 June and then allowed to fade out.[55] It was perhaps frustration at this lack of success that moved Marcellus to challenge Caesar over the status of the Transpadani, whom Caesar wanted to treat as Roman citizens. In dramatic proof of his disagreement, the consul had a senator of Caesar's colony at Novum Comum flogged.[56]

By the middle of summer the optimates had been encouraged by the election to the tribunate for 50 of the young Curio, who was expected to be hostile to Caesar.[57] On 22 July Pompeius was asked in the senate to withdraw from Caesar a legion that he had loaned him in 55.[58] Pompeius agreed to do so, but refused to comply immediately, nor did he say when he would, despite complaints. He was then asked about Caesar's provinces. A debate was impossible at that moment, since Pompeius was on the point of leaving for Ariminum, but the senate decreed that he should return to the city as soon as possible so that the question could be discussed in his presence. So far he had committed himself to nothing more precise than the vague assertion that everyone should obey the senate. Caelius expected that the matter would come up on 13 August, but that no striking development would ensue: either some compromise would be made, perhaps arranged by Pompeius on his trip to Ariminum, or any more drastic proposal would be blocked by tribunician veto. Early in August he was predicting, no doubt to Cicero's disgust, that two years might be taken up in technical skirmishing of this nature.[59]

It is interesting that early in July Cicero heard from Varro that Pompeius was determined to go to Spain.[60] It is hard to believe that he was seriously contemplating such a move at this time. Perhaps he was eager to remind the optimates that his presence in Italy was vital to them and so to elicit protests and demonstrations of support. If so, his tactics certainly produced the desired effect on Cicero at least, who rushed off to persuade Theophanes that Pompeius should do nothing of the kind.[61]

The discussion planned for 13 August was postponed until 1 September.[62] Caelius' impression of that debate was that nothing would be accomplished till the following year. However, Pompeius did make his position rather clearer. He himself declared that no decree of the senate should be passed at the present time, but his father-in-law Metellus Scipio brought in a motion that the Gallic provinces should be discussed, with nothing else on the agenda, on 1 March 50.[63] This proposal alarmed Caesar's friend Cornelius Balbus, who protested to Metellus, and Caelius was led to believe that Pompeius was unwilling to see Caesar use the *absentis ratio* while he was still in control of his provinces and his army.[64] It certainly appears that in spring 50 Pompeius would be prepared to countenance discussion that might lead to Caesar's replacement, whereas in autumn 51 he was not. Recall in 50 would have allowed Caesar five years in Gaul under the *lex Licinia Pompeia* provided that 55 itself was counted as one of the five years. Pompeius could therefore claim to have been fair to Caesar, though certainly not generous. Recall in 51 on the other hand could in no way be passed off as just. If Caesar was replaced in the spring of 50, he would have no opportunity to use the *absentis ratio* in that year while retaining his provinces and army, though he could of course wait outside the city, keeping his *imperium*, until the consular elections and then try to exercise his privilege. This would put him in a very weak position, with little hope of attaining his objective unless Pompeius saw fit to exert his *auctoritas* on his behalf. So, if this plan had succeeded, Caesar would not have been destroyed, for Pompeius was well aware that the *boni* endured his own pre-eminence only through fear of Caesar and that if that fear was allayed they would soon begin to think that he too could be dispensed with. But he would have been rendered totally dependent on Pompeius for his political survival, and that was precisely what Pompeius was hoping to achieve. Those ancient writers who claim that he could tolerate no equal had grasped an important truth,[65] and Pompeius' intrigues at the end of the fifties were designed to ensure, without resort to civil war, that Caesar did not become his equal.

At a further meeting of the senate on 29 September he made his views quite clear: it would be legitimate to replace Caesar at any time after 1 March 50.[66] A decree of the senate was consequently passed on the motion of the consul M. Marcellus, that the consuls of 50, L. Aemilius Paullus and C. Claudius Marcellus, should raise the question of the consular provinces in the senate as the first and only item on the agenda on 1 March 50.[67] It could of course be predicted that, whatever was decided on that day, a tribune would come forward to veto. The senate attempted to guard against this by passing a supplementary decree that anyone who tried to obstruct proceedings should be deemed to be acting against the interests of the state. But inevitably this decree was itself vetoed by four Caesarian tribunes.[68] So too were a further decree providing for the demobilization of those of Caesar's troops whose term of service had expired and a decree to make all other provinces praetorian, so that the Gallic provinces would inevitably fall to the consuls.[69] It is hardly surprising that in this farcical situation men were chiefly concerned about the attitude of Pompeius, which seemed to be of more practical importance than decrees.[70] He declared yet again that he could not in justice come to any decision about Caesar's provinces before 1 March 50, but that after that date he would have no hesitation. He was therefore naturally asked what his reaction would be if any decree passed on 1 March 50 were vetoed. His reply was equally unambiguous: for Caesar to arrange for a tribune to frustrate the senate in this way would be tantamount to a direct refusal on his part to obey the decree if it were passed. The next question was about the *absentis ratio.* What would Pompeius do if Caesar wanted to exercise it while still retaining his army? 'What', said Pompeius very gently, 'would I do if my son wanted to take a stick to me?' This reply puts his position in a nutshell. He saw himself as a father, Caesar as his son. In that there was a message, for the optimates and for Caesar. The optimates could rest assured that Pompeius would act to keep Caesar in his place, subordinate as a son should be to his father, but they were also being warned that he was still not prepared to abandon Caesar, that a bond still existed between them as close as that between a father and his son. Similarly Caesar could read in the words a promise that Pompeius would not forsake him but protect him as a man should his son, but only if he accepted that he owed obedience to Pompeius as to a father.

Thus men were perhaps right to suspect, as Caelius says they did, that Pompeius had done a deal with Caesar, but it is doubtful whether the terms were as favourable to Caesar as he suggests. He believed that Caesar would be prepared either to postpone his use of the *absentis ratio* until 49 provided he could retain his command, or to give up his command provided that he could secure election to the consulship first.[71] Caesar might indeed have been satisfied with either of these alternatives, but it is hard to see how Pompeius could have been, and neither appears compatible with his clear implication that he could not allow Caesar to use the *absentis ratio* while he remained in command of his army. If there was a deal, it can only have been that Pompeius would defend Caesar's right to stand in absence and so escape prosecution, on condition that Caesar first gave up his province and army. If Caesar accepted, it will have been because Pompeius offered him that or nothing, and it is not surprising that, as events were to show, he felt free to work for something better.

The idea that Pompeius might go to Spain, which he had first mooted in July, is mentioned again in October, when Cicero heard from Ap. Claudius that his departure was imminent.[72] But more is said at about this time of another possibility, that Pompeius might be sent to defend Syria against the threat of a major Parthian invasion. In September Cicero felt that the senate would not take the risk of employing Pompeius abroad when the situation at home was so unsettled.[73] Early in October the danger seemed to have receded.[74] But in mid-November Caelius not only raises once again the question of sending Pompeius to the East but also alludes for the first time to the alternative scheme of sending Caesar.[75] The theme continued to exercise Cicero during the winter and spring of 50.[76] In the East men still believed that Pompeius would come to mount a Parthian war, and he appears to have encouraged Cicero in this belief.[77]

Early in the year he had been distracted by the prosecution of his son's father-in-law, Ap. Claudius, on whose behalf he expended considerable effort.[78] February had also brought a great shock: Curio, who had been expected to be a bulwark of the opposition to Caesar, changed sides.[79] His motives have been much discussed, and no certain conclusion is possible.[80] Nevertheless the consul C. Marcellus duly raised the question of the Gallic provinces on 1 March, as he had been instructed to do.[81] However, he received no support from his colleague Paullus, whose ambitious building schemes were being furthered by subventions from Caesar,[82] and a new tactic was introduced by Curio, who now brought forward for the first time his often repeated proposal that both Caesar and Pompeius should give up their extraordinary commands.[83] This move was in the short term a master stroke, but it perhaps did more than any other factor to bring about the confrontation between Pompeius and Caesar that led eventually to war.[84] It was calculated both to win sympathy for Caesar and to undermine Pompeius' superior position. Pompeius had tried to make himself the arbiter of Caesar's destiny, ready to protect him from his enemies in the senate but not prepared to condone contumacy. By treating the Gallic and Spanish commands as equal Curio toppled Pompeius from this perch, and by suggesting that Caesar would be happy to resign if Pompeius would only do the same he implied that it was not Caesar who was the source of tension in the state while Pompeius was the voice of moderation, but that it was rather Pompeius whose desire to stand alone on the pinnacle of power had created the strained situation, while Caesar was the reasonable man eager to put matters right by a fair compromise.

Pompeius was taken aback. In the senate he produced a counter proposal, that Caesar should leave on 13 November.[85] The choice of date has caused many problems, perhaps more than it should, for it may have been picked at random. Whether it was the anniversary of the date on which Crassus set out for Parthia in 55 is uncertain.[86] It is more important to examine the practical consequences if the proposal were put into effect. Curio regarded it as quite intolerable, and Caelius agreed that it constituted an attack on Caesar, though Pompeius tried to claim that he was being fair and that Curio was simply out to stir up trouble. In Caelius' view Pompeius was still afraid that Caesar might secure the consulship before he had given up his provinces and his army.[87] If this were correct, Pompeius' position would not have changed in that respect since the previous summer, but his proposal does not bear out the claim. It would allow Caesar to use the *absentis ratio* for 49 while still in command of his troops, leaving him only six weeks to while away outside the city before entering on his consulship.

Thus although Caesar would have owed his survival to Pompeius' good offices, Pompeius had made a considerable concession and may well have felt sincerely that he was being more than fair to Caesar. But by now the issue had changed and sharpened. Pompeius' claim that he was being fair, if not generous, took for granted his own predominance in the state and in particular his predominance over Caesar. But Curio's response strongly suggests that Caesar had decided no longer to accept Pompeius' superiority, that just as Pompeius was not ready to acknowledge an equal, Caesar was not prepared to tolerate a superior or owe his political survival to Pompeius' charity. By summer of 50 Caesar and Curio had brought civil war much closer. Caelius was well aware that the tension had increased. He predicted that, if an all-out attack on Curio were mounted, Caesar would fight to defend the tribune's veto, while if the optimates got cold feet Caesar would simply stay where he was for as long as he liked. Pompeius could not endure the latter alternative, and to that extent he too can be blamed for hastening the approach of war. But it was Caesar and Curio who had created the situation in which Pompeius was being forced towards a choice he had no wish to make.

M. Marcellus was prepared to negotiate with the tribunes, but the senate would have none of it.[88] Pompeius was uncertain what to do next, for the initiative had been taken out of his hands. His position was made more difficult when Curio followed up his earlier successes by repeating his proposal that both Pompeius and Caesar should give up their commands, innocently claiming that his only objective was to preserve the balance of power between the two and reduce tension in the state.[89] Already it was beginning to seem that the only hope of internal peace for the Roman world was ironically a Parthian war, which might divert the energies of one of the dynasts.[90] In the summer it was decreed that both Pompeius and Caesar should sacrifice one legion to be sent to the East.[91] Pompeius, however, played a trick on Caesar, choosing this moment to ask for the return of the legion he had loaned him, so that in practice Caesar lost two legions and Pompeius none.[92] To underline the deceit, the men were never shipped to the East, but were retained in southern Italy to await developments.

Then came an event which was to have momentous consequences. Pompeius suffered from some recurring fever.[93] Of the precise nature and history of the disease nothing is known, though it may have been malaria contracted in the East. In the summer of 50 he suffered a bad attack, so bad that his life was thought to be in danger. Public response was remarkable. All over Italy prayers were said and vows undertaken to promote his recovery, and when his health was restored rejoicing knew no bounds.[94] There can be no doubt that these demonstrations encouraged Pompeius to face the thought of civil war with equanimity. Though he was not prepared to let Caesar, through Curio, destroy the pre-eminence in the state that meant so much to him, he must have had doubts about the kind of response he could evoke from the people of Italy if Caesar invaded with his highly trained army of veterans. The displays of loyalty and affection which attended his recovery gave him fresh confidence, confidence that was to be proved unfounded. Pompeius made an error which only his vanity can explain: he allowed himself to believe that all those men who had flocked to celebrate his return to health would come forward with equal enthusiasm if he called upon them to fight. His confidence was also boosted by the reports of the officers who had brought the two legions from Gaul: they assured him that morale in Caesar's army was so low that the troops were on the verge of mutiny.[95] It was now that he uttered his famous boast that, wherever he stamped his foot in Italy, companies of foot and horse would spring up from the earth.[96] During his illness he had written to the senate offering to resign his command, an offer which he repeated on his return to Rome. On the latter occasion he promised that his friend Caesar would of course do the same. This ploy was clearly intended to cut the ground from under Curio's feet, but Curio was equal to the challenge. He insisted that Pompeius must make the first move, delivered a scathing attack on his ambition, and crowned his performance by proposing that both men should be declared public enemies if they did not give up their commands.[97]

In August Caelius expressed his conviction that unless the clash could be averted by sending one or other of the dynasts off to fight the Parthians, war was inevitable.[98] Both men in his estimation were prepared for it in both spirit and material resources. The point at issue, as he saw it, was that Pompeius had decided not to allow Caesar to become consul unless he first gave up his army and provinces, while Caesar was convinced that he would not be safe unless he kept his army, though he still offered the compromise suggestion that they should both resign their commands. This assessment appears to be influenced by Curio's demand that Pompeius should be the first to lay down his powers, and confirms the degree to which Caesar now distrusted Pompeius. Cicero too looked forward with gloom to the prospect of war, and in October was much exercised as to the line he himself should take.[99] At this time there were renewed rumours that Pompeius was about to leave the city, and it was also believed that Caesar had already begun to launch an invasion.[100]

Matters came to a head in the senate on 1 December. Curio once more urged that both Pompeius and Caesar should lay down their commands. The consul Marcellus divided the motion, proposing first that Caesar alone should resign, which was passed, then that Pompeius should be deprived of his command, which was not. But then Curio reintroduced his original proposal, that both should give up their provinces, and this was passed by 370 votes to 22. This victory, however, was shortlived, for Marcellus dismissed the senate.[101] Shortly afterwards, exploiting yet another rumour that Caesar was already marching on Italy, Marcellus went to Pompeius and placed a sword in his hands, enjoining him on his own authority to undertake the defence of Rome against Caesar, to assume command of the troops at Capua and any others in Italy, and to conduct levies as required.[102] In this he had the support of both consuls designate for 49, since the elections had turned out badly for Caesar: his candidate Ser. Sulpicius Galba had been defeated, while L. Cornelius Lentulus Crus and C. Claudius Marcellus, brother of the consul of 51, had been elected.[103] Pompeius accepted the task entrusted to him, provided, as he said, that no better solution could be found, and promptly set out to take up command of the two legions that had come from Gaul.[104] Curio demanded that the consuls should issue an edict instructing men to ignore Pompeius' levies, but no notice was taken, and he left the city to join Caesar.[105]

Both Marcellus' action and Pompeius' response to it require explanation.[106] Marcellus' aims will have been threefold: to force the hesitant majority in the senate to adopt a more positive stance by presenting them with proof of what they might well have still doubted, that Pompeius was prepared to take the lead in a war against Caesar, to compel Pompeius to commit himself openly to such a position, and to demonstrate to Caesar the strength and unity of opposition to him at Rome in the hope that this might make him back down without a fight. By replying to the appeal in the manner that Marcellus had hoped, Pompeius too will have reckoned to inspire the senate with the will to resist and to strengthen his own position by gathering fresh support. He too will have seen the move as a warning to Caesar, but he was surely far more eager than Marcellus that Caesar should be frightened into backing down. The consul probably had few regrets that his action had brought war closer, provided that Pompeius and the mass of senators were now committed to fight, but Pompeius' prime objective will have been to try to enforce a peaceful solution while maintaining and indeed enhancing his own supremacy over Caesar.

On 6 December Caesar's secretary Hirtius paid a flying visit to Rome. He did not call on Pompeius, and though Balbus had made an appointment for him to discuss the whole situation with Metellus Scipio on the morning of 9 December, Hirtius did not stay, but left the city that same night.[107] On 9 December Cicero expressed his intention of trying to influence Pompeius in favour of concord.[108] But Pompeius interpreted Hirtius' conduct as the final proof that his breach with Caesar could not be healed, as he told Cicero when they met on the next day. He now maintained that war was inevitable, and as the days passed his attitude did not change. By the end of the month Cicero could write, after another meeting with him on 24 December, that not only was there no hope of peace, Pompeius did not want peace.[109] Pompeius claimed to believe that if Caesar became consul, even if he gave up his command in order to achieve it, this would mean the total overthrow of the state, and he appeared to have decided that war was the only solution. Since Curio's departure M. Antonius had to some extent taken over his role. He too attempted to disrupt the raising of troops and proposed that the two legions brought from Gaul should be sent to Syria to guard it against the Parthians.[110] On 20 December he had delivered a long and virulent attack on Pompeius, embracing his whole career.[111] 'What do you think', Pompeius asked Cicero, 'Caesar himself will be like if he gains control of the state, when his quaestor dares to talk like that?' Yet despite the impression gained by Cicero, it should not be lightly assumed that Pompeius was determined on war.[112] That he faced the prospect calmly is plausible enough: he was still in a confident mood and had not yet been shaken by the problems of recruitment that were soon to arise and the shock of Caesar's sudden advance. But there were still many possibilities,[113] and a peaceful settlement might still be achieved.

On 1 January the senate met under the new consuls. A letter from Caesar, probably brought by Curio, was laid before it, but the tribunes Antonius and Q. Cassius had great difficulty in persuading the consuls to allow it to be read, and were unable to secure a discussion of its contents.[114] In his account Caesar does not say what those contents were, but Cicero describes his tone as harsh and threatening.[115] He rehearsed his achievements in public life from the beginning of his career to the present and repeated his proposal that he and Pompeius should simultaneously lay down their commands. But he insisted that it was unreasonable to expect him to make concessions while Pompeius retained his power, and threatened civil war if Pompeius would not comply.[116] This last menace angered even moderate opinion in the senate, yet the mass of senators was still inclined to peace, for Lentulus found it necessary to stir them to resistance, declaring that he would override the senate if it adopted a policy of conciliation towards Caesar. A similar line was taken by Metellus Scipio, who was assumed to be speaking with Pompeius' approval. He proclaimed that Pompeius would not fail the state, if the senate was prepared to follow his lead, but warned that if they hesitated now and only later changed their minds, they would beg for his help in vain.[117]

Some voices were still raised in favour of moderation. M. Marcellus, with an eye for the realities, advised that the senate should not discuss the matter until levies had been held throughout Italy and armies enrolled. M. Calidius, supported by Caelius, went so far as to propose that Pompeius should go to Spain, so that war might be avoided. But Lentulus was obdurate. He refused to admit Calidius' motion and forced Marcellus too to back down. So, under pressure, the senate passed Scipio's motion, that Caesar should dismiss his army before a fixed day, and that if he failed to do so, he should be deemed to be acting against the interests of the state. Antonius and Cassius promptly vetoed, which gave rise to a further acrimonious discussion.[118] The same evening, after the meeting had broken up, all the senators were summoned by Pompeius. He commended and encouraged those who had been steadfast, rebuked and inspirited those who had not. The city was now filled with his veterans and men from the two legions taken from Caesar. But there were still those who favoured an embassy to Caesar to put the senate's requirements before him, and both L. Piso and the praetor L. Roscius volunteered their services.[119] But Lentulus, Metellus and Cato continued to oppose a stubborn resistance to any suggestion of appeasement or compromise.[120] Pompeius too, according to Caesar, was eager for war, thanks to the influence of Caesar's enemies, with whom he had now become reconciled, his reluctance to see any man his equal in *dignitas*, and his guilty conscience over the trick with the two legions.[121]

Nevertheless, attempts were made during the next few days to bring about a settlement.[122] In these Cicero played a leading part.[123] The initial basis of negotiation was the proposal which Caesar had sent to Rome in the last weeks of December, that he should retain only Cisalpina and Illyricum, with two legions, until his second consulship.[124] There is disagreement in the sources about Pompeius' response. According to Appian he would have accepted these terms but the consuls prevented it, whereas in Plutarch's opinion he too insisted that Caesar must give up all his troops.[125] The latter view is more likely to be right, since Pompeius' objective was still to make Caesar weak enough to be dependent on him for his survival, and this would be achieved if he were stripped of his legions, even if he retained Cisalpine Gaul. The solution next advocated by Cicero involved further concessions by Caesar on both counts: he suggested that all parties might be satisfied if Caesar kept only Illyricum and one legion.[126] Pompeius was allegedly willing to accept this, though to leave Caesar even one legion marked a slight withdrawal from his previous position, but Lentulus, Scipio and Cato overrode him.[127]

On 7 January, the *senatus consultum ultimum* was passed, and the Caesarian tribunes were warned that if they tried to interfere the senate would not be held responsible for their safety. So, accompanied by Curio, they left the city in disguise and made their way to Caesar.[128] The senate continued to meet, now outside the city. Pompeius maintained the posture he had adopted in the previous week, praising the senators for their courage and constancy. He claimed to view the military situation in an optimistic light: he himself had two legions ready for action, and he knew that morale among Caesar's troops was so low that they were likely to mutiny if he tried to lead them against the state.[129] The senate proceeded with its preparations: Pompeius was given authority to draw from the treasury and provinces were allotted with scant regard for the proper formalities.[130] On hearing news of these measures Caesar addressed the men of the thirteenth legion. He was careful to draw a distinction between his enemies and Pompeius, who had, he said, been led astray and corrupted by them even though he had himself always furthered Caesar's rise. He made much of the treatment of Antonius and Cassius, berating Pompeius for inconsistency in his attitude to the tribunate, and claimed that there had been no justification for the passing of the *senatus consultum ultimum*.[131] The legion duly declared itself ready to defend his *dignitas* and the rights of the tribunes, and Caesar set off for Ariminum.[132]

Pompeius probably still did not see war as inevitable or even desirable. Neither he nor the senate trusted each other, both for the best of reasons. Pompeius' main aim was to win sufficient support from a wavering senate to enable him to bring effective pressure to bear on Caesar. The hard core of optimates who wanted war was equally eager to strengthen the morale of the senate, but for a different reason. They suspected that, if Pompeius was not vigorously supported – perhaps indeed if he was not vigorously pushed – he would still try to come to some arrangement with Caesar. Pompeius welcomed the show of strength in the senate on 1 January and encouraged the senators to further demonstrations of firmness, not, as Caesar claimed, because he was now bent on war, but because such a display could only strengthen his hand in any eventual negotiations. Caesar too, in threatening civil war by letter, was chiefly concerned to frighten the bulk of the senate into moderation and so to render Pompeius readier to think in terms of an accommodation. Even the motion of Metellus Scipio, though it presented

Caesar with an ultimatum, had left a period of several months for tempers to cool and a settlement to be reached before it was due to come into effect. But Lentulus, Cato and their friends had been quick to guard against any backsliding on Pompeius' part, and for them the *senatus consultum ultimum* was undoubtedly intended to prevent a peaceful settlement. Yet many of those who voted for it will have seen it not as a declaration of war against Caesar, but as a prophylactic measure designed to put still more pressure on him and bring him to his senses.[133]

13

THE CIVIL WAR

It was Caesar who upset the calculations of both Pompeius and the optimates by invading Italy not only with such speed but also so early in the year.[1] Pompeius' claim to military superiority, if it was not simply a foolish and shortsighted lie to boost public morale, is intelligible only on the assumption that he expected to have much more time at his disposal to make his preparations and assemble his forces. He must have believed that, even if the worst came to the worst, Caesar would wait until the spring before mounting his attack. Nevertheless, at the outset Pompeius held most of the moral and psychological cards. Men feared that Caesar would prove violent and that a Caesarian victory would lead to massacres and confiscations, a fear encouraged by the sharpness of Antonius' tongue.[2] It was only later, when Caesar had given proofs of his clemency and Pompeius' own supporters had begun to utter pronouncements of an alarming nature, that public opinion began to swing in Caesar's favour.

The official attitude not only of the optimates but also of Pompeius himself was that any negotiations with Caesar were out of the question, for to negotiate, on whatever terms, would imply a recognition of Caesar's position that they were not willing to concede.[3] But on a private basis Pompeius was prepared to sound out the possibility of a settlement. Two envoys came to Caesar while he was at Ariminum, neither of whom had any official mandate from the senate: first the young L. Caesar and subsequently L. Roscius, both of whom had been in contact with Pompeius.[4] But while they were absent on their mission there was bitter criticism of Pompeius' lack of preparation, and Favonius sneeringly urged him to stamp his foot and bring forth the armies he had promised. Pompeius replied with a warning that to raise them it might be necessary to abandon not only Rome but Italy too. Then he proclaimed a state of *tumultus*, summoned the senate and magistrates to follow him, declaring that in his eyes anyone who stayed behind would be regarded as an enemy, and on the evening of 17 January left the city for Capua, to be followed over the next two days by the consuls and many senators.[5]

Cicero, who is consistent in his condemnation of the evacuation of Rome, speaks as if it had come to him as a complete surprise when it happened, and repeatedly describes it not as a planned withdrawal but a panic flight.[6] But although this reaction is comprehensible in terms of the difficulty that men may feel in accepting that some unpleasant event has actually happened, even when they have been living with the possibility that it may, his claims cannot be taken at their face value. When he wrote on 1 October 50 that Pompeius might leave the city, he was perhaps referring only to the possibility that he might go to his province.[7] But about 12 December 50 he had had a conversation with Ampius Balbus, in the course of which the evacuation not only of Rome but of Italy too had been discussed.[8] The abandonment of the city may also have been in his thoughts after his talk with Pompeius himself on 25 December.[9] It certainly was on 27 December when he wrote his exhaustive catalogue of the possible courses that events might take.[10] But that letter presents the evacuation of Rome as only one of two possible alternatives: the other is that the city would be defended. Pompeius' behaviour at the end of December and the beginning of January strongly suggests that he still regarded this latter course as a real possibility. When Cicero wrote to Tiro on 12 January that Pompeius was taking steps for the defence of Italy, various regions of which had been assigned to different commanders, there is no hint that the defence of Rome at this point had been abandoned.[11]

Then had come Caesar's lightning advance. Panic-stricken crowds from the surrounding country had flocked into Rome, and in the general confusion Pompeius found it difficult, if not impossible, to get reliable information about Caesar's movements.[12] Nor was he at liberty to use his own judgement. Cato's advice had been ignored; despite the powers that had been voted to him, Pompeius had not been given the supreme command.[13] So the consuls persisted in harassing him with their own views.[14] The key to the evacuation of Rome is given by Dio, who maintains that when Pompeius found that Caesar's forces were advancing on the city, he changed his plan, because the troops he had collected were not sufficient to oppose him and widespread hostility to the war still existed.[15] The conclusion is clear: Pompeius had intended to defend Rome and was compelled to abandon this strategy and evacuate the city, not because it seemed to him the better course but because he had no choice. He had not expected Caesar to move, if he moved at all, until the spring, and so he had made no haste with his preparations. By the time the need for haste became apparent, it was too late: Caesar's speed, the popular desire for peace, and resistance to the levy made the defence of Rome impossible. Pompeius had allowed himself to be caught unprepared, and although the evacuation of Rome had in fact been a contingency plan, the manner in which it was put into effect gave considerable justification to those, like Cicero, who in their fear and anger were moved to label it a flight.

The disadvantages are obvious, and Cicero labours them.[16] That the consuls and senate should be absent from the city caused widespread alarm and consternation, though it also had the immediate effect of hardening opposition to Caesar. Deprived of its emotional rallying-point, the republican cause was weakened, and on a more practical level the contents of the treasury were left to fall eventually into Caesar's hands, though for that Pompeius cannot be blamed, since the removal of the money was entrusted to the consul Lentulus, who had failed to perform this task.[17]

On 22 January Cicero declared that he could tell Atticus nothing of what Pompeius was doing; indeed he doubted if Pompeius knew himself.[18] But there is no need to suppose that Pompeius shared Cicero's confusion; even after the evacuation of Rome, it seems that hopes were cherished of cutting Caesar's lines of supply and communication with his forces in Gaul and so of checking his advance before he reached the city. It was a strategy of this kind that Cicero had seen as the alternative to the defence of the city when he enumerated the possibilities at the end of December.[19] A month later he was still hoping that this would be possible, and both on that occasion and early in February he claimed that Caesar himself was afraid of it.[20] That Pompeius himself was thinking along these lines is extremely likely. But things were not going well. The levy continued to prove slow and difficult, and the only experienced troops he had were the two legions that had come from Caesar. These he was reluctant to trust, while the danger of risking untried conscripts against Caesar's veterans was obvious to all.[21] It is small wonder that he was criticized for his lack of forethought by both Cicero and Cato.[22] The only cheering feature of events at this stage was the arrival at Teanum Sidicinum on 22 January of Labienus, who had decided to desert Caesar and return to his original allegiance.[23]

On the next day L. Caesar arrived to put Caesar's peace proposals before Pompeius and the consuls.[24] His message to Caesar had been that Pompeius wished to clear himself of the charge that he was moved by personal enmity. His only concern, now as throughout his career, had been the welfare of the state, and he appealed to Caesar to follow his example in putting the common good before personal considerations and to shun the risk of harming the republic in an attempt to hurt his private enemies.[25] Caesar insisted that, although these adjurations did nothing to relieve his legitimate grievances, he was eager to keep the possibility of a settlement open. Despite the injustice he had suffered and the hostile response to his earlier efforts to secure peace, he too was prepared to put up with anything to serve the interests of the state. Therefore he suggested that Pompeius should go to Spain, that both of them should disband their armies, that all troops in Italy should be demobilized, that free elections should be held, and that affairs should be restored to the control of the senate and people. The implications of these last two clauses are first that Caesar was now prepared to abandon his claim to stand for the consulship in absence, as is confirmed by Cicero, and secondly that the *senatus consultum ultimum* should be rescinded. Finally he asked Pompeius for a personal meeting to facilitate settlement of the detail of their differences.[26] The reply was as follows: if Caesar evacuated Ariminum, returned to Gaul and disbanded his forces, Pompeius would go to Spain. But until they had received some tangible guarantee that Caesar would keep his promise, the consuls and Pompeius would continue to levy troops.[27]

It is possible that both sides were sincere in their offers. If his terms had been accepted, Caesar would have gained all his political objectives without fighting for them; he must have calculated that his sacrifice of the *absentis ratio* would be safe, that is, that he would not be prosecuted by his enemies during his spell as a private citizen and that he would in fact be elected to the consulship for 48. In this estimate both Cicero and Pompeius would appear to have concurred.[28] It is therefore reasonable to suppose that Caesar intended his offer to be taken seriously and would have been happy if it had been accepted. The attitude of Pompeius and the consuls is more complex.[29] They were ready to concede Caesar's political demands, that is, to accept the prospect of a second consulship. But they found it hard to trust him, and Pompeius in particular must have been eager to avoid any appearance of wanting to make a private deal with Caesar, since he knew that there was no true good faith in his present alliance with Cato and his friends. They were also aware of their military disadvantage, and if Caesar accepted that he must make the first move, then the military situation would be altered greatly in their favour, a useful insurance should things go wrong at a later stage. They would be better prepared for war than they were at the moment, and more important they would without a blow recover Rome, with all the psychological and material benefits that followed. In other words they were asking Caesar to abandon the advantage he had so far gained from speed and surprise. That they were optimistic in hoping that he might comply is perhaps true, but that need not mean they were insincere in making the attempt. Caesar's response can only have confirmed their reluctance to trust him. In his eyes their conditions were totally unfair, and he complained bitterly about them.[30] He felt, perhaps with some justification, that his opponents had no real desire for peace and saw negotiations only as a means of gaining time in which to levy troops, and no doubt he was greatly disappointed at his failure to detach Pompeius from his optimate allies. So the invasion continued.[31]

When Cicero reached Capua on 25 January, just before Pompeius left with Labienus for Larinum,[32] he found a general hope that Caesar would abide by his terms and accept that he must make the first move. Only Favonius now held out for war; even Cato was prepared to make peace, though he expressed a grim desire to be present in the senate when and if the terms were discussed.[33] However, there was an equally general feeling that Caesar had made his offer only to delay the republican mobilization and would not now abide by it.[34] During the last week in January Pompeius wrote to Cicero that in a few days he would have a strong army and that he hoped soon to occupy Picenum; if that happened, Cicero and the other senators would be able to return to Rome.[35] He had apparently been much encouraged by Labienus' tales of the weakness of Caesar's forces. Yet when Cicero visited Capua on 4 February he found an atmosphere of gloom, and Pompeius was soon said to be deeply depressed.[36] On 7 February he sent a message to the consuls at Capua, urging them to go to Rome and remove the money from the treasury. Provoked by the impracticality of the suggestion and the hint that Pompeius was giving him orders, Lentulus replied that he would go to Rome if Pompeius first went to Picenum, a remark not wholly ironical, since at that moment only Cicero knew, thanks to a letter from Dolabella, that the whole of Picenum was already lost to Caesar.[37]

It was at this point, after the fall of Picenum, that Cicero began to express the fear that, whatever his strategy, Pompeius would be driven out of Italy.[38] But news he received on 9 February gave him hope that there might still be a chance of resistance in the North: Domitius Ahenobarbus was said to have a strong army at Corfinium, and the republican forces from Picenum under Spinther and Thermus had rallied to him there. So Caesar might still be cut off before he could reach Rome.[39] Cicero waited on tenterhooks to know how Pompeius would react to this news, but when the answer came it was not encouraging. On 10 February Pompeius wrote to Cicero from Luceria.[40] He had just learned from Q. Fabius that Domitius was planning to leave Corfinium on 9 February and to make his way to Luceria, bringing with him a total of twenty-six cohorts, to be closely followed by a further five under the command of Pompeius' cousin Hirrus. Pompeius advised Cicero too to head for Luceria. Then, on 11 February, Pompeius heard from Vibullius that Domitius had changed his plans and remained where he was. He wrote to him at once.[41] Only if their forces were united, he said, was there any hope of serving the interests of the state, and he could not understand why Domitius had changed his mind. The reason suggested by Vibullius, that Caesar had advanced from Firmum, struck him as quite inadequate, since the closer Caesar came, the more imperative it was that Domitius should link up with him before Caesar was able to cut them off from one another. Therefore he urged Domitius once again, as he claimed to have done repeatedly in earlier letters, to come to Luceria before it was too late.

On 16 February he received a reply, which he in turn answered straight away.[42] Domitius wrote that he proposed to observe Caesar's movements and, if he showed signs of advancing down the coast, to join Pompeius in Samnium, but that if Caesar remained in the North, he would try to hold up his advance. Pompeius, struggling to be polite, complimented Domitius on his courage, but reiterated his belief that the republicans were not strong enough to face Caesar with their forces divided, especially since Caesar would soon be receiving copious reinforcements. So he begged Domitius yet again to join him at Luceria, pointing out that the consuls had now agreed to do so. He then explained what his plans were if Caesar marched directly against him.[43] Unfortunately the text of the vital sentence is uncertain, but it is clear that in the event of Caesar's advancing against him Pompeius had decided to evacuate Italy. The consuls, he said, would withdraw the garrisons from the Italian towns to Sicily, since in order to maintain themselves in Italy the republicans would need either a force strong enough to enable them to break through Caesar's advance or to hold territory that could be successfully defended, and neither condition could be met. The only possible conclusion to be drawn was that Italy would have to be evacuated. On receipt of this letter Domitius could hardly complain that Pompeius was keeping him in the dark about his intentions; the only question is whether Pompeius had informed him earlier of what was in his mind.[44] Before the letter could be sent, a second message arrived from Domitius, asking for help, but Pompeius merely added a postscript, offering his lack of confidence in his legions as grounds for his inability to comply.[45] On the next day he received even more disturbing news from Domitius, who reported that Caesar had encamped outside Corfinium.[46] Pompeius pointed out in his reply that this was exactly what he had warned Domitius against. He did not try to disguise his alarm at the situation, and asked Domitius once more to join him, if it was still possible, before Caesar had time to concentrate all his forces.

This correspondence with Domitius illustrates only too well the impossible nature of Pompeius' position. Unable to give orders, he could only ask for co-operation, and Domitius was plainly determined to try to force his hand and compel him to make a stand in the North.[47] It is equally clear that Pompeius never had any intention of going to Corfinium. Three questions remain. Why did Domitius change his mind? When did Pompeius decide to evacuate Italy? Did he ever contemplate a stand in Italy at all?

The answer to the first question must lie in some event that took place on or immediately before 9 February; hence the attempt to connect Domitius' decision with the arrival of Vibullius and his men.[48] But the mere fact that Vibullius brought more men cannot have had such an effect, for Vibullius had already arrived when Domitius sent Fabius to Pompeius, and at that stage he was still allegedly planning to leave, bringing Vibullius' troops with him.[49] Nor can the reason that Vibullius offered to Pompeius, the advance of Caesar, be seen as anything more than a pretext.[50] There is a further possibility: that Vibullius for the first time made it quite clear to Domitius that the reason Pompeius wanted him to come to Luceria was because he proposed to evacuate Italy.[51] There is much to be said for this suggestion. In his letter of 16 February Pompeius indicated to Domitius that Italy was to be evacuated, yet the way in which he alludes to the subject there makes it very unlikely that in earlier letters he had given Domitius more specific news of this intention.[52] His first request that Domitius should come to Luceria must have been sent by 6 February at the latest,[53] but it need not have included an explanation of his ultimate purpose, and Cicero for one did not deduce that Italy was to be abandoned when the same request was addressed to him. So it is highly likely that Vibullius revealed to Domitius what Pompeius intended, and that Domitius' response was to stay where he was, in the hope of blackmailing Pompeius into changing his plans. Pompeius can be accused of deceiving Domitius only in that he asked him initially to come to Luceria without revealing why he wanted him to do so, and given his lack of authority over Domitius and Domitius' reaction when he realized what was going on, it is hard to blame him.

At the same time as he had been trying to deal with Domitius, Pompeius had been in constant communication with the consuls. Not later than 11

February he had sent them a message through D. Laelius, asking their approval of the following plan: that one of them should join him while the other crossed to Sicily with the troops assembled at Capua, to which Domitius' forces would be joined, while the bulk of the army was shipped from Brundisium to Dyrrachium.[54] After receiving Domitius' final letter he wrote twice more, on 17, then on 18 or 19 February. The first message was a brief covering note with a copy of Domitius' letter, in which he urged the consuls to join him while leaving a garrison at Capua.[55] The second offered a more elaborate account and defence of his dealings with Domitius since 11 February and reiterated his change of plan: now that Domitius was irrevocably cut off, he had decided to take all his troops to Brundisium and asked both consuls to join him there as soon as possible.[56]

By the time Pompeius issued his requests to the republican commanders to assemble at Luceria, probably during the first week in February, he had surely decided to abandon Italy. But when did he come to that decision? Confusion has been created by a remark of Cicero in a letter to Atticus of 18 March, where he claims that Pompeius had planned the evacuation two years before.[57] Much weight, however, cannot be assigned to this outburst, written under the shock of recent events in a highly emotive tone and coloured by suspicion of Pompeius' political intentions.[58] The possibility had certainly been in men's minds for some time. Cicero had expressed his disapproval at the talks that had been held about 12 December, and he and Atticus repeatedly discussed the question of Pompeius' intentions in this regard in their letters of January and February.[59] In a letter of 17 March he speaks of talks at which the blockade of Italy, which presupposes its evacuation, had been mooted.[60] The participants he calls *nostri principes*. If this phrase is to be taken literally, and there is no reason why it should not be, it points to a date before the evacuation of Rome, since afterwards the Pompeian *principes* were scattered over Italy.[61] On 17 January Cicero formed the impression that Pompeius had by then already decided to abandon Italy.[62] This was no doubt premature, but the evacuation of Italy had plainly been discussed as a serious contingency plan by early January at the very latest. For a brief period before and after the evacuation of Rome Pompeius probably intended to make a stand in Italy, but he very soon changed his plans. If his confident predictions of 28 January were sincere, he had by then not yet altered his mind, but by 6 February he had.[63] His new resolve was therefore not a result of the fall of Picenum, since news of the collapse of resistance there did not reach Cicero, who was the first to hear, until 8 February.[64] It must have been taken as soon as he became fully aware of the problems in recruiting and the low morale of the troops in Campania.[65] This, coupled with the speed of Caesar's advance, will have made him feel that resistance would be futile with the forces under his control at the time when the attempt would have to be made. But the messages by which he began to prepare to put his plan into practice were at first characteristically devious and oracular.

Pompeius left Luceria for Brundisium on 19 February.[66] Any suggestion that he still intended to make a stand in Italy rests entirely on Cicero's misinterpretation of his intentions.[67] Cicero had received Pompeius' letter on 15 February.[68] In his reply he had declared his ignorance of Pompeius' purpose, but his comments to Atticus make it clear that he suspected that Pompeius' object in assembling his forces at Luceria was to withdraw them from Italy if Caesar kept up the pressure – and that Caesar would do so could hardly be doubted. His assumption that an effort might be made to hold the coastal region can only be seen as an attempt to persuade Pompeius to change his mind and defend the coastal towns.[69] But by 17 February he had realized that this attempt had been in vain.[70] On 20 February Pompeius wrote to him, urging him now to come to Brundisium, but Cicero still refused to understand what was in his mind.[71] He had misinterpreted completely the point of Pompeius' request to the consuls to leave a garrison at Capua,[72] seeing it as evidence that he intended to take all his forces to the aid of Domitius.[73] Yet on 21 February he was again convinced that Pompeius would abandon both Domitius and Italy, and a couple of days later he acknowledged to Atticus that he had misunderstood Pompeius' designs.[74] On 27 February he wrote to Pompeius himself along similar lines, though with greater circumspection: he had first realized that Pompeius intended to evacuate Italy when he became acquainted with the contents of his message to the consuls through Laelius, but when he saw his subsequent letter to Lentulus he, like everyone else, had concluded that Pompeius now meant to march on Corfinium and that his earlier instruction was therefore cancelled.[75] By the time he received the letter encouraging him to come to Brundisium, he was already cut off.[76]

Though Caesar claims to have been uncertain whether or not Pompeius intended to try to hold Brundisium as a base from which to control the Adriatic there can be no doubt that he was only waiting for ships.[77] As he moved towards Brundisium, Caesar sent a prisoner, N. Magius, to Pompeius, in yet another attempt to open negotiations.[78] His principal aim was still to secure the personal interview which Pompeius had refused to grant him and which he still professed to be sure would enable them to settle all their differences.[79] The terms Magius brought are not recorded, but it is clear that Caesar found them unacceptable. Magius went again to Pompeius, but this time he did not return, so Caesar tried again, sending his legate Caninius Rebilus, who was a friend of Pompeius' close adviser Scribonius Libo.[80] Once more his top priority was a personal interview with Pompeius. But Pompeius sought refuge in technicalities, replying that he could not enter into any discussion concerning a settlement in the absence of the consuls.[81] The attitude of both men is not difficult to understand. That the initiative should come from Caesar is natural enough. He still cherished hopes of detaching Pompeius from the optimate leaders if he could only get the chance of talking to him alone, and he must have wished that the war could be brought to a peaceful conclusion before it spread, as it now inevitably must if agreement could not be reached at once, to the remainder of the empire. Altruism need have played no part in this desire, since on any rational calculation of prospects Caesar would be in desperate straits if Pompeius brought the vast resources of the East into play in the next campaigning season. But for Pompeius peace was at the moment out of the question. He knew that men saw the evacuation first of Rome, then of Italy as a panic flight in the face of Caesar's advance, and so to make peace now would have every appearance of an ignominious surrender to a victorious enemy. That was more than his self-esteem could endure. It was vital for him to reassert himself in the field before he could think of coming to terms with Caesar, and he too must have believed that the coming campaigning season would give him every opportunity to do so.

On 17 March Pompeius crossed to Dyrrachium.[82] His strategy is clearly perceptible through the fumes of Cicero's rhetorical outrage.[83] He intended to use the resources of the East to blockade and if need be to reconquer Italy, though it is hardly likely that the country would have been overrun by all manner of savage barbarians. This plan had been devised by Pompeius and his closest advisers: Cicero singles out Lucceius and Theophanes as particularly responsible for the scheme.[84] But an effective blockade could not be maintained unless Pompeius controlled not only the sea but also the corn-producing provinces. For the moment Caesar had insufficient ships to challenge Pompeius at sea, or indeed even to pursue him, and so he decided to go to Spain, but he sent commanders without delay to try to seize control of Sardinia, Sicily and Africa. Success in this venture would guarantee supplies of corn to Italy, despite Pompeius' overall naval supremacy, provided that the coastal routes could be kept open.[85]

Disquiet about Pompeius' intentions did not extend only to the methods by which he proposed to achieve victory. There was also grave alarm about the ways in which that victory, if it came, might be exploited. Fear of

Pompeius grew as experience of Caesar's clemency gradually soothed men's fears of what he might do.[86] At the end of February Cicero claimed that Pompeius, together with many of his followers, had long been hankering after domination on the Sullan model. In this mood he saw Pompeius and Caesar as more or less equally evil, since both wanted to be king.[87] In the middle of March he repeated the charge and maintained that Pompeius had admitted his desire openly, or at least as openly as he ever admitted to anything.[88] Even in late April, when he had been alarmed by Caesar's ill-concealed impatience with any signs of opposition in the senate and especially by his clash with the tribune L. Metellus, who tried to deny him access to the treasury (an incident which destroyed his image as the defender of tribunician rights and exploded the rumour that the conquest of Gaul had left him the possessor of unlimited ready cash), Cicero was no more moderate in his judgement of Pompeius' ambitions, still insisting that the fate of the republic was no longer an issue. It was now a struggle for monarchy. All that could be said for Pompeius is that he would make the more moderate and honourable king. His victory was essential to preserve the very name of Rome, but it would, if it came, follow the Sullan pattern.[89]

Certainly Pompeius and his followers had uttered grim threats against the towns of Italy that had gone over to Caesar and against all individuals who remained behind in Italy, proclaiming that neutrals would be treated as enemies.[90] But it is very difficult in Pompeius' own case to disentangle the political from the strategic in his pronouncements. Almost always in Cicero's letters the allegation of his eagerness for Sullan *regnum* is closely linked with bitter criticism of the plan to blockade Italy, and Pompeius' most notorious claim – *Sulla potuit, ego non potero?* ('Sulla could do it, shall I not be able to?') – is best interpreted on a purely military level.[91] Just before Pompeius left Brundisium it was reported to Cicero that the talk in his entourage was of nothing but proscriptions. Cicero branded his adherents as nothing but a bunch of Sullas, and the financial situation of some of the more distinguished, including Metellus Scipio, gave every reason to fear that they would welcome proscriptions and confiscations as a means to restoring their fortunes.[92] Caesar himself tried to exploit the feeling created by the rumours of these threats; he reminded men of the cruelties of Pompeius' Sullan youth and cast himself as the avenger of Brutus, Carbo and the rest.[93]

Depression and the feeling that he had been betrayed, sharpened by vanity and the consciousness that he had lost the initiative through his own miscalculations, could easily have loosened Pompeius' tongue against all those from whom he had mistakenly expected enthusiastic support. But these outbursts need not represent his real intentions. The question of what position Pompeius had in mind for himself when he had won the war is difficult to answer, and of course in a sense the answer is of no importance. Yet he must have given the matter some consideration. If the dictatorship had been offered him in 52 he would surely have accepted it, and now the offer would inevitably be made to him, as it had been to Sulla, in the chaos that would ensue after his victorious return from the East. Even those of his supporters who distrusted him most and saw him only as a weapon to be used against Caesar and then discarded would be bound to acquiesce in the short term to ensure the restoration of order and the safe acquisition of their own profits. For all his vanity Pompeius must have been aware that for a large number of the men who were at present on his side he would, once the war was over, have outlived his own usefulness, and that therefore his own security would be a paramount issue. On that score too the dictatorship would be the best safeguard. Sulla's tenure of the office had of course been brief, and Pompeius too might well have preferred to resign as soon as he felt it safe to do so. When, if ever, that might have been, we cannot know, but neither could Pompeius himself, and he may well have resolved to face the problem only when the time came.

Despite the loss of Italy, he still held the moral advantage. Unable to pursue him because of his lack of ships, Caesar had decided to make for Spain and so remove the threat to his back from Pompeius' legates there.[94] On his way he attempted to win over Massilia, which was torn between conflicting obligations and so desired to remain neutral.[95] He urged the city to follow the example of the whole of Italy rather than to submit to the will of a single man,[96] an argument which, however tendentious, shows how the abandonment of Italy could be exploited to give Caesar the appearance of moral legitimacy even before he had secured any legal standing. Political legitimacy was for the moment manifestly on Pompeius' side.[97] Both consuls and many distinguished senators were with him, and although a rump senate remained in Rome, it lacked lustre.[98] More important, with the consuls away there appeared to be nobody competent to hold the elections. This matter had been exercising Caesar even before Pompeius' departure, and his supporters had been toying with the the notion (which aroused Cicero's constitutionalist ire) that the consular elections could legitimately be held by a praetor.[99] It was on his return to Massilia from the conquest of Spain that Caesar heard of the solution that had been devised. Though a praetor could not preside over consular elections, he could, it was argued, bring in a law for the appointment of a dictator. This had duly been done, and Caesar had been proclaimed by the praetor M. Aemilius Lepidus, the future triumvir.[100] When he reached Rome, he held the consular elections and was elected consul for 48, together with P. Servilius Isauricus, son of the consul of 79.[101]

Caesar's supporters, including Curio and Caelius, had always regarded the rapid conquest of Spain as a foregone conclusion.[102] But although Caelius had expressed the view that the fall of Spain would mean the end for Pompeius, Cicero for once showed more military sense when he remarked to Atticus that, whatever the outcome in Spain, that would not be the end of the war.[103] In his judgement Pompeius had never been deeply concerned about holding the Spanish provinces: his conviction that ultimate victory would depend on control of the sea had meant that his chief concern had always been the preparation of naval forces with which to mount his blockade and ultimately his invasion of Italy. In this Cicero is no doubt correct. Despite rumours that he proposed to penetrate Gaul by way of Illyricum and Germany,[104] Pompeius must have seen Caesar's enforced operations in Spain above all as an opportunity for him to gain time in which to organize the resources of the East on the vast scale required.[105] He used his breathing-space well.[106] He assembled ships from Greece, the provinces of Asia Minor, and Egypt, and gave orders that more were to be built. In addition to his regular forces, he amassed auxiliaries from diverse Eastern sources.[107] Money was exacted from the wealthy provinces of Asia and Syria, from all the potentates of the East, and from the cities of Greece. The *publicani* of the Eastern provinces were forced to delve into their coffers, and individuals too made contributions, willingly or otherwise: Cicero's finances were still in chaos in 47 because of his subventions to the Pompeian cause.[108] To complete his preparations Pompeius got together all the available corn from Thessaly, Asia, Egypt, Crete, Cyrene and the other areas under his control.[109]

His immediate objective was to prevent Caesar crossing to confront him, but Caesar's speed and luck brought him through the blockade commanded by Bibulus.[110] The difficulties of his position encouraged him to make yet another attempt to achieve a peaceful settlement.[111] His terms, carried by L. Vibullius, ran as follows: he and Pompeius should both disarm before they suffered any further losses, while they both still had confidence in their strength and seemed to be equal, so that neither would be appearing to surrender and neither would be able to exploit the peace, the details of which should be referred to the senate and people at Rome. Pompeius had by now been granted the republican supreme command, on the motion of Lentulus Crus.[112] But before he had a chance to consider Vibullius' message, the effects of the change in the political balance began to show themselves. First Oricum and then Apollonia opened their gates to Caesar, declaring that they could not refuse entry to the official representative of the Roman people or take a stand that ran counter to that adopted by Rome and the whole of Italy.[113] Pompeius was alarmed by these developments, though Labienus tried to encourage him and the whole army took an oath of loyalty.[114] Further talks were then initiated by Libo and Bibulus. Libo declared – for Bibulus did not trust his temper if he appeared in Caesar's presence and was reluctant to endanger the success of negotiations by a possible outburst – that Pompeius wanted nothing more than a settlement, though he himself could make no concrete offer now that Pompeius had been appointed commander-in-chief. As the discussion proceeded, it became obvious that Libo and Bibulus had nothing to offer and were concerned only with securing a truce to ease their own immediate problems.[115]

Vibullius, however, attempted to carry out his mission in a meeting with Pompeius and his personal advisers Libo, Lucceius and Theophanes.[116] But Pompeius would not even let him speak. He could not, he said, accept either life or citizenship as a gift from Caesar, and, whatever the truth of the matter, that would be what men would think he had done if he returned to Italy by the terms of any agreement.[117] This answer was inevitable, and Caesar can hardly have expected anything else. No doubt he would have been delighted if Pompeius had been ready to make terms, for two superficially contrasting reasons: first, Pompeius was still by far the stronger and on any rational calculation ought to have won the war if it continued; secondly, because of the curious course that the war had so far taken and the general lack of understanding of Pompeius' strategy, peace now, even on equable terms, would be universally regarded as a victory for Caesar. Thus Caesar would win a moral victory in a war that he might otherwise still expect to lose. Despite his attempt to conceal these facts and to pretend that Pompeius would not be conceding defeat, he could not disguise all his own advantages: reference to the senate and people at Rome was something that Pompeius and his supporters could not possibly accept, as events at Oricum and Apollonia had only just driven home. Pompeius was now the prisoner of his own strategy: men thought that he had run away from Italy, and his self-respect and credibility as a leader demanded that he should fight his way back. In this attitude he was no doubt confirmed by loudmouths like Labienus, who proclaimed that Caesar's head was the first condition of any peace.[118]

In March 48 the Pompeian naval blockade failed to prevent Antonius from bringing reinforcements to Caesar, who succeeded over the summer in besieging Pompeius near Dyrrachium. It was not until Pompeius broke the siege that he was once more faced with any real choice about the future conduct of the war. His position as supreme commander ought to have made matters easier for him, but he found it extremely difficult to assert himself and use his own judgement in the face of the pressure put on him by the other republican commanders. There were essentially three courses open to him: he could attempt an invasion of Italy, fight a decisive battle in Greece, or simply prolong the war in the hope of wearing Caesar down.[119] The first was recommended by the old soldier Afranius. It had obvious attractions: for Pompeius the evacuation of Italy had been a great psychological and moral setback, and its recovery would cancel this out. Caesar's grip on Rome and Italy seemed fragile,[120] and it could have been argued that the sooner he was deprived by force of the advantage he enjoyed as the legal representative of the Roman people, the better. But Pompeius was concerned about the immediate effect on public opinion that an invasion would produce, and reluctant to leave Metellus Scipio in Greece to face Caesar alone.[121] His own inclination was to prolong the war, to wear Caesar into submission or at least make him weak enough to prove an easy victim.[122] But his supporters would have none of this. Cicero in retrospect paints a scathing picture of the republican leaders which justifies Caesar's own gleeful strictures.[123] Most of them were burdened with debts and needed victory to restore their fortunes. Cicero tried to persuade Pompeius, first to make peace, then, when that proved impossible, to protract the war. At first Pompeius listened, but after Dyrrachium his judgement failed: from that moment, says Cicero, he was no commander.[124] Another man might perhaps have been able to adhere to the course that he knew to be the wiser, but Pompeius' concern for the good opinion of men betrayed him. He was accused of wanting to prolong the war for his own pleasure and profit, because he enjoyed ordering proconsuls about as if they were his slaves.[125] His own officers nicknamed him 'Agamemnon' and 'King of Kings'. Both they and Pompeius will have been acutely aware that underneath the gibes there was an awkward kernel of fact. Pompeius was supreme commander for the duration of the war. Once it was over, who knew what would become of him? At bottom those who said that he was in no hurry to achieve a final solution must have had truth on their side.

That the Pompeian leaders saw success in a decisive battle as certain is amply attested. Before Pharsalus they were already quarrelling over the prizes of victory: in particular Ahenobarbus, Scipio and Spinther squabbled as to which of them should follow Caesar as *pontifex maximus*.[126] After the

battle, when he had captured the enemy camp, Caesar found that preparations had already been made on a lavish scale for the celebrations.[127] At last
Pompeius gave way, and for personal and political reasons chose the course
which he knew was militarily unsound, to stake everything on a single
battle.[128]

Moreover, there can be no doubt that during the battle of Pharsalus his
nerve cracked:[129] the picture Caesar paints is all the more striking for its
relative restraint. Yet even now there was no need to see his cause as
hopeless: he still had great strength, particularly at sea.[130] Whether he
thought of making a further stand in Greece is unclear. His advice to the
people of Larisa, the first town he came to in his flight from Pharsalus, to
throw themselves on Caesar's mercy suggests not, but the edict issued in his
name at Amphipolis ordering a levy of Roman citizens and Greeks
throughout Macedonia might point to an intention of trying to hold that
province.[131] Too much weight should probably not be assigned to either
piece of evidence: it is unlikely that in his present frame of mind he had
given much consideration even to the most immediate future. At all events
he swiftly withdrew, first to Mytilene, then by way of Attalia to Syhedra in
Cilicia.[132]

There he held a council of war. First he attempted to rally his supporters,
pointing out that they were strong enough to recover from the defeat at
Pharsalus, and in particular that his naval strength was still unimpaired.[133]
Then he offered them the choice between three possible sources of aid,
Parthia, Numidia and Egypt, but made it clear that he did not trust the
kings of Egypt or Numidia, and that Parthia would be his first preference.[134] But his scheme met with general disapproval, and Spinther made
himself the mouthpiece of those who found such a suggestion unendur-
able.[135] He spoke not only of the shame of using Parthian arms against
Rome, but also argued that such help would be of little value, since the
Parthians were militarily effective only when fighting on their own ground
under favourable conditions. Finally he threw his weight behind the
fatal proposal: if Juba could not be trusted, then Pompeius should withdraw to Egypt, where Ptolemy owed him his kingdom.[136]

It might be doubted whether Pompeius really intended to take refuge in
Parthia and use Parthian troops against Rome. He had sent his cousin
Hirrus as an envoy to the Parthian court, from which he had returned
shortly before Pharsalus.[137] Caesar says nothing of the purpose of Hirrus'
mission, but it is hard to believe that before the defeat in Greece Pompeius
was thinking of using Parthia as a base; at the time that Hirrus was sent, he
had not yet succumbed to the pressure from his entourage to fight a

decisive battle in Greece, and contingency plans about a base to which to retire would depend on the existence of a plan to fight in Greece which might lead to a defeat. The most likely explanation of Hirrus' embassy is that Pompeius wanted to make sure that Parthia stayed neutral and did not take advantage of the civil war to invade Rome's eastern provinces.[138] Such a guarantee would be particularly important at a time when, if things went well, the East might be temporarily at least stripped of most of its defences while the Pompeians mounted an invasion of Italy. Nevertheless, if Pompeius did not think after Pharsalus of going to Parthia, it is hard to see where the story that he did can have come from, especially since it does not stem from Caesar. It may have been exaggerated, since Pompeius could hardly have been unaware of the outraged reaction that the mere thought of using Parthian troops against Rome would provoke, but that he considered and indeed advocated withdrawing to Parthia and using it as a base must be accepted.

Now for the last time he gave way to his advisers and sailed by way of Paphos in Cyprus to Pelusium.[139] From there he sent a letter to the young king Ptolemy, asking in the name of his friendship with Ptolemy's father for admission to Alexandria and protection in his hour of defeat.[140] But Ptolemy's advisers, Achillas, Pothinus and Theodotus, saw every reason to reject the appeal. If Pompeius did succeed in re-establishing himself, they were afraid that he might seize control of Egypt and deprive it of its independence – and them of course of their power – while if he failed and they had helped him, he would merely drag Egypt down with him in his ruin. So for its own sake, they argued, Egypt must side with the victor.[141] Accordingly, a friendly message was sent to Pompeius, asking him to come to meet the king, while at the same time preparations were made to assassinate him.[142] One of those entrusted with the task was a Roman, L. Septimius, who had served under Pompeius in the pirate war and had been left in Alexandria by Gabinius after the restoration of Auletes.[143] A small boat, with Septimius and Achillas aboard, was sent out to meet Pompeius' ship and bring him to land. Pompeius suspected a trick, but he had gone too far and was too weary of his fate to draw back now. As he stepped ashore, he was struck down, in full view of Cornelia and his friends.[144] It was the day before his fifty-ninth birthday.[145] His head was taken, to be presented to Caesar on his arrival in Egypt.[146] The body was left unburied on the beach, where it received a makeshift funeral at the hands of Pompeius' freedman Philippus.[147] His ashes were later returned to Cornelia, to be buried on his Alban estate.[148]

14

CONCLUSION

Non possum eius casum non dolere: hominem enim integrum et castum et grauem cognoui. Thus Cicero on learning the news of Pompeius' death.[1] The absence of any judgement on Pompeius as soldier or statesman is striking, but at a time when political life as Cicero knew it seemed to have been brought to a disastrous close in part at least by Pompeius' ambition, his political miscalculations and military errors, it is perhaps understandable that his friend preferred simply to mourn, with some dignity, Pompeius the man.

Most judgements passed on Pompeius in our sources fall into three main categories: of these two relate solely to his aims in the war with Caesar, while the third, though it may be applied to his whole career, is particularly relevant to the chain of events that led up to the civil war.

The first is familiar from Cicero's repeated outbursts during 49 and 48: Pompeius was as bad as Caesar, for he too was bent on seizing supreme power.[2] The charge recurs several times in later tradition. It appealed, not surprisingly, to the acid cynicism of Tacitus, who damned Pompeius as more devious than Marius and Sulla in his quest for domination, but no better.[3] Even the less suspicious Dio, when he came to analyse what was at stake in the civil war, concluded that both men were aiming at monarchy.[4] But before that Cicero's *uterque regnare uult* ('they both want to be king') is echoed by Seneca on more than one occasion.[5] The object of the claim is consistently tendentious: to exalt the memory of Cato as the one man who dared to defy both Caesar and Pompeius and defend the *res publica* against the ambitions of the dynasts. The theme is also prominent in Lucan. Only the sacrifice of liberty will secure peace; the war will merely settle the question *uter imperet urbi* (which of the two should rule over the city).[6] Brutus warns Cato that if he places himself under Pompeius' command, Caesar will be left as the one free man in the world, but Cato offers a more positive response: his presence on the Pompeian side will make Pompeius realize that his victory, if it comes, has not been won for himself alone.[7]

Yet Lucan is at the same time the most eloquent spokesman of the opposite view: that Pompeius died a martyr for freedom and the republic.[8] His cause is that of the fatherland and of the entire senate, he hails his men as champions of the state.[9] This attitude finds its most memorable expression in the aphorism on Pompeius' place in the ranks of the senate in exile: *non Magni partes sed Magnum in partibus esse.*[10] At Pharsalus the lust for *regnum* inspires Caesar's men, while the fear of it drives on his opponents.[11] Nor were the senators fighting for Pompeius, for they were ready to die even after his flight from the field.[12] After his death it could be said that he had always laid down his arms and returned to civilian life, resting content with his triumphs.[13] The timing of this verdict gives the first clue to its significance; a second lies in the paradox that the true and indisputable champion of freedom, Cato, became wholeheartedly Pompeian only when Pompeius had fallen.[14] The game is completely given away by the opening words of the epitaph spoken by Cato: *ciuis obit.*[15] Pompeius had had the good fortune to die before his good intentions could be put to the test.[16] Justice and, more important, the desire to exploit the contrast with men's actual experience of Caesar combined to give him the benefit of the doubt, though fastidious critics might utter the wish that he had died of the fever in 50, for then his good reputation would never have been questioned.[17]

While both these verdicts on Pompeius are to a large degree vitiated by the desire of their authors to propound a schematic antithesis with the virtues of Cato on the one hand or the vices of Caesar on the other, there is more to be said for the third stock judgement: that Pompeius could tolerate no equal in power and esteem, Caesar no superior.[18] This estimate too could be framed in terms of bitter criticism: only Pompeius himself, remarks Seneca, thought that he was not great enough, and Caesar dared to resent the fact that one man stood above him, while the republic could endure the overweening power of two.[19] Velleius makes repeated use of the theme. In his epitaph on Pompeius he observes that he had risen as high as it was possible for man to rise,[20] a remark that points the inevitability of the conflict between him and Caesar, who wanted to rise still higher, and perhaps implies a very discreet comment on Caesar's ambition. Earlier, in his sketch of Pompeius' character, he singles out as almost his only vice his reluctance, in a free state, to see anyone become his equal in *dignitas.*[21] Lucan puts an admission of this into Pompeius' own mouth, in terms that seem to echo Velleius: Pompeius claims that he had risen as high as a citizen, a member of a free people, could do, leaving nothing but monarchy for anyone who wanted to aim higher.[22]

Pompeius then refused to overstep the bounds of constitutional liberty, but at the same time, on his own admission, he extended those bounds to the furthest limit that the freedom of the state and the Roman people would allow. Sceptics might point to his readiness to demonstrate his strength by breaking his own laws, and a philosopher could rail against the lust for power that made him pile command on command,[23] but Pompeius' own claim that, though he had attained every honour sooner than he had expected, he had also laid each down before men had expected it of him,[24] was borne out by the facts. His desire for power was always moderated, as Velleius and Dio noted, by the wish that it should be granted to him with at least the outward appearance of good will.[25] This even Lucan's Cato was ready to concede.[26] He insisted that true freedom had died with Marius and Sulla, and that by the standards of the early republic Pompeius' conduct left much to be desired. Yet he had to admit that Pompeius had always been ready to resign his commands and that his eagerness for honours to be granted him willingly had compelled him to acknowledge the right of senate and people to deny him if they chose. He had wanted to be the dominant figure in the senate, but in a senate that was still the ruler of Rome. So his position had been compatible at least with that measure of *libertas* which still prevailed.

Pompeius then did not want to destroy the republic. Caesar, whatever he wanted, did destroy it. But that must not be allowed to obscure the difficulties that the republic experienced in accommodating Pompeius.[27] His ambitions are fairly clear. He wanted, not to rule as king or dictator, but to be the man to whom senate and people turned, ostensibly of their own accord, whenever there was a military or administrative crisis. Between such missions he wanted no more than to be treated with the respect that his standing and achievements deserved and in consequence to be able to advance and protect his friends and clients as the occasion demanded. To a certain extent these aims were those of any Roman *nobilis*. But Pompeius' character did not make matters easy. His conceit and hypocrisy inspired resentment, his deviousness bred distrust. As a result, even in emergencies, the senate would approach him only with reluctance, and took delight in pricking the bubble of his vanity whenever circumstances allowed. So Pompeius, to maintain his power and prestige, was driven to provoke crises at home and abroad, and the stability of the republic was increasingly undermined.[28] Problems were also inherent in the degree of pre-eminence to which Pompeius laid claim. He had, as Lucan makes him say, left no legitimate field in which Caesar might exercise his ambition. Though Caesar's ambition was too great, it was not only he who might be hampered by Pompeius' conception of his own role. The more modest and legitimate aspirations to glory of men who would never have dreamed of behaving like Caesar were in danger of curtailment by Pompeius. However innocent his ultimate aspirations, he had already grown great enough to alarm any man who believed that in a healthy republic there ought to be many *principes* of roughly equivalent influence and power.

Nor did his career differ from that of the traditional *princeps ciuitatis* only in degree. For most of his life his position in the state was far more anomalous than that of Caesar, who held the usual magistracies at the usual times. It was Pompeius who at twenty-four cast himself as the Roman Alexander,[29] Pompeius who twice triumphed as an *eques*, Pompeius who entered the senate as consul, Pompeius the *priuatus* who was granted the great commands in the East. It was ironical and tragic, both for him and for the senate, that, although he spent so much of his career fighting to defend the senate against its enemies, he and the aristocracy never learned to accept and trust one another. Some of the same problems were to face Augustus, for whom on a practical level Pompeius provided several useful precedents, though Caesar's heir preferred to leave them unacknowledged. Augustus solved them, but by then the republican aristocracy had been shattered by another civil war and was ready, after its experience of Caesar, to settle for dignity without power.

In death Pompeius became a symbolic figure, crudely ambiguous: failed pretender to sole dominion of the Roman world, or martyr in the cause of *libertas* and *auctoritas senatus*. Both images border on caricature: inevitably the man who had done so much to shape the destiny of the dying republic even as it had shaped his own was more complex than that. But by the time such verdicts had crystallized, the doom of the Roman state had been settled once and for all, and there was little encouragement to enquire too deeply or too long into the enigma. It was easier and safer to forget the ambivalent figure, whose political career raised such awkward questions, and remember instead only a cardboard hero, the mighty conqueror who had triumphed over three continents and brought the East under Roman sway. Once that happened, then even as a symbol Pompeius had ceased to matter.

AFTERWORD

In the time that has elapsed since the publication of the first edition of this book there have been no dramatic new discoveries, no fundamental changes of perception or approach in the study of the political history of the late republic. The new edition of the ninth volume of the *Cambridge Ancient History* means that there is now available for the first time a full and up-to-date account of the political, social and military events of which the life of Pompeius forms a vital constituent. Opinions are still divided on the question of the validity or usefulness of historical biography as a genre. For those in favour, one of the most important recent contributions to our understanding of the age of Pompeius' pre-eminence is indeed a biography, that of Clodius by Tatum. However, in one field relatively tangential to the subject matter of this book, the nature of Roman imperialism and the organization (or lack of it) of the Roman provinces, there have been noteworthy shifts in opinion. These obviously affect our understanding of Pompeius' settlement of the East and will be considered in due course. But for the most part what follows is concerned only with detailed points of fact and interpretation suggested by the results of recent research.

The opening chapters, on Pompeius' father and his early career down to the time of Sulla, call for little comment. A broader background is now supplied, not only by the *Cambridge Ancient History*, but also by Keaveney's book on Sulla, which, though excessively disposed in Sulla's favour, considerably enhances understanding of the man, his work and the nature of his support. A few points merit specific notice. In the matter of the divergent accounts of Cinna's death in 84 (p. 26) a clearer case can and should be made in favour of accepting Appian's simpler version against that of Plutarch, with its anachronistic overestimate of Pompeius' importance.[1] A somewhat more detailed account of Pompeius' service in Sulla's civil war

(p. 26) is also possible, though it adds little or nothing to our understanding of Pompeius or his relationship with Sulla.[2]

The negotiations that led to Sulla's acquiescence in Pompeius' request for a triumph in 81 (p. 28) are the subject of an intriguing suggestion by Keaveney.[3] He argues that Pompeius was in a strong position to blackmail Sulla, since Sulla was extremely eager to attach the young man to himself (and, one might add, the Metelli) by a marriage alliance. This would of course mean that Pompeius would have to divorce his current wife Antistia. Keaveney claims that Sulla made the grant of a triumph a condition of his doing so. Other factors will certainly have played a part in determining Sulla's decision, but the notion is attractive and perfectly plausible, though not susceptible of proof.

Further background on various aspects of the rise of Pompeius during the seventies is again to be found in the new *CAH*: on the military details of the rising of M. Lepidus in 78–7 (p. 30) (though the precise course of events remains as uncertain as ever); on events in Rome during Pompeius' absence in Spain (p. 33) (with a less Pompeiocentric focus); and on the campaigns against Sertorius and Spartacus (p. 32).[4]

In particular the military situation in 74 and the response to it at Rome (p. 33) demand reappraisal. First it must be stressed that in 74 Pompeius can have had no hope of securing a command against Mithradates.[5] The chief stimulus for the senate's sudden display of energy in that year, marked by the sending of reinforcements to Spain and the creation of commands against Mithradates and the pirates, will have been not Mithradates' invasion of Bithynia, which did not take place till 73,[6] but the news of the agreement between Mithradates and Sertorius. Up to this point the senate will have felt that it was engaged with three distinct actual or potential enemies. But both Sertorius and Mithradates had already had dealings with the pirates, and the revelation that they might now co-operate with one another will have made it seem that Rome now faced a single unified threat that spanned the Mediterranean world. It was the shock of this that roused the senate from its inertia and provoked a correspondingly unified response.[7]

The motives of L. Lucullus, who stirred himself to ensure that Pompeius and Metellus Pius received the support they needed in Spain (p. 34), may be clarified by the observations of Hillman on relations between Lucullus and Pompeius prior to this time.[8] He dismisses as unconvincing Plutarch's claim that the two men had been enemies ever since Sulla had cut Pompeius out of his will while making Lucullus the guardian of his children.[9] If this is correct, there is no need to assume that circumstances conspired to compel Lucullus to assist an enemy, though he and Pompeius can certainly not be called friends. His behaviour will have been dictated by the public interest – nobody wanted to lose the war in Spain, whatever their opinion of Pompeius – and his own. Desperately eager for a command against Mithradates, he may have feared that, if the worst happened in Spain, he would be forced to go to Cisalpina (the province originally allocated to him) as a precautionary measure.[10]

A certain amount needs to be said about the circumstances of Pompeius' appointment to the great commands against the pirates and Mithradates and the nature of his *imperium* in each case, though agreement on the latter question is unlikely ever to be reached. Recent work on the events that gradually led to the supersession of Lucullus tends, rightly, to see the principal factor as a widespread belief at Rome that the war was virtually over, a belief ironically encouraged by Lucullus' own inflated reports of his successes, after which the failures of 68 and 67, culminating in the disaster at Zela, came as a complete surprise.[11] Certainly there is no reason to posit a campaign by Pompeius or men working on his behalf to denigrate and undermine Lucullus (p. 43).[12] He was in an enviable position: the course of events favoured his ultimate ambition without the need for intervention, direct or indirect, on his part. Nevertheless the part played by L. Quinctius, who of course had his own good reasons to dislike Lucullus, should not be overlooked.[13]

The command assigned to M'. Glabrio on the proposal of Gabinius (p. 43) has been the subject of a thorough investigation by Williams. He is right to reject collusion between Glabrio and Pompeius, and his explanation of Glabrio's inertia when he found himself confronted by a military situation quite different from what he had been led to expect is also convincing.[14] Nor does Gabinius' choice of Glabrio require much explanation: a consul of 67 was the only real possibility, and C. Piso was out of the question.[15] So for Gabinius, Glabrio was the only possible option.

His justifiable desire to deny Pompeius' involvement in the downfall of Lucullus also leads Williams to question the existence of any link between Pompeius and Gabinius before 67.[16] He suggests that Gabinius' marriage to Lollia, daughter (or sister) of the 'Pompeian' M. Lollius Palicanus (p. 41), may not have occurred before 67 or even later. Certainty is impossible, but it seems more likely that the marriage belongs to her father's brief prominence, as tribune in 71, or at the latest to his praetorship of 69, rather than to the moment of his political annihilation by C. Piso in 67.

On events leading up to the passage of the *lex Gabinia* (p. 44), it has been shown by Watkins that Plutarch does not in fact say that Caesar was the only senator to support the bill.[17] What he actually says is that Caesar 'alone of the greatest and most powerful men in the senate' was in favour. The passage is thus a prime example of the tendency of the secondary sources grossly to overestimate the early importance of Caesar in the light of hindsight, but leaves open the possibility that the law enjoyed some support (how much is beyond conjecture) among the rank and file of the senate. This is true and deserves to be pointed out, though it must also be said that the views of such men will have counted for relatively little.

Disagreement on the subject of Pompeius' *imperium* against the pirates (p. 46) continues. Kallet-Marx holds that it was already *maius*, but does not consider the significance for this question of the stand-off between Pompeius' legate L. Octavius and Q. Metellus in Crete.[18] Sherwin-White on the other hand believes that it was *aequum*, and specifically cites the attitude of Metellus as evidence for this view.[19] This still seems to me the more plausible interpretation. On the *lex Manilia* (p. 51) Sherwin-White rightly calls attention to the grotesque misrepresentation of the situation perpetrated by Cicero in his speech to the people.[20] He also remarks, without drawing any conclusions, that both Q. Marcius Rex and M'. Glabrio acquiesced in their premature supersession by Pompeius without offering any resistance.[21] It might be possible to see this fact as a further indication that Pompeius' *imperium* had now been upgraded to *maius*, but the point can hardly be pressed.

Much has been written about Pompeius' settlement of the East; a crucial contribution is that of Freeman, who argues the case for his own radical reinterpretation against the views of earlier scholars. He argues convincingly that the picture of Pompeius' arrangements as a carefully planned and unified whole, in which an inner ring of provinces under direct Roman control was protected by an outer ring of client kingdoms (p. 61), is a complete illusion. Both ancient authors (writing well after the event) and modern scholars have tended to summarize Pompeius' dispositions at the end of an account of his campaigns in the region, as if they had all been conceived as a single package, either at the end of the fighting or even before it started.

This cannot in fact have been the case. Rather, the many individual provisions that go to make up what we perhaps misleadingly call the 'settlement of the East' were devised and executed piecemeal as the occasion demanded and the opportunity offered, while Pompeius was still actively engaged in the field.[22] There is no warrant for the assumption that at any point, whether before, during or after the war, Pompeius ever set himself the task of devising a master-plan for the organization of the Roman East that would solve all its problems for the foreseeable future.

One qualification, however, might perhaps be made. That Pompeius did not set out to establish in the East a nucleus of provinces protected by a ring of client kingdoms must be accepted. Nevertheless the impression created by any modern map that records his achievements is not entirely false. He did not plan in advance to bring about this result; he did not realize in the course of his campaigns that this was what he was doing. Yet at the end of the day it turned out to be what he had done, even if by accident rather than by design. Moreover, his remark about Asia (p. 61) gives a hint that in retrospect at least he understood this fact.

Also relevant, if less directly, to the settlement of the East are Freeman's views on the annexation and organization of provinces.[23] He makes a strong case for the view that neither annexation nor organization as a province can be seen as a single coherent act that follows a more or less standard pattern. In reality things were much more haphazard, dictated by perceived military and administrative needs in a particular area at a particular time. This perception is especially germane to the history of Cilicia at this time. When P. Servilius went there in the early seventies, the name Cilicia merely served roughly to define a sphere of military command; Servilius' only task was to combat Isaurian pirates. When Ap. Claudius and Cicero successively governed Cilicia in the fifties, there was an established assize circuit and civil business took up much of the governor's time, though a man sufficiently desperate for glory could still flush out enough barbarians to slaughter to give him hopes of a triumph. That Cilicia was moving, as it were, along a line from purely military command to primarily civil appointment is clear. But it would now be rash to claim that there was any one single act which made Cilicia a 'province' in the modern administrative sense, or that that act was performed by Pompeius.

Events at Rome during Pompeius' absence in the East call for little comment. The trial of C. Manilius (p. 64) has been the subject of an examination by Ramsey, who highlights the unusual features of the situation.[24] Both the choice of *repetundae*, rather than *maiestas* or *uis*, as a weapon against a *popularis* tribune and the date so late in the year are remarkable, especially as *repetundae* cases usually required a great deal of preparation. His suggested explanation, that this was a charge under the clause *quo ea pecunia peruenerit*, arising out of a case heard earlier in 66, is attractive. He also makes a good case for the view that Cicero's lost speech in favour of Manilius was delivered in 66, when Cicero agreed to undertake Manilius' defence, not at a trial of Manilius in 65.[25]

Greater emphasis should be laid on the stupidity and incompetence of Q. Metellus Nepos at the beginning of his tribunate of 62 (p. 72).[26] Both his behaviour while he was in Rome and his subsequent flight to rejoin Pompeius can only have exacerbated the fears felt by many about how Pompeius would conduct himself on his return; Pompeius cannot have been pleased by Nepos' performance. Tatum goes so far as to suggest that Pompeius' divorce of Mucia was a way of distancing himself from Nepos. There may be an element of truth in this, though it can hardly have been the only or principal motive.

The grounds for the passing of the *senatus consultum ultimum* in 62 (p. 73) have also given rise to discussion. Burckhardt argues that it was not the level of violence involved in the clashes between Nepos and Cato that gave rise to the decree but the strength of the desire to block Nepos' legislation, because of its possible consequences for the senate's chances of maintaining itself against Pompeius.[27] If this is correct, it makes an interesting illustration of the readiness with which the *s.c.u.* could be abused and how far it had lost its original character as a last resort when the welfare of the state was allegedly under immediate physical threat.

The attitude of Pompeius to the Bona Dea affair (p. 77) is only one of several questions concerning Pompeius investigated by Tatum in his study of Clodius. He believes (plausibly enough, though there is no proof) that after his release by the pirates Clodius served under Pompeius in 67.[28] There was therefore, as he says, no reason for Pompeius to adopt a stance hostile to Clodius. Indeed, the tribune Fufius Calenus seems to have hoped for Pompeius' support, since M. Piso was backing Clodius, while such staunch opponents of Pompeius as Catulus, Hortensius, Lucullus and C. Piso were prominent on the other side.[29] But Pompeius, cautious after his experiences with Nepos, did not mention the Bona Dea scandal.[30] After the initial debates he remained aloof, pleasing nobody, as Cicero says.[31] It may be added that if Clodius had indeed hoped that Pompeius would back him, his failure to do so will have given Clodius a reason to distrust him even before they clashed over the fate of Cicero.

Several points may be made about the politics of the year 59 and relations between Clodius and the coalition. The difficulties of the Egyptian king Ptolemy Auletes are highlighted by Braund.[32] The tenuous nature of his hold on his kingdom made him ready to promise vast sums to Pompeius and Caesar as the price for recognition by Rome (p. 88). But ironically this expedient only hastened his downfall, since the stringent fiscal measures he was forced to introduce in the attempt to pay his debt to the dynasts led directly to his expulsion in 58.

The behaviour of Metellus Nepos in 59 draws a comment from Tatum.[33] He rejects the idea of a 'Clodian group' of which Nepos was a member – something for which I should certainly not wish to argue – and claims that Nepos' motive for his declared hostility to the coalition was a straightforward desire to inconvenience Pompeius in revenge for Pompeius' divorce of Mucia and disparagement of Nepos' performance in his tribunate. The point is a valid one. But Nepos was also close to Clodius, and a personal motive for attacking Pompeius is by no means incompatible with a desire at the same time to further the interests of his friend.

It is likely that there will always be as many views on the Vettius affair as there are discussions of it. Most striking among the more recent contributions is that of Marshall.[34] Basing himself on Plutarch, he claims that the plot was an invention of Pompeius, designed to win sympathy. This is part of a more far-reaching argument that Pompeius' notorious fear of assassination was not genuine but a pose, to which Pompeius had recourse to boost his popularity when the need arose. Of the three occasions on which the question arises, Marshall's thesis is plausible enough for 52, but is far less convincing for 59 and 58. Why Caesar should have lent his active support to such a scheme is not made clear.

Wiseman reiterates the common view that Caesar was responsible, since Caesar benefited.[35] Caesar did indeed benefit; no doubt that is why he was prepared to become involved. But Clodius benefited more, and it is hard to imagine why, if the plan was of Caesar's devising, Curio, whose hostility to Caesar at this time was extreme, should have been prepared to undertake such a crucial role. Tatum rejects the authorship of Clodius for lack of evidence, though he admits that Clodius profited from the affair.[36] But if, as I still believe, Cicero never knew that Clodius was behind the business, the lack of evidence becomes explicable. Moreover, the parallel between the Vettius affair and the supposed attempt on the life of Pompeius perpetrated by Clodius in 58 (which Tatum does not consider) remains very striking.[37]

The tribunate of Clodius has also received attention. His proposal to annex Cyprus (p. 103) was inspired not only by political considerations that were relevant in 58 but also by a personal grudge, since Ptolemy of Cyprus had failed to come up with sufficient funds for the ransom when Clodius had been captured by pirates.[38] The decision to annex Cyprus must also be seen as linked with the recognition of Ptolemy Auletes of Egypt by Pompeius and Caesar in the previous year and the alleged bequest to Rome of his kingdom by Ptolemy Alexander, since Cyprus constituted a part of the legacy, if the will was genuine.[39]

Clodius' decision to go on the offensive against Pompeius in 58 (p. 104) remains something of a puzzle. Tatum rejects the notion that Clodius saw both Cato and Pompeius as rivals for popular support and so was eager to neutralize both. He suggests that Clodius believed that a campaign against Pompeius might win him optimate support (as it certainly did in 56). He notes that Clodius chose as his specific targets aspects of the Eastern settlement, which had moved leading optimates to such wrath in the late sixties.[40] The idea is an attractive one, though it must not be forgotten that Clodius had personal motives for choosing these particular points of attack. Tatum himself has pointed to his grudge against Ptolemy of Cyprus, while engineering the escape of the young Tigranes was probably, as I have suggested (p. 103), a *quid pro quo* for the attempt to send Clodius to Armenia in 59. As for Brogitarus, he no doubt paid handsomely for the privilege of replacing Deiotarus at Pessinus. In the same connection Tatum also calls attention to Pompeius' cunning in using Gabinius as a weapon against Clodius.[41] Respectable senators were perhaps more likely than the people to feel that Clodius was going too far in using such a degree of violence against a consul in office, even if he were not the ideal consul. (It is interesting, however, that the *s.c.u.* was not passed.)

Marshall offers an explanation of the supposed attempt to murder Pompeius in August 58 (p. 106) that is consistent with his view of the Vettius affair, that is, that Pompeius himself staged this piece of theatre, deliberately withdrawing from public life in order to prove himself indispensable.[42] This seems implausible. As far as the public knew Pompeius was in hiding since a singularly unconvincing charade had made him so afraid for his life that he did not dare to show his face in public. His retirement must have been seen as a plain admission that he felt himself unable to stand up to Clodius as long as Clodius was in office. It is surely incredible that a man as vain and as concerned for his public image as Pompeius undoubtedly was should even temporarily have courted such a crushing loss of face.

Various events before and after Luca are in need of some reappraisal. Tatum claims that the first proposal to assign to Pompeius the task of restoring Ptolemy Auletes (p. 113) was promulgated by L. Caninius Gallus at the outset of his tribunate.[43] However, there is no dated mention of this bill before the middle of January 56, and the usual view that it was not proposed until the first days of February (though talked about earlier) still seems preferable. The problems encountered by Pompeius in acquiring corn, which were at least in part responsible for his readiness to reopen the question of the Campanian land (p. 110), are linked by Tatum with the burning of the temple of the Nymphs in February or March of 56 by a gang led by Clodius' henchman Sex. Cloelius. The temple had served Pompeius as an office for the administration of grain distributions in the city, and so its destruction may belong to the series of confrontations between him and

Clodius on the subject of the food supply that had begun in connection with the recall of Cicero.[44]

A matter on which Tatum is almost certainly right is the reconciliation between Clodius and Pompeius which took place in the aftermath of Luca (p. 120).[45] He argues convincingly that it must be regarded as sincere. Clodius, moved by family loyalty, sacrificed his own feelings and principal source of amusement in order to further the interests of his brothers, especially the eldest, Appius. Though this view is to be accepted, it may still be the case that the fulsomeness with which Clodius advertised his changed stance was a way of salving his wounded pride and a discreet indication that he was bowing to the force of circumstance.[46]

There is a close connection between Tatum's view of the reconciliation and his solution to another vexed question, the date of the marriage between Pompeius' son Gnaeus and the daughter of Ap. Claudius (p. 127). Here Tatum is in conflict with Hillard. Hillard places the match immediately after Pompeius' return from the East. He bases this conclusion on a passage of Cicero (*har.resp.* 45) which calls Pompeius a relative by marriage of Clodius in 60.[47] This, he says, cannot refer to Mucia since the divorce. Therefore young Gnaeus must already have married Claudia. In the same passage Cicero also calls Pompeius a *sodalis* of Clodius; this Hillard refers to support by Clodius for Pompeius' candidate in the consular elections for 60.[48]

Tatum objects that this dating entails the rejection of the evidence of Dio (38.15.6), which points to a date between 59 and 54.[49] But 58 and 57, when relations between Pompeius and Clodius were at their worst, are obviously out of the question; spring 56, on the other hand, would be politically most appropriate. Tatum must then of course find a way round the Cicero passage. He suggests that the description of Pompeius as an *adfinis* and *sodalis* of Clodius is to be referred not to 60 but to 56, so that Cicero is indeed alluding to the marriage of Pompeius' son, shortly after it took place in spring 56.[50]

The truth may lie in a combination of the two views. Tatum's dating of the marriage to spring 56 is almost certainly correct: the evidence of Dio cannot be simply disregarded. But his explanation of the Cicero passage is surely farfetched. Cicero was talking about 60, not 56, as his parallel allusion to Metellus Celer as consul in the same passage makes clear. It remains to decide on what ground Pompeius could be called an *adfinis* of Clodius in 60. Despite the certainty of Hillard (less vehemently followed by Tatum), it seems to me that the claim could still be based on Pompeius' marriage to Mucia, even after the divorce. Cicero's point is that Clodius met with opposition even from those from whom ties of birth or marriage might have led him to expect support. He would not have shrunk from the degree of distortion involved, if it enabled him to put Pompeius in that category. Tatum's interpretation may have some relevance here. If at the time of delivery of the *de haruspicum responso* Pompeius had just become an *adfinis* of Clodius for a second time, this may have encouraged Cicero to hope that his hearers would forget that he had not in fact been one in 60. If Cicero is indeed speaking about 60, Hillard's interpretation of *sodalis* is probably correct.

Ward's interpretation of Cicero's comment on his embarrassment after Luca (p. 119) has been challenged by Hornblower and defended against Hornblower's criticisms by me. In my view it still holds good.[51]

The performance of Gabinius as governor of Syria and his tribulations on his return to Rome have attracted attention. The view that Gabinius was in the main a good governor, who throughout his career had the interests of the provincials at heart (p. 101), has received welcome support.[52] Tatum notes how many associates of Pompeius joined in the attacks on Gabinius when he returned.[53] This is true and striking. Yet Pompeius' efforts to save Gabinius (p. 128) were undoubtedly sincere and energetic. The lesson is that men of distinction, even if they were linked with Pompeius by alliances of one sort and another, did not on that account feel obliged to concur with his wishes on every issue. Sherwin-White suggests that at his trial for *maiestas* (p. 129) Gabinius had some powerful equestrian support, from bankers such as Rabirius Postumus, who approved of Gabinius' restoration of Auletes because the Egyptian king owed them money.[54] But at his second trial, for *repetundae*, these men may have shown less interest, while the *publicani*, who were baying for Gabinius' blood, will have been strong enough to carry the day.

Of the occasions in the fifties when Pompeius claimed to fear assassination, his alleged suspicion that at the time of his trial Milo was planning to kill him is perhaps the hardest to evaluate (p. 135). Marshall argues yet again that Pompeius was being hypocritical.[55] This is undoubtedly the instance in which he is most likely to be right. Pompeius certainly wanted to get rid of Milo now that he had rendered himself obsolete by liquidating Clodius, but to accomplish that end he had no need to pretend that he thought Milo wanted to kill him. Milo was plainly guilty of murder, and Pompeius took elaborate and effective measures to ensure that the court brought in the desired verdict. It may therefore be the case that his fear of assassination, however neurotic and implausible, was yet again genuine.

Epstein is inclined to take seriously Cicero's claim that Pompeius did not approve of Clodius' murder.[56] His reason is that such approval would have called into question the sincerity of the reconciliation between the two men after Luca. It might be asked whether that still mattered, now that Clodius was safely dead. But even if Pompeius was so punctilious, his scruples would do no more than prevent him from endorsing Milo's action in public. His private opinions would remain unaffected. It would seem not unreasonable to suppose that he was glad both that Clodius was gone and that the manner of his going afforded him the opportunity to dispense with Milo as well (p. 136).

Epstein is on firmer ground when he claims that Pompeius chose Metellus Scipio as his colleague in the consulship of 52 (p. 137) in part to protect Metellus from the charge of *ambitus* brought against him by C. Memmius.[57] It might be fairer to say that Pompeius would have chosen Metellus in any case; but that this saved Metellus from the threat of prosecution was unquestionably a bonus. Epstein's further suggestion that Memmius had himself brought the case to secure immunity from the bribery charge that had been hanging over him since 54 is attractive. He is also surely correct in rejecting the idea that the prosecution of Plancus (p. 139) is to be seen as an attack on Pompeius.[58]

In the complex prelude to the civil war of 49 the idea that Cicero's young friend M. Caelius and others suspected that Pompeius and Caesar had come to some arrangement (p. 143) has been called into question.[59] Wiseman, following Shackleton Bailey, believes that *negotium* in Cael. *Fam.*8.8.9 means not 'a deal', but 'trouble'. This is indeed linguistically possible, but does not seem to me to make any sense in context, since Caelius in his next sentence goes on to speculate about the possible terms of such a deal from Caesar's point of view.

APPENDIX 1
CHRONOLOGICAL TABLE

146	Destruction of Carthage by Scipio Aemilianus.
133	Tribunate and death of Ti. Gracchus.
129	Death of Scipio Aemilianus.
125	Failed attempt of Fulvius Flaccus to enfranchise the Italians. Revolt of Fregellae.
123	First tribunate of C. Gracchus.
122	Second tribunate of C. Gracchus.
121	Death of C. Gracchus; first use of *s.c.u.*
119	Tribunate of C. Marius.
112	Massacre of Italian businessmen at Cirta by Jugurtha.
109	Q. Metellus appointed to command against Jugurtha.
107	First consulship of Marius; appointed to command against Jugurtha.
106	Birth of Pompeius.
105	Jugurtha handed over to Sulla by Bocchus. Cimbri defeat Mallius and Caepio at Arausio.
104– 100	Marius holds five successive consulships.
103	First tribunate of Saturninus.
102	Teutones defeated at Aquae Sextiae.
101	(?Second) tribunate of Glaucia. Cimbri defeated at Vercellae.
100	Second tribunate of Saturninus, praetorship of Glaucia. Deaths of Saturninus and Glaucia.
98	*Lex Caecilia Didia.*
95	Trials of C. Norbanus and Caepio the younger. *Lex Licinia Mucia.*
92	Trial of Rutilius Rufus.
91	Tribunate and death of Livius Drusus the younger. Outbreak of Social War.
90	*Quaestio Varia.*

Lex Iulia on citizenship.

89   Consulship and triumph of Pompeius Strabo.

Lex Plautia Papiria; *lex Pompeia* on Transpadani.

Outbreak of war against Mithradates.

88   First consulship of Sulla.

Tribunate of P. Sulpicius.

Sulla's march on Rome; death of Sulpicius; flight of Marius to Africa; departure of Sulla to Mithradatic War.

Death of Pompeius Strabo.

87   First consulship of Cinna.

Capture of Rome by Cinna, Marius and Sertorius.

86   Seventh consulship and death of Marius; second consulship of Cinna.

Prosecution of Pompeius for *peculatus*.

Marriage of Pompeius and Antistia.

85   Cinna's third consulship, Carbo's first.

Sulla concludes Peace of Dardanus with Mithradates.

84   Fourth consulship and death of Cinna, second consulship of Carbo.

Distribution of new citizens throughout all the tribes.

83   Sulla lands in Italy and is joined by Pompeius and others.

Sertorius flees to Spain.

82   Third consulship of Carbo, consulship of Marius' son.

Battle of the Colline Gate.

Sulla institutes proscriptions.

Sulla appointed dictator.

Marriage of Pompeius and Aemilia.

Pompeius in Sicily.

81   Sulla's legislation.

Death of Aemilia.

Pompeius in Africa, acquires *cognomen* Magnus.

Pompeius' first triumph (12 March).

Marriage of Pompeius and Mucia.

Sulla's abdication.

80   Sulla's second consulship.

Sex. Roscius of Ameria defended by Cicero.

79   Pompeius quarrels with Sulla, is cut out of Sulla's will.

78   Consulship of M. Lepidus.

Death and state funeral of Sulla.

Rising of Lepidus.

77   Pompeius receives praetorian *imperium* to assist Catulus against Lepidus and M. Brutus, puts Brutus to death after fall of Mutina.

Pompeius receives proconsular *imperium* to reinforce Metellus Pius in Spain against Sertorius.

75   The consul C. Cotta reopens higher office to ex-tribunes.

74	Negotiations between Sertorius and Mithradates.
	Mithradatic commands of L. Lucullus and M. Cotta; command of M. Antonius against the pirates.
	Agitation of the tribune L. Quinctius.
73	Verres becomes governor of Sicily.
	Revolt of Spartacus.
	Agitation of the tribune Licinius Macer.
72	Assassination of Sertorius.
	Special command of Crassus against Spartacus.
71	Defeat and death of Spartacus.
	Triumphs of Pompeius and Metellus Pius; ovation of Crassus.
70	First joint consulship of Pompeius and Crassus.
	Restoration of the legislative powers of the tribunes.
	Trial of Verres.
	Reform of juries by the praetor L. Cotta.
	The censors expel 64 senators and complete formal enrolment of new citizens.
69	Trial of M. Fonteius.
68	Agitation of Quinctius against Lucullus.
67	Tribunates of Cornelius and Gabinius.
	Lex Gabinia gives Pompeius command against pirates; Pompeius defeats pirates, clashes with Q. Metellus in Crete.
	Disastrous defeat of Lucullus' forces at Zela.
66	*Lex Manilia* gives Pompeius command against Mithradates; defeat of Mithradates, surrender of Tigranes.
65	Trials of Manilius and Cornelius.
	Trial of Catilina for *repetundae*.
	Unsuccessful attempt by Crassus as censor to annex Egypt.
	Iberian and Albanian campaigns; reduction of Pontus.
63	Consulship of Cicero.
	Agrarian bill of Rullus.
	Trial of Rabirius.
	'Catilinarian Conspiracy'.
	Caesar elected *pontifex maximus*.
	Death of Mithradates.
62	Death of Catilina at battle of Pistoria.
	Praetorship of Caesar, tribunates of Metellus Nepos and Cato.
	Pompeius completes his settlement of the East, returns to Rome and divorces Mucia.
61	Trial of Clodius.
	Pompeius' third triumph.
	Caesar in Spain.
	Agrarian bill of L. Flavius.

60	Caesar returns from Spain, sacrifices triumph, is elected consul for 59, supported by Pompeius and Crassus.
59	Caesar's first consulship.
	Coalition between Caesar, Pompeius and Crassus.
	Caesar's legislation, including land for Pompeius' veterans and ratification of his Eastern *acta*.
	Lex Vatinia gives Caesar his Gallic command.
	Marriage of Pompeius and Julia.
	Clodius becomes a plebeian, is elected tribune.
	The 'Vettius affair'.
58	Tribunate of Clodius.
	Exile of Cicero.
	Commands in Syria and Macedonia for Gabinius and Piso.
	Cato's mission to annex Cyprus.
	Caesar begins Gallic war.
	Pompeius worsted by Clodius, withdraws from public life.
57	Recall of Cicero.
	Pompeius appointed to oversee corn supply.
	Ptolemy Auletes comes to Italy.
56	Campanian land and Egyptian controversies.
	'Conference of Luca'.
55	Second joint consulship of Pompeius and Crassus.
	Lex Trebonia creates commands for Pompeius in Spain, Crassus in Syria.
	Extension of Caesar's Gallic command; first invasion of Britain.
	Dedication of theatre of Pompeius.
	Restoration of Ptolemy Auletes by Gabinius.
54	Death of Julia.
	Trials of Gabinius.
	Caesar's second invasion of Britain.
53	Defeat and death of Crassus at Carrhae.
	Growth of anarchy at Rome.
52	Murder of Clodius by Milo.
	Sole consulship of Pompeius.
	Trial of Milo.
	Marriage of Pompeius and Cornelia.
	Law of ten tribunes; Pompeius' laws on appointment of provincial governors and personal candidature for office.
51	Attempts to remove Caesar from the Gallic command.
	Cicero governor of Cilicia.
50	Further attempts to supersede Caesar.
	Tribunate of Curio.
	Illness and recovery of Pompeius.
	The consul C. Marcellus entrusts the defence of the state to Pompeius.

49   Tribunate of Antonius and Q. Cassius, who flee to Caesar after passing
                of the *s. c. u.*
            Caesar invades Italy.
            Evacuation of Rome and Italy by Pompeius and the consuls.
            Caesar as dictator presides over his own election as consul for 48.
48   Pompeius appointed supreme commander of republican forces.
            Battle of Pharsalus.
            Pompeius murdered on arrival in Egypt.

APPENDIX 2
THE CHRONOLOGY OF CAESAR'S LEGISLATION IN 59

The view that the first agrarian law was not passed until the latter part of April rests on two statements in the secondary sources: that Bibulus' retirement from public life was occasioned by riots connected with this law, and that he spent eight months of the year shut up in his house.[1] The evidence of Cicero compels the rejection of this combination. Letters from the middle of April make it clear that the law had already been in existence long enough for the commission of twenty charged with its administration to have been elected.[2] Before 24 April there was only one comitial day in that month; therefore the law cannot have been passed later than March.[3] It is clear from Cicero's comment in December 60 that it must have been promulgated in January 59, perhaps even earlier if it was formally proposed by Vatinius rather than Caesar himself.[4] The delays narrated in detail by Dio will have occupied the month of January, and if Bibulus in fact spent eleven months shut up in his house, the law must have been forced through at the end of that month.[5]

The earliest reference to the ratification of Pompeius' settlement of the East also comes from the middle of April.[6] The date of this allusion and the fact that the measure was carried without opposition, after resistance had been cowed by the violence used to secure the passage of the agrarian bill, point to a date in middle or late March.[7] The rebate for the *publicani* is not mentioned by Cicero until early May,[8] but the arguments advanced in the text would suggest a date in March for this measure too.[9]

The Campanian land law, first mentioned at the end of April or beginning of May,[10] presumably belongs to the last week in April. The only major problem remaining is the *lex Vatinia*. The case for a date at the end of February or beginning of March is feeble in the extreme.[11] The question of whether the law laid down a precise terminal date for Caesar's tenure will be discussed elsewhere.[12] All that needs to be said here is that, even if the *lex Vatinia* did specify 1 March 54 as the terminal date, there could be various possible reasons for the choice of that date, of which the fact that it was the anniversary of the day on which the law was passed is one of the least cogent that could be imagined. It must therefore be stressed that belief in 1 March 54 as the terminal date under the *lex Vatinia* in no way depends on or entails belief in 1 March 59 as the date of the law's enactment. General arguments all point to a later date. If any weight is to be assigned to Suetonius' statement that the law was passed after the marriages of Caesar to Calpurnia and Pompeius to Julia,[13] this would mean that May was the earliest possible date,[14] while in general terms it is highly unlikely that Caesar would turn to securing his own reward before all those matters in which Pompeius and Crassus had a direct interest had been attended to.[15] The earliest passage of Cicero in which a reference to the law has been detected comes from the beginning of May: the notoriously controversial remark of Pompeius: *oppressos uos tenebo exercitu Caesaris*.[16] Understanding of this utterance has been bedevilled by the unfortunate suggestion that *exercitu* here is metaphorical.[17] This interpretation has nothing to commend it; the parallels cited are all false, since in all of them *exercitus* is qualified in one way or another, and it is always the qualifying word or phrase that gives the whole expression its figurative character. *Exercitus* here must be taken at its face value.[18] Two facts therefore emerge: at the beginning of May Pompeius knew that Caesar would have an army, and that Caesar would be governor of Cisalpine Gaul, the only province, geographically speaking, of which his remark could reasonably be made. The first fact is of no significance: anyone in Rome who stopped to think would realize that Caesar would proceed to some provincial command. The second is more important. It proves that the dynasts had agreed among themselves what Caesar's province was to be and that Pompeius at least did not regard this as a secret. It does not, however, of itself prove that the *lex Vatinia* had been passed or even promulgated.[19] It is true that Cicero does not treat the remark as likely to stimulate surprise or needing any gloss. That might perhaps indicate that the fact behind Pompeius' allusion was already public knowledge, that is, that the law had been promulgated or was at least on the point of being so, but again it might merely show that Cicero thought the point too obvious to require any explanation. Therefore the most plausible date for the *lex Vatinia* remains late May or even early June.[20]

APPENDIX 3
THE TERMINAL DATE
OF CAESAR'S GALLIC COMMAND

The purpose of this appendix is simply to present a clear and succinct statement of the views assumed in the text. It does not purport to offer a full discussion of the subject or of other solutions to the problem.

The obvious question provoked by mention of the *legis dies* is: if there was a terminal date, why does no source say what it was? The evidence is relatively copious, and in it discussions of the subject of Caesar's supersession are often reported at length. In the course of these discussions various persons suggest various dates on or after which it would or would not be fair or expedient to replace Caesar, yet at no point does any party to the dispute appeal plainly to a legally defined terminal date and rest his case upon it. Instead all is confusion, with a string of more or less tendentious proposals made on one side or the other.[1] The natural explanation of this situation is that there was no terminal date specified in the law of Pompeius and Crassus, but to defend this answer it is necessary to examine those texts which have been cited as evidence for the view that the *lex Vatinia*, the *lex Licinia Pompeia* or both did lay down a terminal date.

A single passage of Cicero (*prov.cos.*36f.) is said to indicate the presence of a terminal date, 1 March 54, in the law of Vatinius. It runs as follows:

Nam illae sententiae uirorum clarissimorum minime probandae sunt, quorum alter ulteriorem Galliam decernit cum Syria, alter citeriorem. qui ulteriorem, omnia illa de quibus disserui paulo ante perturbat; simul ostendit eam se tenere legem quam esse legem neget, et, quae pars prouinciae sit cui non possit intercedi, hanc se auellere, quae defensorem habeat, non tangere, simul et illud facit, ut, quod illi a populo datum sit, id non uiolet, quod senatus dederit, id senator properet auferre. alter belli Gallici rationem habet, fungitur officio boni senatoris, legem quam non putat, eam quoque seruat; praefinit enim successori diem. *quamquam* mihi nihil uidetur alienum a dignitate disciplinaque maiorum quam ut, qui consul Kalendis Ianuariis habere prouinciam debet, is ut eam desponsam non decretam habere uideatur. fuerit toto in consulatu sine prouincia cui fuerit, ante quam designatus est, decreta prouincia. sortietur an non? nam et non sortiri absurdum est, et quod sortitus sis non habere. proficiscetur paludatus? quo? quo peruenire ante certam diem non licebit. Ianuario, Februario prouinciam non habebit: Kalendis ei denique Martiis nascetur repente prouincia.

Not all the points made in this tortuously sophistical argument are relevant here. Cicero is combating two proposals, the first to make Transalpina consular, the second to do the same to Cisalpina. In either case the province would be allotted to a consul of 55. About the first proposal he makes the point that it respects the *lex Vatinia*. The reason is clear: Transalpina had been granted to Caesar not by the *lex Vatinia* but by a decree of the senate, so a proposal to reallocate it did not infringe that law. But Cicero says that the second proposal also observes the *lex Vatinia*, because it prescribes in advance a day for Caesar's successor. That day, as emerges from what follows, is 1 March 54, so that some unfortunate consul of 55 will paradoxically be unable to go to his province not only during his year of office but even in January or February 54.

The question to be asked is simple: how did this restriction show respect for the *lex Vatinia*? An obvious answer, and the one usually given, is that the *lex Vatinia* in some sense guaranteed Caesar his province until 1 March 54. However, if there was a terminal date in the *lex Vatinia*, it is highly unlikely that there was not also a terminal date in the *lex Licinia Pompeia*. Yet the confusion of the late fifties militates against this assumption, and as will be seen there is no evidence to support it. It is therefore not unreasonable to ask if this is the only possible explanation. If the *lex Vatinia* said nothing more than that Caesar was to have Cisalpina for five years, the natural interpretation of this, before political chicanery took a hand, would be for five campaigning seasons, those of 58 to 54 inclusive. If this intention was observed, the likely train of events would be as follows: in summer 55, before the consular elections, Cisalpina would be declared consular, to be held by a consul of 54, who would not go out until late 54 or early 53. The significance of 1 March 54 in this schema might be that this would be the normal day for dealing with provincial allocations, perhaps the day on which the consuls drew lots.[2] A consul of 54 might therefore in the normal course of things acquire Cisalpina as his province precisely on 1 March 54. The present proposal, by a devious yet transparent fiction, pretended to respect that intended train of events, since it too allowed a consul to acquire the province on 1 March 54. The vital difference of course was that that consul would be, not one of 54, but one of 55, who would be free to take over control at once. Thus Caesar would be deprived of one campaigning season, and could be succeeded by Domitius Ahenobarbus, who at the time the proposal was made was still expected to secure the consulship for 55. Yet it could be argued that the motion respected the *lex Vatinia*, in that by its terms the province was in one sense being allocated on the day on which it would indeed have been allocated in another sense if Vatinius' intentions had been observed.[3] It may be asked why Cicero did not expose this sophistry and cry out that the *lex Vatinia* was being infringed on a far more important level, since Caesar was being deprived of a whole year in Gaul. The answer is surely that he did not want to appear in so unlikely and uncomfortable a guise as that of earnest defender of the *lex Vatinia*, and had hit upon an adequate, though equally sophistical counter, posing as the champion of consular rights, rights that in the circumstances Ahenobarbus or any other optimate consul might well have been happy to forgo.

Three passages have been said to refer to a terminal date in the *lex Licinia Pompeia*. They are:

> Cic.*Att*.7.7.6: exercitum retinentis cum legis dies transierit rationem haberi placet?
> Cic.*Att*.7.9.4: tenuisti prouinciam per annos decem non tibi a senatu sed a te ipso per uim et per factionem datos; praeteriit tempus non legis sed libidinis tuae, fac tamen legis.
> Caes.*BC* 1.2.6: sic uocibus consulis, terrore praesentis exercitus, minis amicorum Pompei plerique compulsi inuiti et coacti Scipionis sententiam sequuntur: uti ante certam diem Caesar exercitum dimittat; si non faciat, eum aduersus rem publicam facturum uideri.

Exploitation of the first rests on the assumption that *legis dies* must refer to a specific day mentioned in the law. That is not impossible, but neither necessary nor likely. *Legis dies* here can equally well mean exactly the same as *tempus legis* in the second passage, that is, the period allowed by the law.[4] As to the third passage, that undoubtedly does refer to a fixed day: not, however, a day prescribed by the *lex Licinia Pompeia*, but one selected *ad hoc* by Metellus Scipio and perhaps incorporated in his ultimatum.[5]

One final argument needs to be dealt with: the suggestion that there must have been a fixed day in the *lex Vatinia* and the *lex Licinia Pompeia* because the *lex Titia* of 43, which established the triumvirate, specified such a day.[6] The fact is secure, but not the inference: it is more likely that the confusion and uncertainty which resulted from the lack of a terminal date in the fifties taught the Romans a lesson, and that the prescription of a precise date in the *lex Titia* was intended to guard against a recurrence.

If there was no terminal date, it is hardly surprising that confusion reigned. According to preference the first quinquennium could be defined in at least five ways: five campaigning seasons, five calendar years from the passing of the law, from 1 January 58, from Caesar's departure from Rome, or from his arrival in Gaul. The second quinquennium could be even more complex: five campaigning seasons, starting with 55, 54 or 53, the tenth anniversary of any of the above calendar dates, or five calendar years from the passing of the law or from 1 January 54. It has been said that Pompeius would never have allowed such ambiguity, but this is naive: the greater the formal uncertainty, the greater the scope for Pompeius to exercise his *auctoritas* as arbiter and assert his political domination over both Caesar and the optimates – precisely what he wanted.

It is therefore assumed in the text that no answer to the question of when a successor to Caesar might or should be appointed was to be found in either law, since neither contained a precise terminal date.

NOTES

PREFACE

1 Since this book, and these words, were written, there has appeared J. Leach, *Pompey the Great* (London, 1978), which does little to improve the situation. Cf. further *LCM* 3, 1978, 233ff. Another recent publication, B. Rawson, *The Politics of Friendship* (Sydney, 1978), is a useful collection of translated sources with an excellent introduction and linking commentary.

1   CN. POMPEIUS STRABO

1 Numantia: *MRR* I 477, 480; Ti. Gracchus: Plut.*TG* 14, Oros.5.8.4, cf. App.*BC* 1.13.57; censorship: *GC* 16f.

2 Vell.2.21.4. For Pompeius' mother Lucilia, a relative of the poet, cf. Vell.2.29.2; Cichorius, *RS* 68. In general, cf. Gelzer, *Pompeius* 25; Miltner, *RE* 21.2050. On the relationship of the Pompeii Bithynici to the family of Magnus, cf. Badian, *Historia* 12, 1963, 138f., against Taylor, *VD* 244f. and the fantasies of Cichorius, *RS* 185ff. On the identity of the Sex. Pompeius who was at Asculum, cf. Mattingly, *Athen.* n.s. 53, 1975, 262f. Cf. now also Ward, *Crassus* 123 n. 84.

3 On Strabo, cf. above all Gelzer, *KS* II 106ff.; for his quaestorship and attempted prosecution of Albucius, cf. Gruen, *RPCC* 172f.

4 For the Pompeii and Picenum, cf. Gelzer, *KS* II 111; Badian, *FC* 228f. The significance of the tribe: Taylor, *VD* 246.

5 App.*BC* 1.47, Liv.*per.*74, Oros.5.18.10, 17.

6 App.*BC* 1.50.216, Diod.37.2, Vell.2.15.3, Liv.*per.*74, Flor.2.6.14, Oros.5.18.10, 17.

7 App.*BC* 1.52.227, Liv.*per.*76.

8 App.*BC* 1.50.217, Liv.*per.*75, Oros.5.18.24.

9 App.*BC* 1.48.207ff., Vell.2.21.1, Flor.2.6.14, *ILLRP* 1092.

10 Cic.*Phil.*12.27. The assumption of Cichorius (*RS* 181ff., followed by Ward, *Phoen.* 24, 1970, 122f.) that Cicero was a member of Strabo's *consilium* at this time is possible but unproven. Even if true, it would not demonstrate any close link between Cicero and the young Pompeius. Ward's attempt (*art. cit.* 119ff.) to establish such a link for the eighties is supported by no solid evidence.

11 On Pompeius' inherited power in Picenum, cf. Cic.*QF* 2.3.4, *Phil.* 5.44, *BAfr*.22.5, App.*BC* 1.80.366, Vell.2.29.1, Val.Max.5.2.9, Plut.*Pomp*.6, Dio fr.107.1. Note the numerous men from Picenum in Strabo's *consilium* at Asculum: *ILLRP* 515.7ff., cf. Cichorius, *RS* 157f.

12 *ILLRP* 515. For discussion, cf. especially Cichorius, *RS* 130ff.; Criniti, *Epigrafe*.

13 *ILLRP* 515.8.

14 Cic.*Balb*.50; cf. Gelzer, *KS* II 113.

15 Ascon.3; cf. Strabo 5.1.6 on the status of Comum, Plin.*NH* 3.138 on the attribution of certain Cottian tribes to Transpadane towns. Cf. Stevenson, *JRS* 9, 1919, 95ff.

16 Cic.*QF* 2.3.4.

17 Ascon.14, *Fast. Triumph.* (*GC* 156).

18 *MRR* II 393.

19 Val.Max.6.9.9, Plin.*NH* 7.135, Juv.7.199ff., Gell.15.4.3.

20 Despite Val.Max.9.7.*mil.Rom*.2 on his continuing tenure *inuita ciuitate* he had proconsular *imperium* in 87, as is attested by App.*BC* 1.66.303, and it is reasonable to suppose that he assumed it on leaving Rome after his triumph. That he was not prosecuted under the *lex Varia* has been finally demonstrated by Badian, *Historia* 18, 1969, 465ff.

21 App.*BC* 1.56.247, Vell.2.18.6, Liv.*per*.77.

22 Vell.2.21.1: *frustratus spe continuandi consulatus*. If these words are to be given their face value, as rightly recommended by Gelzer, *KS* II 117, they must refer to the consulship of 88. If so, they make sense in the logic of Velleius' account as an explanation of why Strabo was moved to take up in 87 the ambiguous attitude which Velleius goes on to describe and criticize. They cannot on the other hand refer in context to the consulship of 86, since it was in order to secure the office for that year that Strabo embarked in 87 on his intrigues with Octavius and Cinna; he could therefore not be described as frustrated of his hope of the consulship of 86 at the moment of initiating a policy designed to achieve it.

23 Neither a Rufus nor a patrician: cf. Mattingly, *Athen.* n.s. 53, 1975, 264f.

24 Sources for these events: *GC* 160ff.

25 Sall.*Hist.* 2.21, correctly interpreted by Badian, *Hermes* 83, 1955, 107f.; *ex composito* refers of course to an arrangement between Herennius and Strabo.

26 The senate as the source of Rufus' appointment: Val.Max.9.7.*mil.Rom*.2; App.*BC* 1.63.283 speaks of a law, but cf. Gelzer, *KS* II 121.

27 App.*BC* 1.63.283ff., who does not directly accuse Strabo of responsibility. Strabo is blamed by Vell.2.20.1, Liv.*per*.77 and Val.Max.9.7.*mil.Rom*.2, who alone mentions the reason for the gathering.

28 For Sulla's apprehension, cf. App.*BC* 1.64.286.

29 Cf. *MRR* II 36.

30 Vell.2.21.1, Liv.*per*.79.

31 App.*BC* 1.66.303–67.304, Licin.18.

32 Plut.*Pomp*.3. The story has certainly been exaggerated to eulogize Pompeius (cf. Gelzer, *KS* II 122); in particular it seems unlikely that the men who had just killed Rufus to protect Strabo's command should have mutinied against him for no good cause.

33 App.*BC* 1.67.304, Licin.18.

34 App.*BC*.1.68.312, Vell.2.21.1, Licin.18f.

35 Licin.19. Dio 52.13.2 goes so far as to accuse him of seeking absolute power.

36 Thus Badian, *FC* 239.

37 Licin.21; cf. Gelzer, *KS* II 124.

38 Most detail in Licin.22; also App.*BC* 1.68.312, 80.366, Vell.2.21.3, Obseq.56a, Oros.5.19.18. The fact that lightning struck Strabo's tent and killed some of his men no doubt promoted misunderstanding of the phrase *sidere adflatus* to give rise to the improving legend that the gods had shown their hatred of him by smiting him with a thunderbolt. Cf. Gelzer, *KS* II 125.

39 Licin.22. It is regrettable that most of Strabo's reaction to the arrival of Cassius has disappeared in a lacuna.

40 Licin.22f., Vell.2.21.3, Plut.*Pomp*.1. Motives for the riot: Strabo's avarice and treachery (Licin.23); his avarice (Plut.*Pomp*.1); his failure to aid the state (Obseq.56a).

41 Vell.2.53.4, Plin.*NH* 37.13.

42 Vell.2.29.3, cf. Diod.38.9; slightly later: Sall.*Hist*.2.19.

43 *ILLRP* 515.8.

44 Apart from the anecdote of Plut.*Pomp*.3, cf. Dio 36.25.2.

45 This perhaps needs stating in view of such curious oversights as Taylor, *PP* 121; Ward, *Phoen.* 24, 1970, 120.

46 Note the apt and succinct observation of Sen.*Contr*.1.6.4: *Pompeium si hereditariae extulissent imagines, nemo Magnum dixisset* ('if Pompeius had displayed his ancestral portraits, nobody would have called him the Great').

47 The famous comment of Cic.ap.Ascon.89: *hominem dis ac nobilitati perinuisum* ('a man most hated by the gods and the nobility'), unfortunately does not refer to Strabo; nevertheless it fits him perfectly.

48 Cf. above n. 11.

49 According to Plut.*Pomp*.1 and Licin. 23 a major cause of Strabo's unpopularity was his unbridled lust for wealth. Pompeius was to be noted for his *innocentia*: Cic.*leg.Man*.36, 40, Vell.2.29.2.

50 Apart from the disturbances at Strabo's funeral, cf. for the general hatred of him Plut.*Crass*.6, *mor*.203B, 553C. This must surely have contributed to Pompeius' exaggerated desire to be the object of universal affection, or at least of its outward show.

2   POMPEIUS, CINNA AND SULLA

1 Plut.*Pomp*.4; cf. Gruen, *RPCC* 244f., who sees the prosecution as a purely financial measure rather than a personal attack. That Pompeius had every right to the items specifically mentioned by Plutarch is shown by Shatzman, *Historia* 21, 1972, 195.

2 Philippus: Cic.*Brut*.230, Plut.*Pomp*.2; Hortensius: Cic.*Brut*.230; Carbo: Val.Max.5.3.5, 6.2.8. For Pompeius' need of such support, cf. Badian, *FC* 267.

3 Cic.*Brut*.308. Carbo's behaviour here is clearly of greater significance for possible official attitudes to Pompeius than the sacking of his house.

4 Plut.*Pomp*.4. For Antistius, cf. Cic.*Brut*.226f.; Plutarch describes him as praetor, but in fact he was only of aedilician rank at the time of his murder in 83: Vell.2.26.2, cf. Plut.*Pomp*.9.

5 Plut.*Pomp*.5.

6   Plut.*Pomp*.5.
7   Plut.*Pomp*.6.
8   Cic.*leg.Man*.61, App.*BC* 1.80.366. For Pompeius' strength in Picenum now and later, cf. Cic.*QF* 2.3.4, *Phil*.5.43f., B*Afr*.22.5, Vell.2.29.1, Plut.*Pomp*.6, Dio fr.107.1. For Crassus, cf. Plut.*Crass*.4, 6; Ward, *Crassus* 62. For Metellus, cf. App.*BC* 1.80.365.
9   App.*BC* 1.80.366.
10   App.*BC* 1.80.367, Plut.*Pomp*.8, cf. *mor*.806E, Val.Max.5.2.9. Plut.*Crass*.10 alleges that this was the origin of Crassus' jealousy of Pompeius. Gelzer (*Pompeius* 33, cf. *KS* II 130) rightly stresses that Pompeius thus already achieved the special position which was to remain his objective throughout his career.
11   App.*BC* 1.87.396 (with Pius), 88.401, 90.413 (with Crassus), 414, Plut.*Pomp*.7, 8 (with Pius), *mor*.203B, Oros.5.20.5. Cf. Gelzer, *KS* II 128f., 133f.
12   App.*BC* 1.80.367, cf. Plut.*Pomp*. 6. Cf. Gelzer, *Pompeius* 33f.; Miltner, *RE* 21.2067; Badian, *FC* 267.
13   Cf. Plut.*Sull*.33; Badian, *FC* 268ff.
14   On the name, cf. Badian, *JRS* 57, 1967, 227f.
15   Plut.*Pomp*.9, *Sull*.33.
16   Cic.*leg.Man*.61, App.*BC* 1.92.425, 95.440, 96.449, Liv.*per*.89, Eutrop.5.8.2. For Pompeius' *imperium*, cf. Licin.31, also Plut.*Pomp*.10.
17   App.*BC* 1.96.449, Plut.*Pomp*.10, Liv.*per*.89, Eutrop.5.8.2, Oros.5.21.11, 24.16.
18   Pompeius' ingratitude is highlighted by Val.Max.5.3.5, 6.2.8.
19   The date: Val.Max.9.13.2, cf. App.*BC* 1.92.425, Eutrop.5.8.2, which strictly speaking date only Carbo's initial flight to his consulship. Carbo as *proscriptus*: Plut.*Pomp*.10, *uir.ill*.77.1; cf. Luc.2.541ff., who makes Pompeius list Carbo along with Catilina, Lepidus, Sertorius and Spartacus as parallels and precedents for Caesar in 49. The defence is accepted by Gelzer, *Pompeius* 37, *KS* II 135.
20   App.*BC* 1.65.296, Vell.2.20.3, Plut.*Mar*.41, Liv.*per*.79.
21   *uir.ill*.77.1; cf. the language of Plin.*NH* 7.96. For Pompeius' generous treatment of Sicily, cf. Plut.*Pomp*.10; Gelzer, *Pompeius* 38. A *uia Pompeia*: Cic.2*Verr*.5.169; Pompeius' selling of the *decumae* of Sicily: Cic.2*Verr*.3.42.
22   Cf. Badian, *FC* 270f., 304.
23   Plut.*Pomp*.10, *mor*.203C.
24   Cic.2*Verr*.2.83ff., esp. 110, 113, Plut.*Pomp*.10, *mor*.203D, 815E–F. The names of others, with sources, are listed by Badian, *FC* 304.
25   App.*BC* 1.80.368, Plut.*Pomp*.11, Eutrop.5.9.1. Münzer, *RA* 330, conjectures that he was the brother of the eventual consul of 54; though the precise degree of the relationship is uncertain, it must have been close.
26   Plut.*Pomp*.11.
27   Sall.*Hist*.1.53, App.*BC* 1.80.368, Plut.*Pomp*.12, Liv.*per*.89, *uir.ill*.77.2, Oros.5.21.14. Here too Pompeius gave thought to his *clientela*: for enfranchisements, cf. Cic.*Balb*.51.
28   Plut.*Pomp*.10, 12, Eutrop.5.9.1, Oros.5.24.16. For the justice of Pompeius' action, cf. Liv.*per*.89; another line of justification was that Domitius died fighting: Oros.5.21.13. Again note the official and approving echoes of Plin.*NH* 7.96. Cf. Gelzer, *Pompeius* 38, *KS* II 135.
29   Plut.*Pomp*.13.

30 Thus Twyman, *ANRW* I 1.819. Badian, *FC* 274, is more inclined to take Pompeius seriously as a potential military threat to Sulla. But although Sulla's hold on Italy may have been insecure, Pompeius was hardly a plausible person to take advantage of this by presenting himself as the leader of a 'Marian' revival so soon after his actions in the civil war and the suppression of Carbo and Domitius.

31 Plut.*Pomp*.13, Plin.*NH* 7.96; salutation as *imperator*: Plut.*Pomp*.12; for Pompeius and Alexander, cf. Sall.*Hist*.3.88, Plut.*Pomp*.2.

32 Plut.*Pomp*.13, with a touching description of the dutiful Pompeius' struggle to restrain his men.

33 Plut.*Pomp*.13.

34 Plut.*Pomp*.14.

35 App.*BC* 1.80.368, Liv.*per*.89, Licin.31, Eutrop.5.9.1.

36 Plut.*Pomp*.14, *mor*.203E–F, 804E.

37 Plut.*Pomp*.9, *Sull*.33.

38 App.*BC* 1.80.368, Plut.*Pomp*.14.

39 Cic.*leg.Man*.61, App.*BC* 1.80.368, Liv.*per*.89, Licin.31.

40 Plut.*Pomp*.14, *mor*.203F. Pompeius' deliberate inconsistency in the suppression of mutiny is noted by Miltner, *RE* 21.2074.

41 Plut.*Pomp*.14, Plin.*NH* 8.4, Licin.31.

42 Licin.31.

43 Vell.2.53.4, Plin. *NH* 37.13.

44 23: Eutrop.5.9.1; 24: Liv.*per*.89; 25: Licin.31; 26: *uir.ill*.77.2.

45 By Badian, *Hermes* 83, 1955, 107ff.

46 Thus Badian, *loc. cit.* The importance accorded to Sulla's attitude may suggest that he was still dictator. If so, this would be decisive for 81, since Sulla resigned the dictatorship by the end of that year at the latest.

47 Cf. Carcopino, *Sylla* 188ff.; Badian, *FC* 249, 275; Twyman, *ANRW* I 1.835. The precise date is uncertain (cf. Badian, *FC* 249 n. 6), but Ward's suggestion of 80 (*Phoen.* 24, 1970, 126 n. 37) is plausible. On the family relationships, cf. Wiseman, *CQ* 65, 1971, 180ff.

48 Cf. Cic.*leg.Man*.30, *Phil*.5.43f., Schol.Gron.320St., and the words put by Lucan into the mouth of Caesar at 1.325ff., 7.307ff.

49 Cf. Twyman, *ANRW* I 1.826; also Gelzer, *Pompeius* 41.

3   THE RISE TO THE CONSULSHIP

1 Plut.*Pomp*.15, *Sull*.34, 38.

2 Plut.*Sull*.34. For Pompeius' motive, cf. Gelzer, *Pompeius* 43. To posit a link between Pompeius' support of Lepidus and the dropping of a charge against him by two of the younger Metelli, Celer and Nepos (thus Twyman, *ANRW* I 1.837; more tentatively Gruen, *RPCC* 275), is pure fantasy.

3 App.*BC* 1.107.501, Sall.*Hist*.1.55, 1.77.5, Flor.2.11.2f., Licin.34. For Lepidus' attitude to the tribunate, contrast Sall.*Hist*.1.77.14 with Licin.33. In general, cf. Gruen, *LGRR* 12ff.

4   App.*BC* 1.105.491, 493, 107.501, Sall.*Hist.*1.54.

5   For Pompeius' part, cf. Plut.*Pomp.*15, *Sull.*38.

6   Sall.*Hist.*1.65, cf. 1.67 on *Etrusci*, 1.77.5, Licin.34.

7   Sall.*Hist.*1.66, 1.77.1, Licin.34f.

8   Exup.6, cf. Licin.35.

9   Licin.35, cf. Sall.*Hist.*1.77.10.

10   App.*BC* 1.107.502, Sall. *Hist.* 1.77.1f., 5, Licin.35.

11   App.*BC* 1.107.502, Sall.*Hist.*1.77.4, 7, Plut.*Pomp.*16, Liv.*per.*90.

12   App.*BC* 1.107.502f.

13   App.*BC.*1.107.503, Sall.*Hist.*1.77.1ff., 14f., Plut.*Pomp.*16, Flor.2.11.5, Licin.35.

14   Cf. Badian, *FC* 275ff.

15   On the activities in Cisalpina of M. Lepidus, *cos.* 187, cf. Badian, *FC* 276.

16   Sall.*Hist.*1.77.6.

17   Sall.*Hist.*1.77.22.

18   Plut.*Pomp.*16, Flor.2.11.5.

19   Cf. Boak, *AHR* 24, 1918/19, 5; Twyman, *ANRW* I 1.821.

20   Plut.*Pomp.*17.

21   Cf. Sall.*Hist.*1.63 on Lepidus' supporters.

22   App.*BC* 1.107.503f., Flor.2.11.6, Oros.5.22.16.

23   Flor.2.11.6.

24   App.*BC* 1.107.504, Plut.*Pomp.*16, Flor.2.11.7, *uir.ill.*77.3.

25   App.*BC* 1.107.504.

26   Plut.*Pomp.*16, *Brut.*4, Liv.*per.*90, Oros.5.22.17, 24.16. Pompeius is strongly con-
     demned by Last, *CAH* IX 316; Miltner, *RE* 21.2077; Stockton, *Cicero* 54. Gelzer,
     Pompeius 44f. is more lenient.

27   It seems unlikely that Brutus could have served as a legate appointed before Lepidus'
     contumacy if he had been proscribed in 82, as Gelzer, *Pompeius* 45 tentatively suggests.

28   Plut.*Pomp.*17.

29   Badian, *FC* 278 is inclined to take the possible threat from Pompeius more seriously.
     Contra: Twyman, *ANRW* I 1.821.

30   This view is stated, and indeed overstated, at inordinate length and with much
     prosopographical fantasy by Twyman, *ANRW* I 1.816ff. (for 77, cf. esp. 821). The
     general point is undoubtedly correct. Cf. also Ward, *Crassus* 37.

31   On Sertorius, cf. especially Gabba, *Esercito* 284ff.

32   Eutrop.6.1.3, cf. Oros.5.23.5. Denied by Ward, *Crassus* 35. Pius had enjoyed little
     success, cf. Plut.*Sert.*12. Cf. Gruen, *AJP* 92, 1971, 5; Twyman, *ANRW* I 1.822.

33   Cic.*Phil.*11.18.

34   Badian, *FC* 277 sees their election as an attempt to neutralize them, but if they had
     been supporters of Lepidus it would surely have been folly to strengthen their position
     by appointing them to magistracies. If Mam. Lepidus had been suspected of disloyalty,
     the loyal Sullan Curio would not have stood down to facilitate his election (Sall.
     *Hist.*1.86). That Curio was persuaded to withdraw his candidature by Pompeius
     (Twyman, *ANRW* I 1.846) is a needless conjecture. For the refusal to go to Spain as
     a sign of sympathy with Sertorius, cf. Badian, *FC* 277; *contra*: Gelzer, *Pompeius* 46;
     Gruen, *AJP* 92, 1971, 4f., *LGRR* 19; Ward, *Crassus* 21f. Sumner suggests (*JRS* 54,
     1964, 45f.) that they did not want to impair Pius' *dignitas*. But Pius had asked for help,
     and the sending of a consul would surely have impaired his *dignitas* less than the

appointment of a youthful and unqualified *priuatus*. This is not to say that they deliberately opened the way for Pompeius, but they must have realized that there was nobody else. Cf. Twyman, *ANRW* I 1.821, 848.

35 Cf. Schol.Gron.322St.

36 Cic.*leg.Man*.62, *Phil*.11.18, App.*BC* 1.108.508, Val.Max.8.15.8, Liv.*per*.91, Schol. Gron.322St.; garbled: *uir.ill*.77.4. The play on words is untranslatable. The literal meaning of *pro consule* = a proconsul is 'in place of a consul'. Thus although Pompeius was in fact being sent as a proconsul Philippus could say, since the consuls had refused the task, that he was being sent 'not in place of a consul but (both) the consuls'. In *leg.Man*.62f. Cicero claims the *auctoritas* of Catulus for the appointment. Despite the recent clash between the two men this is not impossible: Pompeius was competent, nobody else wanted to go, and the command was free from the objections which dictated Catulus' later opposition to the laws of Gabinius and Manilius.

37 Caes.*BC* 1.29.3, 2.18.7.

38 Sall.*Hist*.2.69, Varro *RR* 3.12.7; cf. Cichorius, *RS* 193f.

39 Schol.Bob.98St.; for the son during the civil war with Caesar, cf. *MRR* II 265, 270, 283.

40 Plut.*Sert*.21, Oros.5.23.12.

41 Plut.*Sert*.19, Oros.5.23.14.

42 Ascon.57.

43 Cic.*Brut*.217, Ps.-Ascon.189St. Sicinius' *praenomen* is uncertain: either Lucius or Gnaeus.

44 Ascon.67, noting the hostility of the *nobilitas*: the reading is secured by Cic.ap.Ascon.78.

45 Thus rightly Last, *CAH* IX 334. Cic.ap.Ascon.78 deliberately minimizes the significance of the law in order to discredit the opposition to it. Cf. his comments on the attitude of Catulus to the tribunate (ap.Ascon.80f.).

46 Sall.*Hist*.3.48.8; cf. the admission put into Cotta's mouth at *Hist*.2.47.4. Cf. Marshall, *RhM* NF 118, 1975, 144ff.

47 Sall.*Hist*.2.45. A desire to distract the attention of the people from the price of corn may have helped to inspire Cotta's law on the tribunician power. For the continuing shortage of corn, which stimulated but was not cured by the *lex Terentia Cassia* of 73, cf. Cic.*2Verr*.3.163, 5.52, 55.

48 Sall.*Hist*.2.47.6f.

49 Sall.*Hist*.2.98, cf. also Plut.*Sert*.21.

50 Sall.*Hist*.2.98.10; Plut.*Pomp*.20 is perhaps even more obscure.

51 Both consuls are mentioned by Sall.*Hist*.2.98.10; for Lucullus, cf. also Plut.*Pomp*.20, *Lucull*.5. For the efforts of Fonteius in Gaul, cf. Cic.*Font*.8, 13, 26.

52 Plut.*Lucull*.6.

53 It is hardly plausible that Pompeius would return from Spain to claim the Mithradatic command, as suggested by Plut.*Pomp*.21, *Lucull*.5 (accepted by van Ooteghem, *Pompée* 122). If he were driven out of Spain by Sertorius, he would be in no position to demand immediate re-employment in a task of even greater magnitude. (Thus rightly Twyman, *ANRW* I 1.851f.) What Lucullus was presumably afraid of was that he might be required to defend Cisalpine Gaul, if not Italy itself.

54 Thus Badian, *FC* 279; Ward, *Latomus* 29, 1970, 64. But the situation in Spain was surely too serious for such tactics, especially as both Pius and Pompeius had thus far enjoyed only very limited success. Rightly denied by Gruen, *AJP* 92, 1971, 8; Ward, *Crassus* 37f., accepts that there was no sabotage, but stresses that help had been very

slow to come and that Pius had got more than Pompeius. Twyman's 'proof' (*ANRW* I 1.848ff.) that in 74 Lucullus was a political ally of Pompeius is one of his choicer flights of fancy.

55 Sall.*Hist*.3.2, Ps-Ascon.259St.

56 Cf. Badian, *FC* 280f. It seems unlikely that after the experience of the eighties Lucullus or anyone else could have expected the war to be particularly short; and if Pompeius did represent a threat, that threat was surely urgent.

57 Plut.*Lucull*.5.

58 App.*Mith*.68.289–70.297.

59 Cic.*Cluent*.110, Ps.-Ascon.189St.

60 Plut.*Lucull*.33, cf. Sall.*Hist*.4.71.

61 Sall.*Hist*.3.48.21.

62 Sall.*Hist*.3.48.23; cf. the expectations expressed in *Hist*.4.42, though these may have owed their genesis to the pronouncements of Palicanus in 71.

63 Cf. Taylor, *PP* 20.

64 Plut.*Sert*.27, *mor*.204A, cf. Cic.*2Verr*.5.152f.

65 Cic.*Balb*.19, 32f., 38. For Pius, cf. Cic.*Arch*.26, *Balb*.50; Badian, *FC* 282. For the consuls' links with Pompeius, cf. Ward, *Crassus* 24f., who suggests that Pius had received the privilege before it was extended to Pompeius by the consular law.

66 Cic.*Balb*.51. Cf. Strabo 3.4.10 on the city of Pompeiopolis, but for doubts as to whether this was in fact a Pompeian foundation from the Sertorian war, cf. Dreizehnter, *Chiron* 5, 1975, 233ff.

67 Cic.*Balb*.5f., 11, 19, 38, 40.

68 Sall.*Hist*.3.89, Strabo 3.4.1, 7, 9, 4.1.3, Plin.*NH* 3.18, cf. 7.96.

69 App.*BC* 1.119.554.

70 Cf. *MRR* II 109f., 116ff.

71 For the date of Crassus' praetorship, cf. Marshall, *Crassus* 26ff. The most likely view of his position in 72 is that he was granted *imperium pro consule* by a decree of the senate and a supporting law: cf. Rubinsohn, *Historia* 19, 1970, 626; Marshall, *Historia* 21, 1972, 670, *Crassus* 26ff. There are, however, no grounds for assuming the existence of a deal between Crassus and the consuls (as Marshall, *Crassus* 30f.; rightly rejected by Ward, *Crassus* 84 n. 2).

72 For Crassus' achievement, cf. esp. Plut.*Crass*.10f., also *Pomp*.21, Vell.2.30.6. For his reluctance to leave any opportunity of glory to Pompeius, cf. App.*BC* 1.119.555.

73 The procedure followed by Metellus Pius later in the year, cf. Sall.*Hist*.4.49.

74 Plut.*Pomp*.21, *Crass*.11. Marshall argues (*Historia* 21, 1972, 669f., *Crassus* 33) that, since Crassus had asked for the recall of Pompeius and M. Lucullus, he cannot have been concerned about losing the credit for the victory to Pompeius. This, however, accords ill with the unanimous verdict of the sources and with Crassus' attitude towards his own ovation and Pompeius' triumph. Cf. also Marshall, *Athen*. n.s. 51, 1973, 109ff.; Ward, *Crassus* 96ff. The story of Crassus' request is rejected, probably rightly, by Ward, *Crassus* 91, n. 24.

75 Plin.*NH* 15.125, Gell.5.6.23; cf. Marshall, *Historia* 21, 1972, 672f., *Crassus* 34.

76 Cic.*Pis*.58, Plut.*Crass*.11; cf. Ward, *Crassus* 96ff.

77 App.*BC* 1.121.561, Liv.*per*.97. The claim that Crassus sought the support of Pompeius and indeed owed his election entirely to it (Plut.*Pomp*.22, *Crass*.12) is at best exaggerated. It is accepted by Gelzer, *Pompeius* 60, *KS* II 166; Miltner, *RE* 21.2089; Marshall,

Crassus 51 (in the context of his general denial of ill-feeling between the two men); Ward, *Crassus* 99f. (a *coitio* to keep out the future Metellus Creticus). It is possible that Crassus made some conciliatory move, whether for safety's sake or to create embarrassment by underlining the abnormality of Pompeius' position. But he was surely not dependent on Pompeius' support, nor will Pompeius have been naive enough to rely on his subsequent co-operation.

78 That Crassus' election was natural and certain is rightly stressed by Garzetti, *Athen.* n.s. 20, 1942, 13.

79 The distinction is brought out by App.*BC* 1.131.560, Val.Max.8.15.8, Liv.*per.*97.

80 Cic.*leg.Man.*62, Plut.*Pomp.*21, *Crass.*12, Liv.*per.*97.

81 Cf. Last, *CAH* IX 333; Gelzer, *Pompeius* 58, *KS* II 147; Taylor, *PP* 20, 103. Rightly denied by Sherwin-White, *JRS* 46, 1956, 6.

82 Both Pompeius and Pius had been eager for the war to be declared *externum* in order to justify their triumphs (Flor.2.10.9). For Pompeius' promise to disband after the triumph, cf. Plut.*Pomp.*21; Gelzer, *KS* II 165; in general Stockton, *Historia* 22, 1973, 206f. On the triumph, cf. Cic.*leg.Man.*62, *Pis.*58, *div.*2.22, App.*BC* 1.121.561, Vell.2.30.2, Luc.7.14ff., Plin.*NH* 7.96, Eutrop.6.5.2. Ward, *Crassus* 44 n. 41, argues cogently (against Gelzer, *Pompeius* 62; Miltner, *RE* 21.2089) that Pius probably did not reach Rome until shortly after Pompeius' triumph. But it is hard to believe, on the strength of the inaccurate and exaggerated remarks in Dio 52.13.2, 56.39.2, that Pompeius or anyone else at Rome was seriously afraid that Pius would try to imitate Sulla.

83 *Contra*: Stockton, *Historia* 22, 1973, 208.

84 Cf. Gruen, *LGRR* 43f. Gelzer's denial that Pompeius was still a Sullan in 71 (*KS* II 148f.) is misleading. His avoidance of the worst excesses of Sulla and his followers did not undermine and would not have obscured his active loyalty throughout the seventies. Nor would the label have turned a majority of the senate against him.

85 For the speech, cf. Sall.*Hist.*4.45f.; for popular expectations, cf. Sall.*Hist.*4.42, 47. Cf. also App.*BC* 1.121.560 (before the consular elections, followed by Gelzer, *Pompeius* 58), Plut.*Pomp.*22.

86 Cic.*Cluent.*61, 77, 79, 136f. On the link between the courts and the tribunate, cf. Cic.*div.Caec.*8, *1Verr.*44; on the general unpopularity of senatorial courts in 70, cf. Cic.*1Verr.*1f., 36, 43, *2Verr.*1.5, 21.

87 Cic.*2Verr.*2.83ff., Plut.*Pomp.*10, *mor.*203D. Gruen's attempt (*AJP* 92, 1971, 11) to deny Pompeius' interest in Sthenius is misconceived and in no way supported by the facts that Verres also attacked men linked with the Metelli, Hortensius, M. Lucullus and Catulus or that Sthenius had other patrons besides Pompeius.

88 Cic.*2Verr.*2.95ff.; cf. Badian, *FC* 282.

89 Cic.*2Verr.*2.100. Badian rightly points out (*FC* 283) that it is uncertain whether Palicanus was acting on Pompeius' orders, but Pompeius could hardly have afforded to disclaim his action. He did not, however, have to take any public stance. For Palicanus and the tribunician power, cf. Ps.-Ascon.189St.; for his Picentine origin, cf. Sall.*Hist.*4.43.

90 For their constant differences during the year, cf. Sall.*Hist.*4.51 (blaming Crassus), Plut.*Pomp.*22, *Crass.*12. For Crassus' dedication to Hercules as a manifestation of his continuing competition with Pompeius, cf. Ward, *Crassus* 101f. That Pompeius wanted a politically memorable consulship, of which his quarrel with Crassus deprived

him (Gelzer, *Pompeius* 65), is unevidenced and unlikely. Contrast *KS* II 147: Pompeius wanted the consulship to be *consularis*; thus also Sherwin-White, *JRS* 46, 1956, 6.

91 Cic.*2Verr*.5.163, ap. Ascon.76, Vell.2.30.4, Plut.*Pomp*.22, Ps.-Ascon. 189St. McDermott, *CP* 72, 1977, 49ff. (followed by Ward, *Crassus* 104), argues that Pompeius alone was responsible for the law. The argument depends on the assumption that the clear statements of Cicero (ap.Ascon.76) and the Epitomator are a lie and a misunderstanding respectively, so that the silence of Cicero elsewhere, when he had no motive for mentioning Crassus, may be regarded as 'decisive'!

92 Cf. Sherwin-White, *JRS* 46, 1956, 7; Twyman, *ANRW* I 1.825.

93 That Pompeius was anxious not to be deprived of the credit might be read into Cicero's defensive answer to the criticism he puts into the mouth of his brother Quintus in *leg*.3.22ff. On Pompeius' motives, cf. Gelzer, *KS* II 160f.

94 Cic.*2Verr*.2.174f., 3.223f., 5.177f. Gelzer, *Cicero* 41, calculates *c*.20 September for the promulgation of the *lex Aurelia*.

95 Note the wording of Plut.*Pomp*.22.; cf. Sherwin-White, *JRS* 46, 1956, 8. This tells against the view of Marshall, *RhM* NF 118, 1975, 148, that Pompeius was responsible for a compromise after an original proposal for total transfer. Cf. also Gelzer, *KS* II 168; van Ooteghem, *Pompée* 146; Stockton, *Historia* 22, 1973, 216ff.

96 Cic.*div.Caec*.8, *1Verr*.49, *2Verr*.1.6, 19, 22. For the idea that this was the last chance, cf. Cic.*div.Caec*.70, *1Verr*.20, 49, *2Verr*.1.6, 23, 3.223f.

97 Cic.*div.Caec*.8, *1Verr*.49, *2Verr*1.22, 2.174, 3.223, 5.177. Nothing supports Ward's conjecture (*Crassus* 107) that Crassus would have liked to see total transfer.

98 Liv.*per*.97, Ps.-Ascon.206St. For talk in the air, cf. Gelzer, *KS* II 172; an actual proposal, cf. van Ooteghem, *Pompée* 147; Marshall, *RhM* NF 118, 1975, 146.

99 Cic.*Phil*.1.20, Schol.Bob.91St.; garbled: Vell.2.32.3. For the two non-senatorial orders treated as one, cf. Cic.*Cluent*.130, Schol.Bob.94St. For detailed discussion, cf. Hill, *RMC* 212ff.; Nicolet, *Ordre* I 593ff.; Wiseman, *Historia* 19, 1970, 71f., 74, 79f.

100 Schol.Gron.328St.; but the notice is very garbled and even Palicanus' involvement cannot be regarded as certain.

101 On the trial of Verres in general, cf. Gelzer, *Cicero* 36ff.; for Pompeius' lack of overt interest, cf. Gelzer, *KS* II 168, *Cicero* 37 n. 8. For the view that Pompeius and Cicero were acting together, cf. Ward, *Latomus* 29, 1970, 60ff., *Crassus* 42ff. For Cicero's provocation of Hortensius, cf. Cic.*div.Caec*.23f., *1Verr*.35, 37, *2Verr*.2.24, 5.174ff.

102 As suggested by Badian, *FC* 283; Ward, *Latomus* 29, 1970, 61; Marshall, *RhM* NF 118, 1975, 147. Nevertheless Cicero received considerable help and hospitality from clients of Pompeius (*2Verr*.4.25) and appeals had been made to Pompeius at the end of 71 and during 70 (Cic.*2Verr*.3.45, 204).

103 Cf. Gelzer, *KS* I 113 = *RN* 113.

104 Cic.*2Verr*.2.64, 138f., 160ff., 3.122f., 152f., 4.146ff., 5.129, Oros.6.3.5.

105 Cic.*1Verr*.26, cf. Quintil.6.5.4. For M. Metellus, cf. Cic.*1Verr*. 21; for Q. Metellus and witnesses, cf. Cic.*1Verr*.27f. Cicero's injunctions to Catulus, who was a juror (*2Verr*.4.69f.), may hint that he too favoured Verres. One well-wisher, C. Curio, congratulated Verres on his acquittal when he heard of Hortensius' election to the consulship (Cic.*1Verr*.18f.); the suggestion that he was merely trying to embarrass Verres' friends (Twyman, *ANRW* I 1.846) is one of the more curious consequences of a fertile prosopographical imagination.

106   A freedman, according to Plut.*Cic*.7.

107   Cf. Taylor, *PP* 52, *VD* 128; in general, Ward, *Crassus* 25.

108   Plut.*Pomp*.22, *mor.* 204A, 815E–F.

109   Cic.*1Verr*.31, Ps.-Ascon.217St.

110   Cic.*Att*.1.18.6, Dio 38.5.1f., cf. Plut.*Lucull*.34. In general, cf. Marshall, *Antichthon* 6, 1972, 43ff., with references to and discussion of earlier views.

111   Gell.14.7.2f.

112   Plut.*Pomp*.23, *Crass*.12. Cf. Ward, *Crassus* 109 with n. 39, who rightly notes that Crassus' praise of Pompeius was two-edged.

4   THE COMMANDS AGAINST THE PIRATES AND MITHRADATES

1   For Pompeius' desire for consular rank, cf. Sherwin-White, *JRS* 46, 1956, 6; on *principes ciuitatis*, cf. Gelzer, *KS* I 53ff. = *RN* 44ff. When Pompeius appeared in public, it was with a retinue that befitted his dignity (Plut.*Pomp*.23).

2   Individuals, particularly younger men, were of course quite ready in the sixties to exploit Pompeius' success for their own advancement only to part company with him again when he had served their turn. Neither their joining Pompeius nor their leaving him need prove anything about their opinion of him as a man or as a political phenomenon.

3   Cic. *Font*.8, 13, 26. There was no other connection between Fonteius and Pompeius; cf. Gruen, *AJP* 92, 1971, 13, against Ward, *Latomus* 27, 1968, 803.

4   Thus Ward, *Latomus* 27, 1968, 803f.

5   Cf. *supra*, p. 38.

6   If M. Fabius were M. Fabius Hadrianus, recorded as a legate of Lucullus in 72 (*MRR* II 119) and 68 (*MRR* II 140), the hand of Lucullus might be discerned, since Fabius might then have been sent home on leave specifically in order to take part. But such a conjectural identification has nothing to recommend it.

7   Ward's view (*Latomus* 27, 1968, 804) that Cicero's references to the testimony of the Metelli at the trial of Q. Pompeius (*Font.* 23, 27) imply that the Metelli were behind the prosecution of Fonteius is needless elaboration; their overt relevance to Cicero's argument is sufficient to explain the presence of the allusions.

8   Cic. *Font*.15, 34, 45f.

9   For Pompeius in Spain, cf. Cic.*Font.Exc.Cus*.6, 8. Support for Fonteius, cf. *Font*.16, 32. That Cicero could go no further is emphasized by Gruen (*AJP* 92, 1971, 12), who perhaps overstates his case, especially as the extant speech is incomplete.

10   Cf. van Ooteghem, *Pompée* 157.

11   Cf. Seager, *Hommages Renard* 683 n. 5.

12   Cf. Seager, *Hommages Renard* 681.

13   Cf. Seager, *Hommages Renard* 684.

14   On the events of Cornelius' tribunate, cf. *MRR* II 142ff. For the order of events, cf. Griffin, *JRS* 63, 1973, 196ff., refuting McDonald, *CQ* 23, 1929, 196ff. For the links with the issues of Pompeius' consulship, cf. Seager, *Hommages Renard* 682ff.; Griffin, *JRS* 63, 1973, 208ff.

15   Ascon.61; cf. Griffin, *JRS* 63, 1973, 203.
16   Cic.ap.Ascon.74f., *Mur.*46, 67, Ascon.75, 88, Dio 36.38f., Schol.Bob.78St.; cf. Seager, *Hommages Renard* 685, Griffin, *JRS* 63, 1973, 208.
17   Val.Max.3.8.3; cf. Seager, *Hommages Renard* 685.
18   On Gabinius, cf. Sanford, *TAPA* 70, 1939, 64ff.; Badian, *Philol.* 103, 1959, 87ff. He was married to a daughter (or sister) of Palicanus.
19   On these events, cf. van Ooteghem, *Lucullus* 139ff.
20   Cf. Gelzer, *Pompeius* 70, *KS* II 179; Frankfort, *FO* 245f.
21   Sall.*Hist.*4.70, Plut.*Lucull.*14, Dio 36.2.1, cf. 16.1, App.*Mith.*90.411. For Metellus, cf. Sall.*BJ* 64.5f., 65.4, Vell.2.11.2.
22   Plut.*Lucull.*7; cf. Badian, *PS* 98.
23   Plut.*Lucull.*20.
24   Plut.*Lucull.*14, cf. Cic.*leg.Man.*22f., Dio 36.16.3.
25   Plut.*Lucull.*36, Dio 36.16.2. Dio makes the point (36.16.3) that Pompeius later had no trouble with the same men.
26   Plut.*Lucull.*33.
27   Sall.*Hist.*4.71, Dio 36.2.2.
28   The mutinies: Plut.*Lucull.*24, 30; reaction at Rome: Plut.*Lucull.*24, Dio 36.2.1.
29   Cf. *MRR* II 103.
30   Plut.*Lucull.*33.
31   Sall.*Hist.*5.12, Plut.*Lucull.*34, Dio 36.14.3f. Clodius was lying about the land grants, since the *lex Plotia* had never been put into effect; cf. *supra*, p. 39.
32   Dio 36.4–11.
33   Dio 36.2.2.
34   Dio 36.15.1f., 17.2.
35   Cic.*leg.Man.*26, Sall.*Hist.*5.13.
36   Dio 36.14.4–15.3.
37   Cic.*leg.Man.*5, Dio 36.17.1.
38   Cf. Frankfort, *FO* 250.
39   Cf. Gelzer, *Pompeius* 70, *KS* II 176f.; also Twyman, *ANRW* I 1.872f., dictated in part by his belief that Lucullus and Pompeius were members of the same 'faction'.
40   Sall.*Hist.*3.2: the text is uncertain, but in support of *nocentior*, cf. Ps.-Ascon.259St.
41   Cf. *MRR* II 87, 90f., 99.
42   The conduct of the pirates: Cic.*leg.Man.*31ff., 53ff., Plut.*Pomp.*24, Dio 36.20–23, App.*Mith.*70.297, 91.413, 92f. In Sicily under Verres: Cic.*2Verr.*3.85, 186, 4.104, 116, 144, 5.62, 87, 90f., 95ff., 137f. Their links with Mithradates: Plut.*Pomp.*24, App.*Mith.*63.262f., 119.586, *Sic.*6.1, Flor.1.41.2. Caesar: cf. Gelzer, *Caesar* 21; Clodius: Dio 36.17.3.
43   Plut.*Pomp.*25, Dio 36.23.1, App.*Mith.*93.423, Liv.*per.*99.
44   Despite Dio's query (36.23.4) there can be no doubt that he was acting in concert with Pompeius.
45   Plut.*Pomp.*25, Dio 36.37.1.
46   Dio 36.23.4, 34.3, 37.1, App.*Mith.*94.428.
47   Vell.2.31.1, Plut.*Pomp.*25, Dio 36.24.3, 36a, App.*Mith.*94.428. Being proconsular, it would not of course be valid in Rome itself.
48   Cic.*leg.Man.*44, Dio 36.23.5, 24.1.

49   Plut.*Pomp*.25. Cf. Taylor, *TAPA* 73, 1942, 14; Gelzer, *Caesar* 29. Strasburger (*Eintritt* 63) is inclined to doubt the statement, arguing (101) that the versions of Plutarch and Dio stem from a single fact, that Caesar supported either the *lex Gabinia* or the *lex Manilia*, and that it is no longer possible to decide which is in error. But support of both laws would be consistent with Caesar's general position at this time. Ward's attempt (*Crassus* 124f.) to minimize the significance of Caesar's support of Pompeius in 67 and 66 is hardly necessary to his justified contention that Caesar was capable of backing Pompeius and Crassus simultaneously or in quick succession, as his own convenience required.

50   Plut.*Pomp*.25.

51   Cic.*leg.Man*.52.

52   Dio 36.24.1 ff.

53   Sall.*Hist*.5.19.

54   Dio 36.24.5f.; cf. Gelzer, *Pompeius* 72.

55   Dio 36.25f.

56   Sall.*Hist*.5.21, Dio 36.27.9.

57   Cic.ap.Ascon.71f., Ascon.72. He may have suggested that Trebellius and Roscius had been bribed, cf. Sall.*Hist*.5.22.

58   Plut.*Pomp*.25, Dio 36.30.1 ff.

59   Dio 36.30.4f.

60   Cf. Cic.*leg.Man*.27, and for the same point in a different context *Font*.42f.

61   Cic.*leg.Man*.59, Sall.*Hist*.5.24, Vell.2.32.1, Val.Max.8.15.9, Dio 36.31–36a. There is no reason to suppose that the crowd's reply was ironical.

62   Cic.*Phil*.11.18, Schol.Bob.98St.

63   Plut.*Pomp*.26, Liv.*per*.99; 4,000 cavalry and 25 legates but only 270 ships in App. *Mith*.94.431. Cf. Groebe, *Klio* 10, 1910, 374ff.; Brunt, *Manpower* 456.

64   Cic.*leg.Man*.44, Plut.*Pomp*.26.

65   Vell.2.31.1 f. Accepted by Boak, *AHR* 24, 1918/19, 12; Gelzer, *Pompeius* 71, *KS* II 185; Ehrenberg, *AJP* 74, 1953, 119; Béranger, *Recherches* 77.

66   Tac.*Ann*.15.25.

67   Cf. Loader, *CR* 54, 1940, 134ff.; Jameson, *Historia* 19, 1970, 539ff.

68   It is quite uncertain whether the fragment Bekker *Anecd*. 157.30 belongs to this speech, nor can its significance be assessed without a context.

69   Plin.*NH* 7.98.

70   Cf. Diod.40.4.1.

71   *Contra*: Boak, *AHR* 24, 1918/19, 13.

72   Cic.*leg.Man*.35, 46, Plut.*Pomp*.29, Dio 36.17a, 18.1, App.*Sic*.6.6, Liv.*per*.99.

73   Plut.*Pomp*.29; according to App.*Sic*.6.6, he even ordered Metellus to leave the island.

74   Plut.*Pomp*.29, Dio 36.19.1 f., App.*Sic*.6.7.

75   Plut.*Pomp*.29.

76   For the list of legates, cf. Groebe, *Klio* 10, 1910, 374ff.; Ormerod, *LAAA* 10, 1923, 46ff.; *MRR* II 148ff.

77   For Varro, cf. Plin.*NH* 3.101, 7.115, 16.7.

78   Plut.*Pomp*.29, App.*Mith*.95.434ff., Flor.1.41.9f.

79   For the date, cf. Cic.*leg.Man*.34f.

80   Cic.*leg.Man*.34.

81   Cic.*leg.Man*.34, 56, *Flacc*.29f., Plut.*Pomp*.29, Dio 36.37.3, App.*Mith*.95.438, Liv.*per*.99, Flor.1.41.15, Eutrop.6.12.1, Oros.6.4.1.

82   Plut.*Pomp*.27, Dio 36.37.2; cf. Gelzer, *Pompeius* 74. Since Piso was consul, his activities prove nothing about the nature of Pompeius' *imperium* in relation to other proconsuls.

83   Plut.*Pomp*.27.

84   App.*Mith*.94.429; for his requisitions in the province of Asia, cf. Cic.*Flacc*.32.

85   Plut.*Lucull*.37.

86   Strabo 14.3.3, Luc.1.121ff., 2.576ff., 8.24ff., Plin.*NH* 7.93, Plut.*Pomp*.28.

87   *SIG*³ 749A/B.

88   Cic.*2Verr*.5.66f., 71.

89   Vell.2.32.4, Plut.*Pomp*.28, Liv.*per*.99, Flor.1.41.14.

90   Dio 36.37.5.

91   Strabo 8.7.5, Plut.*Pomp*.28, Dio 36.37.6, App.*Mith*.96.444, 115.562.

92   Strabo 8.7.5, 14.3.3, Plut.*Pomp*.28, App.*Mith*.96.444. In at least one case it is known that Pompeius' leniency served him well and was remembered with gratitude. The dynast Tarcondimotus, who was loyal to Pompeius in the civil war against Caesar, was himself a former pirate (Luc.9.219ff.).

93   Cf. Gelzer, *Pompeius* 77; Frankfort, *FO* 252f.

94   Dio. 36.la. On Metellus in Crete, cf. *MRR* II 145, 154.

95   Plut.*Pomp*.29, App.*Sic*.6.6, Flor.1.42.5.

96   Plut.*Pomp*.29, Dio 36.18.1–19.1. App.*Sic*.6.7, Flor.1.42.5f. (garbled).

97   Dio 36.45.1.

98   Dio 36.17a, 19.2, App.*Sic*.6.7.

99   Dio 36.19.3.

100 Flor.1.41.15.

101 Cic.*Flacc*.28.

102 Cic.*Flacc*.31f.

103 Dio 39.56.5.

104 Dio 39.59.2.

105 Cf. Frankfort, *FO* 318.

106 On Lucullus' misfortunes in 67, cf. van Ooteghem, *Lucullus* 154ff.

107 Ascon.65, Dio 36.42.2.

108 Ascon.45, 65, Dio 36.42.3.

109 Cic.ap.Ascon.65, *Mur*.34, Ascon.65, Vell.2.33.1, Plut.*Pomp*.30, *Lucull*.35, Liv.*per*.100, Eutrop.6.12.2, Oros.6.4.3.

110 Plut.*Pomp*.30, Dio 36.43.1.

111 Cic.*leg.Man*.51f.

112 Dio 36.43.2. Gelzer, *Caesar* 31, probably overestimates his reluctance: popular support and the favour of Pompeius would both benefit Caesar at this stage of his career. There is no reason to follow Strasburger (*Eintritt* 101) in suspecting that either Dio's statement here or Plutarch's on Caesar's support of the *lex Gabinia* is a doublet of the other.

113 Cic.*leg.Man*.68.

114 Cf. Gelzer, *Pompeius* 80; Gruen, *Historia* 18, 1969, 74.

115 Cic.*Fam*.1.9.11, *comm.pet*.51, Dio 36.43.2.

116 Cic.*leg.Man*.53, 56.

117 Cf. Gelzer, *KS* II 182f.

118 Cic.*leg.Man*.4, 15ff.

119 Cic.*leg.Man*.4, 6f., 14, 21, 32, 45.

120   Cic.*leg.Man*.19.
121   Cic.*leg.Man*.6, 11ff.
122   Cic.*leg.Man*.5, 13.
123   Cic.*leg.Man*.28, 49. For courage, cf. 3, 10, 29ff.; authority: 43; luck: 47f.; moderation and humanity: 13, 36ff., 67f.
124   Cic.*leg.Man*.27.
125   Cic.*leg.Man*.10, 35, 46.
126   Cic.*leg.Man*.10, 20f.
127   Cic.*leg.Man*.22ff., 26.
128   Cic.*leg.Man*.60. Neither example answers Catulus' point, since neither Scipio nor Marius was a private citizen when appointed, as Pompeius had been in 67.
129   Cic.*leg.Man*.60ff. The case is no doubt overstated.
130   Cic.*leg.Man*.63f., cf. 53.
131   Plut.*Pomp*.30, Dio 36.45.1f.
132   App.*Mith*.97.446f.
133   Thus Boak, *AHR* 24, 1918/19, 13.
134   Cf. Ehrenberg, *AJP* 74, 1953, 120f.
135   Cf. Gelzer, *Pompeius* 81.
136   App.*Mith*.97.446f.
137   Cf.*MRR* II 156, 160, 164, 170, 177. The identification of L. Flaccus with the praetor of 63 seems highly unlikely; cf. *MRR* II 156 n. 3.
138   Cf. Cic.*leg.Man*.57f. Despite van Ooteghem, *Pompée* 200ff., it probably would have been improper for Gabinius to occupy a post of his own creation, though the fact that as a tribune in office he could not go abroad would of itself be decisive. In *leg.Man*.58 Cicero is clearly concerned with a claim that Gabinius should not be allowed to serve in 66 under the *lex Manilia*, no doubt urged by those who were reluctant to see him thus escape the threat of prosecution. Van Ooteghem's discussion is marred by the bizarre assertion (202) that Gabinius was not a member of the senatorial order.
139   A failure to give due weight to this fact and a consequent desire to find positive reasons in Pompeius' own behaviour for the changing attitudes to him of families like the Metelli and the Cornelii Lentuli to some extent vitiate the detailed and often valuable treatment of Pompeius' relations with the aristocracy by Gruen, *Historia* 18, 1969, 71ff., esp. 80ff.

5   POMPEIUS IN THE EAST

1   Cf. Cic.*Mur*.34: Pompeius thought the war was not over until Mithradates was dead.
2   Even Cicero could say in 63 (*Mur*. 34) that Pompeius had been chosen to put the finishing touches to the war.
3   Dio 36.45.2.
4   Thus Frankfort, *FO* 259ff., with discussion of other views.
5   Dio 36.3.1ff., App.*Mith*.87.393, Memnon 434F38.8. Lucullus' decision to attack Parthia and his subsequent abandonment of the scheme in the face of mutiny by his troops (Plut.*Lucull*.30f.) probably belong to the realm of contemporary gossip. An

agreement on the Euphrates frontier is suggested by Oros.6.13.2 but denied by implication by Flor.1.46.4, followed by Frankfort, *FO* 242.

6   Dio 36.45.3, Liv.*per.*100.
7   Dio 36.45.3.
8   Dio 36.45.3, App.*Mith.*98.451.
9   Cf. Miltner, *RE* 21.2105.
10 Dio 36.45.4, App.*Mith.*98.452.
11 Dio 36.45.4f.
12 Plut.*Lucull.*35, Dio 36.42.2.
13 Plut.*Pomp.*31, *Lucull.*36, Dio 36.46.2. Among those to suffer for helping Lucullus was the family of Strabo (Strabo 12.3.33).
14 Strabo 12.5.2, Plut.*Lucull.*36, Dio 36.46.1. (Both the name and location of Danala, where the meeting took place, are uncertain.)
15 Plut.*Pomp.*31.
16 Vell.2.33.2ff., Plut.*Pomp.*31, *Lucull.*36, Dio 36.46.1f.
17 Plut.*Pomp.*31, *Lucull.*36.
18 Plut.*Pomp.*32, Dio 36.48.2, 50.1.
19 Dio 36.50.1.
20 Strabo 12.3.28, Plut.*Pomp.*32, Dio 36.50.2.
21 Dio 36.50.3.
22 In favour of Dio's order of events for the campaign of 66, cf. Frankfort, *FO* 267f.
23 Dio 36.51.1.
24 Plut.*Pomp.*33, Dio 36.51.3, App.*Mith.*104.487.
25 Dio 36.51.3.
26 Vell.2.37.3, Val.Max.5.1.9, Plut.*Pomp.*33, *comp.Cim.Lucull.*3, Dio 36.52.2ff., Liv. *per.*101, Flor.1.40.27, Eutrop.6.13, Oros.6.4.8.
27 Plut.*Pomp.*33, Dio 36.53.2, App.*Mith.* 105.491f., Liv.*per.*101, Eutrop. 6.13.
28 Cic.*Sest.*58, Strabo 11.14.10, Vell.2.37.4, Plut.*Pomp.*33, Dio 36.53.2, App. *Mith.*104.490, Eutrop.6.13.
29 Dio 36.53.1.
30 Plut.*Pomp.*33, Dio 36.53.2; App.*Mith.*105.491f. adds Gordyene, against which, cf. Frankfort, *FO* 270.
31 Dio 36.53.3; App.*Mith.*105.493 speaks of an attempt on his father's life.
32 Plut.*Pomp.*33, Dio 36.53.4ff.
33 Cf. Frankfort, *Latomus* 22, 1963, 185ff., *FO* 269.
34 Plut.*Pomp.*33.
35 Plut.*Pomp.*33.
36 Strabo 11.1.6, 3.5, 4.5, Vell.2.40.1, Plut.*Pomp.*34ff., Dio 36.54, 37.1ff., Flor.1.40.28, Eutrop.6.14.1.
37 Dio 36.54.1f.
38 *uir.ill.*77.7.
39 Thus Magie, *RRAM* 359.
40 Cf. Frankfort, *FO* 272.
41 Plin.*NH* 6.52.
42 Though he tested the water which was brought to him (Plin.*NH* 6.51).
43 Plut.*Pomp.*36, Dio 37.5.3.
44 Dio 37.5.2.

45 Plut.*Pomp*.36, Dio 37.5.3f.

46 Dio 37.5.4.

47 Vell.2.38.8, Plut.*Pomp*.38, Liv.*per*.102.

48 App.*Mith*.107.506f.; the chronological position is not clear in Appian's narrative, and the incident may belong as late as Pompeius' sojourn at Damascus in 63.

49 Vell.2.37.4, Plut.*Pomp*.38f., Dio 37.7a, Flor.1.40.29; cf. Downey, *TAPA* 82, 1951, 149ff.

50 Cf. Frankfort, *FO* 289.

51 Cf. Frankfort, *FO* 288.

52 Plut.*Pomp*.39, App.*Mith*.106.497; cf. Frankfort, *FO* 304.

53 Plut.*Crass*.21, Dio 40.20.1; cf. Frankfort, *FO* 311.

54 Cf. Seyrig, *Syria* 27, 1950, 11ff., citing numismatic evidence from Antioch and Apamea.

55 App.*Mith*.106.500.

56 Dio 37.7a, App.*Syr*.49.249f., 70.367, Justin 40.2.2ff.; cf. Frankfort, *FO* 291.

57 Plut.*Pomp*.38, Dio 37.6.2ff.; cf. Frankfort, *FO* 297.

58 Dio 37.7.2 claims he did.

59 Cf. Plut.*Pomp*.41, Dio 37.7.1.

60 Dio 37.7.1, App.*Mith*.106.501.

61 Dio 37.7.3, App.*Mith*.106.501.

62 Dio 37.7.4 says that Phraates did not want to help Rome by crushing Tigranes, but Pompeius would not have stood by and watched this happen, as Phraates must have known. The result of the arbitration is unknown: probably that each side should keep what it held.

63 In general, cf. Burr, *ANRW* I 1.875ff.

64 Jos.*BJ* 1.127ff., *AJ* 14.29ff.

65 Jos.*BJ* 1.131ff., *AJ* 14.40ff., Dio 37.15.3, Diod.40.2.1, Flor 1.40.30.

66 Jos.*AJ* 14.46.

67 Jos.*BJ* 1.133ff., *AJ* 14.48ff., Plut.*Pomp*.41.

68 Jos.*BJ* 1.138, *AJ* 14.53, Dio 37.11f., Oros.6.5ff.

69 Jos.*BJ* 1.139ff., *AJ* 14.55ff., Dio 37.15.3, 16.4.

70 Jos.*BJ* 1.142, *AJ* 14.58, Ps.Sol.17.6ff., 16ff.; the Psalms of Solomon also repeatedly present the Roman conquest as the reward of Jewish impiety (2.3ff., 8.8ff., 25ff.). Whether the Kittim of the Dead Sea commentary on Habakkuk are the Romans under Lucullus and Pompeius is much debated and, though probable, immaterial, since no addition to our knowledge of Pompeius' campaign would accrue from this source.

71 Strabo 16.2.40, Jos.*BJ* 1.149, Tac.*Hist*.5.12, Dio 37.16.1, Eutrop.6.14.2, Oros.6.6.2f., Ps.Sol.2.1, 8.16ff.

72 Jos.*BJ* 1.152, *AJ* 14.71f., Tac.*Hist*.5.9, App.*Syr*.50.252, Ps.Sol.2.2, cf. 20. The Psalms of Solomon not only charge Pompeius with arrogance and impiety (2.29, 32f., 17.13ff.) but also with plundering the temple (2.27f.). The charge is denied by Jos.*BJ* 1.153, *AJ* 14.72; for Pompeius' moderation, cf. Cic.*Flacc*.67f.

73 Strabo 16.2.46 (calling him Herod), Jos.*BJ* 1.153, *AJ* 14.73, 15.180, 15.180, 20.244, Oros.6.6.4; Dio 37.16.4 mistakenly speaks of kingship.

74 Jos.*BJ* 1.159, *AJ* 14.79f.

75 Plut.*Pomp*.42, Dio 37.20.1; for Pompeius' haste, cf. Frankfort, *FO* 306.

76 Dio 37.14.1f., App.*Mith*.113.552ff., 114.558ff.

77 Strabo 11.14.10, App.*Mith*.116.565.

78 Vell.2.18.1, Plut.*Pomp*.42; for Theophanes, cf. also Strabo 11.5.1, 13.2.3.

79   Cic.*Tusc*.2.61, Strabo 11.1.6, Plin.*NH* 7.112, Plut.*Pomp*.42.

80   Plut.*Pomp*.42.

81   In general on the settlement of the East, cf. van Ooteghem, *Pompée* 244ff.

82   Cf. Fletcher, *TAPA* 70, 1939, 17ff.; Jones, *Cities* 157ff.; van Ooteghem, *Pompée* 248f.; Frankfort, *FO* 279ff.

83   Strabo 12.3.1.

84   Strabo 11.8.4, 12.3.37.

85   Strabo 12.3.30f., App.*Mith*.115.561.

86   Strabo 12.3.38.

87   Cf. Dio 37.20.2, App.*Mith*. 115.561f.; for justified scepticism and analysis, cf. Dreizehnter, *Chiron* 5, 1975, 213ff.

88   Strabo 12.3.28, Dio 36.50.3, App.*Mith*.105.494, 115.561.

89   Plin.*Ep*.10.79.1, 112.1, 114.1, 3, 115.

90   Dio 37.20.2.

91   Strabo 12.3.34, App.*Mith*.114.560; cf. Jones, *Cities* 158.

92   Strabo 12.3.1.

93   Strabo 12.3.1, App.*Mith*.114.560.

94   Strabo 12.3.13, App.*Mith*.114.560, *Syr*.50.254. According to Eutrop.6.14.1 Pompeius granted Armenia Minor to Deiotarus; according to Cic.*har.resp*.29, *Deiot*.10, *Phil*.2.94, *div*.2.79 and *BAlex*.67 he received it from the senate. The simplest solution, that Deiotarus received it from Pompeius and that this was then confirmed by the senate in 59, is perhaps the best; cf. Frankfort, *FO* 280f., emending Strabo.

95   App.*Mith*.114.560, Eutrop.6.14.1.

96   App.*Mith*.114.558. He did not, however, receive Gordyene and Sophene, as claimed by App.*Mith*.105.496; cf. Frankfort, *Latomus* 22, 1963, 185ff.

97   Strabo 16.2.3, App. *Mith*.114.559.

98   Strabo 16.2.8, 18, 46, Jos.*BJ* 1.155ff., *AJ* 14.74ff., Eutrop.6.14.2; cf. Jones, *Cities* 257ff.

99   Cf. Frankfort, *FO* 303ff.

100   Jos.*BJ* 1.155, 166, 170, *AJ* 14.74f., 88, 90f.; cf. Jones, *Cities* 257.

101   Plin.*NH* 7.99, Flor.1.40.31; cf. Frankfort, *FO* 316f.

102   Cf. Badian, *RI* 70f.

103   Cf. Frankfort, *FO* 313ff.

104   Honours: *ILS* 8776, 9459, *SIG*³ 338. Cult on Delos: *SIG*³ 749A, *Insc. Délos* 1797. Cf. Crawford, *JRS* 66, 1976, 216.

105   Cf. Badian, *RI* 72ff.

106   Cf. the summaries of his achievements in Plut.*Pomp*.45, App.*Mith*.116.568, and for patronage especially the language of Diod.40.4.1. For the catalogue of Pompeius' Eastern forces in the civil war, cf. Caes.*BC* 3.3f., Cic.*Att*.9.9.2, Vell.2.51.1, Luc.3.169ff., 5.54ff., Flor.2.13.5, Oros.6.15.18ff. For Deiotarus in particular, cf. also Cic.*Deiot*.9, 11, 28, Luc.8.209ff.

6   ROME IN THE ABSENCE OF POMPEIUS

1   Cf. Seager, *Hommages Renard* 685f. Ward, *Crassus* 28, claims that Volcacius was favourable to Pompeius because he testified for Cornelius (Ascon.60). This will not

outweigh Cic.*Fam*.1.1.3, which clearly implies that no previous link between Volcacius and Pompeius was known.

2   Cf. Seager, *Hommages Renard* 685. Ward, *Crassus* 30, tries to link Autronius with Pompeius, but on purely negative grounds. However, he raises reasonable doubts about the identification of P. Sulla as an adherent of Pompeius, preferring the better conclusion that Sulla was the candidate of the optimates (*Crassus* 28f.).

3   Cic.*Sull*.15,*fin*.2.62, Ascon.75. The exclusion of Catilina: Sall.*BC* 18, Ascon.89; cf. Seager, *Historia* 13, 1964, 338ff.; Sumner, *Phoen*.19, 1965, 226ff. For the alleged 'First Catilinarian Conspiracy', cf. Seager, *Historia* 13, 1964, 338ff.

4   Cf. Sumner, *Phoen*. 19, 1965, 230; Seager, *Hommages Renard* 682ff.; and for Torquatus, Ward, *Crassus* 30, though he posits optimate backing for Cotta (*Crassus* 18f.).

5   Ascon.59. Corruption in the text of Ascon.60 makes certainty impossible, but it is unlikely that he assigned responsibility for this disturbance to Manilius; the reference is much more likely to be to the first trial of Manilius himself in January 65.

6   Ascon.60.

7   Cic.ap.Ascon.62; Plut.*Cic*.9 mistakenly suggests *peculatus*. On the trials of Manilius, cf. Phillips, *Latomus* 29, 1970, 595ff.; Ward, *TAPA* 101, 1970, 545ff.

8   Ascon.45.

9   Thus Phillips, *Latomus* 29, 1970, 597.

10   Plut.*Cic*.9, Dio 36.44.1f.

11   Despite Phillips, *Latomus* 29, 1970, 600ff., Cicero's action cannot have been intended to postpone the trial till 65, since if that had been his aim he had only to grant Manilius' original request; cf. Ward, *Crassus* 138 n. 36.

12   He had given no promise to defend Manilius in the speech *pro lege Manilia*: cf. Phillips, *Latomus* 29, 1970, 599, against Gelzer, *Cicero* 60. For Cicero's reluctance, cf. Gelzer, *Cicero* 60; Ward, *TAPA* 101, 1970, 547.

13   The charge is given by Schol.Bob.119St. This evidence is rejected by Phillips, *Latomus* 29, 1970, 605, who believes that both trials of 65 were for *repetundae*, but the text of Ascon.60, on which he bases his argument, is too corrupt to bear the weight he places on it. Gruen, *LGRR* 261f., accepts a trial for *repetundae* at the end of 66, but only one trial for *maiestas* in 65. For the date, cf. Phillips, *Latomus* 29, 1970, 603, 606.

14   Cic.ap.Ascon.65 with Asconius' comment.

15   Ascon.62.

16   Schol.Bob.119St.; cf. Ascon.60, Cic.ap.Ascon.66, perhaps Dio 36.44.2. There is no ground for Ward's conjecture (*TAPA* 101, 1970, 551f.) that Cicero refused to continue with the defence: indeed, it is certain that he spoke at one trial (cf. Gruen, *LGRR* 262 n. 7), though it is not clear which.

17   Ascon.60. The charge was presumably still *maiestas*; for the date, cf. Phillips, *Latomus* 29, 1970, 606.

18   Cf. Ward, *TAPA* 101, 1970, 553.

19   Cic.*Brut*.271, *comm.pet*.51. For the fragments, cf. Kumaniecki, *Discours*. The speeches were published in much the same form as they were delivered in court (Nep.*Cic*.fr.2P). On the trial of Cornelius, cf. Seager, *Hommages Renard* 680ff.; Ward, *TAPA* 101, 1970, 554ff.; Griffin, *JRS* 63, 1973, 211ff.; Gruen, *LGRR* 263ff.

20   Ascon.60, Val.Max.8.5.4. Valerius mistakenly adds the absent L. Lucullus. That the Lepidus involved was Mamercus, not Manius, is demonstrated by Sumner, *JRS* 54, 1964, 41ff.

21 Cic.ap.Ascon.79ff.

22 Ascon.61, Quintil.10.5.13. The correct view of the nature of Cornelius' offence is reaffirmed by Gruen, *LGRR* 263ff., against Bauman, *Crimen* 71ff.

23 Ascon.70, 74f.

24 Quintil.4.3.13, 9.2.55; cf. Seager, *Hommages Renard* 681. He did not criticize Pompeius' father in the speech, cf. Badian, *Historia* 18, 1969, 465ff.

25 Ascon.57, 61. One of the senatorial jurors was Crassus, whose support is politely assumed by Cic.ap.Ascon.76. The acquittal was by a large majority (Ascon.81).

26 Ascon.61.

27 Cic.*Vat*.5f., *comm.pet*.5, 14, 51.

28 Plut.*Lucull*.33, *Cato* 29; for the eventual grant of the triumph, cf. also Cic.*Lucull*.3. Cf. Twyman, *ANRW* I 1.846; Gruen, *LGRR* 266.

29 Suet.*gramm*.14.1. For wider speculation based on these events, cf. Gruen, *Athen*. n.s. 49, 1971, 56ff.

30 Sall.*BC* 19, Ascon.92, *ILS* 875. On the relation between these events and the 'First Catilinarian Conspiracy', cf. Seager, *Historia* 13, 1964, 346; against any exaggeration of Crassus' objectives, cf. Marshall, *Crassus* 70f.

31 Dio 37.9.3. Cf. Marshall, *Crassus* 65; Ward, *Crassus* 128f. The relevance of the *lex Papia* to this issue is obscure: for conflicting views, cf. Gruen, *LGRR* 409ff.; Ward, *Crassus* 130ff.

32 The early career of Pompeius notwithstanding; *contra*: Gelzer, *Caesar* 36. Sumner's conjecture that Pompeius was originally intended to be the beneficiary (*TAPA* 97, 1966, 574) rejects too much evidence for too little gain; cf. Ward, *Historia* 21, 1972, 245f. Cf. also Marshall, *Crassus* 65f., though there is nothing here to support his fundamental thesis that there was no hostility between Crassus and Pompeius; Ward, *Crassus* 132ff.

33 Cic.*leg.agr*.2.44, Suet. *DJ* 11, Plut.*Crass*.13, Schol.Bob.92St.

34 *Comm.pet*.51.

35 *Comm.pet*.4f., cf. Cic.*Att*.1.1.2, Plut.*Cic*.10.

36 Cic.*Att*.1.1.4; cf. Seager, *LCM* 1, 1976, 46.

37 Fear of Cicero's competitors will not, as Gruen says (*LGRR* 138), explain his election, but it is an important consideration.

38 *ILLRP* 515; cf. Cichorius, *RS* 164, 172ff.

39 Catilina's presence in the forum with a weapon on 29 December 66 cannot be pressed. Even if the disturbances were connected with the trial of Manilius, there is no proof that he was acting on Manilius' side. Cf. Gruen, *CP* 64, 1969, 20ff., modifying Seager, *Historia* 13, 1964, 338ff. The prosecution of Catilina in 64 by Pompeius' close friend L. Lucceius (Ascon.91) suggests that Pompeius had by then abandoned any interest in Catilina he might have had; cf. Seager, *Historia* 13, 1964, 347 n. 43.

40 Sall.*BC* 35.1; Oros.6.3.1 ascribes Catilina's escape on the charge of seducing a Vestal *c*.83 to the influence of Catulus.

41 Cic.ap.Ascon.87, 89, 92, Ascon.85; Cic.ap.Ascon.87, 90f. with Asconius' commentary, Ascon.84.

42 Cic.ap.Ascon.88, Ascon.83, 85f.

43 Sources: *MRR* II 168. Cf. in general, Hardy, *JP* 32, 1913, 228ff.; Afzelius, *CM* 3, 1940, 214ff.; Gabba, *Mélanges Piganiol* 769ff.

44 App.*BC* 1.29.132, 30.134, 31.140, 32.143.

45 Cic.*leg.agr*.1.5, 2.23ff., 46, 49ff., 60ff., 99, 3.16.

46 On Cicero's treatment of *popularis* themes in the Rullan speeches, cf. Seager, *CQ* 66, 1972, 330, 332, 334ff.

47 Cic.*leg.agr*.2.49.

48 Cic.*leg.agr*.1.6, 2.51f.

49 Cic.*leg.agr*.1.13, 2.61f.

50 Cic.*leg.agr*.2.23ff., 60.

51 Cic.*leg.agr*. 2.54. Here Cicero appears to hint that Pompeius' life might even be in danger.

52 Cic.*leg.agr*.1.13, 2.61f.

53 The case is cogently stated by Sumner, *TAPA* 97, 1966, 568ff.; for an attempt at refutation, cf. Ward, *Historia* 21, 1972, 255ff., *Crassus* 154ff. Further tentative arguments might be drawn from the exemption of the *ager Recentoricus* (Cic.*leg.agr*.1.10f., 2.57) – Pompeius had clients in Sicily who may have been as relevant as the companions of Aeneas – and of royal lands in Numidia, whose king Hiempsal was Pompeius' client (Cic.*leg.agr*.1.10f., 2.58f.). It is hardly credible that this was intended as a sop to Pompeius in an essentially hostile bill; such concessions would hardly have been sufficient to allay his wrath if the measure as a whole was aimed against him.

54 Cic.*leg.agr*.1.1, 2.25, 44, 3.13, cf. 2.63, 65 on *auaritia*. On the limits of Crassus' positive aims, cf. Marshall, *Crassus* 75f.

55 The technical difficulties presented by the sources are perhaps ultimately insoluble. For a statement of the view that derives from Mommsen, cf. Gelzer, *Cicero* 79 n. 77; the best discussion is that of Meyer, *Caesars Monarchie* 549ff. Two points may be regarded as known: Cicero defended Rabirius for *perduellio* (Cic.*Pis*.4) and he quashed the death penalty in the senate (Cic.*Rab.perd*.10, 17). It is therefore best, despite the difficulties that remain, to assume that Cicero spoke in court on only one occasion, when Rabirius' appeal from the duumviral verdict was heard, by which time the penalty had been reduced to a fine, though the charge was still of course *perduellio*, and that it was this hearing that was brought to a close by Metellus Celer's intervention (Dio 37.27.3–28.3). The second trial, at which Rabirius was acquitted, belongs to the realm of fiction.

56 Cicero is clearly misrepresenting Labienus when he claims that the prosecutor challenged the validity of the *senatus consultum ultimum* (*Rab.perd*.2, 4, 33f., cf. *Pis*.4). Labienus' point was that Saturninus had been killed after Marius had granted him a safe-conduct; cf. Cic.*Rab.perd*.28. For Cicero's exploitation of *popularis* themes in this speech, cf. Seager, *CQ* 66, 1972, 332, 335.

57 Dio 37.27.3–28.3.

58 On Labienus' origins and politics, cf. Syme, *JRS* 28, 1938, 113ff.; Tyrrell, *Historia* 21, 1972, 434ff.

59 Cic.*Rab.perd*.14, 18, 20ff.

60 Sall.*BC* 49.2.

61 Dio 36.54.2ff.

62 For the traditional view of the Catilinarian conspiracy, cf. esp. John, *Jahrb. klass. Phil. Supp.* 8, 1875/6, 706ff.; Hardy, *JRS* 7, 1917, 153ff.; Gelzer, *Cicero* 81ff. For some criticisms, cf. Seager, *Historia* 22, 1973, 240ff. Catilina is said to have wanted to take advantage of Pompeius' absence (Sall.*BC* 16.5, 17.7, Plut.*Cic*.14, 18); this is reasonable enough, whatever attitude Pompeius was likely to adopt on his return.

63 Cic.*Cat*.1.10, 12, 18, 20, 23, 30f., esp. 32; cf. Seager, *Historia* 22, 1973, 245ff.

64 Cic.*Cat*.2.18ff.; cf. Seager, *Historia* 22, 1973, 246.

65 Cic.*Cat*.2.3; cf. Seager, *Historia* 22, 1973, 246.

66 Cic.*Cat*.2.5, 24, *Mur*.78; cf. Seager, *Historia* 22, 1973, 246f.

67 On the prosecution of Murena, cf. Cicero's speech, *Flacc*.98, *fin*.4.74, Plut.*Cato* 21.

68 Cic.*Mur*.20, 37f., 69.

69 Cic.*Mur*.10, 48.

70 Cf. Seager, *Historia* 22, 1973, 246f.

71 Sources: *MRR* II 171.

72 Cf. Taylor, *TAPA* 73, 1942, 19, 23; Gruen, *LGRR* 79f.

73 Vell.2.40.4; Caesar's support is indicated by Dio 37.21.4. Caesar also supported Labie-
    nus' re-enactment of the *lex Domitia* of 104 on the election of priests (Dio 37.37.1),
    although this measure had nothing to do with his own election as *pontifex maximus*, since
    that office had not been affected by Sulla's revival of the principle of co-option.

74 Cic.*Flacc*.98, cf. Sall.*BC* 49.2. Cf. Stockton, *Cicero* 108 n. 60. Syme, *JRS* 28, 1938, 117,
    sees the prosecution of Piso as a service to Pompeius by Caesar, though he tends to
    discount most of Caesar's alleged Pompeian activities of 63.

75 For his service with Pompeius, cf. *MRR* II 148, 160, 164, 170. For his return and
    candidature, cf. Plut.*Cato* 20.

76 Cic.*Sull*.31 (with Schol.Bob.82St.), 34, *Sest*. 11, *Pis*.6f., *Fam*.5.2.7f., Ascon.6, Plut.
    Cic.23, 26, Dio 37.38.2, Schol.Bob.127St. The exchange reported in Plut.*Cic*.26 may
    belong to Nepos' tribunate.

77 It is unlikely, to say the least, that Nepos argued, as Plut.*Cic*.23 claims, that Pompeius
    was needed to check the power of Cicero. Of the two proposals, only the emergency
    recall is mentioned in the copious narrative of Plut.*Cato* 26 and in Dio 37.43.1. Only
    Schol.Bob.134St. has the consulship in absence, but it need not necessarily be rejected
    on that account.

78 Cf. Stockton, *Cicero* 148.

79 Thus Meier, *Athen*. n.s. 40, 1962, 111.

80 The two proposals are thus certainly not contradictory, as urged by Meier, *Athen*. n.s.
    40, 1962, 105.

81 Caesar and Nepos: Suet.*DJ* 16.1, Plut.*Cic*.23, *Cato* 27; Caesar and Catulus: Suet.*DJ* 15,
    which misses the point that Pompeius was to benefit, Dio 37.44.1f.

82 Sall.*BC* 49, Plut.*Caes*.7.

83 Dio's suggestion that Caesar was not really acting in Pompeius' interests rests largely on a
    false dichotomy: of course Caesar was out to boost his own popularity, but at this point his
    own interests could still best be served by cultivating Pompeius. Cf. Stockton, *Cicero* 149.

84 Cic.*Mur*.81, cf. 83, 87, 90, Plut.*Cato* 20, cf. Cic.*Sest*.12. He even went so far as to
    propose a law for the distribution of cheap corn (Plut.*Caes*.8, *Cato* 26).

85 Cic.*Sest*.12, 62. According to Plut.*Cato* 26–29 the context of the struggle was Nepos'
    attempt, with Caesar's support, to force through against Cato's veto his bill recalling
    Pompeius to deal with the Catilinarian crisis. Cato enjoyed the active backing of a
    colleague, Minucius Thermus (Plut.*Cic*.23). Only Dio 37.43.3 specifically mentions
    the *senatus consultum ultimum*. For the suspension of Caesar and Metellus, cf. Suet.*DJ*
    16.1. Dio 37.44.2 appears to suggest that Nepos was suspended from office, Caesar not,
    whereas Nepos' suspension is denied by Plut.*Cato* 29, but is rendered certain by
    Cic.*Fam*.5.2.9, recording its cessation. Cf. also Schol.Bob.134St.

86 Cf. Stockton, *Cicero* 149.

87 Suet.*DJ* 16.1f.

88   Plut.*Cato* 29, Dio 37.43.4. His eventual return to Rome is recorded by Plut.*Cic.*26.
      That he too was eventually reinstated in office is made clear by Cic.*Fam.*5.2.9.
89   Plut.*Pomp.*43.
90   Cic.*Flacc.*32. Cf. Parrish, *Phoen.* 27, 1973, 363, 369; Ward, *Crassus* 193f.
91   Cf. Parrish, *Phoen.* 27, 1973, 369.
92   Cf. Ward, *Crassus* 197f. against the more far-reaching suggestions of Marshall, *Crassus* 93f.
93   Plut.*Pomp.*44, *Cato* 30. Dio 37.44.3 speaks of a postponement which was granted, not
      to allow Pompeius to canvass in person, but to permit Piso to stand. This may be
      garbled, but it is possible that both reports are true, and that a first postponement was
      granted, a second not. It is equally possible, as suggested by Gruen, *LGRR* 85 n. 9, that
      a single postponement was requested for both purposes, but one adequate only for the
      first was conceded.

7   THE RETURN OF POMPEIUS

1   Vell.2.40.3, Plut.*Pomp.*43, Dio 37.20.6, App.*Mith.*116.566.
2   For doubts and fears as to Pompeius' intentions, cf. Vell.2.40.3, Plut.*Pomp.*43, who
      ascribes the demobilization to a desire to dispel alarm.
3   Cic.*Fam.*5.7.1. This passage has been correctly interpreted, with convincing argu-
      ments, by Gruen, *Phoen.* 24, 1970, 237ff. The attempt at refutation by Mitchell,
      Historia 24, 1975, 618ff., misinterprets *otium* and denies *hostes* its proper force, which
      Gruen's view allows.
4   Cic.*Att.*1.12.3, Plut.*Pomp.*42, 44, *Cato* 30.
5   For a recent brief but cogent demonstration of this, cf. Wiseman, *LCM* 1, 1976, 1ff.
      On the meanings of *factio* in general, cf. Seager, *JRS* 62, 1972, 53ff.
6   Plut.*Pomp.*44, *Cato* 30, who sees Pompeius' approach as a direct response to Cato's
      opposition to his request for the postponement of the consular elections. For Servilia,
      cf. Plut.*Brut.*4, Liv.*per.*90.
7   In *Cat.*2.11 Cicero is prepared to equate himself, as leader on the domestic front, with
      Pompeius, in 3.26 he treats his own achievement as equal to that of Pompeius, but in
      4.21 the implication is clear that his own success is greater. His lost poem on his
      consulship took a similar line, cf.*Pis.*72ff., with disingenuous disclaimers. Note Schol.
      Bob.167St. on Pompeius' reaction to Cicero's letter in praise of his own achievements,
      for which cf. also Cic.*Sull.*67.
8   'Nothing obliging, nothing straightforward, nothing transparent in political matters,
      nothing honourable, nothing courageous, nothing open': Cic.*Att.*1.13.4, cf. 1.19.7.
      He later claimed that Pompeius gave him the credit for saving the state at their very first
      meeting in 61 (*Phil.*2.12); cf. also *off.*1.78.
9   In general, cf. Balsdon, *Historia* 15, 1966, 65ff.
10   Cic.*Att.*1.13.3; on Cicero's motives for interfering, cf. *Att.*1.18.2.
11   Cic.*Att.*1.14.1.
12   Cic.*Att.*1.14.2.
13   Cic.*Att.*1.14.2. The meaning of *istae res* in this passage is debated. Some think it refers
      to Cicero's consulship, but that is unlikely (cf. Shackleton Bailey *ad loc.*): Pompeius had
      no occasion to speak of it at all in this context, and even he was not so crude as to allude

to it in such slighting terms. The reference must therefore be to the Bona Dea affair, distinguished by *etiam* from Pompeius' more general reflections. *Suspicarentur* in the following sentence would not make sense if Pompeius had said anything specific, however brief and grudging, about Cicero's consulship.

14 Cic.*Att*.1.14.3.

15 Cic.*Att*.1.15.5f.

16 Cic.*Att*.1.16.2ff., *Pis*.95, *Mil*.13, Val.Max.9.1.7, Sen.*Ep*.97.2f., 6, 9, Dio 37.46.1ff., Schol.Bob.85St. The interpretation of Cic.*Att*.1.16.5 remains problematical: against a reference to Crassus, cf. esp. Wiseman, *Cinna* 147ff.; most recently in favour of an allusion to Crassus, cf. Marshall, *Crassus* 183ff., Ward, *Crassus* 227ff. The arguments on both sides are unsatisfactory, but the burden of proof must lie with those who wish to find a mention of Crassus.

17 Plut.*Cic*.29, who makes it clear that Clodius had a right to expect at least neutrality, if not actual support, from Cicero, Val.Max.8.5.5, Quintil.4.2.88, Schol.Bob.85St.

18 Cic.*Att*.1.16.8ff.

19 Cic.*Att*.1.16.11.

20 Cf. Stockton, *Cicero* 162.

21 Dio 37.49.1.

22 He had hoped for the consulship of 61, but had realized that he had no chance without Pompeius' backing, and so had had to wait (Plut.*mor*.806B).

23 Cic.*Att*.1.16.12f. For Pompeius' bribery on behalf of Afranius, cf. Plut.*Pomp*.44, *Cato* 30.

24 Apart from the detailed sources cited below, cf. *MRR* II 181.

25 Plin.*NH* 7.97, cf. Plut.*Pomp*.45, App.*Mith*.117.576. On the alleged figures for the founding of cities, cf. Dreizehnter, *Chiron* 5, 1975, 215ff., who goes so far as to emend the claims in Plutarch and Appian out of existence.

26 Plin.*NH* 7.98.

27 Cf. Gelzer, *Pompeius* 123.

28 Diod.40.1.4.

29 Plut.*Pomp*.45, cf. App.*Mith*.116.568.

30 Strabo 12.3.31, Plin.*NH* 33.151, 37.11, App.*Mith*.116.569f.

31 Dio 37.21.2, App.*Mith*.117.574ff.

32 Plin.*NH* 12.20, 111.

33 Dio 37.21.2f.

34 Plut.*Pomp*.45, App.*Mith*.117.571ff.

35 App.*Mith*.117.577, with open disbelief.

36 App.*Mith*. 117.578.

37 Badian, *PS* 100, points out that competition will have been especially fierce for the first contracts since the establishment of peace. Cf. Schol.Bob.157St.

38 Cic.*Att*.1.17.9, *Planc*.34, Schol.Bob.157St., mistakenly assuming, as 159, that Caesar was present in 61. On the ways in which senators could enjoy an interest in equestrian business operations, cf. Badian, *PS* 101ff. Cf. Marshall, *Crassus* 97f.; Ward, *Crassus* 211f., refuting (n. 53) the views of Parrish, *Phoen*. 27, 1973, 374ff.

39 Cic.*Att*.1.17.9. For the threat to *concordia ordinum*, cf. *Att*.1.18.3, 1.19.6, 2.1.7f., *off*.3.88. Cf. his later criticism of the opposition to the *equites* (*Planc*.24).

40 Cic.*Att*.1.17.10.

41 Cic.*Att*.1.17.8, 2.1.8.

42   Cic.*Att*.1.18.6, Dio 37.49.2, 50.1; for Flavius, Pompeius and Caesar in 59, cf. Cic.*QF* 1.2.11. On Afranius, cf. Cic.*Att*.1.18.3, 5, 1.19.4, 1.20.5, Dio 37.49.3. He may have come from Cupra Maritima in Picenum, cf. *ILS* 878; Taylor, *VD* 188.

43   Plut.*Pomp*.46, *Lucull*.42, *Cato* 31, though he claims (*Lucull*.41) that the two men remained on good terms in private, Dio 37.49.3–50.1, App.*BC* 2.9.31f. Cf. Vell.2.40.6, Suet.*DJ* 19.2. For Lucullus' earlier withdrawal from public life, cf. Plut. *Lucull*.38. Crassus' part, which indicates that he had come to no positive arrangement with Pompeius in 62, is accepted by Ward, *Crassus* 204, rejected, but without good reason, by Marshall, *Crassus* 96f.; it is, however, true that Crassus does not seem to have played a prominent role.

44   Cic.*Att*.1.19.4.

45   Cic.*Att*.1.19.4. Shackleton Bailey *ad loc.* offers no convincing reason for reading *actorem* instead of *auctorem*.

46   Cic.*Att*.2.1.8, Dio 37.50.1ff.

47   Cic.*Att*.1.18.7, cf. *off*.3.88, Dio 38.7.4.

48   Cic.*Att*.1.19.7, 1.20.2, 2.1.6.

49   Cic.*Att*.2.1.6 (Flavius), 2.1.8 (Asian taxes).

50   Cic.*Att*.2.1.6.

51   Cic.*Att*.1.20.2f., 2.1.6.

52   Cic.*Att*.2.1.8, 2.9.1f., cf. Plut.*Lucull*.42, *Cato* 30.

53   Cic.*Att*.2.1.6.

54   Cic.*Att*.1.17.11, cf. 2.1.9. For the sense of 1.17.11, cf. Shackleton Bailey *ad loc.*; Stanton–Marshall, *Historia* 24, 1975, 217.

55   Cf. Dio 37.52.3f.

56   Plut.*Caes*.13, *Cato* 31, Dio 37.54.1f. (confused), App.*BC* 2.8.28f. Caesar's haste to return is noted by Suet.*DJ* 18.1, Dio 37.54.1, who remark that he left his province before his successor's arrival.

57   Plut.*Caes*.13, *Cato* 31, App.*BC* 2.8.30, Suet.*DJ* 18.2 without naming Cato.

58   Plut.*Caes*.13, *Cato* 31, Dio 37.54.3, Suet.*DJ* 18.2.

59   Suet.*DJ* 19.1.

60   Suet.*DJ* 19.1.

61   Pompeius: Plut.*Cato* 31; Crassus: Plut.*Caes*.11, *Crass*.7, Suet.*DJ* 18.1 without naming him; both: Plut.*Pomp*.47, *Caes*.13, *Crass*.14, Dio 37.54.3, Suet.*DJ* 19.2. Cf. Marshall, *Crassus* 99ff.; Ward, *Crassus* 213ff.

62   Vell.2.44.2, App.*BC* 2.9.33, Suet.*DJ* 19.2.

63   Cf. Hor.*Carm*.2.1.1ff., Luc.1.84ff., Plut.*Lucull*.42, *Cato* 30, Flor. 2.13.8f. The judgement is ascribed to Cato himself by Plut.*Pomp*.47.

64   Cf. the remarks of Gruen, *LGRR* 142f.

65   Suet.*DJ* 19.2. For the essentials of the view expounded here, cf. Balsdon, *JRS* 29, 1939, 180ff.

66   Cic.*Att*.1.19.2ff.

67   Cic.*Att*.1.20.5.

68   This view has recently been challenged by Stanton–Marshall, *Historia* 24, 1975, 205ff., cf. Marshall, *Crassus* 99ff. Their arguments are not convincing. That Pompeius and Crassus were in general terms much stronger than Caesar in 60 is true, but both needed a consul in office to attain their ends. That they could have arranged a reconciliation of their own accord without Caesar's mediation is also true, but provides no ground for

rejecting the evidence for Caesar's part and suggesting that Balbus was deliberately deceiving Cicero: the attempt to evade the natural meaning of Cic.*Att*.2.3.3 is impossibly strained. Cf. Ward, *Crassus* 215 n. 61.

69 Plut.*Crass*.14, cf. Suet.*DJ* 19.2. On the relative position of the partners, cf. Dio 37.56.3ff., Flor.2.13.10ff.

70 Cf. Meier, *RPA* 280; Stockton, *Cicero* 182.

71 Stanton–Marshall, *Historia* 24, 1975, 210, rightly stress Plutarch's error (*Crass*.14) in placing Caesar's reconciliation of Pompeius and Crassus before the consular elections. Suet.*DJ* 19.2 is unclear; he appears to put all Caesar's dealings with Pompeius and Crassus after the elections, or at least after the decree on *siluae callesque*, which can hardly be right. Liv.*per*.103 assigns the reconciliation to the time when Caesar was a candidate for the consulship, but the epitomator's chronology is more than usually vague at this point and the degree of abridgement even more acute than normal. The clearest statements are in Vell.2.44.1, who dates the formation of the coalition to 59 itself, and Dio 37.55.1 (cf. 54.3, 56.1), who places the reconciliation of Pompeius and Crassus after Caesar's election.

72 Cf. Ward, *Crassus* 215.

73 Cic.*Att*.2.3.3f., cf. *prov.cos*.41, *Pis*.79.

8   THE CONSULSHIP OF CAESAR

1 A powerful case for Vatinius' authorship is made by Pocock, *Commentary* 161ff., *CQ* 19, 1925, 16ff. On the chronology of Caesar's legislation, cf. Appendix 2.

2 Dio 38.2.1.

3 Dio 38.2.2f.; for Cato, cf. Gell.4.10.8, Plut.*Cato* 31f., Dio 38.3.1.

4 Dio 38.2.3.

5 Dio 38.3.2f., Val.Max.2.10.7 (who confuses the occasion), Sen.*Ep*.14.13, Suet.*DJ* 20.4, Gell.4.10.8.

6 Dio 38.4.1ff.

7 Dio 38.3.2.

8 Dio 38.4.4–5.5, Plut.*Pomp*.47, *Caes*.14, App.*BC* 2.10.36 (confusing the two agrarian laws).

9 Dio 38.6.1ff., Plut.*Pomp*.48, *Cato* 32, App.*BC* 2.11.37ff. (again confused), Suet.*DJ* 20.1.

10 Dio 38.6.4, Plut.*Pomp*.48, *Cato* 32, Sen.*Ep*.14.13, *Dial*.2.1.3.

11 Dio 38.6.4, Suet.*DJ* 20.1.

12 Dio 38.6.5ff., Vell.2.44.5, Plut.*Pomp*.48, *Caes*.14, Suet.*DJ* 20.1; cf. Cic.*Fam*.1.9.7. For Vatinius' part, cf. Cic.*Vat*.21, Dio 38.6.6.

13 Cf. Dio 38.1.4ff.

14 Cf. *MRR* II 191f. for the known members.

15 Cf. Gelzer, *Pompeius* 136.

16 *ILS* 46.

17 Dio 38.7.1f., Plut.*Cato* 32.

18 Cic.*Rab.Post*.6, Luc.8.518f., 595, Dio 39.12.1.

19 Suet.*DJ* 54.3. On Ptolemy's wealth, cf. Plin.*NH* 33.136 from Varro.

20 Cic.*Att*.2.9.1, *Sest*.135, Dio 38.7.4ff., Plut.*Pomp*.48, App.*BC* 2.13.46ff., Suet.*DJ* 20.3, Schol.Bob.159St. In the suitable context of *Planc*.35 Cicero expresses guarded approval of the tax rebate.

21 Dio 38.7.3, Vell.2.44.4, Plut.*Cato* 33, App.*BC* 2.10.35, Suet.*DJ* 20.3.

22 Cic.*Phil*.2.101. There is no warrant for Meier's claim (*RPA* 284) that the *ager Campanus* was intended principally for veterans, despite Plut.*Caes*.26.

23 Cic.*Att*.2.18.2. Laterensis' refusal to swear is mistakenly associated with the first law by Schol.Bob.162St. Plut.*Cato* 33, cf. *Caes*.14, tells a story of attempted opposition by Cato which led to his arest by one tribune and subsequent release by another, both at Caesar's behest. It is unclear whether this is a doublet of the earlier incident in the senate or a separate and authentic event; it is accepted as the latter by Gelzer, *Caesar* 72f.

24 This seems the most economic way of reconciling the available evidence. The boundary stone of Ti. Gracchus' commission (*ILS* 24) found near Capua indicates, provided that its provenance can be trusted, that Ti. Gracchus did not formally exempt the *ager Campanus*. Certain land was, however, exempted from distribution by C. Gracchus (*l.agr*.6). If this included, as conjectured here, the Campanian land, that would be enough to justify Cicero's claim, in a polemical context (*leg.agr*.2.81), that neither Gracchus had dared to interfere with Campania. For its financial importance, cf. Suet.*DJ* 20.3.

25 Cic.*leg.agr*.1.21, 2.80ff.; cf. his halfhearted praise of Pompeius and Caesar in *Pis*.4.

26 Cic.*Att*.2.16.1.

27 Cic.*Att*.2.16.1.

28 Dio 38.8.5, Suet.*DJ* 22.1. Plut.*Pomp*.48, *Caes*.14 merges the *lex* and the subsequent *senatus consultum* (as do Vell.2.44.5, App.*BC* 2.13.49) and speaks of four legions. For Vatinius' interference with senatorial prerogatives, cf. Cic.*Vat*.36.

29 Cf. *supra*, p. 72.

30 Dio 38.34.3.

31 Caes.*BG* 1.5.4, 10.3.

32 Suet.*DJ* 28.3.

33 Cf. Vulić, *RE* 9.1087.

34 Cic.*Att*.8.3.3, Dio 38.8.5. Suet.*DJ* 22.1 distinguishes the grant from the *lex Vatinia* but erroneously refers it to Gallia Comata; so too Oros.6.7.1. This grant presumably had to be renewed annually; cf. Gelzer, *KS* II, 226.

35 Caes.*BG* 1.33.3f.

36 For Clodius' desire to secure the tribunate and his efforts to make *transitio ad plebem* in 60, cf. Cic.*Att*.2.1.6, 8f., 2.9.1f., Plut.*Lucull*.42, *Cato* 30. P. Sulpicius, *tr.pl*.88, did not provide a precedent: he was never a patrician, cf. Mattingly, *Athen*. n.s. 53, 1975, 264f. On relations between Clodius, Pompeius and Cicero in 59, cf. Seager, *Latomus* 24, 1965, 519ff.

37 On these aspects of the trial, cf. Gruen, *Latomus* 32, 1973, 301ff. The charge is uncertain: *repetundae* according to Schol.Bob.94St.

38 Cic.*Att*.1.12.1.

39 Ascon.84; cf. Cicero's comment on the timing of Vatinius' law *de alternis consiliis reiciendis* (*Vat*.27f.).

40 Cf. *MRR* II 126f.

41 Cic.*Att*.1.12.1.

42 Suet. *DJ* 20.4. Dio 38.10.1ff. misplaces the incident after the marriages of Pompeius and Caesar and the Vettius affair.

43 Cic.*Sest*.15f., *har.resp*.45, *prov.cos*.42, *Att*.8.3.3, Plut.*Cato* 33, Dio 38.12.2 (amid much fantasy). For the synchronism, cf. Cic.*dom*.41, Suet.*DJ* 20.4.

44 Cf. Seager, *Latomus* 24, 1965, 519ff.

45 Cic.*Att*.2.4.2, 2.7.2; cf. Seager, *Latomus* 24, 1965, 521.

46 Cic.*Att*.2.7.2f.

47 Cic.*Att*.2.4.2, 2.5.1; he was also offered a place on the agrarian commission after the death of Cosconius: *Att*.2.19.4, 9.2a.1, *prov.cos*.41.

48 Cic.*Att*.2.5.1.

49 Cic.*Att*.2.7.3. Cf. the general reflections of Lucan on the instability of the coalition (1.92ff.).

50 Cic.*Att*.2.5.2.

51 Cic.*Att*.2.5.2, 2.7.3; cf. Ward, *Crassus* 222.

52 Cic.*Att*.2.5.2, 2.7.3.

53 Cic.*Att*.2.7.3, 2.8.1. On the conduct of Curio in 59, cf. Seager, *Latomus* 24, 1965, 522f.

54 Cic.*Att*.2.7.4.

55 Cic.*Att*.2.8.1.

56 Cic.*Att*.2.9.1, 2.15.2.

57 Cic.*Att*.2.9.1.

58 Cic.*Att*.2.9.2.

59 Cic.*Att*.2.12.2. For the interpretation of Clodius' action, cf. Seager, *Latomus* 24, 1965, 521f.; Lintott, *GR*^{2} 14, 1967, 166, *Violence* 146.

60 Cic.*Att*.2.12.1f.

61 Cic.*Att*.2.12.2.

62 Cf. Seager, *Latomus* 24, 1965, 521f.

63 Cic.*Att*.2.13.2; cf. 2.6.2 on Antium, with Shackleton Bailey's comment.

64 Cf. Luc.1.131ff. on Pompeius' love of popular acclaim.

65 Cic.*Att*.2.14.1, cf. 2.17.2 (early May). On the critical nature of the political situation at this time, cf. Meier, *Historia* 10, 1961, 70f.

66 Cic.*Att*.2.16.2. On Caesar's need to bind Pompeius to him at this point, cf. Gelzer, *Caesar* 72.

67 Cic.*Att*.2.17.1, 8.3.3, Vell.2.44.3, Plut.*Pomp*.47, *Caes*.14, *Cato* 31, Dio 38.9.1, Suet.*DJ* 21. For criticism of Pompeius, cf. Suet.*DJ* 50.1. On the importance of the marriage as a new and more durable commitment to Caesar on Pompeius' part, cf. Meier, *RPA* 285.

68 Plut.*Pomp*.47, *Caes*.14, Dio 38.9.1, App.*BC* 2.14.50, Suet.*DJ* 21. It is unclear, and fortunately not vital here, whether the victim was the man we know as M. Brutus or his adoptive father; for the former view, cf. Münzer, *RA* 337ff.

69 Plut.*Pomp*.47, *Caes*.14, Dio 38.9.1, App.*BC* 2.14.51, Suet.*DJ* 21.

70 Suet.*DJ* 21, Gell.4.10.5.

71 Suet.*DJ* 83.1: Pompeius retained this position until 49.

72 Cic.*Vat*.30ff., Schol.Bob.149f.St. Cf. Marshall, *Crassus* 105; Ward, *Crassus* 222ff.

73 Cic.*Att*.2.21.4. It is not, however, necessary to see the hand of Crassus behind the activities of Clodius and Curio in the latter half of 59, as do Marshall, *Crassus* 106; Ward, *Crassus* 231ff.

74 Cic.*Att*.2.18.3, *prov.cos*.41f., Vell.2.45.2. Plut.*Cic*.30 mistakenly suggests that the initiative came from Cicero, who then changed his mind.

75   Cic.*Att*.2.19.1, 4f.

76   Dio 38.8.1, Schol.Bob.97St.

77   Cic.*Att*.2.18.1.

78   Cic.*Att*.2.18.2, cf. Schol.Bob.162St., mistakenly associating Laterensis' action with the first agrarian law.

79   Cic.*Att*.2.18.2, 2.19.2.

80   Cic.*Att*.2.19.3, Val.Max.6.2.9; whether the corrupt Tac.*Dial*.40.1 refers to this is uncertain.

81   Cic.*Att*.2.19.3.

82   Cic.*Att*.2.19.3.

83   Cic.*Att*.2.19.2, 2.20.4, Plut.*Pomp*.48, Suet.*DJ* 20.1, 49.2.

84   Suet.*DJ* 49.2.

85   Cic.*Att*.2.19.4.

86   Cic.*Att*.2.19.5.

87   Cic.*Att*.2.20.lf.

88   Cic.*Att*.2.20.3f., 2.21.1.

89   Cic.*Att*.2.21.3.

90   Cic.*Att*.2.21.3f.

91   Cic.*Att*.2.21.1, 4.

92   Cic.*Att*.2.20.6, 2.21.4f.

93   Cic.*Att*.2.21.5. Vatinius' alleged attempt to force Bibulus to leave his house (*Vat*.22) may belong in this context.

94   Cic.*Att*.2.22.1.

95   Cic.*Att*.2.21.6, 2.22.2, cf. *Sest*.15.

96   Cic.*Att*.2.22.4f. Crassus too appears to have interceded with Clodius at this time, cf. Ward, *Crassus* 243, on Cic.*Att*.2.22.5.

97   Cic.*Att*.2.22.6, 2.23.2.

98   Cic.*Att*.2.23.2.

99   Cic.*Att*.2.23.3. At this time the tribunician elections were imminent, and Clodius' success was certain. They presumably took place at the very end of July or perhaps in August. Oost, *AJP* 77, 1956, 25f., claims that they too were postponed till October, but Cic.*QF* 1.2.16, from which he argues, proves only that the elections had taken place before 22 October.

100   Cf. Seager, *Latomus* 24, 1965, 524.

101   The date of the Vettius affair is disputed. The attempt of Taylor, *Historia* 1, 1950, 45ff., to rearrange the traditional order of Cicero's letters was challenged by Brunt, *CQ* 47, 1953, 62ff., not fully disposed of by Taylor, *CQ* 48, 1954, 181f. For further conclusive arguments in favour of the traditional chronology, cf. Meier, *Historia* 10, 1961, 90ff.; Seager, *Latomus* 24, 1965, 525 n. 1 (though what is said there about the date of the tribunician elections requires amendment); Shackleton Bailey, *Letters* I 395.

102   Cic.*Att*.2.24.lff., *Sest*.132, *Vat*.24ff.

103   For the interpretation of the Vettius affair given here and discussion of other views, cf. Seager, *Latomus* 24, 1965, 525ff. Ward, *Crassus* 237f., argues that Clodius would not risk exposing Curio to prosecution. But the danger would not have been great, given Curio's part in making the matter public. Ward also claims that the ascription of responsibility to Clodius depends largely on names in Vettius' second list. The point

has little weight, since it can hardly have been a major objective for Clodius to discredit his own *inimici*, and there is in any case no reason to suppose, as Ward does, that the whole of the second list owed its inspiration to Caesar. His own view (*Crassus* 238ff.) that Pompeius himself was responsible is not unattractive, but does not fully account for Curio's role and makes the Vettius affair fit less well into the overall pattern of events during the year.

104　Cf. McDermott, *TAPA* 80, 1949, 364 n. 29.

105　That the trial was later than the Vettius affair appears from Cic.*Flacc.*96. Cf. Seager, *Latomus* 24, 1965, 529f.

106　Cic.*Att.*2.25.1, cf. *Flacc.*41, 54.

107　Cic.*Flacc.*2, Sall.*Hist.*2.31, Frontin.*Strat.*2.5.31, Obseq.58, Schol.Bob.98St. He himself followed Pompeius in the civil war: Cic.*Att.*8.11d.1, 8.12a.3, Caes.*BC* 3.5.3, 7.1.

108　Cic.*Flacc.*14.

109　Schol.Bob.93St. For the possible identification, cf. Val.Max.7.8.7; Münzer, *RE* 4.1262f. Another possibility is L. Herennius Balbus, friend of Clodius, cf. Cic. *Cael.*27, 49, 53, 56, Ascon.34.

110　Cic.*Flacc.*83.

111　Cic.*Flacc.* 2, 5, 14f., 94ff., Schol.Bob.98St.

112　Cic.*dom.*28 (no names), *Sest.*41 (anonymous), 67, 132 (Vatinius), *Pis.*76f. For Clodius' assistance to Vatinius in 58, cf. Cic.*Sest.*135, *Vat.*33f., Schol.Bob.140, 150St.

113　Cic.*Sest.*41.

114　Cic.*Pis.*3, Plut.*Pomp.*48, *Cato* 33, App.*BC* 2.14.51.

115　Cic.*QF* 1.2.15. This despite *Att.*2.25.2, of uncertain date but later than the trial of Flaccus, which suggests that the dynasts were still uniformly loathed. Gabinius later claimed to owe his escape to Clodius' gangs (Cic.*Sest.*18). The role ascribed to Crassus by Ward, *Crassus* 242, is pure conjecture.

116　Cic.*QF* 1.2.16.

9   THE EXILE OF CICERO

1　For the legislation, cf. esp. Ascon.7ff.; other sources: *MRR* II 195f.

2　On Clodius, cf. Meyer, *Caesars Monarchie* 103; Gruen, *Phoen.* 20, 1966, 120ff.; Lintott, *GR*² 14, 1967, 157ff.; Ward, *Crassus* 232, 256.

3　The best discussion of Clodius and the *leges Aelia et Fufia* remains that of McDonald, *JRS* 19, 1929, 164ff.

4　Cic.*dom.*21, Vell.2.45.1, Plut.*Cic.*30, Dio 38.14.4, App.*BC* 2.15.54, Liv.*per.*103.

5　Cic.*red.sen.*10, 18, 32, *red.Quir.*11, 13, 21, *dom.*23f., 55, 60, 66, 70, 93, 124, *Sest.*24f., 31, 44, 53ff., 67ff., *har.resp.*58, *prov.cos.*2ff., 17, *Pis.*28, 31, 37, 49, 56f., *Rab.Post.*20, Plut.*Cic.*30, App.*Syr.*51.257ff., *uir.ill.*81.4, Schol.Bob.168St. The change from Cilicia to Syria: Cic.*dom.*23, *Sest.*55. The synchronism: Cic.*red.sen.*17f., *Sest.*25, 53.

6　Cic.*red.sen.*10ff., 31f., *red.Quir.*11ff., *dom.*55, 62, 66, 70, 124, *Sest.* 18, 20, 24ff., 53ff., 69f., 93f., *har.resp.*3f., *Pis.*8, 11, 13ff., 48, 64, 72, 77, *Planc.*86f., *Fam.*11.16.2, 12.29.1, Ascon.7, 9, Plut.*Pomp.*49, *Cic.*31, Dio 38.16.3ff., 30.2, Schol.Bob.127f., 168St.

7　Cf. Fantham, *Historia* 24, 1975, 430, against Badian, *PS* 103.

8　Cic.*dom.*66.

9   Cf. Seager, *Latomus* 24, 1965, 531. Cicero's schematic comment in *Phil*.2.23 that in 59 he tried to detach Pompeius from Caesar, but instead Caesar detached Pompeius from him, does scant justice to the complex factors involved in Pompeius' decision.

10 Cic.*Att*.8.3.3. For Clodius' claim that Pompeius approved of his actions, cf. Cic. *dom*.66, *Sest*.39f., 42, 52, *har.resp*.47.

11 Cic.*Att*.3.15.4, *QF* 1.4.4.

12 Cf. Cic.*Att*.3.9.2, 3.15.2, *QF* 1.3.8, *Fam*.1.9.13f., *har.resp*.38, Dio 38.12.6f. Denied: Cic.*dom*.95.

13 Plut.*Cic*.31, Dio 38.17.3 (less extreme). For the continuation of the whispering campaign, cf. Cic.*Sest*.41, 67, *Pis*. 76f. Cf. Gelzer, *Cicero* 138 n. 39.

14 Cic.*Pis*.77; slanted to exculpate Pompeius: *Sest*.41. For the attitudes of Gabinius and Piso, cf. Plut.*Cic*.31. Schol.Bob.122St. confuses Marcellinus with Spinther.

15 For his account of his motives, cf. esp. Cic.*red.sen*.33, *dom*.96ff., *Sest*.42ff., *Vat*.6.

16 Cic.*red.sen*.32, *dom*.5, 131, *Sest*.40ff., 52 (exaggerating the number of troops), *har. resp*.47, Plut.*Caes*.14, Suet.*DJ* 23.1, Schol.Bob.130, 146St.

17 Cic.*dom*.20, 52f., 65, 129, *Sest*.57, 59, 62, 84, *har.resp*.58, Vell. 2.45.4f., Plut.*Pomp*.48, *Cato* 34, *Caes*.21, Dio 38.30.5, Liv.*per*.104; other sources: *MRR* II 198. For Cato's conduct in Cyprus, cf. Vell.2.38.6, 45.5, Plut.*Cato* 36ff., *Brut*.3, Dio 39.22.2ff. For his title, cf. Balsdon, *JRS* 52, 1962, 135; for the sequence of events leading to his appointment, cf. Badian, *JRS* 55, 1965, 116f.

18 Cic.*Sest*.60, Plut.*Cato* 40, *Cic*.34; cf. Caesar's alleged congratulations to Clodius: Cic.*dom*.22.

19 Cic.*dom*. 129, *Sest*.56, 62, 84, *har.resp*.28f., 58f.

20 Cic.*dom*.66, *Mil*.18, 37, Ascon.47, Plut.*Pomp*.48, Dio 38.30.1f., Schol.Bob.118f.St.

21 Cic.*dom*.66, *Pis*.27, Dio 38.30.2.

22 Cic.*red.Quir*.14, *dom*.124, *Pis*.28, Dio 38.30.2.

23 Dio 38.30.3, cf. Cic.*Mil*.87, Plut.*Cic*.33.

24 Cf. Lintott, *GR*² 14, 1967, 166, *Violence* 191ff.

25 Cf. Cic.*har.resp*.46, 50ff., *prov.cos*.44f., 47.

26 Cic.*prov.cos*.46. Ward, *Crassus* 247, sees this as a response to, rather than the stimulus for, Clodius' attack on Caesar's legislation; this is by no means impossible. Cf. the proposal that Antonius' acceptable laws be re-enacted without breach of the auspices (Cic.*Phil*.5.10).

27 Cic.*Att*.2.8.1, 2.12.1f., cf. Seager, *Latomus* 24, 1965, 521f.

28 Cic.*dom*.40, *har.resp*.48. For Cicero's unconvincing rejoinder and his repeated claim that Clodius' tribunate was invalid, cf. *dom*.34, 36, 38f., 42. Cf. Gelzer, *Cicero* 144. There is no good reason to date Clodius' threat to Caesar's legislation late in the year, as a response to the law of the eight tribunes, as Grimal, *CRAI* 1966, 103.

29 Cic.*Att*.3.8.3f.

30 Cic.*red.sen*.3, *Sest*.67f. (not so flattering to Pompeius), Dio 38.30.3f. For Ninnius' earlier support of Cicero, cf. Cic.*Sest*.26, Dio 38.14.1f., 16.3; for his consecration of Clodius' property, cf. Cic.*dom*.125.

31 Cic.*Att*.3.9.2.

32 Cic.*Att*.3.10.1, 3.12.1, *QF* 1.3.8.

33 Cic.*Att*.3.13.1, 3.14.1, 3.18.1.

34 Cf. Cic.*Att*.3.13.1, *QF* 1.4.3, 5, *Fam*.14.2.2.

35 Cic.*dom*.129, *Sest*.69, *har.resp*.49, *Pis*.28, *Mil*.18f., 37, Ascon.46, Plut.*Pomp*.49.

36 Cic.*red.sen*.4, 29, *red.Quir*.14, *dom*.67, 110, *Sest*.69, 84, *har.resp*.49, 58, *Pis*.16, 29, *Mil*.18f., 73, ap.Schol.Bob.170, 172St., Ascon.46f.

37 Cic.*Att*.3.15.1, 3.18.1.

38 Plut.*Pomp*.49.

39 Cic.*Att*.3.15.3, 3.18.1.

40 Cic.*Sest*.71, giving an approximate date, cf. *Pis*.80, *Fam*.1.9.9.

41 Cic.*Att*.3.22.2, 3.23.1, *Fam*.14.1.2, 14.2.2, *red.sen*.8, *dom*.70, *sest*.70. For Caesar's assistance to Spinther, cf. Caes.*BC* 1.22.4.

42 Cic.*Att*.3.15.5f., 3.20.3, 3.23.1ff., *red.sen*.4, *Sest*.69.

43 Cic.*Att*.3.23.1, 3.24.2, *Fam*.1.9.16, *red.Quir*.15. For the difference in their attitudes, cf. Cic.*dom*.87, *Sest*.72, 87. In April 57 Cicero wrote an awkward letter of thanks to Nepos (*Fam*.5.4).

44 Cf. Cic.*red.sen*.5, 8, *red.Quir*.11f., *dom*.70, *Sest*.72, *Pis*.34, *Mil*.39. Dio 39.6.3 overprolongs Nepos' hostility.

45 Cic.*dom*.68f., *Sest*.73f., *leg*.3.45.

46 Messius: Cic.*red.sen*.21; Fabricius: Cic.*red.sen*.6f., 22, *red.Quir*.14, *Sest*.75ff., *Mil*.38, Dio 39.7.2f.

47 Plut.*Pomp*.49, *Cic*.33. For the contribution of Sestius and Milo, cf. Cic.*red.sen*.19f., 30, *red.Quir*.15, *Sest*.86ff., *Mil*.94, Vell.2.45.3, Dio 39.6.2, App.*BC* 2.16.59 (confused), Liv.*per*.104.

48 Cic.*red.sen*.29, 31, *dom*.25, 30, *Pis*.25, 27, 80, *Mil*.39. Vell. 2.45.3 is malicious, but hardly unfair. Cicero repeatedly highlights Pompeius' efforts on his behalf in an attempt to justify his own services to the coalition after Luca (cf. ch. 10 below): *Planc*.93, *Pis*.76ff.

49 Cf. Cic.*red.sen*.9, 24, 26f., 31, *red.Quir*.15ff., *dom*.7, 14, 30, 70ff., 85, *Sest*.107, 109, 128f., *har.resp*.14, 46, *prov.cos*.22, 43, *Pis*.34ff., *Mil*.38f., *Fam*.1.9.16. Nepos yielded in part to the influence of Servilius Isauricus, cf. Cic.*red.sen*.25, *Sest*.130, *prov.cos*.22, Dio 39.8.2f.

50 Cic.*Att*.4.1ff, *red.sen*., *red.Quir.passim*, *dom*.76, *Pis*.51f.

51 Ascon.48, Dio 39.9.2.

52 Cic.*Att*.4.1.6, *dom*.6, 11ff.

53 Cic.*dom*.7, 9f., 15f., 27, Plut.*Pomp*.49, Dio 39.9.3.

54 Cic.*dom*.4, 18ff., 26, Plut.*Pomp*.49. Wiseman, *JRS* 59, 1969, 64 with n. 48, suggests very plausibly that the burning of the temple of the Nymphs, used by Pompeius as an office, by Sex. Cloelius (Cic.*Cael*.78, *har.resp*.57, *Mil*.73, *parad*.31) was intended to destroy the list which Pompeius eventually prepared (Dio 39.24.1f.) of those eligible to receive the corn dole.

55 Cic.*dom*.8; cf. Clodius' claim (*dom*.3, 31) that Cicero had angered the *pontifices* by proposing a command for Pompeius.

56 Cic.*Att*.4.1.7.

57 Cic.*Att*.4.1.7, Plut.*mor*.204C, Dio 39.9.3, App.*BC* 2.18.67 (twenty legates, dated to 53!), Liv.*per*.104.

58 Cf. Miltner, *RE* 21.2138; *contra*: Stockton, *Cicero* 195, who sees Messius' proposal as a springboard for Pompeius to intervene in Egypt.

59 Cf. Cic.*QF* 2.5.3, *Fam*.1.9.9, 13.75.2, Plut.*mor*.204C.

60 Cf. Cic.*QF* 2.3.3, *Fam*.1.9.7.

61 Thus Plut.*Pomp*.50, *mor*.240C, records his sailing to Sicily, Sardinia and Africa.

62 Cic.*Att.*4.1.7, 4.2.6, 4.19.2, *QF* 2.2.1, 2.3.7, 2.5.3, *Fam.*1.9.9, *Scaur.*39.

63 Cf.Plin.*Pan.*29.1.

64 Ward, *Crassus* 245, assigns Crassus a more active role. If this were correct, it could only have strengthened Pompeius' feeling that the coalition had no further value.

10   THE CONFERENCE OF LUCA

1 In general, cf. Cary, *CQ* 17, 1923, 103ff.; Stockton, *TAPA* 93, 1962, 471ff.

2 Cf. Cic.*leg.agr.* 1.21, 2.80ff.

3 Cic.*Phil.*2.101.

4 Cf. Stockton, *Cicero* 207.

5 Cf. Cic.*Fam.* 1.1.3f.; *contra*: Stockton, *TAPA* 93, 1962, 474.

6 Cic.*QF* 2.1.1.

7 Dio 39.12.2f., Liv.*per.* 104.

8 Cic.*Fam.*1.1.3, *Rab.Post.*6, *Pis.*50, Dio 39.12.3. According to Plut.*Pomp.*49 some thought Spinther had backed Pompeius' corn commission in order to keep him too occupied to take an interest in Egypt.

9 Cic.*Fam.*1.1.1, 4, *QF* 2.2.3, *Cael.*18, *Rab.Post.*6, Plut.*Pomp.*49, Dio 39.12.3 (before the appointment of Spinther).

10 Cic.*Cael.*23ff., 51, 54, *har.resp.*34, Strabo 17.1.11, Dio 39.13.1ff.

11 Cic.*Rab.post.*6, Strabo 17.1.11, Dio 39.14.3.

12 Cic.*Fam.*1.1.1, *QF* 2.2.3; for the date and the part played by C. Cato, cf. Dio 39.15.1ff.

13 Cf. Cic.*Fam.*1.4.2.

14 Cic.*Fam.*1.1.2.

15 Cic.*Fam.*1.1.2f., Dio 39.16.1.

16 Cic.*Fam.*1.1.3.

17 Cic.*Fam.*1.1.3f. It is noteworthy that it was the attitude of Afranius that was the giveaway: clearly Volcacius himself was not known as a 'Pompeian'. Cf. Cic.*QF* 2.2.3, Dio 39.16.1.

18 Cic.*Fam.*1.2.1.

19 Cic.*Fam.*1.2.1f. Rutilius was no doubt afraid that because of Pompeius' public stance Hortensius' motion might pass: cf. Stockton, *Cicero* 200ff.

20 Cic.*Fam.*1.2.3f., cf. 1.4.2, 1.5a.2, *QF* 2.2.3.

21 Plut.*Pomp.*49.

22 Cic.*Fam.*1.5a.2f., *QF* 2.3.1, 4, *Sest.*144.

23 Cic.*Fam.*1.4.1.

24 Cic.*QF* 2.2.3.

25 Cic.*Fam.*1.5a.3. Despite Cicero's oracular turn of phrase and the deficiencies of the text the overall sense seems clear.

26 Cic.*QF* 2.3.1, *Mil.*40.

27 Cic.*Fam.*1.5b.1, *QF* 2.3.1f., Ascon.48. The chronology adopted in the text depends on the assumption that the date of 6 February for the riot is correctly transmitted in *Fam.*1.5b.1. This involves four emendations to dates in *QF* 2.3.1–3. It is equally possible that the days concerned were 7, 8 and 9 February rather than 6, 7 and 8. This would require emendation in *Fam.*1.5b.1, but only two changes in *QF* 2.3.3. The matter is happily of no importance whatsoever.

28 Cf. Ward, *Crassus* 252; on the text and meaning of Cic.*QF* 2.3.2, cf. *ibid*. n. 66.

29 Cic.*Fam*. 1.5b.1, *QF* 2.3.2, cf. *Mil*.40, 68, Schol.Bob.122St. In general terms, cf. Plut.*Pomp*.48, Dio 39.19.1f.

30 Cf. Cicero's comments on the attitude of the optimates in *har.resp*.46, 50ff., *prov. cos*.44f., 47, *Fam*. 1.9.10.

31 Cic.*Fam*.l.5b.1, *QF* 2.3.3.

32 Cic.*Fam*.l.5b.1, *QF* 2.3.3, cf. *Att*.1.14.3.

33 Cic.*QF* 2.3.4.

34 Cic.*Fam*.1.5b.1. It appears from *Fam*.1.7.4 that Servilius' motion was eventually passed, vetoed and recorded as an *auctoritas*; when exactly this happened is unclear. Dio 39.55.1 probably refers not to this but merely to the earlier decision not to allow the use of force.

35 Cic.*QF* 2.3.4. On the link between Milo and Sestius, cf. Cic.*Sest*.92, *Vat*.41.

36 Cic.*Fam*.1.9.7, *QF* 2.4.1; for his insistence that in attacking Vatinius he was not criticizing Caesar, cf. *Vat*.13, 15, 38f.

37 Cic.*QF* 2.3.5, 2.4.1, *Sest*. 3, 14, Schol.Bob.125St.; for the charge of *praeuaricatio*, cf. Cic.*Vat*.3, 41.

38 Cic.*QF* 2.4.4f.

39 Cic.*QF* 2.4.5; note also Marcellinus' attack on Pompeius' excessive power in a *contio* (Val.Max.6.2.6).

40 Cic.*QF* 2.4.6. On the name, cf. Shackleton Bailey, *CQ* 54, 1960, 41f.

41 Cic.*QF* 2.4.6, *Cael*.78.

42 Cic.*QF* 2.4.5.

43 Cic.*Fam*.1.9.8., *QF* 2.5.1; there is no evidence that Pompeius was present, *pace* Marshall, *Crassus* 126.

44 Cic.*QF* 2.5.1. For the continuing high price of corn at the time of the *de haruspicum responso*, cf. *har.resp*.31.

45 Cic.*Fam*.1.9.9, *QF* 2.5.3. Cicero visited him after dinner on 8 April (reading *a.d.vi* rather than *vii* in *QF* 2.5.2) and learned that he was planning to leave Rome on 11 April.

46 Cic.*Fam*.1.9.6f.

47 Cic.*Fam*.1.9.8.

48 Cic.*Fam*.1.9.9. Crassus' part in these events invites speculation. The suggestion that he deliberately engineered the crisis to force Pompeius into a new agreement (thus Marshall, *Crassus* 124ff.; Ward, *Crassus* 262ff.) underestimates Cicero's role in bringing matters to a head (acknowledged by Marshall, *Crassus* 125), which Crassus could hardly have predicted, and the obviously hastily improvised nature of proceedings at Ravenna and Luca. It seems more likely that Crassus had merely intended to make sure, in as unpleasant a manner as could be contrived, that Pompeius derived no profit from the Egyptian affair. When Cicero tried to exploit the situation, Crassus was compelled to extemporize at top speed, and did so brilliantly.

49 Plut.*Pomp*.51, *Caes*.21, *Crass*.14, *Cato* 41, App.*BC* 2.17.62, Suet.*DJ* 24.1.

50 Crassus' presence is accepted by Marshall, *Crassus* 127; Ward, *Crassus* 263f. Doubts are expressed, but not argued, by Gelzer, *Caesar* 109f., *Cicero* 167 n. 5, *KS* II 200f. The view expressed in the text is derived from Jackson, *LCM* 3, 1978, 175ff. The best general discussion of Luca is that of Luibheid, *CP* 65, 1970, 88ff., to be preferred to Lazenby, *Latomus* 18, 1959, 67ff.

51 Cic.*Fam*.1.9.9.
52 Cf. Plut.*Pomp*. 51, *Caes*.21, *Crass*.14, *Cato* 41, App.*BC* 2.17.63, Suet.*DJ* 24.1.
53 Cic.*Fam*.1.9.9f., 12.
54 Cic.*Fam*.1.9.9f., 12.
55 Cic.*QF* 2.6.2. On the meaning of *in hac causa mihi aqua haeret* in this passage (lit. 'in this matter water sticks to me'), cf. the attractive suggestion of Ward, *Crassus* 260 n. 9.

11 THE SECOND CONSULSHIP AND THE GROWTH OF ANARCHY

1 Cic.*har.resp*.51f., Dio 39.29.1; cf. Schol.Bob.170St. on Clodius' abject plea to Pompeius for a reconciliation, which probably belongs in this context. For the view that this was a consequence of Luca cf. Lenaghan, *Commentary* 26, 180. Wiseman, *Cinna* 163f., claims that Pompeius was already reconciled with Clodius at the time of his talk with Cicero on 8 April, and that Clodius' *contio*, at which this was revealed, may be as early as 12 April. This is unconvincing. The *contio* may well have been earlier than is supposed by Lenaghan, *Commentary* 180, but there is no cogent ground for putting it before Luca and some evidence against. The only indication of time in Cicero (*har.resp*.8: *paulo ante*) is too vague to be of use. However, Dio's account of 56 is not a chronological whole, but falls into three main sections: 39.15.1–16.3, 39.18.1–23.4, and 39.24.1–30.4. He mentions a *contio* of Clodius, probably that of *har.resp*.8, in the second section, at 39.20.3, and Clodius' reconciliation with Pompeius in the third section, at 39.29.1. Unfortunately it is impossible to establish any relationship between events dealt with in the second section and those treated in the third. However, within the third section itself Dio dates the reconciliation as occurring during events that are subsequent to Luca (which would, if he had mentioned it, have appeared in his narrative at 39.27.1). The clearest indication of the date of the *de haruspicum responso* is precisely the allusion to Clodius' reconciliation with Pompeius as recent. Cicero's oracular remarks on discord (54f.) also appear to be directed against any attempt to set Pompeius and Caesar at each other's throats and in general against baiting Pompeius. They too are therefore consistent with his own position immediately after Luca. The overall trend of the speech, however, suggests that the arrangements made at Luca were not yet fully understood and that the reconciliation of the dynasts had not yet had its full impact. A date before 15 May seems the most likely, perhaps 14 May. Cf. Lenaghan, *Commentary* 22ff., who deals with other views; Wiseman, *Cinna* 161 n. 18, 165.
2 Cic.*Att*.4.5.1ff., cf. *Fam*.1.9.5, 10, 13f., 17.
3 Cic.*Att*.4.5.1f., *Fam*.1.7.10, *prov.cos*.26ff., *Balb*.61, Suet.*DJ* 24.3. In the last matter Cicero had at least the consolation of pressing instead for the recall of Gabinius and Piso (*prov.cos*.1ff., 17, Ascon.2), as he had threatened to do immediately after his return from exile. For his public comments on Caesar at this time, cf. *prov.cos*.18, 20, 23, 38f., 44f., 47.
4 Cic.*Att*.4.6.1f., *Fam*.1.7.10, 1.8.2f.
5 Cic.*Fam*.1.7.3ff. (claiming Pompeius' blessing), 1.8.5.
6 Cf. Cic.*Balb*.6, 11, 19, 38. The prosecution as an attack on Pompeius: Cic.*Balb*.6, 58ff., 62, 65.

7   Praise of Pompeius for his speech: Cic.*Balb*.2f., 17, 59; in general: Cic.*Balb*.5, 8ff., 13, 15f. Defence of Cicero's own actions in the context of an appeal for concord: Cic.*Balb*.60ff. Pompeius' challenge: Cic.*Balb*.59. For Crassus, cf. Cic.*Balb*.3, 17, 50.

8   Plut.*Pomp*.52, *Crass*.15, *Cato* 41f., App.*BC* 2.17.64, Suet.*DJ* 24.1.

9   Plut.*Pomp*.51, *Crass*.15; a slightly different version in Dio 39.30.1f.

10   Dio 39.27.2f.

11   They employed the services of C. Cato, who seems to have followed Clodius' lead in revising his attitudes after Luca (Dio 39.27.2–30.4, Liv.*per*.105, cf. Val.Max.6.2.6).

12   Plut.*Pomp*.52, *Crass*.15, *Cato* 41, Dio 39.31.1f., App.*BC* 2.17.64–18.65, cf. Vell.2.46.1. For interregal elections, cf. Staveley, *Historia* 3, 1954/5, 193ff.

13   Plut.*Pomp*.52, *Cato* 42, Dio 39.32.1f., Liv.*per*.105, Val.Max.7.5.6, Sen.*Dial*.1.3.14, 2.1.3, 12.13.5, *Ben*.5.17.2, Quintil.9.2.25.

14   Cic.*QF* 2.7.3, Plut.*Cato* 42 (technically inaccurate, as Cicero makes clear).

15   Plut.*Pomp*.53 (undated), Dio 39.32.2.

16   Cf. Gruen, *LGRR* 230ff.

17   Cic.*Planc*.49, which also records how Pompeius held the aedilician elections unexpectedly, to minimize opportunities for bribery, *Pis*.94, *Mil*.5, *Phil*.1.20, Ps.-Sall.*Ep*.2.3.3, 7.11, Ascon.17, Dio 39.37.1. Pompeius' raising of the question of *repetundae* in the senate in 55 (Cic.*Rab.Post*.13) may belong in this context.

18   Cic.*Planc*.36ff., *Fam*.8.2.1, Schol.Bob.152St. On the motives for the law, cf. Ward, *Crassus* 271; Marshall, *Crassus* 131, thinks that the aim was in fact to make bribery easier.

19   Cic.*Att*.4.10.2, 4.9.1.

20   Cic.*Att*.4.9.1; on the meaning of *iactans*, cf. Shackleton Bailey *ad loc.*

21   Cic.*Att*.4.9.1.

22   Vell.2.46.2, 48.1, Plut.*Crass*. 15, Dio 38.33.2, Liv.*per*.105. Plut.*Pomp*.52, *Caes*.28, *Cato* 43, like App.*BC* 2.18.65, erroneously assigns Africa to Pompeius, while *Cato* 43 also gives Egypt to Crassus.

23   If Plut.*Crass*.15 is correct, the consuls drew lots, but manipulation of the lot to produce the desired result was never difficult.

24   Plut.*Crass*.16, Dio 40.12.1, to be preferred to Plut.*Pomp*.52, Liv.*per*.105. Cf. Ward, *Crassus* 275; *contra:* Marshall, *Crassus* 142ff.

25   Plut.*Cato* 43, Dio 39.33.2.

26   Plut.*Cato* 43, Dio 39.34–36.1, Liv.*per*.105.

27   Cic.*Att*.8.3.3, Vell.2.46.2, Plut.*Crass*.15, *Cato* 43, Dio 39.36.2. In 39.33.3 and 44.43.2 Dio insists that the extension was for only three years. Plut.*Pomp*.52 suggests that the so-called *lex Licinia Pompeia* was in fact a *lex Trebonia*, which is by no means unlikely; cf. Pocock, *Commentary* 164f. This is not excluded by Hirt.*BG* 8.53.1, cited by Ward, *Crassus* 276, which need indicate no more than their general responsibility. There is no reason to suppose that the law made any mention of the conquest of Britain as a justification for the additional term.

28   Cic.*Phil*.2.24, Plut.*Cato* 43.

29   Cic.*off*.2.60.

30   Plin.*NH* 7.34, 35.114, 36.41, Tac.*Ann*.14.20, Plut.*Pomp*.52, Dio 39.38.1.

31   Cic.*Pis*.65, *off*.2.57, Ascon.1f., 16, Plin.*NH* 8.20f., 53, Plut.*Pomp*.52, Dio 39.38.2.

32   Cic.*Fam*.7.1.4. Caninius may have been condemned, cf. Val.Max.4.2.6; Gruen, *LGRR* 313.

33 Val.Max.6.2.8; cf. Gruen, *LGRR* 314.
34 Cic.*leg*.2.6; the date is conjectural, cf. Gruen, *LGRR* 314.
35 Plut.*Cato* 44.
36 Cic.*Pis*.48ff., *Rab*.*Post*.19ff., Strabo 17.1.11, Jos.*AJ* 14.82, *BJ* 1.160, Dio 39.55ff., App.*Syr*.51.258, Liv.*per*.105, Schol.Bob.168, 177St. Cf. Ward, *Crassus* 278f. on Crassus' attitude; Marshall, *Crassus* 140ff. is less convincing.
37 Strabo 12.3.34, 17.1.11, Jos.*AJ* 14.98, 102, *BJ* 1.175f., App.*Syr*.51.257, Justin 42.4.1f.
38 Cic.*Fam*.1.9.20, Dio 39.60.1.
39 Cic.*Fam*.1.9.20.
40 Dio 39.60.4.
41 Cic.*Att*.4.13.2, Vell.2.46.3, Plut.*Crass*.16, Dio 39.39.5ff., App.*BC* 2.18.66, Oros. 6.13.1. Ateius was later blamed by Ap. Claudius as censor for causing the disaster of Carrhae (Cic.*div*.1.29f.). Cf. Ward, *Crassus* 285 with n. 50, refuting Simpson, *TAPA* 69, 1938, 532ff.
42 Vell.2.48.1, Dio 39.39.4 (use of the corn commission as an excuse). The result is put neatly enough by *uir*.*ill*.77.8: Crassus held Syria, Caesar Gaul, and Pompeius the city.
43 Suet.*Nero* 2.2.
44 Cic.*Fam*.5.8.1, cf. 1.9.20.
45 Cic.*QF* 2.11.2; for Gabinius and the *publicani*, cf. Cic.*Pis*.41, 45, 48, Dio 39.59.2.
46 Cic.*QF* 2.13.5; cf. Plut.*Caes*.28, without any clear chronological context.
47 Cic.*Att*.4.16.5, 4.15.4, Ascon.19; C. Cato was defended by Scaurus (Ascon.18). Cf. Gruen, *LGRR* 314ff.
48 Cic.*Att*.4.16.5.
49 Cic.*Att*.4.15.9.
50 Cic.*QF* 2.3.2.
51 Cic.*QF* 2.15.3, cf. Ascon.18, Val.Max.4.2.4, Plut.*Cic*.26, Schol.Bob.160St. It was Spinther's displeasure at this incident that inspired Cicero's defence of his conduct in *Fam*.1.9. For the part played by Pompeius and Caesar, cf. Cic.*Fam*.1.9.19.
52 Cic.*QF* 3.9.5, *Att*.11.5.4, 11.9.2, *Fam*.5.9f.
53 Cic.*Att*.4.16.6, 4.15.7; cf. the excellent discussion of Gruen, *Hommages Renard* II 311ff.
54 Cic.*Att*.4.16.6, 4.15.9, Ascon.18f.
55 Cic.*Att*.4.9.1; for his continuing hostility, cf. *Att*.4.15.7.
56 Cic.*Sest*.113, Schol.Bob.135, 146, 151St., cf. Cic.*Vat*.16, Dio 38.6.1.
57 Cic.*Att*.4.16.6, 4.15.7.
58 Cic.*Att*.4.15.7, *QF* 2.14.4. In general on the growth of *ambitus*, cf. Luc.1.178ff.
59 Cic.*Att*.4.15.7, *QF* 2.14.4.
60 Cic.*Att*.4.15.7.
61 Cf. Gruen, *Hommages Renard* II 317f.
62 Cic.*QF* 2.15.2f.
63 Cic.*Att*.4.15.9, *QF* 2.15.3.
64 Cic.*Att*.4.17.2, *QF* 3.1.16.
65 Cic.*Att*.4.17.2.
66 Cic.*Att*.4.17.2. The marriage of one of Appius' daughters to Pompeius' son Gnaeus cannot yet have taken place, given Appius' attitude to Gabinius in Cic.*QF* 3.2.3. Cf. Gruen, *Historia* 18, 1969, 101ff. Appius' part in the prosecution of Scaurus, also cited by Gruen, is less significant. The earliest reference to the marriage in Cicero's correspondence comes from early June 51 (*Fam*.3.4.2).

67 Cic.*Att*.4.17.4. The date is given by Ascon.18. On the trial, cf. Gruen, *LGRR* 333ff.

68 Ascon.19.

69 Ascon.19f.

70 On the uses of *factio*, cf. Seager, *JRS* 62, 1972, 53ff.

71 Ascon.20, 28, Val.Max.8.1.*abs*.10. Sardinians who owed their citizenship to Pompeius also testified in Scaurus' favour (Cic.*Scaur*.43).

72 Cic.*QF* 3.1.15. In general on the trials of Gabinius, cf. Fantham, *Historia* 24, 1975, 425ff.; Gruen, *LGRR* 322ff.

73 Cic.*QF* 3.1.15, cf. Dio. 39.62.2.

74 Cf.Cic.*Vat*.25.

75 Cic.*QF* 3.1.15.

76 Cic.*QF* 3.1.24, Dio 39.62.1.

77 Cic.*QF* 3.2.1.

78 Cic.*QF*.3.2.1.

79 Cic.*QF* 3.2.2.

80 Cic.*QF* 3.2.3.

81 Cic.*Att*.4.18.3, *QF* 3.3.2.

82 Cic.*QF* 3.3.3; for Pompeius' efforts, cf. also Dio 39.63.3f.

83 Cic.*Att*.4.18.1, *QF* 3.4.1, Dio 39.55.4f., 62.2f. On the grounds for the *maiestas* charge, cf. Cic.*Pis*.48ff., Dio 39.56.4, App.*BC* 2.24.90. For elements of the prosecution and Gabinius' defence, cf. Cic. *Rab.Post*.20f.

84 Cic.*QF* 3.4.2.

85 Cic.*Att*.4.18.3, *QF* 3.4.1.

86 Cic.*QF* 3.4.1.

87 Cic.*QF* 3.4.2, 3.9.1; Dio 39.62.2 appears to state that Cicero spoke for the prosecution, but this could merely be an exaggerated account of his testimony.

88 Cic.*QF* 3.4.3, cf. 3.5.5, 3.9.1 on his refusal to defend Gabinius on the *maiestas* charge.

89 Cic.*Att*.4.5.2, 4.18.2, *Fam*.1.7.10, 1.8.1ff., *QF* 2.7.3, 3.4.2.

90 Cic.*Rab.Post*.19, Val.Max.4.2.4, Dio 39.63.2, 5. For the gibes of the prosecutor Memmius and Cicero's embarrassment, cf. Cic.*Rab.Post*.32f.

91 Cic.*Rab.Post*.31ff.

92 For the attempt to shelter Gabinius by D. Laelius (Val.Max.8.1.*abs*.3) cf. Fantham, *Historia* 24, 1975, 434. For Pompeius' evidence, cf. Cic.*Rab.Post*.34. For the hatred of the *publicani* for Gabinius, cf. Cic.*Pis*. 41, 45, 48, *Rab.Post*.8, 10, 12, 38, Dio 39.55.5, 59.2, 63.2, 5. Cicero naturally claimed to have done his best (*Rab.Post*.19). But it is hard to believe Dio's claim (39.55.6) that Gabinius' condemnation came as a great surprise to Pompeius. There seems no good reason for postponing the *repetundae* trial until midsummer 53, as Lintott, *JRS* 64, 1974, 67f.

93 Cic.*QF* 3.1.17 mentions the event in September; Dio 39.64.1 synchronizes it with the trial of Gabinius.

94 Vell.2.47.2, Plut.*Pomp*.53, *Caes*.23 (Caesar received news of her death on his return from the second invasion of Britain in 54), App.*BC* 2.19.68, Suet.*DJ* 26.1, Liv.*per*.106, Flor.2.13.13.

95 Vell.2.47.2, Dio 41.6.3f., Val.Max.4.6.4, Flor.2.13.13, Luc.1.111ff.

96 Cf. Gruen, *LGRR* 450f.

97 Cic.*Att*.4.17.5, 4.18.3, *QF* 3.2.3, 3.3.2.

98 Cic.*QF* 3.2.3, 3.3.2.

99   Cic.*QF* 3.8.3.
100 Cic.*QF* 3.8.3.
101 Cic.*QF* 3.8.4, cf. App.*BC* 2.19.71–20.73.
102 Cic.*QF* 3.8.4, Plut.*Pomp*.54.
103 Cic.*QF* 3.8.6, 3.9.2.
104 Cic.*QF* 3.9.3. Already in this year Cato had accused Pompeius of deliberately fostering anarchy in order to pave the way to dictatorship (Plut.*Cato* 45).
105 Cf. Plut.*Pomp*.54, Dio 40.45.5, who claims (40.46.1) that the dictatorship was actually offered to Pompeius, but refused.
106 Dio 40.45.1ff.
107 Vell.2.46.4, Plut.*Pomp*.53, *Caes*.28, App.*BC* 2.18.66, Dio 40.27, Liv.*per*. 106, Flor. 2.13.13, Eutrop.6.18.1.
108 For the implication, cf.Plut.*Pomp*.53, *Caes*.28, but grossly ante-dating the determination of both Caesar and Pompeius to liquidate one another and exaggerating the role of Crassus. Also Luc.1.99f., Flor.2.13.13.
109 Suet.*DJ* 27.1.
110 Plut.*Pomp*.55, giving the date, Dio 40.51.3.
111 Cf. Gruen, *LGRR* 453.

12   THE THIRD CONSULSHIP AND THE APPROACH OF CIVIL WAR

1   That the violence began in 53 in made clear by Ascon.48, Dio 40.46.3.
2   The best narrative is that of Ascon.30ff.; cf. also Dio 40.46.3, Liv.*per*.107, Schol. Bob.169St.
3   For Pompeius and Hypsaeus, cf. Cic.*Flacc*.20.
4   Ascon.30f., Plut.*Cato* 47, cf. Cic.*Mil*.32, 89. Later, when Clodius' death had made Milo unpopular, Hypsaeus and Scipio tried to bring pressure to bear on M. Lepidus to hold the elections illegally, cf. Ascon.43, Schol.Bob.116St.
5   Ascon.31f., App.*BC* 2.21.75f., Schol.Bob.111f.St.
6   Ascon.32, 53, Vell.2.47.4, Dio 40.48.2, Liv.*per*.107.
7   Ascon.32f., 42, 49, Dio 40.48.3–49.1, Schol.Bob.115St.
8   Cic.*Mil*.33, 91, Ascon.7, 33, 46, 55, Dio 40.49.1ff., App.*BC* 2.21.77f., Liv.*per*. 107, Schol.Bob.111St.
9   Cic.*Mil*.13, 61, 67f., 70, Ascon.34, 51f., Liv.*per*.107. For the date, cf. Dio 40.49.5: not excluded by Ascon.34, where *factum erat* suggests that the decree is mentioned out of its proper chronological sequence.
10 Caes.*BG* 7.1.1, Ascon. 52, Dio 40.50.1.
11 Cic.*Mil*.91, Ascon.33.
12 Ascon.34.
13 Cic.*Mil*.65f., Ascon.51.
14 Ascon.35, 52.
15 Ascon.35.
16 Ascon.35.
17 Ascon.34f.; for the *pro Milone* composed by Brutus as a rhetorical exercise, cf. Ascon.41, Quintil.3.6.93, 10.1.23.

18 Ascon.35, Dio 40.50.3, App.*BC* 2.23.84; cf. the hostile comment of Brutus recorded by Quintil.9.3.95.

19 Ascon.36, Vell.2.47.3, Val.Max.8.15.8, Plut.*Pomp*.54, *Caes*.28, *Cato* 47, Dio 40.50.4, App.*BC* 2.23.84, Suet.*DJ* 26.1, Liv.*per*.107. For Pompeius and Cato in 52, cf. Plut. *Pomp*.54, *Cato* 48.

20 Ascon.36, Plut.*Pomp*.54.

21 Cf. Gruen, *LGRR* 153.

22 Cf. App.*BC* 2.23.84. Nevertheless Pompeius' power in 52 should not be underestimated, cf. Cicero's comment in *fin*.2.57.

23 Cic.*Mil*.15, *fin*.4.1, *Brut*.324, Ascon.36, Vell.2.47.3, Tac.*Dial*.38.2, Plut.*Pomp*.55, Dio 40.52.1ff., 55.2, App.*BC* 2.23.87f., Schol.Bob.112St. For Cicero's later criticism of the setting up of a special court, cf. *Phil*.2.22. Caesar is flattering at *BG* 7.6.1, critical at *BC* 3.1.4.

24 Cic.*Mil*.14, Ascon.44f. For the support of Rufus and Sallustius for Pompeius' law, cf. Ascon.49f.

25 Ascon.36.

26 Ascon.36, 50. Note Cicero's guarded criticism of Pompeius' readiness to believe rumours at *Mil*.61.

27 Cic.*Mil*.12, 47, 58, Ascon.37.

28 Ascon.38.

29 Cic.*Mil*.22, Ascon.38.

30 Cic.*Mil*.21, Ascon.38f., Dio 40.52.1. For Milo's eventual condemnation in absence on the subsidiary charges, cf. Ascon.54.

31 Ascon.40, 42, 52.

32 Cic.*Mil*.3, 71, Ascon.30, App.*BC* 2.24.89.

33 Ascon.41f.

34 Cicero denies the significance of the presence of the troops at *Mil*.2, 15, 21, 31, 70f., though he admits to fear of Pompeius' suspicions at *Mil*.67f.; later he claimed that Pompeius did not resent his stand (*Fam*.3.10.10). Cf. also Vell.2.47.4, Luc.1.320ff., Dio 40.53.2f., Quintil.4.2.25, Schol.Bob.112St.

35 Ascon.42, Plut.*Cic*.35, Dio 40.54.2ff., Schol. Bob.112St.

36 Ascon.53f., Liv.*per*.107.

37 Ascon.54ff.

38 Plut.*Pomp*.55, Dio 40.51.3, App.*BC* 2.24.94–25.95. It is to Pompeius' conduct here and at the trial of Plancus that the famous condemnation of Tac.*Ann*.3.28 alludes.

39 Val.Max.9.5.3, Plut.*Pomp*.55, Dio 40.51.3, 53.2, App.*BC* 2.24.93; cf. Gruen, *LGRR* 345f.

40 Val.Max.9.5.3, Plut.*Pomp*.55, Dio 40.53.1, App.*BC* 2.24.90.

41 Suet.*DJ* 26.1, cf. Flor.2.13.16, Dio 40.51.2 (claiming that Pompeius would have been reluctant to have Caesar as a colleague), App.*BC* 2.25.96. For the problem of the terminal date of Caesar's Gallic command, cf. Appendix 3.

42 For Pompeius' support, cf. Cic.*Att*.7.3.4, 8.3.3, *Fam*.6.6.5, Flor.2.13.16. For Cato's opposition, cf. Caes.*BC* 1.32.3, Liv.*per*.107. Cicero too claimed to have advised Pompeius against this step, cf. *Phil*.2.24.

43 For the decree, cf. Dio 40.46.2; for the law, Dio 40.56.1.

44 Dio 40.56.1.

45 Dio 40.56.2, Suet.*DJ* 28.3; cf. Cic.*Att.*8.3.3: *lege quadam sua*. Balsdon argues (*JRS* 52, 1962, 141) that the law cannot have invalidated Caesar's privilege or the tribunes would have opposed it. But this is incompatible with the attitude of Caesar's friends at the time, the fact that Pompeius did add a codicil, and the subsequent behaviour of Caesar's enemies. Nor is it easy to believe that the original inconsistency was merely the innocent result of careless drafting (as Gelzer, *Pompeius* 178f.). Cf. Meyer, *Caesars Monarchie* 243f.

46 Suet.*DJ* 28.2.

47 Gell.10.1.7, with a delightful anecdote of Pompeius' concern for good grammar and Cicero's tact.

48 Plut.*Pomp.*55 (four years), *Caes.*28, Dio 40.44.2, 56.2, App.*BC* 2.24.92.

49 Cic.*Fam.*7.2.2f., Val.Max.6.2.5, Plut.*Pomp.*55, *Cato* 48, Dio 40.55; cf. Gruen, *LGRR* 346f.

50 Hirt.*BG* 8.53.1, cf. Dio 40.59.1, App.*BC* 2.25.97, 26.99, Liv.*per.*108. Cf. Gruen, *LGRR* 463.

51 Suet. *DJ* 28.2.

52 The text of Suetonius is corrupt, but the sense can hardly be in doubt.

53 Cic.*Fam.*4.1.1, 4.2.3, 6.1.6, Dio 40.59.1, Suet.*DJ* 29.1, Liv.*per.*108.

54 Cic.*Att.*8.3.3, cf. Dio 40.59.3, App.*BC* 2.26.99.

55 Cael.*Fam.*8.1.2, 8.2.2; for the senate's rejection of Marcellus' proposals, cf. Hirt.*BG* 8.53.1.

56 Cic.*Att.*5.2.3, 5.11.2 (highly critical), Plut.*Caes.*29, App.*BC* 2.26.98, Suet.*DJ* 28.3. There is confusion in the sources concerning the exact status of the victim, but common sense suggests that he will not have been an ex-magistrate, since in that case his position would not have depended on Vatinius' law of 59, the validity of which Marcellus wished to impugn.

57 Cael.*Fam.*8.4.2, App.*BC* 2.26.100.

58 Cael.*Fam.*8.4.4; for the loan, cf. Caes.*BG* 6.1.2, Plut.*Pomp.*52, *Cato* 45, Dio 40.65.1.

59 Cael.*Fam.*8.4.4, 8.5.2, cf. Cic.*Att.*5.19.1.

60 Cic.*Att.*5.11.3.

61 Theophanes, as Cicero remarks, was very easily convinced.

62 Cael.*Fam.*8.9.2.

63 Cael.*Fam.*8.9.5.

64 Cael.*Fam.*8.9.5; despite corruption in the text, the general sense of Caelius' view of Pompeius' position remains clear.

65 Caes.*BC* 1.4.4, Vell.2.29.2, Luc.1.121ff., Sen.*Ep.*94.65, Flor.2.13.14, Ps.-Sall.*Ep.*1.2.3; cf. Gelzer, *Pompeius* 180. Lucan makes Pompeius state Caesar's problem in a nutshell when he has him claim that nobody could excel him by peaceful means (2.562ff.).

66 Cael.*Fam.*8.8.4, cf. Dio 40.59.3, App.*BC* 2.26.99.

67 Cael.*Fam.*8.8.5.

68 Cael.*Fam.*8.8.6.

69 Cael.*Fam.*8.8.7f. On the motives for the veto, cf. Raaflaub, *Chiron* 4, 1974, 297ff.

70 Cael.*Fam.*8.8.9.

71 Cael.*Fam.*8.8.9. For the view that *hoc anno* refers to 50, cf. e.g. Stevens, *AJP* 59, 1938, 173; Sealey, *CM* 18, 1957, 94. For 51, cf. Stockton, *Historia* 24, 1975, 238.

72 Cic.*Fam.*3.8.10.

73 Cic.*Att.*5.18.1.

74   Cic.*Fam*.3.8.10, cf. 2.10.4 (14 November).

75   Cael.*Fam*.8.10.2.

76   Cic.*Att*.5.21.2f. (February), *Fam*.2.11.1 (April), *Att*.6.2.6 (May).

77   Cic.*Att*.6.1.3, 14.

78   Cael.*Fam*.8.6.1, 3, cf. Cic.*Att*.6.2.10, *Fam*.2.13.2, 3.10.10, 3.12.1, Quintil.9.3.41. Appius was apparently well satisfied, cf. Cic.*Fam*.3.11.3. The date of the marriage is uncertain: the earliest reference to it is 4 June 51 (Cic.*Fam*.3.4.2) and there is no reason to suppose that it was not recent. Cf. Gruen, *Historia* 18, 1969, 102, and on the trial *LGRR* 353f.

79   Cael.*Fam*.8.6.5, cf. Cic.*Att*.6.3.4, Liv.*per*.109. Cicero later claimed to have expected this (*Fam*.2.13.3). For Curio's earlier hostility, cf. Cael.*Fam*.8.8.10 (October 51), 8.10.3f. (November), where he is said to have threatened to reopen the question of the *ager Campanus*.

80   Cf.Vell.2.48.4, Val.Max.9.1.6, Luc.4.819f., Plut.*Pomp*.58, *Caes*.29, Dio 40.60.3, 61.3, 62.1f., App.*BC* 2.26.101, 27.102f., Suet.*DJ* 29.1.

81   Cic.*Att*.5.20.7, App.*BC* 2.27.103, Suet.*DJ* 29.1.

82   Plut.*Pomp*.58, *Caes*.29, App.*BC* 2.26.101f., Suet.*DJ* 29.1; on Paullus, cf. Cic.*Att*.6.3.4.

83   Vell.2.48.2, Plut.*Pomp*.58, *Caes*.30, *Cato* 51, Dio 40.62.3, App.*BC* 2.27.104ff., Liv. *per*.109. For the Caesarian angle, cf. Hirt.*BG* 8.52.4, correctly dated to the spring by Raaflaub, *Chiron* 4, 1974, 302f.

84   Cf. Vell.2.48.3.

85   Cael.*Fam*.8.11.3. It is impossible to determine the precise chronological relationship between Curio's proposals and this move by Pompeius (cf. Raaflaub, *Chiron* 4, 1974, 306), but that suggested in the text seems plausible.

86   Cf. Adcock, *CQ* 26, 1932, 24ff.

87   Cael.*Fam*.8.11.3. For a less favourable estimate of Pompeius' proposal, cf. Stockton, *Historia* 24, 1975, 240f.

88   Cael.*Fam*.8.13.2; cf. Cicero's later criticism of the senate's attitude in *Att*.7.7.5.

89   App.*BC* 2.28.110–29.113.

90   Cic.*Att*.6.2.6, 6.3.2, 6.5.3.

91   Cic.*Fam*.2.17.5, Hirt.*BG* 8.54.1, Dio 40.65.2, App.*BC* 2.29.114.

92   Hirt.*BG* 8.54.1–55.1, Caes.*BC* 1.2.3, 4.5, 9.4, 32.6, Plut.*Pomp*.56, *Caes*.29, Dio 40.65.3–66.1, App.*BC* 2.29.115.

93   Cf. Cicero's fears for Pompeius' health in June (*Att*.6.3.4).

94   Cic.*Att*.8.16.1 (hysterically claiming that the demonstrations had been insincere), 9.5.4, Vell.2.48.2, Plut.*Pomp*.57, Dio 41.6.3f., App.*BC* 2.28.107; moralizing: Sen. *Dial*.6.20.4, Juv.10.283ff.

95   Plut.*Pomp*.57, *Caes*.29, App.*BC* 2.30.116ff.

96   Plut.*Pomp*.57, cf. 60.

97   App.*BC* 2.28.107ff.

98   Cael.*Fam*.8.14.2, 4.

99   Cic.*Att*.7.1.1ff.

100 Cic.*Att*.6.8.2, 6.9.5.

101 App.*BC* 2.30.118f., to be preferred to Plut.*Pomp*.58, who makes Curio, not Marcellus, propose that Caesar alone should give up his command, but adds, perhaps rightly, that Marcellus was eager to have Caesar declared a *hostis* if he defied the senate.

102 Hirt.*BG* 8.52.5, Plut.*Pomp*.59, Dio 40.64.4, 66.1, App.*BC* 2.31.120f., Oros.6.15.1; cf. Raaflaub, *DC* 33ff.

103 Plut.*Pomp*.59 (only Lentulus), Dio 40.66.2 (both); for the elections, cf. Hirt.*BG* 8.50.4.

104 Hirt.*BG* 8.55.1, Dio 40.66.3, App.*BC* 2.31.122 (giving Pompeius' proviso), Oros.6.15.1 (placing the two legions at Luceria).

105 Dio 40.66.5, App.*BC* 2.31.123.

106 Cf. Raaflaub, *DC* 38ff., who rightly stresses that various motives may have operated both here and in the case of the *senatus consultum ultimum* in January 49.

107 Cic.*Att*.7.4.2.

108 Cic.*Att*.7.3.4f. (severely critical of Pompeius' behaviour); cf. in retrospect *Marc*.15, *Phil*.2.24.

109 Cic.*Att*.7.8.4.

110 Plut.*Ant*.5.

111 Cic.*Att*.7.8.5.

112 Cf. Raaflaub, *DC* 52f.

113 Catalogued by Cic.*Att*.7.9.2 (27 December).

114 Caes.*BC* 1.1.1, Plut.*Pomp*.59, *Caes*.30, *Ant*.5, Dio 41.1.1, App.*BC* 2.32.127f.

115 Cic.*Fam*.16.11.2.

116 Plut.*Pomp*.59, *Caes*.30, Dio 41.1.3f., App.*BC* 2.32.127ff.

117 Caes.*BC* 1.1.2–2.1.

118 Caes.*BC* 1.2.2ff., Plut.*Caes*.30, Dio 41.3.4 (erroneously placed after the *senatus consultum ultimum* and the departure of the tribunes). The *certa dies* was probably, as Raaflaub, *DC* 56 n. 219, suggests, that prescribed for personal *professio* at the elections of 49.

119 Caes.*BC* 1.3.

120 Caes.*BC* 1.4.1ff.

121 Caes.*BC* 1.4.4f.

122 Cf. Raaflaub, *DC* 64ff. It is uncertain whether in the first week of January there took place a repetition of the proceedings of 1 December 50. Caesar may be believed that there was no such debate on 1 January, but it is possible that on a subsequent day the motion that both men should resign their commands was again brought and again divided with the same result as before, and that the part played by Antonius and Cassius not only increased the hostility felt towards them but also provoked the senate's vote to don military dress. Cf. Plut.*Caes*.30, *Ant*.5, Dio 41.2.1 (misdated to 1 January); Raaflaub, *Chiron* 4, 1974, 306ff.

123 Cic.*Att*.8.11D.6f., 8.9.1, 9.11A.2, *Fam*.6.6.4.ff., 16.12.2, *Deiot*.29, *Marc*.14f., *Phil*.2.24, 37, Plut.*Pomp*.59. Cf. his comments to Tiro (*Fam*.16.11.2); he felt, with justice, that there were men on both sides who wanted war.

124 Plut.*Caes*.31, App.*BC* 2.32.126, Suet.*DJ* 29.2. Plut.*Pomp*.59 omits Cisalpina. For the date, cf. Raaflaub, *Chiron* 4, 1974, 312ff. Despite the ambiguity of Suetonius, it is clear that Caesar was insisting on retaining his *imperium* until the end of 49, i.e. that the six months of Caes.*BC* 1.9.2 are the second half of 49, not the first. Cf. Cic.*Att*.7.9.3, *Fam*.6.6.5, Flor.2.13.15ff.; Raaflaub, *DC* 66, 129 n. 94.

125 Plut.*Caes*.31, cf. *Pomp*.59, App.*BC* 2.32.127.

126 Plut.*Pomp*.59 assumes that the original proposal was Illyricum and two legions, the amended version Illyricum and one legion; in *Caes*.31 the original proposal is correctly given, but Cicero suggests only one legion while leaving Caesar both

provinces. The correct sequence is stated by Suet.*DJ* 29.2, implied by Vell.2.49.4. Cf. Raaflaub, *DC* 66 n. 269.

127   Plut.*Pomp*.59, *Caes*.30f., *Ant*.5.

128   Caes.*BC* 1.5, Cic.*Fam*.16.11.2, *Phil*.2.51, Luc.1.266ff., Plut.*Caes*.31, *Ant*.5, Dio 41.3.2f., App.*BC* 2.33.130ff., Liv.*per*.109, Oros.6.15.2. For general exaggeration of Antonius' role in these events, cf. Cic.*Phil*.2.53f.

129   Caes.*BC* 1.6.1f.

130   Caes.*BC* 1.6.3ff., Cic.*Fam*.16.11.3, Dio 41.3.3f., App.*BC* 2.34.135. The appointment of Ahenobarbus is anticipated by App.*BC* 2.32.129.

131   Caes.*BC* 1.7.1ff.

132   Caes.*BC* 1.7.8–8.1.

133   Cf. Raaflaub, *DC* 78ff.

13   THE CIVIL WAR

1   App.*BC* 2.34.134, Suet.*DJ* 31. Cf. Raaflaub, *Chiron* 5, 1975, 266, *DC* 53.

2   Cic.*Att*. 7.7.7, 7.8.5, 7.20.2, 7.22.1, Luc.2.453f. On Caesar's supporters, cf. Cic.*Att*. 7.3.5, *Fam*.8.4.2, *Phil*. 2.78.

3   Caes.*BC* 1.32.8, Plut.*Pomp*.60, Dio 41.12.2, App.*BC* 2.36.143ff. Cf. Raaflaub, *DC* 262f.

4   Caes.*BC* 1.8.2, 4, Dio 41.5.2. On the nature of their mission, cf. Shackleton Bailey, *JRS* 50, 1960, 80ff.; Raaflaub, *Chiron* 5, 1975, 251, *DC* 265ff.

5   Caes.*BC* 1.14.3, Cic.*Att*. 7.11.3, 7.12.2, 8.3.3, 9.10.2, Plut.*Pomp*.60f., *Caes*.33, Dio 41.6.1f., 9.7, App.*BC* 2.37.146ff., Suet.*DJ* 75.1.

6   Cic.*Att*. 7.10, 7.11.3f., 7.13.1, 8.3.3, Vell.2.49.5, Luc.1.511ff., Plut.*Pomp*.61, *Caes*.34, Dio 41.7ff., Suet.*DJ* 34.1, *uir.ill*.77.9, 78.5, Eutrop.6.19.3.

7   Cic.*Att*.6.8.2. Thus Shackleton Bailey *ad loc.*; *contra*: Franklin, *Groups* 59, who rightly says that Pompeius could hardly withdraw to Spain if Caesar invaded. Pompeius might, however, at this stage have made the suggestion for the same reason as in July 51.

8   Cic.*Fam*. 2.16.3; for the date, cf. Shackleton Bailey on *Att*. 7.8.5.

9   Cic.*Att*. 7.8.5. The text is unfortunately corrupt.

10   Cic.*Att*. 7.9.2.

11   Cic.*Fam*.16.11.3. Cf. Franklin, *Groups* 60, 62.

12   Luc.1.469ff., Plut.*Pomp*.60. Cf. von Fritz, *TAPA* 72, 1941, 125ff.; Rambaud, *Déformation* 134ff.

13   Plut.*Pomp*.61, *Cato* 52, *mor*.810C.

14   App.*BC* 2.36.142, cf. Plut.*Pomp*.61.

15   Dio 41.5.1, 6.1, App.*BC* 2.36.143ff. On the difficulties of the levy at this time and a little later, cf. Cic.*Att*.7.13.2, 7.14.2, 7.21.1, Plut.*Pomp*.59. Cf. Franklin, *Groups* 64.

16   Cic.*Att*.7.10, 7.11.3f., 7.12.5, 7.13.1, 8.3.4. Cf. Luc.3.91f. on Caesar's amazement that Rome was not defended.

17   Cic.*Att*.7.13.1, 7.15.3, 8.3.4. For Lentulus' responsibility, cf. Caes.*BC* 1.14.1. In general, cf. Dio 41.6.3ff.

18   Cic.*Att*.7.12.1, cf. 7.10, 7.11.3.

19 Cic.*Att*.7.9.2.

20 Cic.*Fam*.16.12.4.

21 Cic.*Att*.7.12.2, 7.14.1, Pomp.*Att*.8.12C.2,4, 8.12D.1f., cf. Cael.*Fam*.8.15.1 and Caesar's words in Luc. 1.311ff. On the forces of both sides during the civil war, cf. Brunt, *Manpower* 473ff.

22 Caes.*BC* 1.30.2, Cic.*Att*.7.15.3, 7.20.2, 8.8.1. Later: Cic.*Att*.11.9.1, *Fam*.6.6.6.

23 Cic.*Att*.7.12.5, 7.13.1, 7.13a.3, 7.15.3, 7.16.1, *Fam*.16.12.4, Plut.*Pomp*.64, *Caes*.34, Dio 41.4.2ff. On Labienus and his motives, cf. Syme, *JRS* 28, 1938, 120ff.; Tyrrell, *Historia* 21, 1972, 424ff., with some implausible speculations.

24 Cic.*Att*.7.14.1, cf. 7.13a.3.

25 Caes.*BC* 1.8.3.

26 Caes.*BC* 1.9.1ff., Cic.*Fam*.16.12.3, Vell.2.49.4. Cf. Raaflaub, *Chiron* 5, 1975, 261ff.

27 Caes.*BC* 1.10, Cic.*Fam*.16.12.3, cf. Dio 41.6.1, 5. Cf. Raaflaub, *Chiron* 5, 1975, 272ff., *DC* 268ff.

28 For Pompeius, cf. Cic.*Att*.7.26.2, for Cicero, *Att*.7.15.3. Cf. Raaflaub, *Chiron* 5, 1975, 268ff. That Caesar had originally feared prosecution is obvious from his insistence on obtaining and retaining the *absentis ratio*, and that he had good cause is proved by his opponents' eagerness to deprive him of it. (Cf. Raaflaub, *DC* 144ff. Rowland, *LCM* 2, 1977, 165f., is sound for the period during which Caesar was insisting on the *absentis ratio*, but ignores this offer to abandon it.) He must now have assumed that the *auctoritas* of Pompeius and the gratitude of all and sundry to him for calling off the invasion would force the optimates to abide by any agreement or at all events cause them to fail if they tried to break it. Once his overtures had been rejected, he was from his own point of view fully justified in reverting to the attitude that finds expression in his famous remark on the field of Pharsalus (Suet.*DJ* 30.3f., Plut.*Caes*. 46).

29 Cf. von Fritz, *TAPA* 72, 1941, 142ff.; Raaflaub, *Chiron* 5, 1975, 272ff., 278.

30 Caes.*BC* 1.11.1ff. On Caesar's reasons for refusing, cf. Raaflaub, *Chiron* 5, 1975, 276ff.

31 Caes.*BC* 1.11.4.

32 Cic.*Att*.7.13a.3, 7.15.3.

33 Cic.*Att*.7.15.2.

34 Cic.*Att*.7.15.3.

35 Cic.*Att*.7.16.2.

36 Cic.*Att*.7.20.1, 7.21.1.

37 Cic.*Att*.7.21.2; for the absence of Marcellus, cf. 7.21.1.

38 Cic.*Att*.7.21.2, 7.22.1, 7.23.1.

39 Cic.*Att*.7.23.1, 3. On the chronology of events at Corfinium and Pompeius' correspondence with Domitius, cf. Shackleton Bailey, *JRS* 46, 1956, 57ff.

40 Pomp.*Att*.8.11A.

41 Pomp.*Att*.8.12B. Vibullius must have written two letters on 9 February, cf. Shackleton Bailey, *JRS* 46, 1956, 58. If any weight is to be assigned to Dio 41.11.1f., who says that Domitius was preparing to obey orders (a formulation which of course completely misrepresents the situation), it must be held to refer to Domitius' original intention and to ignore his change of plan.

42 Pomp.*Att*.8.12C. For Domitius' objectives, cf. Luc.2.489f.

43 Pomp.*Att*.8.12C.3. If *aut* in this passage is to be retained, it might be defended on the grounds that originally only one of the consuls was to go to Sicily and it was not certain

which, cf. Pomp.*Att*.8.12A.3. But it seems better to read *et*, despite Shackleton Bailey, *JRS* 46, 1956, 59; cf. Franklin, *Groups* 85f.

44 Cf. Franklin, *Groups* 86f. For a different view of Pompeius' letter, cf. Shackleton Bailey, *JRS* 46, 1956, 58f., who believes that he deliberately deceived Domitius in the hope of persuading him to comply.

45 Pomp.*Att*.8.12C.4; cf. Shackleton Bailey, *JRS* 46, 1956, 59.

46 Pomp.*Att*.8.12D, cf. Caes.*BC* 1.19.4.

47 Cf. Burns, *Historia* 15, 1966, 84.

48 Pomp.*Att*.8.11A, cf. Caes.*BC* 1.15.4ff. The crucial period is identified by Burns, *Historia* 15, 1966, 83.

49 Pomp.*Att*.8.11A, 8.12B.1; cf. Franklin, *Groups* 83.

50 Pomp.*Att*.8.12B.1; cf. Franklin, *Groups* 83.

51 Cf. Burns, *Historia* 15, 1966, 83; *contra*: Franklin, *Groups* 88, who thinks the information may have come from Hirrus (which is quite possible), but was more probably included in one of Pompeius' earlier letters (highly unlikely).

52 Pomp.*Att*.8.12C.3; *contra*: Franklin, *Groups* 87, 90.

53 Cf. Franklin, *Groups* 87.

54 Pomp.*Att*.8.12A.3, cf. Cic.*Att*.8.3.7. For the date, cf. Franklin, *Groups* 84.

55 Pomp.ap.Cic.*Att*.8.6.2.

56 Pomp.*Att*.8.12A.1f., 4, cf. Plut.*Caes*.35.

57 Cic.*Att*.9.10.6.

58 The connection between the alleged plan and Pompeius' supposed Sullan inclinations is specifically drawn in Cic.*Att*.9.10.6.

59 The meeting: Cic.*Fam*.2.16.3; for the date, cf. Shackleton Bailey on *Att*.7.8.5. The possibility that Cicero might be sent to Sicily, mentioned on 19 December (*Att*.7.7.4), need not, however, presuppose the evacuation of Italy; cf. Franklin, *Groups* 68. For later discussion between Cicero and Atticus, cf. *Att*.7.10, 7.12.2, 7.17.1, 7.20.2, 7.21.2, 7.22.1, 7.24, 8.1.2, 8.3.1, and for Atticus' views 9.10.4ff.

60 Cic.*Att*.9.9.2.

61 Cf. Franklin, *Groups* 72.

62 Cic.*Att*.9.10.2

63 Contrast Cic.*Att*.7.16.2 with 7.21.1.

64 Cic.*Att*.7.21.2.

65 Cf. Caes.*BC* 1.14.3, Cic.*Att*.7.21.1. 7.22.1. Dio 41.10.3 ascribes Pompeius' decision to abandon Italy to the news that Domitius was being besieged at Corfinium while others were deserting to Caesar. On morale at this time, cf. Luc.2.596ff. Cf. Franklin, *Groups* 78.

66 Cic.*Att*.8.9a.2.

67 Cf. Franklin, *Groups* 88f.

68 Cic.*Att*.8.11B.1.

69 For Cicero's alleged ignorance, cf. *Att*.8.11B.3; for his suspicions, cf. *Att*.8.1.2. That he understood the purport of *Att*.8.11A perfectly well is made clear by his comment on it in *Att*.8.1.1.

70 Cic.*Att*.8.2.3.

71 Pomp.*Att*.8.11C.

72 Pomp.*Att*.8.12A.4, Cic.*Att*.8.6.2, 8.11D.3.

73 Cic.*Att*.8.8.2, 8.7.1, 8.11D.3. Whether this conviction was as universal as Cicero claims may be doubted.

74 Cic.*Att*.8.7.1, 8.8.2, cf. 8.4.3.

75 Cic.*Att*.8.11D.1, 3.

76 Cic.*Att*.8.11D.4, cf. 3.

77 Caes.*BC* 1.25.3, 27.1, cf. App.*BC* 2.40.159.

78 Caes.*BC* 1.24.4f., *Att*.9.7C.2 (very guarded), cf. Balbus and Oppius on Caesar's desire for peace (*Att*.9.7A.1, 9.7B.1), Plut.*Pomp*.63. Caesar's claim that the initiative had come from Pompeius (*Att*.9.13A.1, cf. Cic.*Att*.9.13.8) is to be rejected. Cf. Raaflaub, *Chiron* 5, 1975, 291ff., *DC* 273ff.

79 Caes.*BC* 1.24.5. Cf. Cic.*Att*.8.13.1 on the slender hope of peace if Caesar caught up with Pompeius before he left Brundisium. Atticus had expressed the same hope, but in *Att*.8.15.3 Cicero is less optimistic. Cf. also *Att*.9.9.2, 9.10.3.

80 Caes.*BC* 1.26.2f.

81 Caes.*BC* 1.26.5, cf. Dio 41.12.2; Raaflaub, *DC* 275. Cicero's fears increased when he heard that the consuls had already left Brundisium, since he rightly took the view that this would prove a fatal obstacle to any agreement (Cic.*Att*.9.9.2, cf.8.15.3, Caes.*BC* 1.27.1, Plut.*Caes*.35, Dio 41.12.1).

82 For the various rumours and false alarms concerning Pompeius' escape, cf. Cic. *Att*.9.6.3, 9.11.3, 9.13a.1, 9.14.3, 9.15.6 (the truth).

83 Cic.*Att*.8.11.2, 8.16.2, 9.6.7, 9.7.4, 9.9.2, 9.10.2f., 9.13.3, 11.6.2, cf. Dio 41.13.3, App.*BC* 2.38.151. His departure is presented as flight by Luc.2.687ff., 699ff., 708, 730. For Pompeius and Themistocles, cf. Cic.*Att*.7.11.3, Plut.*Pomp*.63, *comp.Ages. Pomp*.4, *mor*.205C, App.*BC* 2.37.146.

84 Cic.*Att*.9.1.3, 9.11.3.

85 Caes.*BC* 1.29–30.2, 3.73.3, Cic.*Att*.9.2a.3, 9.9.2, cf. 9.7.4, Plut.*Caes*.35, Dio 41.18.1, App.*BC* 2.40.161f., cf. 54.222, Luc.3.59, 64ff., Flor.2.13.22.

86 Cic.*Att*. 8.13.2, 8.16.1f., 9.5.4, 9.13.4, 9.15.3, cf. Caes.*Att*.9.7C.1.

87 Cic.*Att*.8.11.2, cf. Sen.*Ep*.14.13, Luc.2.61.

88 Cic.*Att*.9.7.3, cf. 9.10.6.

89 Cic.*Att*.10.7.1. For Caesar and Metellus and his utterances at Rome, cf. Caes.*BC* 1.32.7, Cic.*Att*.10.4.8, 10.8.6, Cael.*Fam*.8.16.1, Plut.*Pomp*.62, *Caes*.35, Dio 41.17.1ff., App.*BC* 2.41.164, Luc.3.114ff., Flor.2.13.21.

90 Caes.*BC* 1.33.2, Suet.*DJ* 75.1, cf. *Nero* 2.3. In retrospect, cf. Cic.*Att*.11.6.2, 6, *Fam*.4.9.2f., 4.14.2, 9.6.3, *Marc*.17f.

91 Cic.*Att*.8.11.2, 9.7.3f., 9.10.2. Cf. Gelzer, *Pompeius* 201; Pocock, *GR*^{2} 6, 1959, 79.

92 Cic.*Att*.9.11.3f., cf. Vell.2.49.3.

93 Cic.*Att*.9.14.2, cf. the words put into Caesar's mouth by Luc.1.330ff., and 7.307ff.

94 Caes.*BC* 1.29–30.1, Dio 41.15.1, App.*BC* 2.40.160.

95 Caes.*BC* 1.34.3, 35.4f., Strabo 4.1.5, Dio 41.19.2, Luc.3.333ff.

96 Caes.*BC* 1.35.1.

97 Cf. Dio 41.18.5f., 43.2ff. Minimized by Vell.2.49.2. For a different light on the same facts, cf. Brutus' speech in Luc.2.277ff.

98 Cf. Cic.*Phil*.13.29, Vell.2.49.2. On the allegiance of members of the *nobilitas* and the senate in the civil war, cf. Shackleton Bailey, *CQ* 54, 1960, 253ff.

99 Cic.*Att*.9.9.3.

100 Caes.*BC* 2.21.5, Dio 41.36.1; for Cicero's opinion, cf. *Att*.9.15.2.

101 Caes.*BC* 3.1.1, Dio 41.39.1, 43.1, App.*BC* 2.48.196, Luc.5.381ff., Flor.2.13.21. Cf. Gelzer, *Pompeius* 217.

102 Cic.*Att*.10.4.8, Cael.*Fam*.8.16.2f., 5.

103 Cic.*Att*.10.8.4.

104 Cic.*Att*.10.6.3, 10.9.1.

105 Dio 41.10.4.

106 For catalogues of Pompeius' Eastern forces, cf. Caes.*BC* 3.3ff., Cic.*Att*.9.9.2, App.*BC* 2.49.201ff., Luc.3.169ff.

107 Caes.*BC* 3.4.2ff., Cic.*Deiot*.9, 11ff., 28, *div*.1.15, 2.79, Vell.2.51.1, App.*BC* 2.71.294f., Luc.5.54ff., 9.219ff., Flor.2.13.5, Oros.6.15.18ff.

108 Cic.*Att*.11.13.4.

109 Caes.*BC* 3.5.1.

110 Caes.*BC* 3.5.2–6.3, Dio 41.44.2f.

111 Caes.*BC* 3.10.1ff., Plut.*Pomp*.65 (garbled); cf. Raaflaub, *DC* 280ff.

112 Probably on 1 January 48, since the problem of the relationship between a proconsul with *imperium maius* and consuls in office would cease to exist at the end of 49. Cf. Caes.*BC* 3.16.3f., Luc.5.45ff. In general on the constitution and activities of the senate in exile, cf. Cic.*Phil*. 13.26, 28, Plut.*Pomp*.64, Dio 41.18.5, 43.2, 44.1, Luc. 5.9ff.

113 Caes.*BC* 3.11.4, 12.2, App.*BC* 2.54.224.

114 Caes.*BC* 3.13.1ff.

115 Caes.*BC* 3.15.6–16.3, 17.6. Cf. Raaflaub, *DC* 285ff.

116 Caes.*BC* 3.18.3.

117 Caes.*BC* 3.18.4. Cf. Raaflaub, *DC* 283f.

118 Caes.*BC* 3.19.8.

119 Cic.*Fam*.4.9.2, Plut.*Pomp*.66, App.*BC* 2.65.270ff., Vell.2.52.1, Luc.6.317ff., Flor. 2.13.43. For Afranius, cf. also Plut.*Caes*.41. The possibility of an invasion of Italy is considered by Caes.*BC* 3.78.3.

120 Cic.*Att*.10.8.7 (April 49) optimistically predicted that Caesar could not retain control for more than six months. But for trouble at Rome in 48, cf. Caes.*BC* 3.20ff., Dio 42.22ff., and the admittedly prejudiced remarks of Caelius in *Fam*.8.17.2.

121 Plut.*Pomp*.66, Dio 41.52.3, App.*BC* 2.65.272f., Luc.6.319ff.

122 Plut.*Pomp*.67, Caes.40f., App.*BC* 2.66.275.

123 Caes.*BC* 3.82.3–83.4, Cic.*Fam*.7.3.2 with the bitter summing-up *nihil boni praeter causam* ('nothing good except the cause', with a play on words: cf. glossary s.v. *bonus*). For Cicero in Pompeius' camp, cf. Cic.*Phil*.2.39, Plut.*Cic*.38.

124 Cic.*Fam*.7.3.2. For a more cynical estimate of the effects of Dyrrachium on Pompeius' judgement, cf. Caes.*BC* 3.79.4.

125 Caes.*BC* 3.82.2, Plut.*Pomp*.67, *Caes*.41, Dio 42.5.5, App.*BC* 2.67.278, cf. Flor.2.13.43.

126 Cic.*BC* 3.82.3, 83.1, 4, Plut.*Pomp*.67, *Caes*.42, App.*BC* 2.69.285.

127 Caes.*BC* 3.96.1, Plut.*Pomp*.72.

128 Caes.*BC* 3.86.1, Plut.*Pomp*.67, Dio 42.1.3, App.*BC* 2.67.276ff., Luc.7.45ff., with Pompeius' defence of his own preference at 7.97ff. It is possible that financial difficulties played a part in encouraging the desire to fight without delay, cf. the rumour reported in Plut.*Comp.Ages.Pomp*.4.

129 Caes.*BC* 3.94.5f., 96.3f., Cic.*Fam*.7.3.2, Plut.*Pomp*.72, *Caes*.45, Dio 42.1.1, 4, App.*BC* 2.81.339, Luc.7.683ff.

130 Plut.*Pomp*.76, Dio 42.2.1, App.*BC* 2.87, Luc.8.262ff.

2.2f., Val.Max.4.5.5, Dio 42.2.3, cf. Luc.7.712ff.

2.4f., Plut.*Pomp*.74, 76, Dio 42.2.3–3.1, App.*BC* 2.83.349, Luc.8.120ff. ; the opposite opinion of Pompeius' prospects at this point was later by Cicero (*Att*.11.6.5).

.76, App.*BC* 2.83.349f., Vell.2.53.1, Luc.8.276ff.; rejected by Dio 42.2.5f. proposal at Attalia to send Deiotarus to Parthia, cf. Luc.8.209ff. It is possible mpeius had already visited Egypt in 67 or 66, cf. Piganiol, *Studi Calderini Pan____i* I 135ff. Caesar appears to place the decision to seek help in Egypt during Pompeius' stay at Paphos, after he had heard of the hostile attitude of Antioch and Rhodes, before which he had been considering a stand in Syria (*BC* 3.102.6–103.1, cf. Cic.*Fam*.12.14.3). That the decision was taken in Cyprus may also be the implication of Plut.*Pomp*.77.

135 Luc.8.327ff.

136 Thus Luc.8.443; Plut.*Pomp*.76 makes Theophanes the prime mover, while Vell.2.53.1 wrongly gives Egypt as Pompeius' own first choice. Cf. also App.*BC* 2.83.351.

137 Caes.*BC* 3.82.4. A request for aid is mentioned by Dio 41.55.3f., 42.2.5, who claims that Orodes asked for Syria as the price of his support and imprisoned the envoy.

138 Cf. Franklin, *Groups* 107.

139 Caes.*BC* 3.103.1, Plut.*Pomp*.77, Dio 42.3.1, App.*BC* 2.84.352.

140 Caes.*BC* 3.103.3, Dio 42.3.2, App.*BC* 2.84.353.

141 Caes.*BC* 3.104.1, Plut.*Pomp*.77, App.*BC* 2.84.354, Luc.8.480ff., 520f.

142 Caes.*BC* 3.104.1f., Plut.*Pomp*.77, Dio 42.3.3f., App.*BC* 2.84.355.

143 Caes.*BC* 3.104.3, Plut.*Pomp*.78, Dio 42.3.3, App.*BC* 2.84.356, garbling the name.

144 Caes.*BC* 3.104.3, Cic.*div*.2.22, *Tusc*.3.66, Strabo 16.2.33, 17.1.11, Vell.2.53.3, Val. Max.5.1.10, Plut.*Pomp*.79, Dio 42.4.1ff., App.*BC* 2.84.355ff., Liv.*per*.112, Flor. 2.13.52, Eutrop.6.21.3, Oros.6.15.28.

145 So Vell.2.53.3. On his birthday: Plut.*Camill*.19; his birthday or the day before: *mor*.717D; the day after: *Pomp*.79. Imprecise: Dio 42.5.2, App.*BC* 2.86.363.

146 Val.Max.5.1.10, Plin.*NH* 5.68, Plut.*Pomp*.80, *Caes*.48, Dio 42.7f., App.*BC* 2.86.361, Liv.*per*.112, *uir.ill*.77.9, 78.6, Eutrop.6.21.3, Oros.6.15.29.

147 Val.Max.1.8.9, Plut.*Pomp*.80, Dio 42.5.6, App.*BC* 2.86.361, Ps.Sol.2.26ff.; Luc. 8.712ff. speaks of a quaestor Cordus, cf. *uir.ill*.77.9.

148 Plut.*Pomp*.80.

14   CONCLUSION

1 'I cannot but lament his fate, for I knew him as a man of integrity, decency and weight.' Cic.*Att*.11.6.5; for partial confirmation of his judgement, cf. Vell.2.29.2, Luc.9.197f., 201f. Cf. Stockton, *Cicero* 265.

2 Cic.*Att*.8.11.2, 9.7.3, 9.10.2, 10.7.1.

3 Tac.*Hist*.2.38: *occultior non melior*, 'less blatant, not better'.

4 Dio 41.53.2; qualifications are added at 54.1, but their practical significance is denied in 54.2f.

5 Sen.*Ep*.14.13, 95.70, 104.29ff.

6 Luc.1.670: *cum domino pax ista uenit* ('that peace comes with a master'), 2.61.

7   Luc.2.279ff., 302f., 319ff.
8   To a certain extent the judgements expressed in Lucan are of course determined by the contexts in which they occur and the speakers into whose mouths they are put. Nevertheless, the ambiguity of Pompeius' character in the poem is so deep rooted that it is hard to resist the conclusion that Lucan had been unable to make up his own mind where the truth lay.
9   Luc.2.519f., cf. 560f.; 2.532f.
10   Luc.5.14: 'not the party of Magnus but Magnus one of that party'.
11   Luc.7.386.
12   Luc.7.696f.
13   Luc.8.813ff.: *dic semper ab armis/ciuilem repetisse togam, ter curribus actis/contentum multos patriae donasse triumphos.*
14   Luc.9.19ff.
15   'He died a citizen', Luc.9.190. Cf. also Cato's sermon to the troops at 9.256ff.
16   Luc.7.706: *uincere peius erat*; cf. Syme, *RR* 51.
17   Vell.2.48.2, Sen.*Dial*.6.20.4, Juv.10.283ff. For the effect of the inevitable contrast with Caesar, cf. App.*BC* 2.86.363.
18   Thus Luc.1.125f., Flor. 2.13.14; cf. Ps.-Sall.*Ep*.1.2.3. Caes.*BC* 1.4.4 is understandably onesided. A different and less accurate formulation in Dio 41.54.1.
19   Sen.*Ep*.94.65.
20   Vell.2.53.4: *in id euecti, super quod ascendi non potest.*
21   Vell.2.29.2, cf. 2.33.3.
22   Luc.2.562ff.: *quo potuit ciuem populus perducere liber/ascendi, supraque nihil nisi regna reliqui./ non priuata cupis, Romana quisquis in urbe/Pompeium transire paras.* So at the end of the speech he is made to summarize the effect of his own achievements thus (595): *quod socero bellum praeter ciuile reliqui?* 'What war have I left for my father-in-law except a civil war?'
23   Tac.*Ann*.3.28: *suarumque legum auctor idem ac subuersor* ('at once maker and breaker of his own laws'), Plut.*Comp.Ages.Pomp*.2; Sen.*Ep*.94.64f.
24   Plut.*Pomp*.54, *mor.* 204D, confirmed by Vell.2.33.3.
25   Vell.2.29.2: *potentiae quae honoris causa ad eum deferretur, non ui ab eo occuparetur cupidissimus*, Dio 41.54.1. Cf. Gelzer, *Pompeius* 158; Badian, *RI* 78.
26   Luc.9.190ff.
27   That he had no answer to its social and political problems (cf. Caldwell, *Studies Robinson* II 959) is relatively unimportant; neither did the optimates or Caesar (cf. Gelzer, *Pompeius* 245f.; Pocock, *GR*^{2} 6, 1959, 74).
28   In general, cf. the estimates of Miltner, *RE* 21.2147f., 2207; Caldwell, *Studies Robinson* II 957ff.; Gelzer, *Pompeius* 140, 159; Meier, *RPA* 143f., 289f.
29   On Pompeius and Alexander, cf. Richard, *Mélanges Boyancé* 659ff., with references to further literature.

AFTERWORD

1   Seager, *CAH* IX^2 184.
2   Seager, *CAH* IX^2 190ff.
3   Keaveney, *Sulla* 195.

4   Seager, *CAH* IX² 208f., 210, 215ff.
5   Thus Keaveney, *Lucullus* 53.
6   Cf. Kallet-Marx, *Hegemony* 301f.; *contra*: Keaveney, *Lucullus* 188ff.
7   Seager, *CAH* IX² 212f.
8   Hillman, *CP* 86, 1991, 315ff.
9   Plut.*Lucull*.4.5.
10   Keaveney, *Lucullus* 53.
11   Thus Sherwin-White, *RFPE* 186ff., Kallet-Marx, *Hegemony* 312ff.
12   Cf. Williams, *Phoen.* 38, 1984, 228ff.
13   As it is by Kallet-Marx, *Hegemony* 312ff., Williams, *Phoen.* 38, 1984, 223.
14   Williams, 225f.
15   Williams, 232.
16   Williams, 224 n. 60.
17   Watkins, *Historia* 36, 1987, 120f.
18   Kallet-Marx, *Hegemony* 317ff.
19   Sherwin-White, *CAH* IX² 249f.
20   Sherwin-White, *RFPE* 188f., *CAH* IX² 251.
21   Sherwin-White, *RFPE* 188.
22   Freeman, *Studies*, 146f., 153ff., 171ff., 177f.
23   Freeman, 144, 165ff.
24   Ramsey, *Phoen.* 34, 1980, 326ff.
25   Ramsey, 332f.
26   Thus briefly Wiseman, *CAH* IX² 359f.; more fully Tatum, *Clodius* 62f.
27   Burckhardt, *PS* 155f.
28   Tatum, *Clodius* 50.
29   Tatum, *Clodius* 69f., 76f.
30   Tatum, *Clodius* 77 n. 114, may well be right in interpreting *de istis rebus* (Cic.*Att*.1.14.2) in very general terms, with no specific reference to either Cicero's consulship or the Bona Dea affair. Pompeius will surely have done his best to avoid speaking about anything specific at all.
31   Tatum, *Clodius* 85.
32   Braund, *Rome* 26, 59f.
33   Tatum, *Clodius* 110.
34   Marshall, *Chiron* 17, 1987, 121ff.
35   Wiseman, *CAH* IX² 375.
36   Tatum, *Clodius* 112.
37   As is realized by Marshall, *Chiron* 17, 1987, 121ff., 124f., though his explanation is very different: not that Clodius was responsible on both occasions, but that both plots were invented by Pompeius.
38   Sherwin-White, *RFPE* 268f., Tatum, *Clodius* 50.
39   Braund, *Rome* 134f., Sherwin-White, *RFPE* 270.
40   Tatum, *Clodius* 167f.
41   Tatum, *Clodius* 171ff.
42   Marshall, *Chiron* 17, 1987, 124f.
43   Tatum, *Clodius* 197, citing the relevant sources.
44   Tatum, *Clodius* 211. He also suggests that the disturbance at the Megalesia was also a food riot. This, and his dating before 5 April, are conjectural but by no means

implausible. There is certainly no cogent reason to date the riot after Cicero's departure on 8 April.

45   Tatum, *Clodius* 214f.
46   One might compare the way in which Cicero, in a not dissimilar situation after Luca, exaggerates Caesar's achievements in Gaul to the point of absurdity in *de prouinciis consularibus*.
47   Hillard, *BSR* 37, 1982, 35ff.
48   Hillard, 42ff.
49   Tatum, *Klio* 73, 1991, 126ff.
50   Tatum, *Klio* 73, 1991, 128.
51   Hornblower, *LCM* 5, 1980, 109; Seager, *LCM* 5, 1980, 133ff. For objections to my view, cf. Watt, *LCM* 5, 1980, 157, and for a reply to Watt, cf. Seager, *LCM* 5, 1980, 185.
52   Sherwin-White, *RFPE* 272ff., esp. 276, *CAH* IX^2 273.
53   Tatum, *Clodius* 234.
54   Sherwin-White, *RFPE* 278.
55   Marshall, *Chiron* 17, 1987, 128ff.
56   Epstein, *PE* 6f.
57   Epstein, 125.
58   Epstein, 111f.
59   Wiseman, *CAH* IX^2 417.

APPENDIX 2

1   Retirement of eight months' duration: Plut.*Pomp.*48; retirement linked with the first law: Suet.*DJ* 20.1. Plut.*Caes.*14 is obscure, but seems to imply that Bibulus' retirement was later than the passage of the first agrarian law. The view that Bibulus in fact remained at home for eleven months, not eight, is argued by Taylor, *AJP* 72, 1951, 261, *Historia* 17, 1968, 181. Shackleton Bailey, *Letters* I 406ff., offers an alternative. He assumes that Bibulus' retirement lasted for eight months and connects it with the *lex Campana* rather than the first law. He claims that the reference to Bibulus' activity in Cic.*Att.*2.15.2 (which, as he rightly says, cannot allude to postponement of the elections) is odd if Bibulus had been acting in this way since February. This is at first sight impressive; but Cicero may have been looking back over the spring as a whole, and Atticus' praise of Bibulus (*ista magnitudo animi*) may have been recent. His other argument is drawn from *Att.*2.16.2, which he says indicates that Bibulus did enter the forum at the time that the Asian tax contract was being dealt with. I confess that I do not understand his reasoning: the Latin seems to me quite plainly to state the opposite. This view also neglects the vital evidence of Cic.*dom.*39, that Bibulus was already engaged in watching the sky at the time of Clodius' *transitio ad plebem*, that is in March. I therefore accept Taylor's solution.
2   Cic.*Att.*2.6.2, 2.7.3 and for the *Vuiri* 2.7.4; cf. Taylor, *AJP* 72, 1951, 255.
3   Cf. Taylor, *AJP* 72, 1951, 257.
4   Cic.*Att.*2.3.3; cf. Pocock, *Commentary* 161ff., esp. 175ff.
5   Thus Taylor, *AJP* 72, 1951, 255ff., who opts for 28 January; the attempted refutation of Meier, *Historia* 10, 1961, 69 n. 2, is unconvincing.

6 Cic.*Att.*2.9.1.
7 *Contra*: Taylor, *AJP* 72, 1951, 264, who postpones it until late April, denying that Cic.*Att.*2.9.1 refers to the ratification. But it is politically implausible to separate the ratification from the revision of the Asian tax contract, especially in a way that would mean that Crassus was catered for before Pompeius.
8 Cic.*Att.*2.16.2.
9 Cf. Taylor, *AJP* 72, 1951, 263.
10 Cic.*Att.*2.16.1f. Taylor, *AJP* 72, 1951, 256, suggests 1 May for its promulgation.
11 The view on the date put forward here is essentially that of Gelzer, *KS* II 206ff.
12 Cf. Appendix 3.
13 Suet.*DJ* 22.1, also Plut.*Caes.*14, less clearly *Pomp.*47f.
14 Cf. Gottlieb, *Chiron* 4, 1974, 246. The validity of this argument is denied by Meier, *Historia* 10, 1961, 73.
15 Cf. Gelzer, *KS* II 207; *contra*: Meier, *Historia* 10, 1961, 86f., but although Caesar might have been able to secure his own interests without satisfying Pompeius and Crassus first, as Meier argues, it would have been tactless as well as unnecessary for him to do so, especially since Pompeius was so nervous and unhappy.
16 'I shall keep you held down with Caesar's army': Cic.*Att.*2.16.2. The earliest reference to Caesar's offer of a legateship for Cicero (*Att.*2.18.3) comes from late June or early July. Cf. Gelzer, *KS* II 212; Gottlieb, *Chiron* 4, 1974, 245.
17 Cf. Gelzer, *KS* II 208ff., followed e.g. by Taylor, *AJP* 72, 1951, 265; Gottlieb, *Chiron* 4, 1974, 247. Against, cf. Meier, *Historia* 10, 1961, 80ff., who, however, mistakenly assumes on the strength of Cic.*Att.*2.16.2 that the law must have been promulgated by 4 April. Taylor's revised view, *Historia* 17, 1968, 185, is that *exercitus* has its literal meaning, but she too assumes that the law must already have been promulgated. Since this is not so, her explanation of why it is not mentioned in Cic.*Att.*2.4–15 (because it was already familiar) becomes otiose as well as unconvincing.
18 Thus rightly Shackleton Bailey, *Letters* I 408.
19 Thus rightly Shackleton Bailey, *Letters* I 408.
20 Cf. Gelzer, *KS* II 212 (June); Taylor, *AJP* 72, 1951, 268 (early June), *Historia* 17, 1968, 187 (second half of May).

APPENDIX 3

1 Cf. Gruen, *LGRR* 492.
2 Cf. Balsdon, *JRS* 29, 1939, 66.
3 Such a claim may have been facilitated by the ambiguity inherent in *succedere*, to which attention is drawn by Cuff, *Historia* 7, 1958, 458ff.
4 Cf. Lewis & Short, s.v. *dies* II A 3.
5 Probably the day by which *professio* had to be made in person for the elections of 49; cf. Raaflaub, *DC* 56 n. 219.
6 Cf. *MRR* II 338. The explanation accepted here is that of Balsdon, *JRS* 29, 1939, 72.

GLOSSARY

absentis ratio   the right to stand for office in absentia.

aedile   magistrates (four each year: two curule, two plebeian) in charge of roads, markets, public works, public order. The games given by an aedile could affect his later career.

ambitus   bribery at elections.

auctore Pompeio   with the formal support of Pompeius.

auctoritas   authority, influence, weight based on birth, achievement, wealth, connections rather than on formal power.

auctoritas senatus   the collective *auctoritas* of the senate as a body; also a technical term for a decree of the senate passed, then vetoed but nevertheless recorded.

augurs   one of the major colleges of priests, particularly concerned with omens.

bellum externum   a war against a foreign enemy, therefore eligible to qualify the commander for a triumph (q.v.).

bonus   lit. a good man/citizen, used by themselves and their supporters of those who in general supported the collective supremacy of the senate, 'law and order' and the sanctity of private property.

capite censi   lit. 'counted by the head': the members of the lowest class in the centuriate assembly, who had either no property or insufficient to qualify them for membership of the fifth (lowest) property class, and so had been ineligible for military service until the reforms of Marius.

censors   two magistrates elected from ex-consuls (q.v.) every five years to update the lists of citizens, senators and *equites* (q.v.), let public contracts, conduct certain purificatory rituals, etc.

clientela   individuals or groups under the patronage of one or more leading Romans; the institution of patronage seen from the point of view of the recipient.

collegia   associations akin in various ways to trade guilds, religious fraternities and friendly societies, politicized by Clodius to form the nucleus of his private army in the fifties.

concilium plebis   an assembly of the plebs, from which patricians were therefore excluded; in the middle and late republic, however, its decisions (*plebiscita*) were binding on the whole people. It was convened by a tribune of the plebs (q.v.) and in addition to its quasi-legislative function elected tribunes and plebeian aediles (q.v.).

consilium   an advisory body, e.g. the senate, a jury, a provincial governor's staff, a commander's officers, a family council.

consul the highest annual magistrates, two in number; in the late republic they commanded troops only in emergencies and normally did little more than preside in the senate and at elections.

consularis an ex-consul; consulars formed an elite within the senate, also called *principes ciuitatis* ('leading men of the state') and were sometimes consulted collectively by magistrates in office.

contio an informal public meeting summoned by a magistrate or tribune of the plebs.

contra rem publicam against the interests of the commonwealth.

cura annonae charge of the corn supply.

curia the senate house.

dictator a magistrate appointed in time of crisis, with no colleague of equal power and immune from veto. Long obsolete until revived in unprecedented form by Sulla and then by Caesar.

dignitas a man's worth or dignity, his claim to respect and recognition based on birth, wealth and personal achievement: a highly individualistic and hence potentially disruptive concept.

diuinatio a procedure to determine which of competing candidates should have the right to conduct a criminal prosecution.

elogium a funerary inscription.

eques (pl. *equites*) a word with various interlinked senses. (a) a cavalryman; (b) a member of the eighteen equestrian centuries in the centuriate assembly; (c) a member of the equestrian order (*ordo equester*), that segment of the upper class which refrained from the pursuit of magistracies and consequent membership of the senate. To call them a 'middle class' or 'business class' is misleading. The *publicani* (q.v.) were the most politically visible and active element of the order, but many more were rural landowners.

factio a pejorative term, sometimes meaning 'clique', far more often 'intrigue'; the perception of Roman politics as a struggle between competing factions is a modern construct without foundation in Latin usage.

fasces the bundles of rods, tied with a cord and outside the city containing an axe, carried by the lictors who attended a magistrate vested with *imperium* (q.v.) and symbolizing the power to bind, beat and execute inherent in *imperium*. Origin of modern 'fascist'.

gens a Roman family or 'clan', the source of an individual's *nomen* (e.g. Caecilius, Cornelius), often subdivided into *stirpes* from which the *cognomen* (e.g. Metellus, Scipio) may be drawn.

gratia influence, gratitude.

hospitium guest friendship.

hostis a foreign enemy; a citizen formally declared a public enemy.

imperator a salutation bestowed on a commander by his troops after success in battle; a holder of *imperium*.

imperium (a) the power of command vested in the higher magistrates and promagistrates, as symbolized in the *fasces* (q.v.); (b) the Roman empire, sc. those areas of the world under direct (provinces) or indirect (e.g. client kingdoms) Roman control.

imperium aequum *imperium* declared equal to that of any other holder of such power with whom the possessor might come into contact.

imperium maius *imperium* declared greater than than of any other holder of such power with whom the possessor might come into contact.

interrex a magistrate (who had to be a patrician and held office for only five days) charged with the holding of consular elections when the outgoing consuls had been unable to do so.

legate   (a) a holder of *imperium* (q.v.) whose power derived directly from that of the superior (usually a consul or proconsul) who appointed him; (b) an envoy.

legis dies   the day laid down in the law; the period of time mentioned in the law.

lex annalis   the law prescribing the minimum ages at which the various magistracies could be held and the intervals that should elapse between iterations of the same office.

lex curiata   a law formally enabling a governor to proceed to his province.

libera legatio   a 'free embassy': a device allowing senators to travel abroad at the public expense, ostensibly for some such purpose as the payment of a vow.

ludi Romani   the most ancient of Roman games, celebrated on 4 September.

maiestas   lit. 'greaterness', a characteristic revealingly ascribed to the Roman people in its relationship with the world at large. The formal title for the charge of treason in the late republic was *maiestas populi Romani minuta* ('diminution of the majesty of the Roman people'). (An alternative formulation, *maiestas laesa*, gives rise to the modern term 'lèse-majesté'.)

maior potestas   greater power, e.g. that of a consul in relation to that of a praetor (q.v.).

nobilis   a member of the *nobilitas*, a 'noble': a descendant of a man who had held the consulship (or possibly any curule magistracy).

operae Clodianae   Clodius' gangs.

optimates   lit. the best men, a term applied to themselves by those who in general upheld the senate's authority against both the excessive claims of individual aristocrats and popular agitation. They never constituted a political 'party' in any modern sense of that term.

otium   internal peace in a socio-political sense; abstention from public life.

peculatus   embezzlement of public funds.

perduellio   an archaic form of treason charge, largely replaced by *maiestas* (q.v.).

pomoerium   the city limit of Rome.

pontifex maximus   the elective chief priest of Rome.

popularis   one who, for whatever ultimate end, claimed to champion the interests of the common people against oppression by the senate and the upper classes generally. The term is applied to a series of more or less distinguished individuals who introduced similar legislation which they defended on similar grounds; there was no 'party' of the *populares*.

portoria   customs and harbour dues.

praetor   (a) magistrates (ten each year since Sulla), vested with *imperium* (q.v.), who supervised civil lawsuits and acted as presidents of the various standing criminal courts, but could also command troops if required; (b) also used as a generic term for a provincial governor.

praeuaricator   a collusive prosecutor in a criminal case.

princeps senatus   a difficult term to translate (lit. 'leading man of the senate'). The *princeps senatus* was nominated by the censors (q.v.) on the grounds of seniority and distinction; he did not convene or preside at its meetings. The practice of nominating a *princeps senatus* may have been abandoned after Sulla.

priuatus   a private citizen, particularly as contrasted with one already holding some public office.

pro quaestore pro praetore   one holding formal rank equivalent to that of a quaestor but with the powers of a praetor (including *imperium*) (qq.v.).

proconsul   a man, usually an ex-praetor or ex-consul, holding *imperium* (qq.v.) for one or more years as governor of a province.

professio   formal declaration of one's candidature for an office.

proscription   the practice of publishing lists of one's political opponents, whose lives and property were declared forfeit and whose descendants suffered various civil disabilities; instituted by Sulla and imitated by the triumvirs Antony, Octavian and Lepidus.

prouocatio ad populum   appeal to the people against the decision of a magistrate.

province   the sphere of activity assigned to a magistrate or promagistrate, definable as either a task or a geographical area according to circumstances.

publicani   those who bid for public contracts, particularly those to farm the taxes of a province; they were the most visible and politically active element of the equestrian order.

quaestio   (a) a standing criminal court, with juries drawn at various times from the senatorial order, the *equites* (q.v.), or both, with the addition from 70 of the *tribuni aerarii* (q.v.); (b) a special court established to deal with cases arising from a specific emergency.

quaestor   the most junior magistrates (twenty each year since Sulla); they performed various administrative duties, notably at the treasury, and acted as aides to provincial governors.

quo ea pecunia peruenerit   lit. 'where that money ended up', a clause in the law on *res repetundae* (q.v.) designed to enable the prosecution of supposed accomplices of the original defendant in any given case.

regnum   monarchy.

(res) repetundae   lit. 'things to be recovered': the designation of the law and the court set up by it which were concerned with extortion by provincial governors and some other forms of financial irregularity.

senate   a body consisting of all ex-magistrates which constituted the deliberative element in Roman politics. Formally it was no more than the advisory *consilium* (q.v.) of the summoning magistrate (usually a consul) and its decrees had no binding legal force, but in practice it was rare for a magistrate to act without taking the senate's advice or to ignore that advice once given.

senatus consultum ultimum   (abbrev. *s.c.u.*) lit. 'the senate's last decree'. Passed in alleged emergencies, it normally instructed the consuls to ensure that the state came to no harm. The consuls and others could nevertheless be called to account later for actions taken under the decree, which conspicuously failed to name any specific act as legitimate or illegitimate.

sodalicia   associations or societies of any kind, including those designed for questionable political purposes.

subscriptor   an assistant prosecutor in a criminal case.

supplicatio   a thanksgiving to the gods in honour of a commander's military successes.

tabernae   shops, stalls, workshops, taverns.

toga praetexta   a toga with a purple border worn by office-holders.

transitio ad plebem   the procedure whereby a patrician was adopted into a plebeian family (thus rendering him eligible to stand for the tribunate of the plebs) (q.v.).

transuectio equitum   a ceremonial parade of the cavalry held by the censors, obsolete by 70 when it was revived to flatter Pompeius.

tribune of the plebs (*tribunus plebis*)   one of ten (in the late republic) annual officials elected by the plebeian assembly (*concilium plebis*, q.v.); only plebeians were eligible. Their original function had been to protect plebeians against ill usage by magistrates, patricians and the upper class in general. They could veto the actions of their colleagues and of other magistrates and also decrees of the senate, and could introduce legislation through the plebeian assembly.

tribuni aerarii originally treasury officials, whose obsolete title was revived in 70 to designate the third panel of jurors established by the *lex Aurelia*. Virtually nothing is known of them beyond the fact that they possessed the equestrian census.

triumph the procession, in a horsedrawn chariot, of a victorious commander to the temple of Jupiter on the Capitol, including prisoners, booty and illustrative floats. The criteria for the granting of a triumph included the killing of at least 5,000 opponents in the course of the successful conclusion of a formally declared war against a foreign enemy.

tumultus a state of emergency declared in the face of an attack from within Italy or by Gauls, giving rise to the cancellation of leave and the holding of emergency levies.

uenatio a wild beast hunt in the arena.

uincere peius erat 'it was worse to be victorious'.

uis public violence.

Vuir a (gris) d (andis) a (ssignandis) i (udicandis) member of a board of five to distribute, assign and make judicial decisions concerning land allotments.

SELECT BIBLIOGRAPHY

Adcock, F. E., The legal term of Caesar's governorship in Gaul, *CQ* 26, 1932, 14ff.

Afzelius, A., Das Ackerverteilungsgesetz des P. Servilius Rullus, *CM* 3, 1940, 214ff.

Anderson, J. G. C., Pompey's treatment of Pontus, *Studies Buckler*, Manchester, 1939, 3ff.

Anderson, W. S., *Pompey, his friends, and the literature of the first century B.C.*, Berkeley/Los Angeles, 1963.

Badian, E., *Foreign clientelae (264–70 B.C.)*, Oxford, 1958.

—— *Roman imperialism in the late republic*, Pretoria, 1967.

—— *Publicans and sinners*, Ithaca, 1972.

—— The date of Pompey's first triumph, *Hermes* 83, 1955, 107ff.

—— The early career of A. Gabinius (*cos.* 58 B.C.), *Philol.* 103, 1959, 87ff.

—— Servilius and Pompey's first triumph, *Hermes* 89, 1961, 254ff.

—— Notes on Roman senators of the republic, *Historia* 12, 1963, 129ff.

—— M. Porcius Cato and the annexation and early administration of Cyprus, *JRS* 55, 1965, 110ff.

—— Review of A. E. Douglas, *Cicero, Brutus, JRS* 57, 1967, 223ff.

—— Quaestiones Variae, *Historia* 18, 1969, 447ff.

Bailey, D. R. S., *Cicero's letters to Atticus*, Cambridge, 1965–70.

—— Expectatio Corfiniensis, *JRS* 46, 1956, 57ff.

—— Sex. Clodius – Sex. Cloelius, *CQ* 54, 1960, 41f.

—— The Roman nobility in the second civil war, *CQ* 54, 1960, 253ff.

—— The credentials of L. Caesar and L. Roscius, *JRS* 50, 1960, 80ff.

Balsdon, J. P. V. D., Consular provinces under the late republic, *JRS* 29, 1939, 57ff., 167ff.

—— Roman history, 65–50 B.C.: five problems, *JRS* 52, 1962, 134ff.

—— Fabula Clodiana, *Historia* 15, 1966, 65ff.

Bardt, C., Die Übergabe des Schwertes an Pompeius im December 50 v.Chr., *Hermes* 45, 1910, 337ff.

Bauman, R. A., *The crimen maiestatis in the Roman republic and Augustan principate*, Johannesburg, 1967.

Béranger, J., *Recherches sur l'aspect idéologique du principat*, Basel, 1953.

——A propos d'un *imperium infinitum*, *Mélanges Marouzeau*, Paris, 1948, 19ff.

Boak, A. E. R., The extraordinary commands from 80 to 48 B.C., *AHR* 24, 1918/19, 1ff.

Braund, D. C., *Rome and the friendly king*, London, 1984.

Broughton, T. R. S., *The magistrates of the Roman republic*, New York, 1951–60.

——More notes on Roman magistrates, *TAPA* 79, 1948, 63ff.

Brunt, P. A., *Italian manpower 225 B.C.–A.D. 14*, Oxford, 1971.

——Cicero *Ad Atticum* 2.24, *CQ* 47, 1953, 62ff.

Burckhardt, L. A., *Politische Strategien der Optimaten in der späten römischen Republik*, Stuttgart, 1988.

Burns, A., Pompey's strategy and Domitius' stand at Corfinium, *Historia* 15, 1966, 74ff.

Burr, V., Rom und Judäa im 1. Jahrhundert v.Chr. (Pompeius und die Juden), *ANRW* I 1.875ff.

Caldwell, W. E., An estimate of Pompey, *Studies Robinson* II, St Louis, 1953, 954ff.

Cambridge Ancient History IX, Cambridge, 1932.

Cambridge Ancient History IX^2 (ed. J. A. Crook, A. W. Lintott, E. Rawson), Cambridge, 1994.

Carcopino, J., *Sylla ou la monarchie manquée*, Paris, 1947.

Cary, M., 'Asinus germanus', *CQ* 17, 1923, 103ff.

Cichorius, C., *Römische Studien*, Berlin/Leipzig, 1922.

Crawford, M. H., Review of E. S. Gruen, *The Last Generation of the Roman Republic*, *JRS* 66, 1976, 214ff.

Criniti, N., *L'epigrafe di Asculum di Gn. Pompeo Strabone*, Milano, 1970.

Cuff, P. J., The terminal date of Caesar's Gallic command, *Historia* 7, 1958, 445ff.

Dessau, H., Gaius Rabirius Postumus, *Hermes* 46, 1911, 613ff.

Downey, G., The occupation of Syria by the Romans, *TAPA* 82, 1951, 149ff.

Dreizehnter, A., Pompeius als Städtegrunder, *Chiron* 5, 1975, 213ff.

Ehrenberg, V., 'Imperium maius' in the Roman republic, *AJP* 74, 1953, 113ff.

Epstein, D. F., *Personal enmity in Roman politics 218–43 B.C.*, London, 1987.

Fantham, E., The trials of Gabinius in 54 B.C., *Historia* 24, 1975, 425ff.

Fletcher, W. G., The Pontic cities of Pompey the Great, *TAPA* 70, 1939, 17ff.

Frankfort, T. (Liebmann-), *La frontière orientale dans la politique extérieure de la république romaine*, Bruxelles, 1969.

——La Sophène et Rome, *Latomus* 22, 1963, 181ff.

Franklin, A.J., *Political groups and their influence, 49 B.C.–44 B.C.*, Diss. Liverpool, 1974.

Freeman, P. W. M., Pompey's eastern settlement: a matter of presentation? *Studies in Latin Literature and Roman History VII* (ed. Deroux), Bruxelles, 1994, 143ff.

Fritz, K. von, The mission of L. Caesar and L. Roscius in January 49 B.C., *TAPA* 72, 1941, 125ff.

——Pompey's policy before and after the outbreak of the civil war of 49 B.C., *TAPA* 73, 1942, 145ff.

Gabba, E., *Appiani Bellorum Civilium Liber Primus*, Firenze, 1958.

——Nota sulla rogatio agraria di P. Servilio Rullo, *Mélanges Piganiol* II, Paris, 1966, 769ff.

——*Esercito e società nella tarda repubblica romana*, Firenze, 1973.

Garzetti, A., M. Licinio Crasso, *Athen.* n.s. 19, 1941, 1ff.; 20, 1942, 12ff.; 22/3, 1944/5, 1ff.

Gelzer, M., *Pompeius*[2], München, 1959.

——*Caesar der Politiker und Staatsmann*[6], Wiesbaden, 1960.

——*Cicero, ein biographischer Versuch*, Wiesbaden, 1969.

——*The Roman nobility*, Oxford, 1969.

——*Kleine Schriften*, Wiesbaden, 1962–4.

Gesche, H., Die quinquennale Dauer und der Endtermin der gallischen Imperien Caesars, *Chiron* 3, 1973, 179ff.

Gottlieb, G., Zur Chronologie in Caesars erstem Konsulat, *Chiron* 4, 1974, 243ff.

Greenidge, A. H. J. and Clay, A. M., *Sources for Roman history 133–70 B.C.*[2] (ed. E. W. Gray), Oxford, 1960.

Grenade, P., Le mythe de Pompée et les Pompéiens sous les Césars, *REA* 52, 1950, 28ff.

Griffin, M., The tribune C. Cornelius, *JRS* 63, 1973, 196ff.

Grimal, P., Le contenu historique du *Contre Pison*, *CRAI* 1966, 95ff.

Groebe, P., Zum Seeräuberkriege des Pompeius Magnus (67 v.Chr.), *Klio* 10, 1910, 374ff.

Gruen, E. S., *Roman politics and the criminal courts, 149–78 B.C.*, Cambridge, MA, 1968.

——*The last generation of the Roman republic*, Berkeley/Los Angeles, 1974.

——P. Clodius: instrument or independent agent? *Phoen.* 20, 1966, 120ff.

——Notes on the 'First Catilinarian Conspiracy', *CP* 64, 1969, 20ff.

——Pompey, the Roman aristocracy, and the conference of Luca, *Historia* 18, 1969, 71ff.

——Pompey and the Pisones, *CSCA* 1, 1969, 155ff.

——The consular elections for 53 B.C., *Hommages Renard* II, Bruxelles, 1969, 311ff.

——*Veteres hostes, novi amici*, *Phoen.* 24, 1970, 237ff.

——Some criminal trials of the late republic: political and prosopographical problems, *Athen.* n.s. 49, 1971, 54ff.

——Pompey, Metellus Pius, and the trials of 70–69 B.C.: the perils of schematism, *AJP* 92, 1971, 1ff.

——The trial of C. Antonius, *Latomus* 32, 1973, 301ff.

Hardy, E. G., The policy of the Rullan proposal in 63 B.C., *JP* 32, 1913, 228ff.

——The Catilinarian conspiracy in its context: a re-study of the evidence, *JRS* 7, 1917, 153ff.

Hayne, L., M. Lepidus (cos.78): a re-appraisal, *Historia* 21, 1972, 661ff.

Hill, H., *The Roman middle class in the republican period*, Oxford, 1952.

Hillard, T. W., P. Clodius Pulcher 62–58 B.C.: 'Pompeii adfinis et sodalis', *BSR* 37, 1982, 35ff.

Hillman, T. P., The alleged *inimicitiae* of Pompeius and Lucullus: 78–74, *CP* 86, 1991, 315ff.

Hornblower, S., 'in hac causa mihi aqua haeret' (Cicero, ad Q.f.2.6.2): a note, *LCM* 5, 1980, 109.

Jackson, J., Cicero, *Fam*.1.9.9, and the conference of Luca, *LCM* 3, 1978, 175ff.

Jameson, S., Pompey's imperium in 67: some constitutional fictions, *Historia* 19, 1970, 539ff.

——The intended date of Caesar's return from Gaul, *Latomus* 29, 1970, 638ff.

John, C., Die Entstehungsgeschichte der catilinarischen Verschwörung, *Jahrb. klass. Phil. Supp.* 8, 1876, 703ff.

Jones, A. H. M., *The cities of the Eastern Roman provinces*[2], Oxford, 1971.

Kallet-Marx, R. M., *Hegemony to empire*, Berkeley/Los Angeles, 1995.

Keaveney, A., *Sulla, the last republican*, London, 1982.

——*Lucullus*, London, 1992.

Knight, D. W., Pompey's concern with pre-eminence after 60 B.C., *Latomus* 27, 1968, 878ff.

Kumaniecki, K., *Les discours égarés de Cicéron 'Pro Cornelio'*, Brussel, 1970.

——Ciceros Rede de haruspicum responso, *Klio* 37, 1959, 135ff.

Lacey, W. K., The tribunate of Curio, *Historia* 10, 1961, 318ff.

Laurand, L., Cicéron et Pompée-le-Grand, *REA* 28, 1926, 10ff.

Lazenby, J. F., The conference of Luca and the Gallic war, a study in Roman politics 57–55 B.C., *Latomus* 18, 1959, 67ff.

Lenaghan, J. O., *A commentary on Cicero's oration De haruspicum responso*, The Hague/Paris, 1969.

Lewis, C. T. and Short, C., *A Latin dictionary*, Oxford, 1879.

Lintott, A. W., *Violence in republican Rome*, Oxford, 1968.

——P. Clodius Pulcher – *felix Catilina? GR*[2] 14, 1967, 157ff.

——Cicero and Milo, *JRS* 64, 1974, 62ff.

Loader, W. R., Pompey's command under the lex Gabinia, *CR* 54, 1940, 134ff.

Luibheid, C., The Luca conference, *CP* 65, 1970, 88ff.

McDermott, W. C., Vettius ille, ille noster index, *TAPA* 80, 1949, 153ff.

——Lex de tribunicia potestate (70 B.C.), *CP* 72, 1977, 49ff.

McDonald, W., The Tribunate of Cornelius, *CQ* 23, 1929, 196ff.

——Clodius and the *lex Aelia Fufia*, *JRS* 19, 1929, 164ff.

Magie, D., *Roman rule in Asia Minor to the end of the third century after Christ*, Princeton, 1950.

Marshall, B.A., *Crassus, a political biography*, Amsterdam, 1976.

Marshall, B.A., Crassus' ovation in 71 B.C., *Historia* 21, 1972, 669ff.

—— The *lex Plotia agraria, Antichthon* 6, 1972, 43ff.

—— Crassus and the command against Spartacus, *Athen.* n.s. 51, 1973, 109ff.

—— Pompeius' temple of Hercules, *Antichthon* 8, 1974, 80ff.

—— Q. Cicero, Hortensius and the lex Aurelia, *RhM* NF 118, 1975, 136ff.

—— Pompeius' fear of assassination, *Chiron* 17, 1987, 119ff.

Mattingly, H. B., The *consilium* of Cn. Pompeius Strabo in 89 B.C., *Athen.* n.s. 53, 1975, 262ff.

Meier, C., *Res publica amissa*, Wiesbaden, 1966.

—— Zur Chronologie und Politik in Caesars erstem Konsulat, *Historia* 10, 1961, 68ff.

—— Pompeius' Ruckkehr aus dem Mithridatischen Kriege und die Catilinarische Verschwörung, *Athen.* n.s. 40, 1962, 103ff.

Meyer, E., *Caesars Monarchie und das Principat des Pompeius*[3], Stuttgart/Berlin, 1922.

Mitchell, T., Veteres hostes, novi amici (Cic.Fam.V.7.1), *Historia* 24, 1975, 618ff.

Münzer, F., *Römische Adelsparteien und Adelsfamilien*, Stuttgart, 1920.

Nicolet, C., *L'ordre équestre à l'époque républicaine (312–43 av.J.C.)* I, Paris, 1966.

Oost, S. I., Cato Uticensis and the annexation of Cyprus, *CP* 50, 1955, 98ff.

—— The date of the *lex Iulia de repetundis, AJP* 77, 1956, 19ff.

Ooteghem, J. van, *Pompée le grand bâtisseur d'empire*, Bruxelles, 1954.

—— *Lucius Licinius Lucullus*, Bruxelles, 1959.

Ormerod, H. A., The distribution of Pompeius' forces in the campaign of 67 B.C., *LAAA* 10, 1923, 46ff.

Parrish, E. J., Crassus' new friends and Pompey's return, *Phoen.* 27, 1973, 357ff.

Phillips, E.J., Cicero and the prosecution of C. Manilius, *Latomus* 29, 1970, 595ff.

Piganiol, A., Un épisode inconnu de la vie de Pompée, *Studi Calderini Paribeni* I, Milano, 1956, 135ff.

Pocock, L. G., *A commentary on Cicero In Vatinium*, London, 1926.

—— Publius Clodius and the acts of Caesar, *CQ* 18, 1924, 59ff.

—— *Lex de actis Cn. Pompeii confirmandis: lex Iulia* or *lex Vatinia? CQ* 19, 1925, 16ff.

—— A note on the policy of Clodius, *CQ* 19, 1925, 182ff.

—— *Pompeiusve parem, CP* 22, 1927, 301ff.

—— What made Pompeius fight in 49 B.C.? *GR*[2] 6, 1959, 68ff.

Raaflaub, K., *Dignitatis contentio*, München, 1974.

—— Zum politischen Wirken der caesarfreundlichen Volkstribunen am Vorabend des Bürgerkrieges, *Chiron* 4, 1974, 293ff.

—— Caesar und die Friedensverhandlungen zu Beginn des Bürgerkrieges von 49 v.Chr., *Chiron* 5, 1975, 247ff.

Rambaud, M., *L'art de la déformation historique chez César*[2], Paris, 1966.

—— L'apologie de Pompée par Lucan au livre VII de la *Pharsale, REL* 33, 1955, 258ff.

Ramsey, J. T., The prosecution of C. Manilius in 66 B.C. and Cicero's *pro Manilio*, *Phoen.* 34, 1980, 323ff.

Reynolds, J., Cyrenaica, Pompey and Cn. Cornelius Lentulus Marcellinus, *JRS* 52, 1962, 97ff.

Richard, J.-C., Alexandre et Pompée: à propos de Tite-Live IX, 16, 19–19, 17, *Mélanges Boyancé*, Rome, 1974, 653ff.

Rowland, R. J., Crassus, Clodius and Curio in the year 59 B.C., *Historia* 15, 1966, 217ff.

——Caesar's fear of prosecution in 49 B.C., *LCM* 2, 1977, 165f.

Rubinsohn, Z., A note on Plutarch, Crassus X, 1, *Historia* 19, 1970, 624ff.

Sanford, E. M., The career of Aulus Gabinius, *TAPA* 70, 1939, 64ff.

Seager, R., The first Catilinarian conspiracy, *Historia* 13, 1964, 338ff.

——Clodius, Pompeius and the exile of Cicero, *Latomus* 24, 1965, 519ff.

——The tribunate of Cornelius: some ramifications, *Hommages Renard* II, Bruxelles, 1969, 680ff.

——Cicero and the word *popularis*, *CQ* 66, 1972, 328ff.

——*Factio*: some observations, *JRS* 62, 1972, 53ff.

——Iusta Catilinae, *Historia* 22, 1973, 240ff.

——L. Domitius Ahenobarbus and Cicero's election to the consulship, *LCM* 1, 1976, 46.

——On sticking water (Cicero QF 2.6.2), *LCM* 5, 1980, 133ff.

——'Aqua araneae non haeret': a postscript on Cicero, QF 2.6.2, *LCM* 5, 1980, 185.

Sealey, R., 'Habe meam rationem', *CM* 18, 1957, 75ff.

Seyrig, H., Antiquités syriennes, *Syria* 27, 1950, 5ff.

Shatzman, I., The Roman general's authority over booty, *Historia* 21, 1972, 177ff.

——The Egyptian question in Roman politics, *Latomus* 30, 1971, 363ff.

Sherwin-White, A. N., *Roman foreign policy in the East 168 B.C. to A.D. 1*, London, 1984.

——Violence in Roman politics, *JRS* 46, 1956, 1ff.

Simpson, A. D., The departure of Crassus for Parthia, *TAPA* 69, 1938, 532ff.

Smith, R. E., The *lex Plotia agraria* and Pompey's Spanish veterans, *CQ* 51, 1957, 82ff.

——Pompey's conduct in 80 and 77 B.C., *Phoen.* 14, 1960, 1ff.

Stanton, G. R. and Marshall, B. A., The coalition between Pompeius and Crassus 60–59 B.C., *Historia* 24, 1975, 205ff.

Staveley, E. S., The conduct of elections during an *interregnum*, *Historia* 3, 1954/5, 193ff.

Stevens, C. E., The terminal date of Caesar's command, *AJP* 59, 1938, 169ff.

Stevenson, G. H., Cn. Pompeius Strabo and the franchise question, *JRS* 9, 1919, 95ff.

Stockton, D., *Cicero, a political biography*, Oxford, 1971.

——Cicero and the *ager Campanus*, *TAPA* 93, 1962, 471ff.

Stockton, D., The first consulship of Pompey, *Historia* 22, 1973, 205ff.

—— 'Quis iustius induit arma?' *Historia* 24, 1975, 232ff.

Strasburger, H., *Caesars Eintritt in die Geschichte*, München, 1938.

Sumner, G. V., Manius or Mamercus? *JRS* 54, 1964, 41ff.

—— The consular elections of 66 B.C., *Phoen.* 19, 1965, 226ff.

—— Cicero, Pompeius and Rullus, *TAPA* 97, 1966, 568ff.

Syme, R., *The Roman revolution*, Oxford, 1939.

—— The allegiance of Labienus, *JRS* 28, 1938, 113ff.

Tatum, W. J., *The patrician tribune Publius Clodius Pulcher*, Chapel Hill, 1999.

—— The marriage of Pompey's son to the daughter of Ap. Claudius Pulcher, *Klio* 73, 1991, 123ff.

Taylor, L. R., *Party politics in the age of Caesar*, Berkeley/Los Angeles, 1949.

—— *The voting districts of the Roman republic*, Rome, 1960.

—— Caesar and the Roman nobility, *TAPA* 73, 1942, 1ff.

—— The date and meaning of the Vettius affair, *Historia* 1, 1950, 45ff.

—— On the chronology of Caesar's first consulship, *AJP* 72, 1951, 254ff.

—— On the date of *Ad Atticum* 2.24, *CQ* 48, 1954, 181f.

—— The dating of major legislation and elections in Caesar's first consulship, *Historia* 17, 1968, 173ff.

Twyman, B., The Metelli, Pompeius and prosopography, *ANRW* I 1. 816ff.

Tyrrell, W. B., Labienus' departure from Caesar in January 49 B.C., *Historia* 21, 1972, 424ff.

—— The trial of C. Rabirius in 63 B.C., *Latomus* 32, 1973, 285ff.

Ward, A. M., *Marcus Crassus and the late Roman republic*, Columbia, MO, 1977.

—— Cicero's support of Pompey in the trials of M. Fonteius and P. Oppius, *Latomus* 27, 1968, 802ff.

—— The early relationships between Cicero and Pompey until 80 B.C., *Phoen.* 24, 1970, 119ff.

—— Cicero and Pompey in 75 and 70 B.C., *Latomus* 29, 1970, 58ff.

—— Politics in the trials of Manilius and Cornelius, *TAPA* 101, 1970, 545ff.

—— Cicero's fight against Crassus and Caesar in 65 and 63 B.C., *Historia* 21, 1972, 244ff.

Watkins, O. D., Caesar solus? Senatorial support for the Lex Gabinia, *Historia* 36, 1987, 120ff.

Watt, W. S., Cicero, QF 2.7 (olim 6).2, *LCM* 5, 1980, 157.

Wellesley, K., The extent of the territory added to Bithynia by Pompey, *RhM* NF 96, 1953, 293ff.

Williams, R. S., The appointment of Glabrio (*cos.* 67) to the eastern command, *Phoen.* 38, 1984, 221ff.

Wiseman, T. P., *New men in the Roman senate 139 B.C.–A.D. 14*, Oxford, 1971.

—— *Cinna the poet*, Leicester, 1974.

—— The census in the first century B.C., *JRS* 59, 1969, 59ff.

—— The definition of 'eques Romanus' in the late republic and early empire, *Historia* 19, 1970, 67ff.

—— Celer and Nepos, *CQ* 65, 1971, 180ff.

—— Factions and family trees, *LCM* 1, 1976, 1f.

INDEX